CHRISTMAS

CHRISTMAS

IN

RITUAL AND TRADITION
CHRISTIAN AND PAGAN

BY

CLEMENT A. MILES

WITH 21 ILLUSTRATIONS

T. FISHER UNWIN

1912

Republished by Omnigraphics ● Penobscot Building ● Detroit ● 1990

Library of Congress Cataloging-in-Publication Data

Miles, Clement A.
    Christmas in ritual and tradition, Christian and Pagan / by
Clement A. Miles.
        p.   cm.
    Reprint. Originally published: London : T.F. Unwin, 1912.
    Includes bibliographical references (p.   ).
    ISBN 1-55888-896-9 (lib. bdg. : alk. paper)
    1. Christmas.   2. Christmas — History.   I. Title.
GT4985.M5   1990
394.2'68282 — dc20   89-29299
                                                                  CIP

  ∞
This book is printed on acid-free paper meeting the ANSI Z39.48
Standard. The infinity symbol that appears above indicates that the
paper in this book meets that standard.

Printed in the United States of America

PREFACE

In this volume I have tried to show how Christmas is or has been kept in various lands and ages, and to trace as far as possible the origin of the pagan elements that have mingled with the Church's feast of the Nativity.

In Part I. I have dealt with the festival on its distinctively Christian side. The book has, however, been so planned that readers not interested in this aspect of Christmas may pass over Chapters II.–V., and proceed at once from the Introduction to Part II., which treats of pagan survivals.

The book has been written primarily for the general reader, but I venture to hope that, with all its imperfections, it may be of some use to the more serious student, as a rough outline map of the field of Christmas customs, and as bringing together materials hitherto scattered through a multitude of volumes in various languages. There is certainly room for a comprehensive English book on Christmas, taking account of the results or modern historical and folk-lore research.

The writer of a work of this kind necessarily owes an immense debt to the labours of others. In my bibliographical notes I have done my best to acknowledge the sources from which I have drawn. It is only right that I should express here my special obligation, both for information and for suggestions, to Mr. E. K. Chambers's "The Mediaeval Stage," an invaluable storehouse of fact, theory, and bibliographical references. I also owe much to the important monographs of Dr. A. Tille, "Die Geschichte der deutschen Weihnacht" and "Yule and Christmas"; to Dr. Feilberg's Danish work, "Jul," the fullest account of Christmas

5

PREFACE

customs yet written ; and of course, like every student of folk-
lore, to Dr. Frazer's "The Golden Bough."

References to authorities will be found at the end ot the
volume, and are indicated by small numerals in the text ; notes
requiring to be read in close conjunction with the text are
printed at the foot of the pages to which they relate, and are
indicated by asterisks, &c.

I have to thank Mr. Frank Sidgwick for most kindly reading
my proofs and portions of my MS., and for some valuable suggestions.

C. A. M.

CONTENTS

7

CONTENTS

CHAPTER IV

CHAPTER V

PART II

PAGAN SURVIVALS

CHAPTER VI

CONTENTS

CHAPTER VII

CHAPTER VIII

CHAPTER IX

CHAPTER X

CONTENTS

CHAPTER XI

CHAPTER XII

CHAPTER XIII

CHAPTER XIV

CONTENTS

CHAPTER XV

CHAPTER XVI

ILLUSTRATIONS

CHAPTER I
INTRODUCTION

CHAPTER I

INTRODUCTION

The Origin and Purpose of Festivals—Ideas suggested by Christmas—Pagan and Christian Elements—The Names of the Festival—Foundation of the Feast of the Nativity—Its Relation to the Epiphany—December 25 and the *Natalis Invicti*—The Kalends of January—Yule and Teutonic Festivals—The Church and Pagan Survivals—Two Conflicting Types of Festival—Their Interaction—Plan of the Book.

IT has been an instinct in nearly all peoples, savage or civilized, to set aside certain days for special ceremonial observances, attended by outward rejoicing. This tendency to concentrate on special times answers to man's need to lift himself above the commonplace and the everyday, to escape from the leaden weight of monotony that oppresses him. "We tend to tire of the most eternal splendours, and a mark on our calendar, or a crash of bells at midnight maybe, reminds us that we have only recently been created."*[1] That they wake people up is the great justification or festivals, and both man's religious sense and his joy in life have generally tended to rise " into peaks and towers and turrets, into superhuman exceptions which really prove the rule." [2] It is difficult to be religious, impossible to be merry, at every moment of life, and festivals are as sunlit peaks, testifying, above dark valleys, to the eternal radiance. This is one view of the purpose and value of festivals, and their function of cheering people and giving them larger perspectives has no doubt been an important reason for their maintenance in the past. If we could trace the custom of festival-keeping back to its origins in primitive society

* For an explanation of the small numerals in the text see Preface.

we should find the same principle of specialization involved, though it is probable that the practice came into being not for the sake of its moral or emotional effect, but from man's desire to lay up, so to speak, a stock of sanctity, magical not ethical, for ordinary days.

The first holy-day-makers were probably more concerned with such material goods as food than with spiritual ideals, when they marked with sacred days the rhythm of the seasons.3 As man's consciousness developed, the subjective aspect of the matter would come increasingly into prominence, until in the festivals of the Christian Church the main object is to quicken the devotion of the believer by contemplation of the mysteries of the faith. Yet attached, as we shall see, to many Christian festivals, are old notions of magical sanctity, probably quite as potent in the minds of the common people as the more spiritual ideas suggested by the Church's feasts.

In modern England we have almost lost the festival habit, but if there is one feast that survives among us as a universal tradition it is Christmas. We have indeed our Bank Holidays, but they are mere days of rest and amusement, and for the mass of the people Easter and Whitsuntide have small religious significance— Christmas alone has the character of sanctity which marks the true festival. The celebration of Christmas has often little or nothing to do with orthodox dogma, yet somehow the sense of obligation to keep the feast is very strong, and there are few English people, however unconventional, who escape altogether the spell of tradition in this matter.

Christmas—how many images the word calls up : we think of carol-singers and holly-decked churches where people hymn in time-honoured strains the Birth of the Divine Child ; of frost and snow, and, in contrast, of warm hearths and homes bright with light and colour, very fortresses against the cold ; of feasting and revelry, of greetings and gifts exchanged ; and lastly of vaguely superstitious customs, relics of long ago, performed perhaps out of respect for use and wont, or merely in jest, or with a deliberate attempt to throw ourselves back into the past, to re-enter for a moment the mental childhood of the race. These are a few of

INTRODUCTION

the pictures that rise pell-mell in the minds of English folk at the mention of Christmas; how many other scenes would come before us if we could realize what the festival means to men of other nations. Yet even these will suggest what hardly needs saying, that Christmas is something far more complex than a Church holy-day alone, that the celebration of the Birth of Jesus, deep and touching as is its appeal to those who hold the faith of the Incarnation, is but one of many elements that have entered into the great winter festival.

In the following pages I shall try to present a picture, sketchy and inadequate though it must be, of what Christmas is and has been to the peoples of Europe, and to show as far as possible the various elements that have gone into its make-up. Most people have a vague impression that these are largely pagan, but comparatively few have any idea of the process by which the heathen elements have become mingled with that which is obviously Christian, and equal obscurity prevails as to the nature and meaning of the non-Christian customs. The subject is vast, and has not been thoroughly explored as yet, but the labours of historians and folk-lorists have made certain conclusions probable, and have produced hypotheses of great interest and fascination.

I have spoken of "Christian"* and "pagan" elements. The distinction is blurred to some extent by the clothing of heathen customs in a superficial Christianity, but on the whole it is clear enough to justify the division of this book into two parts, one dealing with the Church's feast of the Holy Birth, the other with those remains of pagan winter festivals which extend from November to January, but cluster especially round Christmas and the Twelve Days.

Before we pass to the various aspects of the Church's Christmas, we must briefly consider its origins and its relation to certain

* "Christianity," as here used, will stand for the system of orthodoxy which had been fixed in its main outlines when the festival of Christmas took its rise. The relation of the orthodox creed to historical fact need not concern us here, nor need we for the purposes of this study attempt to distinguish between the Christianity of Jesus and ecclesiastical accretions around his teaching.

pagan festivals, the customs of which will be dealt with in detail in Part II.

The names given to the feast by different European peoples throw a certain amount of light on its history. Let us take five of them—*Christmas*, *Weihnacht*, *Noël*, *Calendas*, and *Yule*—and see what they suggest.

I. The English *Christmas* and its Dutch equivalent *Kerstmisse*, plainly point to the ecclesiastical side of the festival ; the German *Weihnacht* 4 (sacred night) is vaguer, and might well be either pagan or Christian ; in point of fact it seems to be Christian, since it does not appear till the year 1000, when the Faith was well established in Germany.5 *Christmas* and *Weihnacht*, then, may stand for the distinctively Christian festival, the history of which we may now briefly study.

When and where did the keeping of Christmas begin ? Many details of its early history remain in uncertainty, but it is fairly clear that the earliest celebration of the Birth of Christ on December 25 took place at Rome about the middle of the fourth century, and that the observance of the day spread from the western to the eastern Church, which had before been wont to keep January 6 as a joint commemoration of the Nativity and the Baptism of the Redeemer.*

The first mention of a Nativity feast on December 25 is found in a Roman document known as the Philocalian Calendar, dating from the year 354, but embodying an older document evidently belonging to the year 336. It is uncertain to which date the Nativity reference belongs ; † but further back than 336 at all events the festival cannot be traced.

From Rome, Christmas spread throughout the West, with the

* Whether the Nativity had previously been celebrated at Rome on January 6 is a matter of controversy ; the affirmative view was maintained by Usener in his monograph on Christmas,6 the negative by Monsignor Duchesne.7 A very minute, cautious, and balanced study of both arguments is to be found in Professor Kirsopp Lake's article on Christmas in Hastings's " Encyclopædia of Religion and Ethics," 8 and a short article was contributed by the same writer to *The Guardian*, December 29, 1911. Professor Lake, on the whole, inclines to Usener's view. The early history of the festival is also treated by Father Cyril Martindale in " The Catholic Encyclopædia " (article " Christmas ").

† Usener says 354, Duchesne 336.

INTRODUCTION

conversion of the barbarians. Whether it came to England through the Celtic Church is uncertain, but St. Augustine certainly brought it with him, and Christmas Day, 598, witnessed a great event, the baptism of more than ten thousand English converts.9 In 567 the Council of Tours had declared the Twelve Days, from Christmas to Epiphany, a festal tide ; 10 the laws of Ethelred (991–1016) ordained it to be a time of peace and concord among Christian men, when all strife must cease.11 In Germany Christmas was established by the Synod of Mainz in 813 ; 12 in Norway by King Hakon the Good about the middle of the tenth century.13

In the East, as has been seen, the Birth of the Redeemer was at first celebrated not on December 25, but on January 6, the feast of the Epiphany or manifestation of Christ's glory. The Epiphany can be traced as far back as the second century, among the Basilidian heretics, from whom it may have spread to the Catholic Church. It was with them certainly a feast of the Baptism, and possibly also of the Nativity, of Christ. The origins of the Epiphany festival 14 are very obscure, nor can we say with certainty what was its meaning at first. It may be that it took the place of a heathen rite celebrating the birth of the World or Æon from the Virgin on January 6.* At all events one of its objects was to commemorate the Baptism, the appearance of the Holy Dove, and the Voice from heaven, " Thou art my beloved son, in whom I am well pleased " (or, as other MSS. read, " This day have I begotten thee ").

* The eastern father, Epiphanius (fourth century), gives a strange account of a heathen, or perhaps in reality a Gnostic, rite held at Alexandria on the night of January 5–6. In the temple of Kore—the Maiden—he tells us, worshippers spent the night in singing and flute-playing, and at cockcrow brought up from a subterranean sanctuary a wooden image seated naked on a litter. It had the sign of the cross upon it in gold in five places—the forehead, the hands, and the knees. This image was carried seven times round the central hall of the temple with flute-playing, drumming, and hymns, and then taken back to the underground chamber. In explanation of these strange actions it was said : " To-day, at this hour, hath Kore (the Maiden) borne the Æon." 15 Can there be a connection between this festival and the Eleusinian mysteries ? In the latter there was a nocturnal celebration with many lights burning, and the cry went forth, " Holy Brimo (the Maiden) hath borne a sacred child, Brimos." 16 The details given by Miss Harrison in her " Prolegomena " of the worship of the child Dionysus 17 are of extraordinary interest, and a minute comparison of this cult with that of the Christ Child might lead to remarkable results.

CHRISTMAS

In some circles of early Christianity the Baptism appears to have been looked upon as the true Birth of Christ, the moment when, filled by the Spirit, He became Son of God ; and the carnal Birth was regarded as of comparatively little significance. Hence the Baptism festival may have arisen first, and the celebration of the Birth at Bethlehem may have been later attached to the same day, partly perhaps because a passage in St. Luke's Gospel was supposed to imply that Jesus was baptized on His thirtieth birthday. As however the orthodox belief became more sharply defined, increasing stress was laid on the Incarnation of God in Christ in the Virgin's womb, and it may have been felt that the celebration of the Birth and the Baptism on the same day encouraged heretical views. Hence very likely the introduction of Christmas on December 25 as a festival of the Birth alone. In the East the concelebration of the two events continued for some time after Rome had instituted the separate feast of Christmas. Gradually, however, the Roman use spread : at Constantinople it was introduced about 380 by the great theologian, Gregory Nazianzen ; at Antioch it appeared in 388, at Alexandria in 432. The Church of Jerusalem long stood out, refusing to adopt the new feast till the seventh century, it would seem.[18] One important Church, the Armenian, knows nothing of December 25, and still celebrates the Nativity with the Epiphany on January 6.[19] Epiphany in the eastern Orthodox Church has lost its connection with the Nativity and is now chiefly a celebration of the Baptism of Christ, while in the West, as every one knows, it is primarily a celebration of the Adoration by the Magi, an event commemorated by the Greeks on Christmas Day. Epiphany is, however, as we shall see, a greater festival in the Greek Church than Christmas.

Such in bare outline is the story of the spread of Christmas as an independent festival. Its establishment fitly followed the triumph of the Catholic doctrine of the perfect Godhead of Christ at the Council of Nicea in 325.

II. The French *Noël* is a name concerning whose origin there has been considerable dispute ; there can, however, be little doubt that it is the same word as the Provençal *Nadau* or *Nadal*, the Italian *Natale*, and the Welsh *Nadolig*, all obviously derived from the Latin *natalis*, and meaning " birthday." One naturally takes this as referring to the Birth of Christ, but it may at any rate remind us of another birthday celebrated on the same date by the Romans of the Empire, that of the unconquered Sun, who on December 25, the winter solstice according to the Julian calendar, began to rise to new vigour after his autumnal decline.

Why, we may ask, did the Church choose December 25 for the celebration of her Founder's Birth ? No one now imagines that the date is supported by a reliable tradition ; it is only one of various guesses of early Christian writers. As a learned eighteenth-century Jesuit [20] has pointed out, there is not a single month in the year to which the Nativity has not been assigned by some writer or other. The real reason for the choice of the day most probably was, that upon it fell the pagan festival just mentioned.

The *Dies Natalis Invicti* was probably first celebrated in Rome by order of the Emperor Aurelian (270-5), an ardent worshipper of the Syrian sun-god Baal.[21] With the *Sol Invictus* was identified the figure of Mithra, that strange eastern god whose cult resembled in so many ways the worship of Jesus, and who was at one time a serious rival of the Christ in the minds or thoughtful men.* [22] It was the sun-god, poetically and philosophically conceived, whom the Emperor Julian made the centre of his ill-fated revival of paganism, and there is extant a fine prayer of his to "King Sun." [23]

What more natural than that the Church should choose this day to celebrate the rising of her Sun of Righteousness with healing in His wings, that she should strive thus to draw away to His worship some adorers of the god whose symbol and representative was the earthly sun ! There is no direct evidence of deliberate substitution, but at all events ecclesiastical writers soon after the foundation of Christmas made good use of the idea

* Mithraism resembled Christianity in its monotheistic tendencies, its sacraments, its comparatively high morality, its doctrine of an Intercessor and Redeemer, and its vivid belief in a future life and judgment to come. Moreover Sunday was its holy-day dedicated to the Sun.

that the birthday of the Saviour had replaced the birthday of the sun.*

Little is known of the manner in which the *Natalis Invicti* was kept; it was not a folk-festival, and was probably observed by the classes rather than the masses.²⁴ Its direct influence on Christmas customs has probaby been little or nothing. It fell, however, just before a Roman festival that had immense popularity, is of great importance for our subject, and is recalled by another name for Christmas that must now be considered.

III. The Provençal *Calendas* or *Calenos*, the Polish *Kolenda*, the Russian *Kolyáda*, the Czech *Koleda* and the Lithuanian *Kalledos*, not to speak of the Welsh *Calenig* for Christmas-box, and the Gaelic *Calluinn* for New Year's Eve, are all derived from the Latin *Kalendae*, and suggest the connection of Christmas with the Roman New Year's Day, the Kalends or the first day of January, a time celebrated with many festive customs. What these were, and how they have affected Christmas we shall see in some detail in Part II.; suffice it to say here that the festival, which lasted for at least three days, was one of riotous life, of banqueting and games and licence. It was preceded, moreover, by the *Saturnalia* (December 17 to 23) which had many like features, and must have formed practically one festive season with it. The word *Saturnalia* has become so familiar in modern usage as to suggest sufficiently the character of the festival for which it stands.

---

* This is the explanation adopted by most scholars (cf. Chambers, " M. S.," i., 241–2). Duchesne suggests as an explanation of the choice of December 25 the fact that a tradition fixed the Passion of Christ on March 25. The same date, he thinks, would have been assigned to His Conception in order to make the years of His life complete, and the Birth would come naturally nine months after the Conception. He, however, " would not venture to say, in regard to the 25th of December, that the coincidence of the *Sol novus* exercised no direct or indirect influence on the ecclesiastical decision arrived at in regard to the matter." ²⁵ Professor Lake also, in his article in Hastings's " Encyclopædia," seeks to account for the selection of December 25 without any deliberate competition with the *Natalis Invicti*. He points out that the Birth of Christ was fixed at the vernal equinox by certain early chronologists, on the strength of an elaborate and fantastic calculation based on Scriptural data, and connecting the Incarnation with the Creation, and that when the Incarnation came to be viewed as beginning at the Conception instead of the Birth, the latter would naturally be placed nine months later.

INTRODUCTION

Into the midst of this season of revelry and licence the Church introduced her celebration of the beginning of man's redemption from the bondage of sin. Who can wonder that Christmas contains incongruous elements, for old things, loved by the people, cannot easily be uprooted.

IV. One more name yet remains to be considered, *Yule* (Danish *Jul*), the ordinary word for Christmas in the Scandinavian languages, and not extinct among ourselves. Its derivation has been widely discussed, but so far no satisfactory explanation of it has been found. Professor Skeat in the last edition of his Etymological Dictionary (1910) has to admit that its origin is unknown. Whatever its source may be, it is clearly the name of a Germanic season—probably a two-month tide covering the second half of November, the whole of December, and the first half of January.[26] It may well suggest to us the element added to Christmas by the barbarian peoples who began to learn Christianity about the time when the festival was founded. Modern research has tended to disprove the idea that the old Germans held a Yule feast at the winter solstice, and it is probable, as we shall see, that the specifically Teutonic Christmas customs come from a New Year and beginning-of-winter festival kept about the middle of November. These customs transferred to Christmas are to a great extent religious or magical rites intended to secure prosperity during the coming year, and there is also the familiar Christmas feasting, apparently derived in part from the sacrificial banquets that marked the beginning of winter.

We have now taken a general glance at the elements which have combined in Christmas. The heathen folk-festivals absorbed by the Nativity feast were essentially life-affirming, they expressed the mind of men who said "yes" to this life, who valued earthly good things. On the other hand Christianity, at all events in its intensest form, the religion of the monks, was at bottom pessimistic as regards this earth, and valued it only as a place of discipline for the life to come ; it was essentially a religion of renunciation that said "no" to the world. The

25

CHRISTMAS

Christian had here no continuing city, but sought one to come. How could the Church make a feast of the secular New Year; what mattered to her the world of time? her eye was fixed upon the eternal realities—the great drama of Redemption. Not upon the course of the temporal sun through the zodiac, but upon the mystical progress of the eternal Sun of Righteousness must she base her calendar. Christmas and New Year's Day—the two festivals stood originally for the most opposed of principles.

Naturally the Church fought bitterly against the observance of the Kalends; she condemned repeatedly the unseemly doings of Christians in joining in heathenish customs at that season; she tried to make the first of January a solemn fast; and from the ascetic point of view she was profoundly right, for the old festivals were bound up with a lusty attitude towards the world, a seeking for earthly joy and well-being.

The struggle between the ascetic principle of self-mortification, world-renunciation, absorption in a transcendent ideal, and the natural human striving towards earthly joy and well-being, is, perhaps, the most interesting aspect of the history of Christianity; it is certainly shown in an absorbingly interesting way in the development of the Christian feast of the Nativity. The conflict is keen at first; the Church authorities fight tooth and nail against these relics of heathenism, these devilish rites; but mankind's instinctive paganism is insuppressible, the practices continue as ritual, though losing much of their meaning, and the Church, weary of denouncing, comes to wink at them, while the pagan joy in earthly life begins to colour her own festival.

The Church's Christmas, as the Middle Ages pass on, becomes increasingly "merry"—warm and homely, suited to the instincts of ordinary humanity, filled with a joy that is of this earth, and not only a mystical rapture at a transcendental Redemption. The Incarnate God becomes a real child to be fondled and rocked, a child who is the loveliest of infants, whose birthday is the supreme type of all human birthdays, and may be kept with feasting and dance and song. Such is the Christmas of popular tradition, the Nativity as it is reflected in the carols, the cradle-rocking, the mystery plays of the later Middle Ages. This

INTRODUCTION

Christmas, which still lingers, though maimed, in some Catholic regions, is strongly life-affirming ; the value and delight of earthly, material things is keenly felt ; sometimes, even, it passes into coarseness and riot. Yet a certain mysticism usually penetrates it, with hints that this dear life, this fair world, are not all, for the soul has immortal longings in her. Nearly always there is the spirit of reverence, of bowing down before the Infant God, a visitor from the supernatural world, though bone of man's bone, flesh of his flesh. Heaven and earth have met together ; the rough stable is become the palace of the Great King.

This we might well call the " Catholic " Christmas, the Christmas of the age when the Church most nearly answered to the needs of the whole man, spiritual and sensuous. The Reformation in England and Germany did not totally destroy it ; in England the carol-singers kept up for a while the old spirit ; in Lutheran Germany a highly coloured and surprisingly sensuous celebration of the Nativity lingered on into the eighteenth century. In the countries that remained Roman Catholic much of the old Christmas continued, though the spirit of the Counter-Reformation, faced by the challenge of Protestantism, made for greater " respectability," and often robbed the Catholic Christmas of its humour, its homeliness, its truly popular stamp, substituting pretentiousness for simplicity, sugary sentiment for naïve and genuine poetry.

Apart from the transformation of the Church's Christmas from something austere and metaphysical into something joyous and human, warm and kindly, we shall note in our Second Part the survival of much that is purely pagan, continuing alongside of the celebration of the Nativity, and often little touched by its influence. But first we must consider the side of the festival suggested by the English and French names : *Christmas* will stand for the liturgical rites commemorating the wonder of the Incarnation —God in man made manifest—*Noël* or " the Birthday," for the ways in which men have striven to realize the human aspect or the great Coming.

How can we reach the inner meaning of the Nativity feast, its significance for the faithful ? Better, perhaps, by the way of poetry than by the way of ritual, for it is poetry that reveals the emotions at the back of the outward observances, and we shall understand these better when the singers of Christmas have laid bare to us their hearts. We may therefore first give attention to the Christmas poetry of sundry ages and peoples, and then go on to consider the liturgical and popular ritual in which the Church has striven to express her joy at the Redeemer's birth. Ceremonial, of course, has always mimetic tendencies, and in a further chapter we shall see how these issued in genuine drama ; how, in the miracle plays, the Christmas story was represented by the forms and voices of living men.

CHAPTER II

CHRISTMAS POETRY

I

MADONNA ENTHRONED WITH SAINTS AND ANGELS.   PESELLINO
(Empoli Gallery)

CHAPTER II

CHRISTMAS POETRY (I) * ¹

Ancient Latin Hymns, their Dogmatic, Theological Character—Humanizing Influence of Franciscanism—Jacopone da Todi's Vernacular Verse—German
Catholic Poetry—Mediaeval English Carols.

CHRISTMAS, as we have seen, had its beginning at the middle
of the fourth century in Rome. The new feast was not long in
finding a hymn-writer to embody in immortal Latin the emotions
called forth by the memory of the Nativity. " Veni, redemptor
gentium " is one of the earliest of Latin hymns—one of the few
that have come down to us from the father of Church song,
Ambrose, Archbishop of Milan (d. 397). Great as theologian
and statesman, Ambrose was great also as a poet and systematizer
of Church music. " Veni, redemptor gentium " is above all
things stately and severe, in harmony with the austere character
of the zealous foe of the Arian heretics, the champion of monasticism. It is the theological aspect alone of Christmas, the
redemption of sinful man by the mystery of the Incarnation and
the miracle of the Virgin Birth, that we find in St. Ambrose's
terse and pregnant Latin ; there is no feeling for the human
pathos and poetry of the scene at Bethlehem—

> " Veni, redemptor gentium,
> Ostende partum virginis ;
> Miretur omne saeculum :
> Talis decet partus Deum.

---

* Cf. chap. xviii. of Dr. Yrjö Hirn's " The Sacred Shrine" (London, 1912). Dr.
Hirn finds a solitary anticipation of the Franciscan treatment of the Nativity in the
Christmas hymns of the fourth-century eastern poet, Ephraem Syrus.

THE CHRISTIAN FEAST

Non ex virili semine,
Sed mystico spiramine,
Verbum Dei factum caro,
Fructusque ventris floruit." * 2

. . . .

Another fine hymn often heard in English churches is of a
slightly later date. "Corde natus ex Parentis" ("Of the
Father's love begotten") is a cento from a larger hymn by the
Spanish poet Prudentius (c. 348–413). Prudentius did not write
for liturgical purposes, and it was several centuries before "Corde
natus" was adopted into the cycle of Latin hymns. Its elaborate
rhetoric is very unlike the severity of "Veni, redemptor gentium,"
but again the note is purely theological; the Incarnation as
a world-event is its theme. It sings the Birth of Him who is

"Corde natus ex Parentis
Ante mundi exordium,
Alpha et O cognominatus,
Ipse fons et clausula.
Omnium quae sunt, fuerunt,
Quaeque post futura sunt
            Saeculorum saeculis." † 3

Other early hymns are "A solis ortus cardine" ("From east
to west, from shore to shore"), by a certain Coelius Sedulius
(d. c. 450), still sung by the Roman Church at Lauds on Christmas Day, and "Jesu, redemptor omnium" (sixth century), the
office hymn at Christmas Vespers. Like the poems of Ambrose
and Prudentius, they are in classical metres, unrhymed, and based
upon quantity, not accent, and they have the same general
character, doctrinal rather than humanly tender.

In the ninth and tenth centuries arose a new form of hymnody,
the Prose or Sequence sung after the Gradual (the anthem
between the Epistle and Gospel at Mass). The earliest writer
of sequences was Notker, a monk of the abbey of St. Gall, near

* No. 55 in "Hymns Ancient and Modern" (Ordinary Edition).
† No. 56 in "Hymns Ancient and Modern" (Ordinary Edition).

32

the Lake of Constance. Among those that are probably his work is the Christmas "Natus ante saecula Dei filius." The most famous Nativity sequence, however, is the " Laetabundus, exsultet fidelis chorus " of St. Bernard of Clairvaux (d. 1153), once sung all over Europe, and especially popular in England and France. Here are its opening verses :—

> " Laetabundus,
> Exsultet fidelis chorus ;
> Alleluia !
> Regem regum
> Intactae profudit thorus ;
> Res miranda !
>
> Angelus consilii
> Natus est de Virgine,
> Sol de stella !
> Sol occasum nesciens,
> Stella semper rutilans,
> Semper clara." * 4

The "Laetabundus " is in rhymed stanzas ; in this it differs from most early proses. The writing of rhymed sequences, however, became common through the example of the Parisian monk, Adam of St. Victor, in the second half of the twelfth century. He adopted an entirely new style of versification and music, derived from popular songs ; and he and his successors in

> * " Come rejoicing,
> Faithful men, with rapture singing
> Alleluya !
> Monarch's Monarch,
> From a holy maiden springing,
> Mighty wonder !
>
> Angel of the Counsel here,
> Sun from star, he doth appear,
> Born of maiden :
> He a sun who knows no night,
> She a star whose paler light
> Fadeth never."
> (Translation in "The English Hymnal," No. 22.)

the thirteenth and fourteenth centuries wrote various proses for the Christmas festival.

If we consider the Latin Christmas hymns from the fourth century to the thirteenth, we shall find that however much they differ in form, they have one common characteristic: they are essentially theological—dwelling on the Incarnation and the Nativity as part of the process of man's redemption—rather than realistic. There is little attempt to imagine the scene in the stable at Bethlehem, little interest in the Child as a child, little sense of the human pathos of the Nativity. The explanation is, I think, very simple, and it lights up the whole observance of Christmas as a Church festival in the centuries we are considering: *this poetry is the poetry of monks, or of men imbued with the monastic spirit.*

The two centuries following the institution of Christmas saw the break-up of the Roman Empire in the west, and the incursions of barbarians threatening the very existence of the Christian civilization that had conquered classic paganism. It was by her army of monks that the Church tamed and Christianized the barbarians, and both religion and culture till the middle of the twelfth century were predominantly monastic. "In writing of any eminently religious man of this period" [the eleventh century], says Dean Church, "it must be taken almost as a matter of course that he was a monk."5 And a monastery was not the place for human feeling about Christmas; the monk was—at any rate in ideal—cut off from the world; not for him were the joys of parenthood or tender feelings for a new-born child. To the monk the world was, at least in theory, the vale of misery; birth and generation were, one may almost say, tolerated as necessary evils among lay folk unable to rise to the heights of abstinence and renunciation; one can hardly imagine a true early Benedictine filled with "joy that a man is born into the world." The Nativity was an infinitely important event, to be celebrated with a chastened, unearthly joy, but not, as it became for the later Middle Ages and the Renaissance, a matter upon which human affection might lavish itself, which imagination might deck with vivid concrete detail. In the later Christmas the pagan and the Christian spirit, or delight in earthly things and joy in the invisible, seem to meet and mingle ; to the true monk of the Dark and Early Middle Ages they were incompatible.

What of the people, the great world outside the monasteries ? Can we imagine that Christmas, on its Christian side, had a deep meaning for them ? For the first ten centuries, to quote Dean Church again, Christianity " can hardly be said to have leavened society at all. . . . It acted upon it doubtless with enormous power ; but it was as an extraneous and foreign agent, which destroys and shapes, but does not mingle or renew. . . . Society was a long time unlearning heathenism ; it has not done so yet ; but it had hardly begun, at any rate it was only just beginning, to imagine the possibility of such a thing in the eleventh century."[6]

" The practical religion of the illiterate," says another ecclesiastical historian, Dr. W. R. W. Stephens, " was in many respects merely a survival of the old paganism thinly disguised. There was a prevalent belief in witchcraft, magic, sortilegy, spells, charms, talismans, which mixed itself up in strange ways with Christian ideas and Christian worship. . . . Fear, the note of superstition, rather than love, which is the characteristic of a rational faith, was conspicuous in much of the popular religion. The world was haunted by demons, hobgoblins, malignant spirits of divers kinds, whose baneful influence must be averted by charms or offerings."[7]

The writings of ecclesiastics, the decrees of councils and synods, from the fourth century to the eleventh, abound in condemnations of pagan practices at the turn of the year. It is in these customs, and in secular mirth and revelry, not in Christian poetry, that we must seek for the expression of early lay feeling about Christmas. It was a feast of material good things, a time for the fulfilment of traditional heathen usages, rather than a joyous celebration of the Saviour's birth. No doubt it was observed by due attendance at church, but the services in a tongue not understanded of the people cannot have been very full of meaning to them, and we can imagine

their Christmas church-going as rather a duty inspired by fear
than an expression of devout rejoicing. It is noteworthy that
the earliest of vernacular Christmas carols known to us, the
early thirteenth-century Anglo-Norman "Seignors, ore entendez
à nus," is a song not of religion but of revelry. Its last verse
is typical :

> "Seignors, jo vus di par Noël,
> E par li sires de cest hostel,
>   Car bevez ben ;
> E jo primes beverai le men,
> E pois aprèz chescon le soen,
>   Par mon conseil ;
> Si jo vus di trestoz, 'Wesseyl !'
> Dehaiz eit qui ne dirra, 'Drincheyl !' " *[8]

Not till the close of the thirteenth century do we meet with
any vernacular Christmas poetry of importance. The verses
of the *troubadours* and *trouvères* of twelfth-century France had
little to do with Christianity ; their songs were mostly of
earthly and illicit love. The German Minnesingers of the
thirteenth century were indeed pious, but their devout lays
were addressed to the Virgin as Queen of Heaven, the ideal
of womanhood, holding in glory the Divine Child in her arms,
rather than to the Babe and His Mother in the great humility
of Bethlehem.

The first real outburst of Christmas joy in a popular tongue
is found in Italy, in the poems of that strange "minstrel of the
Lord," the Franciscan Jacopone da Todi (b. 1228, d. 1306).
Franciscan, in that name we have an indication of the change
in religious feeling that came over the western world, and

> * "Lords, by Christmas and the host
>   Of this mansion hear my toast—
>   Drink it well—
>   Each must drain his cup of wine,
>   And I the first will toss off mine :
>   Thus I advise.
>   Here then I bid you all *Wassail*,
>   Cursed be he who will not say, *Drinkhail* ! "
>
> (Translation by F. Douce.)

especially Italy, in the thirteenth century. 9   For the twenty
all-too-short years of St. Francis's apostolate have passed, and
a new attitude towards God and man and the world has become
possible.   Not that the change was due solely to St. Francis;
he was rather the supreme embodiment of the ideals and tendencies of his day than their actual creator ; but he was the spark
that kindled a mighty flame.   In him we reach so important
a turning-point in the history of Christmas that we must linger
awhile at his side.

Early Franciscanism meant above all the democratizing, the
humanizing of Christianity ; with it begins that " carol spirit "
which is the most winning part of the Christian Christmas, the
spirit which, while not forgetting the divine side of the Nativity,
yet delights in its simple humanity, the spirit that links the
Incarnation to the common life of the people, that brings human
tenderness into religion.   The faithful no longer contemplate
merely a theological mystery, they are moved by affectionate
devotion to the Babe of Bethlehem, realized as an actual living
child, God indeed, yet feeling the cold of winter, the roughness
of the manger bed.

St. Francis, it must be remembered, was not a man of high
birth, but the son of a silk merchant, and his appeal was made
chiefly to the traders and skilled workmen of the cities, who, in
his day, were rising to importance, coming, in modern Socialist
terms, to class-consciousness.   The monks, although boys of low
birth were sometimes admitted into the cloister, were in sympathy one with the upper classes, and monastic religion and
culture were essentially aristocratic.   The rise of the Franciscans
meant the bringing home of Christianity to masses of town-
workers, homely people, who needed a religion full of vivid
humanity, and whom the pathetic story of the Nativity would
peculiarly touch.

Love to man, the sense of human brotherhood—that was the
great thing which St. Francis brought home to his age.   The
message, certainly, was not new, but he realized it with infectious
intensity.   The second great commandment, " Thou shalt love
thy neighbour as thyself," had not indeed been forgotten by

mediaeval Christianity ; the common life of monasticism was an attempt to fulfil it ; yet for the monk love to man was often rather a duty than a passion. But to St. Francis love was very life ; he loved not by duty but by an inner compulsion, and his burning love of God and man found its centre in the God-man, Christ Jesus. For no saint, perhaps, has the earthly life of Christ been the object of such passionate devotion as for St. Francis ; the Stigmata were the awful, yet, to his contemporaries, glorious fruit of his meditations on the Passion ; and of the ecstasy with which he kept his Christmas at Greccio we shall read when we come to consider the *Presepio.* He had a peculiar affection for the festival of the Holy Child; "the Child Jesus," says Thomas of Celano, "had been given over to forgetfulness in the hearts of many in whom, by the working of His grace, He was raised up again through His servant Francis." [10]

To the Early Middle Ages Christ was the awful Judge, the *Rex tremendae majestatis,* though also the divine bringer of salvation from sin and eternal punishment, and, to the mystic, the Bridegroom of the Soul. To Francis He was the little brother of all mankind as well. It was a new human joy that came into religion with him. His essentially artistic nature was the first to realize the full poetry of Christmas—the coming of infinity into extremest limitation, the Highest made the lowliest, the King of all kings a poor infant. He had, in a supreme degree, the mingled reverence and tenderness that inspire the best carols.

Though no Christmas verses by St. Francis have come down to us, there is a beautiful "psalm" for Christmas Day at Vespers, composed by him partly from passages of Scripture. A portion of Father Paschal Robinson's translation may be quoted :—

> "Rejoice to God our helper.
> Shout unto God, living and true,
> With the voice of triumph.
> For the Lord is high, terrible :
> A great King over all the earth.
> For the most holy Father of heaven,

JACOPONE IN ECSTASY BEFORE THE VIRGIN.

From "Laude di Frate Jacopone da Todi" (Florence, 1490).

To face p. 39.

ITALIAN CHRISTMAS POETRY

> Our King, before ages sent His Be-
> loved Son from on high, and He
> was born of the Blessed Virgin,
> holy Mary.

> .   .   .   ,   .

> This is the day which the Lord
> hath made : let us rejoice and be
> glad in it.
> For the beloved and most holy
> Child has been given to us and
> born for us by the wayside.
> And laid in a manger because He
> had no room in the inn.
> Glory to God in the highest : and
> on earth peace to men of good will." [11]

It is in the poetry of Jacopone da Todi, born shortly after the death of St. Francis, that the Franciscan Christmas spirit finds its most intense expression. A wild, wandering ascetic, an impassioned poet, and a soaring mystic, Jacopone is one of the greatest of Christian singers, unpolished as his verses are. Noble by birth, he made himself utterly as the common people for whom he piped his rustic notes. "Dio fatto piccino" ("God made a little thing") is the keynote of his music ; the Christ Child is for him "our sweet little brother"; with tender affection he rejoices in endearing diminutives—"Bambolino," "Piccolino," "Jesulino." He sings of the Nativity with extraordinary realism.* Here, in words, is a picture of the Madonna and her Child that might well have inspired an early Tuscan artist :—

> " Veggiamo il suo Bambino
> Gammettare nel fieno,
> E le braccia scoperte
> Porgere ad ella in seno,

---

* It is difficult to be sure of the authenticity of the verse attributed to Jacopone. Many of the poems in Tresatti's edition, from which the quotations in the text are taken, may be the work of his followers.

THE CHRISTIAN FEAST

> Ed essa lo ricopre
> El meglio che può almeno,
> Mettendoli la poppa
> Entro la sua bocchina.

> . . . .

> A la sua man manca,
> Cullava lo Bambino,
> E con sante carole
> Nenciava il suo amor fino . . .
> Gli Angioletti d' intorno
> Se ne gian danzando,
> Facendo dolci versi
> E d' amor favellando." * 12

But there is an intense sense of the divine, as well as the human, in the Holy Babe ; no one has felt more vividly the paradox of the Incarnation :—

> " Ne la degna stalla del dolce Bambino
> Gli Angeli cantano d' intorno al piccolino ;
> Cantano e gridano gli Angeli diletti,
> Tutti riverenti timidi e subietti,

* " Come and look upon her child
Nestling in the hay !
See his fair arms opened wide,
On her lap to play !
And she tucks him by her side,
Cloaks him as she may !
Gives her paps unto his mouth,
Where his lips are laid.

. . . .

She with left hand cradling
Rocked and hushed her boy,
And with holy lullabies
Quieted her toy. . . .
Little angels all around
Danced, and carols flung ;
Making verselets sweet and true,
Still of love they sung."

(Translation by John Addington Symonds in "The Renaissance in Italy. Italian Literature" [1898 Edn.], Part I., 468.)

ITALIAN CHRISTMAS POETRY

Al Bambolino principe de gli eletti,
Che nudo giace nel pungente spino.

.   .   .   .   .

Il Verbo divino, che è sommo sapiente,
In questo dì par che non sappia niente,
Guardal su' l fieno, che gambetta piangente,
Como elli non fusse huomo divino." * [13]

Here, again, are some sweet and homely lines about preparation for the Infant Saviour :—

" Andiamo a lavare
La casa a nettare,
Che non trovi bruttura.
    Poi el menaremo,
Et gli daremo
Ben da ber' e mangiare.
    Un cibo espiato,
Et d' or li sia dato
Senza alcuna dimura.
    Lo cor adempito
Dagiamoli fornito
Senza odio ne rancura." † [14]

---

* " In the worthy stable of the sweet baby the angels are singing round the little
one ; they sing and cry out, the beloved angels, quite reverent, timid and shy round the
little baby Prince of the Elect who lies naked among the prickly hay. . . . The Divine
Verb, which is highest knowledge, this day seems as if He knew nothing of anything.
Look at Him on the hay, crying and kicking as if He were not at all a divine man."
(Translation by Vernon Lee in " Renaissance Fancies and Studies," 34.)

† " Sweep hearth and floor ;
Be all your vessel's store
Shining and clean.
Then bring the little guest
And give Him of your best
Of meat and drink. Yet more
Ye owe than meat.
One gift at your King's feet
Lay now. I mean
A heart full to the brim
Of love, and all for Him,
And from all envy clean."
(Translation by Miss Anne Macdonell, in " Sons of Francis," 372.)

THE CHRISTIAN FEAST

There have been few more rapturous poets than Jacopone ; men deemed him mad ; but, " if he is mad," says a modern Italian writer, " he is mad as the lark "—" Nessun poeta canta a tutta gola come questo frate minore. S' è pazzo, è pazzo come l' allodola."

To him is attributed that most poignant of Latin hymns, the " Stabat Mater dolorosa "; he wrote also a joyous Christmas pendant to it :—

> " Stabat Mater speciosa,
>   Juxta foenum gaudiosa,
>   Dum jacebat parvulus.
>   Cujus animam gaudentem,
>   Laetabundam ac ferventem,
>   Pertransivit jubilus." * 15

In the fourteenth century we find a blossoming forth of Christmas poetry in another land, Germany.16   There are indeed Christmas and Epiphany passages in a poetical Life of Christ by Otfrid of Weissenburg in the ninth century, and a twelfth-century poem by Spervogel, " Er ist gewaltic unde starc," opens with a mention of Christmas, but these are of little importance for us.   The fourteenth century shows the first real outburst, and that is traceable, in part at least, to the mystical movement in the Rhineland caused by the preaching of the great Dominican, Eckhart of Strasburg, and his followers.   It was a movement towards inward piety as distinguished from, though not excluding, external observances, which made its way largely by sermons listened to by great congregations in the towns.   Its impulse came not from the monasteries proper, but from the convents of Dominican friars, and it was for Germany in the fourteenth century something like what Franciscanism had been for Italy in the thirteenth.   One of the central doctrines of the school

---

* " Full of beauty stood the Mother,
    By the Manger, blest o'er other,
      Where her little One she lays.
    For her inmost soul's elation,
    In its fervid jubilation,
      Thrills with ecstasy of praise."

(Translation by J. M. Neale.)

was that of the Divine Birth in the soul of the believer; according to Eckhart the soul comes into immediate union with God by "bringing forth the Son" within itself; the historic Christ is the symbol of the divine humanity to which the soul should rise: "when the soul bringeth forth the Son," he says, "it is happier than Mary."[17] Several Christmas sermons by Eckhart have been preserved; one of them ends with the prayer, "To this Birth may that God, who to-day is new born as man, bring us, that we, poor children of earth, may be born in Him as God; to this may He bring us eternally! Amen."[18] With this profound doctrine of the Divine Birth, it was natural that the German mystics should enter deeply into the festival of Christmas, and one of the earliest of German Christmas carols, "Es komt ein schif geladen," is the work of Eckhart's disciple, John Tauler (d. 1361). It is perhaps an adaptation of a secular song :—

> "A ship comes sailing onwards
>   With a precious freight on board;
> It bears the only Son of God,
>   It bears the Eternal Word."

The doctrine of the mystics, "Die in order to live," fills the last verses :—

> "Whoe'er would hope in gladness
>   To kiss this Holy Child,
> Must suffer many a pain and woe,
>   Patient like Him and mild;
>
> Must die with Him to evil
>   And rise to righteousness,
> That so with Christ he too may share
>   Eternal life and bliss."[19]

To the fourteenth century may perhaps belong an allegorical carol still sung in both Catholic and Protestant Germany :—

> "Es ist ein Ros entsprungen
>   Aus einer Wurzel zart,

THE CHRISTIAN FEAST

Als uns die Alten sungen,
Von Jesse kam die Art,
Und hat ein Blümlein bracht,
Mitten im kalten Winter,
Wohl zu der halben Nacht.
Das Röslein, das ich meine,
Davon Jesajas sagt,
Hat uns gebracht alleine
Marie, die reine Magd.
Aus Gottes ew'gem Rat
Hat sie ein Kind geboren
Wohl zu der halben Nacht." * [20]

In a fourteenth-century Life of the mystic Heinrich Suso it is told how one day angels came to him to comfort him in his sufferings, how they took him by the hand and led him to dance, while one began a glad song of the child Jesus, "In dulci jubilo." To the fourteenth century, then, dates back that most delightful of German carols, with its interwoven lines of Latin. I may quote the fine Scots translation in the "Godlie and Spirituall Sangis" of 1567 :—

"*In dulci Jubilo*, Now lat us sing with myrth and jo
Our hartis consolatioun lyis *in praesepio*,
And schynis as the Sone, *Matris in gremio*,
Alpha es et O, Alpha es et O.
O *Jesu parvule!* I thrist sore efter thé,

* "A spotless Rose is blowing,
    Sprung from a tender root,
  Of ancient seers' foreshowing,
    Of Jesse promised fruit ;
  Its fairest bud unfolds to light
    Amid the cold, cold winter,
  And in the dark midnight.

  The Rose which I am singing,
    Whereof Isaiah said,
  Is from its sweet root springing
    In Mary, purest Maid ;
  For through our God's great love and might
    The Blessed Babe she bare us
  In a cold, cold winter's night."
(Translation by C. Winkworth, "Christian Singers," 85.)

44

Confort my hart and mynde, *O puer optime,*
God of all grace sa kynde, *et princeps gloriae*
Trahe me post te, Trahe me post te.
Ubi sunt gaudia, in ony place bot thair,
Quhair that the Angellis sing *Nova cantica,*
Bot and the bellis ring *in regis curia,*
God gif I war thair, God gif I war thair." [21]

The music of " In dulci jubilo " * has, with all its religious
feeling, something of the nature of a dance, and unites in a
strange fashion solemnity, playfulness, and ecstatic delight. No
other air, perhaps, shows so perfectly the reverent gaiety of
the carol spirit.

The fifteenth century produced a realistic type of German carol.
Here is the beginning of one such :—

"Da Jesu Krist geboren wart,
do was es kalt ;
in ain klaines kripplein
er geleget wart.
Da stunt ain esel und ain rint,
die atmizten über das hailig kint
gar unverborgen.
Der ain raines herze hat, der darf nit sorgen." † [22]

It goes on to tell in naïve language the story of the wanderings
of the Holy Family during the Flight into Egypt.

This carol type lasted, and continued to develop, in Austria and
the Catholic parts of Germany through the sixteenth, seventeenth,
and eighteenth centuries, and even in the nineteenth. In
Carinthia in the early nineteenth century, almost every parish
had its local poet, who added new songs to the old treasury. [23]
Particularly popular were the *Hirtenlieder* or shepherd songs,
in which the peasant worshippers joined themselves to the
shepherds of Bethlehem, and sought to share their devout

---

* The tune is often used in England for Neale's carol, " Good Christian men,
rejoice."

† "When Jesus Christ was born, then was it cold ; in a little crib He was laid.
There stood an ass and an ox which breathed over the Holy Child quite openly. He
who has a pure heart need have no care."

emotions. Often these carols are of the most rustic character and in the broadest dialect. They breathe forth a great kindliness and homeliness, and one could fill pages with quotations. Two more short extracts must, however, suffice to show their quality.

How warm and hearty is their feeling for the Child :—

> " Du herzliabste Muater, gib Acht auf dös Kind,
> Es is ja gar frostig, thuas einfatschen gschwind.
> Und du alter Voda, decks Kindlein schen zua,
> Sonst hats von der Kölden und Winden kan Ruah.
> Hiazt nemen mir Urlaub, o gettliches Kind,
> Thua unser gedenken, verzeich unser Sünd.
> Es freut uns von Herzen dass d'ankomen bist ;
> Es hätt uns ja niemand zu helfen gewist." * 24

And what fatherly affection is here :—

> " Das Kind is in der Krippen glögn,
> So herzig und so rar !
> Mei klâner Hansl war nix dgögn,
> Wenn a glei schener war.
> Kolschwarz wie d'Kirchen d'Augen sein,
> Sunst aber kreidenweiss ;
> Die Händ so hübsch recht zart und fein,
> I hans angrürt mit Fleiss.
>
> Aft hats auf mi an Schmutza gmacht,
> An Höscheza darzue ;
> O warst du mein, hoan i gedacht,
> Werst wol a munter Bue.
> Dahoam in meiner Kachelstub
> Liess i brav hoazen ein,
> Do in den Stâl kimt überâl
> Der kalte Wind herein." † 25

---

* " Dearest mother, take care of the Child ; it is freezing hard, wrap Him up quickly. And you, old father, tuck the little one up, or the cold and the wind will give Him no rest. Now we must take our leave, O divine Child, remember us, pardon our sins. We are heartily glad that Thou art come ; no one else could have helped us."

† " The Child is laid in the crib, so hearty and so rare ! My little Hans would be nothing by His side, were he finer than he is. Coal-black as cherries are His eyes, the

MEDIAEVAL ENGLISH CAROLS

We have been following on German ground a mediaeval tradition that has continued unbroken down to modern days ; but we must now take a leap backward in time, and consider the beginnings of the Christmas carol in England.

Not till the fifteenth century is there any outburst of Christmas poetry in English, though other forms of religious lyrics were produced in considerable numbers in the thirteenth and early fourteenth centuries. When the carols come at last, they appear in the least likely of all places, at the end of a versifying of the whole duty of man, by John Awdlay, a blind chaplain of Haghmon, in Shropshire. In red letters he writes :—

> " I pray you, sirus, boothe moore and lase,
> Sing these caroles in Cristëmas,"

and then follows a collection of twenty-five songs, some of which are genuine Christmas carols, as one now understands the word.[26]

A carol, in the modern English sense, may perhaps be defined as a religious song, less formal and solemn than the ordinary Church hymn—an expression of popular and often naïve devotional feeling, a thing intended to be sung outside rather than within church walls. There still linger about the word some echoes of its original meaning, for " carol " had at first a secular or even pagan significance : in twelfth-century France it was used to describe the amorous song-dance which hailed the coming of spring ; in Italian it meant a ring- or song-dance ; while by English writers from the thirteenth to the sixteenth century it was used chiefly of singing joined with dancing, and had no necessary connection with religion. Much as the mediaeval Church, with its ascetic tendencies, disliked religious dancing, it could not always suppress it ; and in Germany, as we shall see, there was choral dancing at Christmas round the cradle of the Christ Child. Whether Christmas carols were ever danced to in Eng-

rest of Him is white as chalk. His pretty hands are right tender and delicate, I touched Him carefully. Then He gave me a smile and a deep sigh too. If you were mine, thought I, you'd grow a merry boy. At home in the kitchen I'd comfortably house you ; out here in the stable the cold wind comes in at every corner."

land is doubtful ; many of the old airs and words have, however, a glee and playfulness as of human nature following its natural instincts of joy even in the celebration of the most sacred mysteries. It is probable that some of the carols are religious parodies of love-songs, written for the melodies of the originals, and many seem by their structure to be indirectly derived from the choral dances of farm folk, a notable feature being their burden or refrain, a survival of the common outcry of the dancers as they leaped around.

Awdlay's carols are perhaps meant to be sung by " wassailing neighbours, who make their rounds at Christmastide to drink a cup and take a gift, and bring good fortune upon the house " 27 —predecessors of those carol-singers of rural England in the nineteenth century, whom Mr. Hardy depicts so delightfully in " Under the Greenwood Tree." Carol-singing by a band of men who go from house to house is probably a Christianization of such heathen processions as we shall meet in less altered forms in Part II.

It must not be supposed that the carols Awdlay gives are his own work ; and their exact date it is impossible to determine. Part of his book was composed in 1426, but one at least of the carols was probably written in the last half of the fourteenth century. They seem indeed to be the later blossomings of the great spring-time of English literature, the period which produced Chaucer and Langland, an innumerable company of minstrels and ballad-makers, and the mystical poet, Richard Rolle of Hampole.*

Through the fifteenth century and the first half of the six-teenth, the flowering continued ; and something like two hundred carols of this period are known. It is impossible to attempt here anything like representative quotation ; I can only sketch in

* Richard Rolle, poet, mystic, and wandering preacher, in many ways reminds us of Jacopone da Todi. Though he has left no Christmas verses, some lovely words of his show how deeply he felt the wonder and pathos of Bethlehem : " Jhesu es thy name. A ! A ! that wondryrfull name ! A ! that delittabyll name ! This es the name that es above all names. . . . I yede [went] abowte be Covaytyse of riches and I fand noghte Jhesu. I satt in companyes of Worldly myrthe and I fand noghte Jhesu. . . . Therefore I turnede by anothire waye, and I rane a-bowte be Poverte, and I fande Jhesu pure, borne in the worlde, laid in a crybe and lappid in clathis." 28

roughest outline the main characteristics of English carol literature, and refer the reader for examples to Miss Edith Rickert's
comprehensive collection, " Ancient English Carols, MCCCC-
MDCC," or to the smaller but fine selection in Messrs. E. K.
Chambers and F. Sidgwick's " Early English Lyrics." Many
may have been the work of *goliards* or wandering scholars, and a
common feature is the interweaving of Latin with English words.

Some, like the exquisite " I sing of a maiden that is makeles," [29]
are rather songs to or about the Virgin than strictly Christmas
carols ; the Annunciation rather than the Nativity is their
theme. Others again tell the whole story of Christ's life. The
feudal idea is strong in such lines as these :—

> " Mary is quene of allë thinge,
> And her sone a lovely kinge.
> God graunt us allë good endinge !
> *Regnat dei gracia.*" [30]

On the whole, in spite of some mystical exceptions, the
mediaeval English carol is somewhat external in its religion ;
there is little deep individual feeling ; the caroller sings as a
member of the human race, whose curse is done away, whose
nature is exalted by the Incarnation, rather than as one whose
soul is athirst for God :—

> " Now man is brighter than the sonne ;
> Now man in heven an hie shall wonne ;
> Blessëd be God this game is begonne
> And his moder emperesse of helle." [31]

Salvation is rather an objective external thing than an inward
and spiritual process. A man has but to pray devoutly to the
dear Mother and Child, and they will bring him to the heavenly
court. It is not so much personal sin as an evil influence in
humanity, that is cured by the great event of Christmas :—

> "It was dark, it was dim,
> For men that levëd in gret sin ;
> Lucifer was all within,
> Till on the Cristmes day.

> There was weping, there was wo,
> For every man to hell gan go.
> It was litel mery tho,
>   Till on the Cristmes day." [32]

But now that Christ is born, and man redeemed, one may be
blithe indeed :—

> " Jhesus is that childës name,
> Maide and moder is his dame,
> And so oure sorow is turned to game.
>   *Gloria tibi domine.*

> .   .   .   .

> Now sitte we downe upon our knee,
> And pray that child that is so free ;
> And with gode hertë now sing we
>   *Gloria tibi domine.*" [33]

Sometimes the religious spirit almost vanishes, and the carol
becomes little more than a gay pastoral song :—

> " The shepard upon a hill he satt ;
> He had on him his tabard and his hat,
> His tarbox, his pipe, and his flagat ;
> His name was called Joly Joly Wat,
>   For he was a gud herdës boy.
>   Ut hoy !
> For in his pipe he made so much joy.

> .   .   .   .   .

> Whan Wat to Bedlem cum was,
> He swet, he had gone faster than a pace ;
> He found Jesu in a simpell place,
> Betwen an ox and an asse.
>   Ut hoy !
> For in his pipe he made so much joy.

> ' Jesu, I offer to thee here my pipe,
> My skirt, my tar-box, and my scripe ;
> Home to my felowes now will I skipe,
> And also look unto my shepe.'
>   Ut hoy !
> For in his pipe he made so much joy." [34]

But to others again, especially the lullabies, the hardness of the Nativity, the shadow of the coming Passion, give a deep note of sorrow and pathos; there is the thought of the sword that shall pierce Mary's bosom :—

> "This endris night I saw a sight,
>   A maid a cradell kepe,
> And ever she song and seid among
>   'Lullay, my child, and slepe.'
>
> 'I may not slepe, but I may wepe,
>   I am so wo begone ;
> Slepe I wold, but I am colde
>   And clothës have I none.
>
>   .   .   .   .   .
>
> 'Adam's gilt this man had spilt ;
>   That sin greveth me sore.
> Man, for thee here shall I be
>   Thirty winter and more.
>
>   .   .   .   .   .
>
> 'Here shall I be hanged on a tree,
>   And die as it is skill.
> That I have bought lesse will I nought ;
>   It is my fader's will.' " 35

The lullabies are quite the most delightful, as they are the most human, of the carols. Here is an exquisitely musical verse from one of 1530 :—

> "In a dream late as I lay,
>   Methought I heard a maiden say
>   And speak these words so mild :
>   'My little son, with thee I play,
>   And come,' she sang, 'by, lullaby.'
>   Thus rockëd she her child.
>
> *By-by, lullaby, by-by, lullaby,*
>   *Rockëd I my child.*
> *By-by, by-by, by-by, lullaby,*
>   *Rockëd I my child."* 36

CHAPTER III

CHRISTMAS POETRY

II

CHAPTER III

CHRISTMAS POETRY (II)

The French *Noël*—Latin Hymnody in Eighteenth-century France—Spanish Christmas Verse—Traditional Carols of Many Countries—Christmas Poetry in Protestant Germany—Post-Reformation Verse in England—Modern English Carols.

THE Reformation marks a change in the character of Christmas poetry in England and the larger part of Germany, and, instead of following its development under Protestantism, it will be well to break off and turn awhile to countries where Catholic tradition remained unbroken. We shall come back later to Post-Reformation England and Protestant Germany.

In French [1] there is little or no Christmas poetry, religious in character, before the fifteenth century ; the earlier carols that have come down to us are songs rather of feasting and worldly rejoicing than of sacred things. The true *Noël* begins to appear in fifteenth-century manuscripts, but it was not till the following century that it attained its fullest vogue and was spread all over the country by the printing presses. Such *Noëls* seem to have been written by clerks or recognized poets, either for old airs or for specially composed music. "To a great extent," says Mr. Gregory Smith, "they anticipate the spirit which stimulated the Reformers to turn the popular and often obscene songs into good and godly ballads." [2]

Some of the early *Noëls* are not unlike the English carols of the period, and are often half in Latin, half in French. Here are a few such "macaronic" verses :—

> " Célébrons la naissance
> *Nostri Salvatoris,*

55

Qui fait la complaisance
Dei sui Patris.
Cet enfant tout aimable,
In nocte mediâ,
Est né dans une étable,
De castâ Mariâ.

.   .   .   .

Mille esprits angéliques,
Juncti pastoribus,
Chantent dans leur musique,
Puer vobis natus,
Au Dieu par qui nous sommes,
Gloria in excelsis,
Et la paix soit aux hommes
Bonae voluntatis.

.   .   .   .

Qu'on ne soit insensible !
Adeamus omnes
A Dieu rendu passible,
Propter nos mortales,
Et tous, de compagnie,
Deprecemur eum
Qu'à la fin de la vie,
Det regnum beatum." [3]

The sixteenth century is the most interesting *Noël* period ; we find then a conflict of tendencies, a conflict between Gallic realism and broad humour and the love of refined language due to the study of the ancient classics. There are many anonymous pieces of this time, but three important *Noëlistes* stand out by name : Lucas le Moigne, Curé of Saint Georges, Puy-la-Garde, near Poitiers ; Jean Daniel, called " Maître Mitou," a priest-organist at Nantes ; and Nicholas Denisot of Le Mans, whose *Noëls* appeared posthumously under the pseudonym of " Comte d'Alsinoys."

Lucas le Moigne represents the *esprit gaulois*, the spirit that is often called " Rabelaisian," though it is only one side of the genius of Rabelais. The good Curé was a contemporary of

THE ADORATION OF THE SHEPHERDS.

By Fouquet.

(Musée Condé, Chantilly.)

To face p. 56.

the author of "Pantagruel." His "Chansons de Noëls nouvaulx"
was published in 1520, and contains carols in very varied styles,
some naïve and pious, others hardly quotable at the present day.
One of his best-known pieces is a dialogue between the Virgin
and the singers of the carol : Mary is asked and answers questions
about the wondrous happenings of her life. Here are four verses
about the Nativity :—

> "Or nous dites, Marie,
> Les neuf mois accomplis,
> Naquit le fruit de vie,
> Comme l'Ange avoit dit ?
> — Oui, sans nulle peine
> Et sans oppression,
> Naquit de tout le monde
> La vraie Rédemption.
>
> Or nous dites, Marie,
> Du lieu impérial,
> Fut-ce en chambre parée,
> Ou en Palais royal ?
> — En une pauvre étable
> Ouverte à l'environ
> Ou n'avait feu, ni flambe
> Ni latte, ni chevron.
>
> Or nous dites, Marie,
> Qui vous vint visiter ;
> Les bourgeois de la ville
> Vous ont-ils confortée ?
> — Oncque, homme ni femme
> N'en eut compassion,
> Non plus que d'un esclave
> D'étrange région.
>
> .   .   .   .
>
> Or nous dites, Marie,
> Des pauvres pastoureaux
> Qui gardaient ès montagnes
> Leurs brebis & aigneaux.

THE CHRISTIAN FEAST

> — Ceux-là m'ont visitée
> Par grande affection ;
> Moult me fut agréable
> Leur visitation." [4]

The influence of the "Pléiade," with its care for form, its respect for classical models, its enrichment of the French tongue with new Latin words, is shown by Jean Daniel, who also owes something to the poets of the late fifteenth century. Two stanzas may be quoted from him :—

> "C'est ung très grant mystère
> Qu'ung roy de si hault pris
> Vient naistre en lieu austère,
> En si meschant pourpris :
> Le Roy de tous les bons espritz,
> C'est Jésus nostre frère,
> Le Roy de tous les bons espritz,
> Duquel sommes apris.
>
> Saluons le doulx Jésuchrist,
> Notre Dieu, notre frère,
> Saluons le doulx Jésuchrist,
> Chantons Noel d'esprit !
>
> .   .   .   .
>
> En luy faisant prière,
> Soyons de son party,
> Qu'en sa haulte emperière
> Ayons lieu de party ;
> Comme il nous a droict apparty,
> Jésus nostre bon frère,
> Comme il nous a droict apparty
> Au céleste convy.
> Saluons, etc.
> Amen. Noel." [5]

As for Denisot, I may give two charming verses from one of his pastorals :—

> "Suz, Bergiez, en campaigne,
> Laissez là vos troppeaux,

Avant qu'on s'accompaigne,
Enflez vos chalumeaux.

.   .   .   .

Enflez vos cornemuses,
Dansez ensemblement,
Et vos doucettes muses,
Accollez doucement."[6]

One result of the Italian influences which came over
France in the sixteenth century was a fondness for diminutives. Introduced into carols, these have sometimes a very
graceful effect :—

" Entre le boeuf & le bouvet,
        Noel nouvellet,
Voulust Jésus nostre maistre,
En un petit hostelet,
        Noel nouvellet,
En ce pauvre monde naistre,
        O Noel nouvellet !

Ne couche, ne bercelet,
        Noel nouvellet,
Ne trouvèrent en cette estre,
Fors ung petit drappelet,
        Noel nouvellet,
Pour envelopper le maistre,
        O Noel nouvellet ! "[7]

These diminutives are found again, though fewer, in a
particularly delightful carol :—

" Laissez paître vos bestes
Pastoureaux, par monts et par vaux ;
    Laissez paître vos bestes,
    Et allons chanter Nau.

J'ai ouï chanter le rossignol,
Qui chantoit un chant si nouveau,
        Si haut, si beau,
        Si résonneau,

59

THE CHRISTIAN FEAST

> Il m'y rompoit la tête,
> Tant il chantoit et flageoloit :
> Adonc pris ma houlette
> Pour aller voir Naulet.
> Laissez paître, etc." [8]

The singer goes on to tell how he went with his fellow-shepherds and shepherdesses to Bethlehem :—

> "Nous dîmes tous une chanson
> Les autres en vinrent au son,
> Chacun prenant
> Son compagnon :
> Je prendrai Guillemette,
> Margot tu prendras gros Guillot ;
> Qui prendra Péronelle ?
> Ce sera Talebot.
> Laissez paître, etc.
>
> Ne chantons plus, nous tardons trop,
> Pensons d'aller courir le trot.
> Viens-tu, Margot ?—
> J'attends Guillot.—
> J'ai rompu ma courette,
> Il faut ramancher mon sabot.—
> Or, tiens cette aiguillette,
> Elle y servira trop.
> Laissez paître, etc.
>
> .   .   .   .
>
> Nous courumes de grand' roideur
> Pour voir notre doux Rédempteur
> Et Créateur
> Et Formateur,
> Qui était tendre d'aage
> Et sans linceux en grand besoin,
> Il gisait en la crêche
> Sur un botteau de foin.
> Laissez paître, etc.

THE FRENCH NOËL

> Sa mère avecque lui était:
> Et Joseph si lui éclairait,
>   Point ne semblait
>   Au beau fillet,
> Il n'était point son père ;
> Je l'aperçus bien au cameau (*visage*)
>   Il semblait à sa mère,
>   Encore est-il plus beau.
>   Laissez paître, etc."

This is but one of a large class of French *Noëls* which make the Nativity more real, more present, by representing the singer as one of a company of worshippers going to adore the Child. Often these are shepherds, but sometimes they are simply the inhabitants of a parish, a town, a countryside, or a province, bearing presents of their own produce to the little Jesus and His parents.   Barrels of wine, fish, fowls, sucking-pigs, pastry, milk, fruit, firewood, birds in a cage—such are their homely gifts. Often there is a strongly satiric note : the peculiarities and weaknesses of individuals are hit off ; the reputation of a place is suggested, a village whose people are famous for their stinginess offers cider that is half rain-water ; elsewhere the inhabitants are so given to law-suits that they can hardly find time to go to Bethlehem.

Such *Noëls*, with their vivid local colour, are valuable pictures of the manners of their time.   They are, unfortunately, too long for quotation here, but any reader who cares to follow up the subject will find some interesting specimens in a little collection of French carols that can be bought for ten *centimes*.9   They are of various dates ; some probably were written as late as the eighteenth century.   In that century, and indeed in the seventeenth, the best Christmas verses are those of a provincial and rustic character, and especially those in *patois* ; the more cultivated poets, with their formal classicism, can ill enter into the spirit of the festival.   Of the learned writers the best is a woman, Françoise Paschal, of Lyons (b. about 1610) ; in spite of her Latinity she shows a real feeling for her subjects.   Some of her *Noëls* are dialogues between the sacred personages ; one presents

61

THE CHRISTIAN FEAST

Joseph and Mary as weary wayfarers seeking shelter at all the inns of Bethlehem and everywhere refused by host or hostess :—

" Saint Joseph.

Voyons la *Rose-Rouge*.
Madame de céans,
Auriez-vous quelque bouge
Pour de petites gens ?

L'Hôtesse.

Vous n'avez pas la mine
D'avoir de grands trésors ;
Voyez chez ma voisine,
Car, quant à moi, je dors.

Saint Joseph.

Monsieur des *Trois-Couronnes*,
Avez-vous logement,
Chez vous pour trois personnes,
Quelque trou seulement.

L'Hôte.

Vous perdez votre peine,
Vous venez un peu tard,
Ma maison est fort pleine,
Allez quelqu'autre part." [10]

The most remarkable of the *patois Noëlistes* of the seventeenth century are the Provençal Saboly and the Burgundian La Monnoye, the one kindly and tender, the other witty and sarcastic. Here is one of Saboly's Provençal *Noëls* :—

"Quand la mièjonue sounavo,
Ai sautà dóu liech au sòu ;
Ai vist un bèl ange que cantavo
Milo fes pu dous qu'un roussignòu.

Lei mastin dóu vesinage
Se soun toutes atroupa ;

62

THE FRENCH NOËL

N'avien jamai vist aquéu visage
Se soun tout-d'un-cop mes à japa.

Lei pastre dessus la paio
Dourmien coume de soucas ;
Quand an aussi lou bru dei sounaio
Au cresegu qu'ero lou souiras.

S'eron de gent resounable,
Vendrien sèns èstre envita :
Trouvarien dins un petit estable
La lumiero emai la verita." * 11

As for La Monnoye, here is a translation of one of his satirical verses :—" When in the time of frost Jesus Christ came into the world the ass and ox warmed Him with their breath in the stable. How many asses and oxen I know in this kingdom of Gaul ! How many asses and oxen I know who would not have done as much ! " 12

Apart from the rustic *Noëls*, the eighteenth century produced little French Christmas poetry of any charm. Some of the carols most sung in French churches to-day belong, however, to this period, *e.g.*, the " Venez, divin Messie " of the Abbé Pellegrin.13

One cannot leave the France of the seventeenth and eighteenth centuries without some mention of its Latin hymnody. From a date near 1700, apparently, comes the sweet and solemn " Adeste, fideles " ; by its music and its rhythm, perhaps, rather than by its actual words it has become the best beloved of Christmas hymns. The present writer has heard it sung with equal reverence and heartiness in English, German, French, and Italian churches, and no other hymn seems so full of the spirit of Christmas devotion—

* " When midnight sounded I leapt from my bed to the floor, and I saw a beautiful angel who sang a thousand times sweeter than a nightingale. The watch-dogs of the neighbourhood all came up. Never had they seen such a sight, and they suddenly began to bark. The shepherds under the straw were sleeping like logs : when they heard the sound of the barking they thought it was the wolves. They were reasonable folk ; they came without waiting to be asked. They found in a little stable the Light, even the Truth."

63

wonder, awe, and tenderness, and the sense of reconciliation between Heaven and earth. Composed probably in France, " Adeste, fideles " came to be used in English as well as French Roman Catholic churches during the eighteenth century. In 1797 it was sung at the chapel of the Portuguese Embassy in London ; hence no doubt its once common name of " Portuguese hymn." It was first used in an Anglican church in 1841, when the Tractarian Oakley translated it for his congregation at Margaret Street Chapel, London.

Another fine Latin hymn of the eighteenth-century French Church is Charles Coffin's " Jam desinant suspiria." [14] It appeared in the Parisian Breviary in 1736, and is well known in English as " God from on high hath heard."

The Revolution and the decay of Catholicism in France seem to have killed the production of popular carols. The later nineteenth century, however, saw a revival of interest in the *Noël* as a literary form. In 1875 the bicentenary of Saboly's death was celebrated by a competition for a *Noël* in the Provençal tongue, and something of the same kind has been done in Brittany. [15] The *Noël* has attracted by its aesthetic charm even poets who are anything but devout ; Théophile Gautier, for instance, wrote a graceful Christmas carol, " Le ciel est noir, la terre est blanche."

On a general view of the vernacular Christmas poetry of France it must be admitted that the devotional note is not very strong ; there is indeed a formal reverence, a courtly homage, paid to the Infant Saviour, and the miraculous in the Gospel story is taken for granted ; but there is little sense of awe and mystery. In harmony with the realistic instincts of the nation, everything is dramatically, very humanly conceived ; at times, indeed, the personages of the Nativity scenes quite lose their sacred character, and the treatment degenerates into grossness. At its best, however, the French *Noël* has a gaiety and a grace, joined to a genuine, if not very deep, piety, that are extremely charming. Reading these rustic songs, we are carried in imagination to French countrysides ; we think of the long walk through the snow to the Midnight Mass, the cheerful *réveillon* spread on the return, the family gathered round the hearth, feasting on wine and chestnuts and *boudins*, and singing in traditional strains the joys of *Noël*.

Across the Pyrenees, in Spain, the late sixteenth and early seventeenth centuries saw a great output of Christmas verse. Among the chief writers were Juan López de Ubeda, Francisco de Ocaña, and José de Valdivielso.[16] Their *villancicos* remind one of the paintings of Murillo ; they have the same facility, the same tender and graceful sentiment, without much depth. They lack the homely flavour, the quaintness that make the French and German folk-carols so delightful ; they have not the rustic tang, and yet they charm by their simplicity and sweetness.

Here are a few stanzas by Ocaña :—

> " Dentro de un pobre pesebre
> y cobijado con heno
> yace Jesus Nazareno.
>
> En el heno yace echado
> el hijo de Dios eterno,
> para librar del infierno
> al hombre que hubo criado,
> y por matar el pecado
> el heno tiene por bueno
> nuestro Jesus Nazareno.
>
> Está entre dos animales
> que le calientan del frio,
> quien remedia nuestros males
> con su grande poderío :
> es su reino y señorío
> el mundo y el cielo sereno,
> y agora duerme en el heno.
>
> Tiene por bueno sufrir
> el frio y tanta fortuna,
> sin tener ropa ninguna
> con que se abrigar ni cubrir,

65   E

y por darnos el vivir
padeció frio en el heno,
nuestro Jesus Nazareno." * 17

More of a peasant flavour is found in some snatches of
Christmas carols given by Fernan Caballero in her sketch, " La
Noche de Navidad."

> " Ha nacido en un portal,
> Llenito de telarañas,
> Entre la mula y el buey
> El Redentor de las almas.
>
> .   .   .   .
>
> En el portal de Belen
> Hay estrella, sol y luna :
> La Virgen y San José
> Y el niño que está en la cuna.
>
> En Belen tocan á fuego,
> Del portal sale la llama,
> Es una estrella del cielo,
> Que ha caido entre la paja.
>
> Yo soy un pobre gitano
> Que vengo de Egipto aquí,
> Y al niño de Dios le traigo
> Un gallo quiquiriquí
>
> Yo soy un pobre gallego
> Que vengo de la Galicia,
> Y al niño de Dios le traigo
> Lienzo para una camisa.

---

* " Within a poor manger and covered with hay lies Jesus of Nazareth. In the
hay lies stretched the Eternal Son of God ; to deliver from hell man whom He had
created, and to kill sin, our Jesus of Nazareth is content with the hay. He rests
between two animals who warm Him from the cold, He who remedies our ills with
His great power ; His kingdom and seigniory are the world and the calm heaven, and
now He sleeps in the hay. He counts it good to bear the cold and fare thus, having no
robe to protect or cover Him, and to give us life He suffered cold in the hay, our Jesus
of Nazareth."

CHRISTMAS POETRY IN SPAIN

Al niño recien nacido
Todos le traen un don;
Yo soy chico y nada tengo;
Le traigo mi corazon." * [18]

In nearly every western language one finds traditional Christmas carols. Europe is everywhere alive with them; they spring up like wild flowers. Some interesting Italian specimens are given by Signor de Gubernatis in his "Usi Natalizi." Here are a few stanzas from a Bergamesque cradle-song of the Blessed Virgin :—

"Dormi, dormi, o bel bambin,
Re divin.
Dormi, dormi, o fantolin.
Fa la nanna, o caro figlio,
Re del Ciel,
Tanto bel, grazioso giglio.

Chiüdi i lümi, o mio tesor,
Dolce amor,
Di quest' alma, almo Signor;
Fa la nanna, o regio infante,
Sopra il fien,
Caro ben, celeste amante.

Perchè piangi, o bambinell,
Forse il giel
Ti dà noia, o l'asinell?
Fa la nanna, o paradiso
Del mio cor,
Redentor, ti bacio il viso." † [19]

* "In a porch, full of cobwebs, between the mule and the ox, the Saviour of souls is born. . . . In the porch at Bethlehem are star, sun, and moon: the Virgin and St. Joseph and the Child who lies in the cradle. In Bethlehem they touch fire, from the porch the flame issues; it is a star of heaven which has fallen into the straw. I am a poor gipsy who come hither from Egypt, and bring to God's Child a cock. I am a poor Galician who come from Galicia, and bring to God's Child linen for a shift. To the new-born Child all bring a gift; I am little and have nothing; I bring him my heart."

† "Sleep, oh sleep, dear Baby mine,
King Divine;

With this lullaby may be compared a singularly lovely and quite untranslatable Latin cradle-song of unknown origin :—

"Dormi, fili, dormi ! mater
        Cantat unigenito :
Dormi, puer, dormi ! pater,
        Nato clamat parvulo :
Millies tibi laudes canimus
        Mille, mille, millies.

Lectum stravi tibi soli,
        Dormi, nate bellule !
Stravi lectum foeno molli :
        Dormi, mi animule.
Millies tibi laudes canimus
        Mille, mille, millies.

.   .   .   .

Ne quid desit, sternam rosis,
        Sternam foenum violis,
Pavimentum hyacinthis
        Et praesepe liliis.
Millies tibi laudes canimus
        Mille, mille, millies.

Sleep, my Child, in sleep recline ;
Lullaby, mine Infant fair,
        Heaven's King,
        All glittering,
Full of grace as lilies rare.

Close thine eyelids, O my treasure,
        Loved past measure,
Of my soul, the Lord, the pleasure ;
Lullaby, O regal Child,
        On the hay
        My joy I lay ;
Love celestial, meek and mild.

Why dost weep, my Babe ? alas !
        Cold winds that pass
Vex, or is't the little ass ?
Lullaby, O Paradise ;
        Of my heart
        Thou Saviour art ;
On thy face I press a kiss." [20]

(Translation by Countess Martinengo-Cesaresco.)

THE FLIGHT INTO EGYPT : THE REST BY THE WAY

MASTER OF THE SEVEN SORROWS OF MARY (ALSO ATTRIBUTED TO JOACHIM PATINIR)

(*Vienna : Imperial Gallery*)

POPULAR CHRISTMAS SONGS

> Si vis musicam, pastores
> Convocabo protinus ;
> Illis nulli sunt priores ;
> Nemo canit castius.
> Millies tibi laudes canimus
> Mille, mille, millies." [21]

Curious little poems are found in Latin and other languages, making a dialogue of the cries of animals at the news of Christ's birth.[22] The following French example is fairly typical :—

> " Comme les bestes autrefois
> Parloient mieux latin que françois,
> Le coq, de loin voyant le fait,
> S'écria : *Christus natus est.*
> Le bœuf, d'un air tout ébaubi,
> Demande : *Ubi? Ubi? Ubi?*
> La chèvre, se tordant le groin,
> Répond que c'est à *Béthléem.*
> Maistre Baudet, *curiosus*
> De l'aller voir, dit : *Eamus ;*
> Et, droit sur ses pattes, le veau
> Beugle deux fois : *Volo, Volo !* " * [23]

In Wales, in the early nineteenth century, carol-singing was more popular, perhaps, than in England ; the carols were sung to the harp, in church at the *Plygain* or early morning service on Christmas Day, in the homes of the people, and at the doors of the houses by visitors.[24] In Ireland, too, the custom of carol-singing then prevailed.[25] Dr. Douglas Hyde, in his " Religious Songs of Connacht," gives and translates an interesting Christmas hymn in Irish, from which two verses may be quoted. They set forth the great paradox of the Incarnation :—

> " Little babe who art so great,
> Child so young who art so old,

* A Bas-Querçy bird-carol of this kind is printed by Mr. H. J. L. J. Massé in his delightful " Book of Old Carols," [26] a collection of the words and music of Christmas songs in many languages—English, Latin, German, Flemish, Basque, Swedish, Catalan, Provençal, and French of various periods and dialects.

> In the manger small his room,
>   Whom not heaven itself could hold.
>
> .   .   .   .   .
>
> Father—not more old than thou ?
>   Mother—younger, can it be ?
> Older, younger is the Son,
>   Younger, older, she than he." [27]

Even in dour Scotland, with its hatred of religious festivals, some kind of carolling survived here and there among Highland folk, and a remarkable and very "Celtic" Christmas song has been translated from the Gaelic by Mr. J. A. Campbell. It begins :—

> " Sing hey the Gift, sing ho the Gift,
> Sing hey the Gift of the Living,
> Son of the Dawn, Son of the Star,
> Son of the Planet, Son of the Far [twice],
> Sing hey the Gift, sing ho the Gift." [28]

Before I close this study with a survey of Christmas poetry in England after the Reformation, it may be interesting to follow the developments in Protestant Germany. The Reformation gave a great impetus to German religious song, and we owe to it some of the finest of Christmas hymns. It is no doubt largely due to Luther, that passionate lover of music and folk-poetry, that hymns have practically become the liturgy of German Protestantism ; yet he did but give typical expression to the natural instincts of his countrymen for song. Luther, though a rebel, was no Puritan ; we can hardly call him an iconoclast ; he had a conservative mind, which only gradually became loosened from its old attachments. His was an essentially artistic nature : "I would fain," he said, "see all arts, especially music, in the service of Him who has given and created them," and in the matter of hymnody he continued, in many respects, the mediaeval German tradition. Homely, kindly, a lover of children, he had a deep feeling for the festival of Christmas ; and not only did he translate into German " A solis ortus cardine" and "Veni, redemptor

SINGING "VOM HIMMEL HOCH" FROM A CHURCH TOWER AT CHRISTMAS.

By Ludwig Richter.

The custom is still kept up in some German towns.

To face p. 71.

gentium," but he wrote for his little son Hans one of the most delightful and touching of all Christmas hymns—"Vom Himmel hoch, da komm ich her."

"Vom Himmel hoch, da komm ich her,
Ich bring euch gute neue Mär,
Der guten Mär bring ich so viel,
Davon ich singen und sagen will.

Euch ist ein Kindlein heut gebor'n
Von einer Jungfrau auserkor'n,
Ein Kindelein so zart und fein,
Das soll eu'r Freud und Wonne sein.

.   .   .   .

Merk auf, mein Herz, und sieh dort hin:
Was liegt doch in dem Kripplein drin?
Wess ist das schöne Kindelein?
Es ist das liebe Jesulein.

.   .   .   .   .

Ach Herr, du Schöpfer aller Ding,
Wie bist du worden so gering,
Dass du da liegst auf dürrem Gras,
Davon ein Rind und Esel ass?

.   .   .   .

Ach, mein herzliebes Jesulein,
Mach dir ein rein sanft Bettelein,
Zu ruhen in mein's Herzens Schrein,
Dass ich nimmer vergesse dein.

.   .   .   .

Davon ich allzeit fröhlich sei,
Zu springen, singen immer frei
Das rechte Lied dem Gottessohn
Mit Herzenslust, den süssen Ton." * 29

* "I come from heaven to tell
   The best nowells that ever befell;
   To you thir tidings true I bring,
   And I will of them say and sing.

   This day to you is born ane child,
   Of Mary meek and virgin mild,
   That blessed bairn, benign and kind,
   Sall you rejoice, baith heart and mind.

"Vom Himmel hoch" has qualities of simplicity, directness, and warm human feeling which link it to the less ornate forms of carol literature. Its first verse is adapted from a secular song ; its melody may, perhaps, have been composed by Luther himself. There is another Christmas hymn of Luther's, too—"Vom Himmel kam der Engel Schar"—written for use when "Vom Himmel hoch" was thought too long, and he also composed additional verses for the mediaeval "Gelobet seist du, Jesu Christ."

"Gelobet seist du, Jesu Christ,
Dass du Mensch geboren bist
Von einer Jungfrau, das ist wahr,
Des freuet sich der Engel Schar.
Kyrieleis !

Des ew'gen Vaters einig Kind
Jetzt man in der Krippe find't,
In unser armes Fleisch und Blut
Verkleidet sich das ewig Gut.
Kyrieleis !

My soul and life, stand up and see
What lies in ane crib of tree [wood].
What Babe is that, so gude and fair ?
It is Christ, Goddis Son and Heir.

O God ! that made all creature,
How art Thou now become so puir,
That on the hay and stray will lie,
Among the asses, oxen, and kye ?

O, my dear heart, young Jesus sweet,
Prepare Thy cradle in my spreit,
And I sall rock Thee in my heart,
And never mair from Thee depart

But I sall praise Thee ever moir,
With sangis sweet unto Thy gloir ;
The knees of my heart sall I bow,
And sing that richt Balulalow." [30]

72

Den aller Weltkreis nie beschloss,
Der lieget in Marie'n Schoss;
Er ist ein Kindlein worden klein,
Der alle Ding' erhält allein.
Kyrieleis! " * 31

The first stanza alone is mediaeval, the remaining six of the hymn are Luther's.

The Christmas hymns of Paul Gerhardt, the seventeenth-century Berlin pastor, stand next to Luther's. They are more subjective, more finished, less direct and forcible. Lacking the finest qualities of poetry, they are nevertheless impressive by their dignity and heartiness. Made for music, the words alone hardly convey the full power of these hymns. They should be heard sung to the old chorales, massive, yet sweet, by the lusty voices of a German congregation. To English people they are probably best known through the verses introduced into the " Christmas Oratorio," where the old airs are given new beauty by Bach's marvellous harmonies. The tone of devotion, one feels, in Gerhardt and Bach is the same, immeasurably greater as is the genius of the composer; in both there is a profound joy in the Redemption begun by the Nativity, a robust faith joined to a deep sense of the mystery of suffering, and a keen sympathy with childhood, a tender fondness for the Infant King.

* " Now blessed be Thou, Christ Jesu,
Thou art man born, this is true;
The angels made a merry noise,
Yet have we more cause to rejoice,
Kirieleyson.

The blessed Son of God only,
In a crib full poor did lie,
With our poor flesh and our poor blood,
Was clothed that everlasting Good.
Kirieleyson.

He that made heaven and earth of nought,
In our flesh hath our health brought,
For our sake made He Himself full small,
That reigneth Lord and King over all.
Kirieleyson." 32

73

THE CHRISTIAN FEAST

The finest perhaps of Gerhardt's hymns is the Advent "Wie soll ich dich empfangen?" ("How shall I fitly meet Thee?"), which comes early in the "Christmas Oratorio." More closely connected with the Nativity, however, are the *Weihnachtslieder*, "Wir singen dir, Emanuel," "O Jesu Christ, dein Kripplein ist," "Fröhlich soll mein Herze springen," "Ich steh an deiner Krippen hier," and others. I give a few verses from the third :—

> "Fröhlich soll mein Herze springen
> Dieser Zeit,
> Da für Freud
> Alle Engel singen.
> Hört, hört, wie mit vollen Choren
> Alle Luft
> Laute ruft :
> Christus ist geboren.
>
> .   .   .   .
>
> Nun, er liegt in seiner Krippen,
> Ruft zu sich
> Mich und dich,
> Spricht mit süssen Lippen :
> Lasset fahrn, O lieben Brüder
> Was euch quält,
> Was euch fehlt ;
> Ich bring alles wieder.
>
> .   .   .   .
>
> Süsses Heil, lass dich umfangen ;
> Lass mich dir,
> Meine Zier,
> Unverrückt anhangen.
> Du bist meines Lebens Leben ;
> Nun kann ich
> Mich durch dich
> Wohl zufrieden geben." * 33

* " All my heart this night rejoices,
As I hear,
Far and near,
Sweetest angel voices ;

GERMAN PROTESTANT HYMNS

One more German Christmas hymn must be mentioned, Gerhard Tersteegen's "Jauchzet, ihr Himmel, frohlocket, ihr englischen Chöre." Tersteegen represents one phase of the mystical and emotional reaction against the religious formalism and indifference of the eighteenth century. In the Lutheran Church the Pietists, though they never seceded, somewhat resembled the English Methodists; the Moravians formed a separate community, while from the "Reformed" or Calvinistic Church certain circles of spiritually-minded people, who drew inspiration from the mediaeval mystics and later writers like Böhme and Madame Guyon, gathered into more or less independent groups for religious intercourse. Of these last Tersteegen is a representative singer. Here are three verses from his best known Christmas hymn :—

> " Jauchzet, ihr Himmel, frohlocket, ihr englischen Chöre,
> Singet dem Herrn, dem Heiland der Menschen, zur Ehre :
> Sehet doch da !
> Gott will so freundlich und nah
> Zu den Verlornen sich kehren.

.   .   .   .   .

> ' Christ is born,' their choirs are singing,
> Till the air
> Everywhere
> Now with joy is ringing.
>
> Hark ! a voice from yonder manger,
> Soft and sweet,
> Doth entreat,
> ' Flee from woe and danger ;
> Brethren, come, from all doth grieve you
> You are freed,
> All you need
> I will surely give you.'
>
> Blessed Saviour, let me find Thee !
> Keep Thou me
> Close to Thee,
> Call me not behind Thee !
> Life of life, my heart Thou stillest,
> Calm I rest
> On Thy breast,
> All this void Thou fillest." [34]

75

König der Ehren, aus Liebe geworden zum Kinde,
Dem ich auch wieder mein Herz in der Liebe verbinde;
    Du sollst es sein,
    Den ich erwähle allein,
    Ewig entsag' ich der Sünde.

Treuer Immanuel, werd' auch in mir neu geboren;
Komm doch, mein Heiland, und lass mich nicht länger ver-
    loren;
    Wohne in mir,
    Mach mich ganz eines mit dir,
    Den du zum Leben erkoren." * 35

The note of personal religion, as distinguished from theological doctrine, is stronger in German Christmas poetry than in
that of any other nation—the birth of Christ in the individual
soul, not merely the redemption of man in general, is a central
idea.

We come back at last to England. The great carol period is,
as has already been said, the fifteenth, and the first half of the
sixteenth, century; after the Reformation the English domestic
Christmas largely loses its religious colouring, and the best carols
of the late sixteenth and early seventeenth centuries are songs of

* " Triumph, ye heavens! rejoice ye with high adoration!
    Sing to the Lord, to the Saviour, in glad exultation!
        Angels, give ear!
        God unto man hath drawn near,
        Bringing to lost ones salvation.

    .   .   .   .   .   .

    King of the Glory! what grace in Thy humiliation!
    Thou wert a child! who of old wert the Lord of creation.
        Thee will I own,
        Thee would I follow, alone,
        Heir of Thy wondrous salvation.

    Faithful Immanuel! let me Thy glories be telling,
    Come, O my Saviour, be born, in mine inmost heart dwelling,
        In me abide.
        Make me with Thee unified,
        Where the life-fountain is welling." 36

CHRISTMAS IN ENGLISH POETRY

feasting and pagan ceremonies rather than of the Holy Child and His Mother. There is no lack of fine Christmas verse in the Elizabethan and early Stuart periods, but for the most part it belongs to the oratory and the chamber rather than the hall. The Nativity has become a subject for private contemplation, for individual devotion, instead of, as in the later Middle Ages, a matter for common jubilation, a wonder-story that really happened, in which, all alike and all together, the serious and the frivolous could rejoice, something that, with all its marvel, could be taken as a matter of course, like the return of the seasons or the rising of the sun on the just and on the unjust.

English Christmas poetry after the mid-sixteenth century is, then, individual rather than communal in its spirit ; it is also a thing less of the people, more of the refined and cultivated few. The Puritanism which so deeply affected English religion was abstract rather than dramatic in its conception of Christianity, it was concerned less with the events of the Saviour's life than with Redemption as a transaction between God and man ; St. Paul and the Old Testament rather than the gospels were its inspiration. Moreover, the material was viewed not as penetrated by and revealing the spiritual, but as sheer impediment blocking out the vision of spiritual things. Hence the extremer Puritans were completely out of touch with the sensuous poetry of Christmas, a festival which, as we shall see, they actually suppressed when they came into power.

The singing of sacred carols by country people continued, indeed, but the creative artistic impulse was lost. True carols after the Reformation tend to be doggerel, and no doubt many of the traditional pieces printed in such collections as Bramley and Stainer's * 37 are debased survivals from the Middle Ages, or perhaps new words written for old tunes. Such carols as "God rest you merry, gentlemen," have unspeakably delightful airs, and the words charm us moderns by their quaintness and rusticity, but they are far from the exquisite loveliness of the mediaeval

---

* A few of the best traditional pieces have been published by Mr. F. Sidgwick in one of his charming "Watergate Booklets" under the title of "Popular Carols." The two next quotations are from this source.

things. Gleams of great beauty are, however, sometimes found amid matter that in the process of transmission has almost ceased to be poetry. Here, for instance, are five stanzas from the traditional " Cherry-tree Carol " :—

> " As Joseph was a-walking,
>   He heard an angel sing :
> ' This night shall be born
>   Our heavenly King.
>
> ' He neither shall be born
>   In housen nor in hall,
> Nor in the place of Paradise,
>   But in an ox's stall.
>
> ' He neither shall be clothed
>   In purple nor in pall,
> But all in fair linen
>   As wear babies all.
>
> ' He neither shall be rocked
>   In silver nor in gold,
> But in a wooden cradle
>   That rocks on the mould.
>
> ' He neither shall be christened
>   In white wine nor red,
> But with fair spring water
>   With which we were christened.' "

The old carols sung by country folk have often not much to do with the Nativity ; they are sometimes rhymed lives of Christ or legends of the Holy Childhood. Of the latter class the strangest is " The Bitter Withy," discovered in Herefordshire by Mr. Frank Sidgwick. It tells how the little Jesus asked three lads to play with Him at ball. But they refused :—

> " ' O we are lords' and ladies' sons,
>   Born in bower or in hall ;
> And you are but a poor maid's child,
>   Born in an oxen's stall.'

CHRISTMAS IN ENGLISH POETRY

'If I am but a poor maid's child,
    Born in an oxen's stall,
I will let you know at the very latter end
    That I am above you all.'

So he built him a bridge with the beams of the sun,
    And over the sea went he,
And after followed the three jolly jerdins,
    And drowned they were all three.

Then Mary mild called home her child,
    And laid him across her knee,
And with a handful of green withy twigs
    She gave him slashes three.

'O the withy, O the withy, O bitter withy,
    That causes me to smart !
O the withy shall be the very first tree
    That perishes at the heart.' "

From these popular ballads, mediaeval memories in the rustic
mind, we must return to the devotional verse of the late sixteenth
and early seventeenth centuries.   Two of the greatest poets of the
Nativity, the Roman priests Southwell and Crashaw, are deeply
affected by the wave of mysticism which passed over Europe in
their time.   Familiar as is Southwell's " The Burning Babe,"
few will be sorry to find it here :—

"As I in hoary winter's night
    Stood shivering in the snow,
Surprised I was with sudden heat,
    Which made my heart to glow ;
And lifting up a fearful eye
    To view what fire was near,
A pretty Babe all burning bright
    Did in the air appear ;
Who, scorchèd with excessive heat,
    Such floods of tears did shed,
As though His floods should quench His flames,
    Which with His tears were fed.

79

THE CHRISTIAN FEAST

'Alas!' quoth He, 'but newly born,
    In fiery heats I fry,
Yet none approach to warm their hearts
    Or feel my fire, but I!
My faultless breast the furnace is,
    The fuel, wounding thorns;
Love is the fire, and sighs the smoke,
    The ashes, shame and scorns;
The fuel Justice layeth on,
    And Mercy blows the coals,
The metal in this furnace wrought
    Are men's defilèd souls,
For which, as now on fire I am,
    To work them to their good,
So will I melt into a bath,
    To wash them in my blood.'
With this he vanished out of sight,
    And swiftly shrunk away:
And straight I callèd unto mind
    That it was Christmas Day." [38]

As for Crashaw,

"That the great angel-blinding light should shrink
His blaze to shine in a poor shepherd's eye,
That the unmeasured God so low should sink
As Pris'ner in a few poor rags to lie,
That from His mother's breast He milk should drink
Who feeds with nectar heaven's fair family,
    That a vile manger His low bed should prove
    Who in a throne of stars thunders above:

That He, whom the sun serves, should faintly peep
Through clouds of infant flesh; that He the old
Eternal Word should be a Child and weep,
That He who made the fire should fear the cold:
That heaven's high majesty His court should keep
In a clay cottage, by each blast controll'd:
    That glory's self should serve our griefs and fears,
    And free Eternity submit to years—" [39]

such are the wondrous paradoxes celebrated in his glowing
imagery. The contrast of the winter snow with the burning

heat of Incarnate Love, of the blinding light of Divinity with the night's darkness, indeed the whole paradox of the Incarnation —Infinity in extremest limitation—is nowhere realized with such intensity as by him. Yet, magnificent as are his best lines, his verse sometimes becomes too like the seventeenth-century Jesuit churches, with walls overladen with decoration, with great languorous pictures and air heavy with incense; and then we long for the dewy freshness of the early carols.

The representative Anglican poets of the seventeenth century, Herbert and Vaughan, scarcely rise to their greatest heights in their treatment of Christmas, but with them as with the Romanists it is the mystical note that is dominant. Herbert sings :—

> "O Thou, whose glorious, yet contracted, light,
> Wrapt in night's mantle, stole into a manger;
> Since my dark soul and brutish is Thy right,
> To man, of all beasts, be not Thou a stranger.
>
> Furnish and deck my soul, that thou may'st have
> A better lodging than a rack or grave." [40]

And Vaughan :—

> "I would I had in my best part
> Fit rooms for Thee ! or that my heart
> Were so clean as
> Thy manger was !
> But I am all filth, and obscene :
> Yet, if Thou wilt, Thou canst make clean.
>
> Sweet Jesu ! will then. Let no more
> This leper haunt and soil thy door !
> Cure him, ease him,
> O release him !
> And let once more, by mystic birth,
> The Lord of life be born in earth." [41]

In Herrick—how different a country parson from Herbert !— we find a sort of pagan piety towards the Divine Infant which,

THE CHRISTIAN FEAST

though purely English in its expression, makes us think of some French *Noëliste* or some present-day Italian worshipper of the *Bambino* :—

> "Instead of neat enclosures
> Of interwoven osiers,
> Instead of fragrant posies
> Of daffodils and roses,
> Thy cradle, kingly Stranger,
>   As gospel tells,
>   Was nothing else
> But here a homely manger.
>
> But we with silks not crewels,
> With sundry precious jewels,
> And lily work will dress Thee ;
> And, as we dispossess Thee
> Of clouts, we'll make a chamber,
>   Sweet Babe, for Thee,
>   Of ivory,
> And plaster'd round with amber." [42]

Poems such as Herrick's to the Babe of Bethlehem reveal in their writers a certain childlikeness, an *insouciance* without irreverence, the spirit indeed of a child which turns to its God quite simply and naturally, which makes Him after its own child-image, and sees Him as a friend who can be pleased with trifles —almost, in fact, as a glorious playmate. Such a nature has no intense feeling of sin, but can ask for forgiveness and then forget ; religion for it is rather an outward ritual to be duly and gracefully performed than an inward transforming power. Herrick is a strange exception among the Anglican singers of Christmas.

Milton's great Nativity hymn, with its wondrous blending of pastoral simplicity and classical conceits, is too familiar for quotation here ; it may be suggested, however, that this work of the poet's youth is far more Anglican than Puritan in its spirit.

Sweet and solemn Spenserian echoes are these verses from Giles Fletcher's "Christ's Victory in Heaven" :—

" Who can forget—never to be forgot—
The time, that all the world in slumber lies,
When, like the stars, the singing angels shot
To earth, and heaven awakèd all his eyes
To see another sun at midnight rise
  On earth ? Was never sight of pareil fame,
  For God before man like Himself did frame,
But God Himself now like a mortal man became.

A Child He was, and had not learnt to speak,
That with His word the world before did make ;
His mother's arms Him bore, He was so weak,
That with one hand the vaults of heaven could shake,
See how small room my infant Lord doth take,
  Whom all the world is not enough to hold !
  Who of His years, or of His age hath told ?
Never such age so young, never a child so old." 43

The old lullaby tradition is continued by Wither, though the infant in the cradle is an ordinary human child, who is rocked to sleep with the story of his Lord :—

  "A little Infant once was He,
    And strength in weakness then was laid
  Upon His virgin-mother's knee,
    That power to thee might be conveyed.
      Sweet baby, then, forbear to weep ;
      Be still, my babe ; sweet baby, sleep.
    . . . . .

  Within a manger lodged thy Lord,
    Where oxen lay and asses fed ;
  Warm rooms we do to thee afford,
    An easy cradle or a bed.
      Sweet baby, then, forbear to weep ;
      Be still, my babe ; sweet baby, sleep." 44

When we come to the eighteenth century we find, where we might least expect it, among the moral verses of Dr. Watts, a charming cradle-song conceived in just the same way :—

THE CHRISTIAN FEAST

" Hush, my dear, lie still and slumber,
 Holy angels guard thy bed !
Heavenly blessings without number
 Gently falling on thy head.

. . . . .

Soft and easy is thy cradle ;
 Coarse and hard thy Saviour lay.
When His birthplace was a stable,
 And His softest bed was hay.

. . . . .

Lo He slumbers in His manger
 Where the hornèd oxen fed ;
—Peace, my darling, here's no danger ;
 Here's no ox a-near thy bed." [45]

It is to the eighteenth century that the three most popular of English Christmas hymns belong. Nahum Tate's " While shepherds watched their flocks by night "—one of the very few hymns (apart from metrical psalms) in common use in the Anglican Church before the nineteenth century—is a bald and apparently artless paraphrase of St. Luke which, by some accident, has attained dignity, and is aided greatly by the simple and noble tune now attached to it. Charles Wesley's " Hark, the herald angels sing," or—as it should be—" Hark, how all the welkin rings," is much admired by some, but to the present writer seems a mere piece of theological rhetoric. Byrom's " Christians, awake, salute the happy morn," has the stiffness and formality of its period, but it is not without a certain quaintness and dignity. One could hardly expect fine Christmas poetry of an age whose religion was on the one hand staid, rational, unimaginative, and on the other " Evangelical " in the narrow sense, finding its centre in the Atonement rather than the Incarnation.

The revived mediaevalism, religious and aesthetic, of the nineteenth century, produced a number of Christmas carols. Some, like Swinburne's " Three damsels in the queen's chamber," with its exquisite verbal music and delightful colour, and William Morris's less successful "Masters, in this hall," and "Outlanders, whence come ye last ? " are the work of unbelievers and bear witness only to the aesthetic charm of the Christmas story ; but there are others, mostly from Roman or Anglo-Catholic sources, of real religious inspiration.*   The most spontaneous are Christina Rossetti's, whose haunting rhythms and delicate feeling are shown at their best in her songs of the Christ Child.   More studied and self-conscious are the austere Christmas verses of Lionel Johnson and the graceful carols of Professor Selwyn Image.   In one poem Mr. Image strikes a deeper and stronger note than elsewhere ; its solemn music takes us back to an earlier century :—

"Consider, O my soul, what morn is this !
    Whereon the eternal Lord of all things made,
For us, poor mortals, and our endless bliss,
    Came down from heaven ; and, in a manger laid,
    The first, rich, offerings of our ransom paid :
Consider, O my soul, what morn is this ! " [46]

.   .   .   .   .

Not a few contemporary poets have given us Christmas carols or poems.   Among the freshest and most natural are those of Katharine Tynan, while Mr. Gilbert Chesterton has written some Christmas lyrics full of colour and vitality, and with a true mystical quality.   Singing of Christmas, Mr. Chesterton is at his best ; he has instinctive sympathy with the spirit of the festival, its human kindliness, its democracy, its sacramentalism, its exaltation of the child :—

"The thatch of the roof was as golden
    Though dusty the straw was and old ;
The wind had a peal as of trumpets,
    Though blowing and barren and cold.

* Browning's great poem, " Christmas Eve," is philosophical rather than devotional, and hardly comes within the scope of this chapter.

THE CHRISTIAN FEAST

> The mother's hair was a glory,
>   Though loosened and torn ;
> For under the eaves in the gloaming
>   A child was born." 47

Thus opens a fine poem on the Nativity as symbolizing the miracle of birth, of childhood with its infinite possibilities, its eternal renewal of faith and hope.

CHAPTER IV
CHRISTMAS IN LITURGY
AND POPULAR DEVOTION

CHAPTER IV

CHRISTMAS IN LITURGY AND POPULAR
DEVOTION

Advent and Christmas Offices of the Roman Church—The Three Masses of Christmas,
their Origin and their Celebration in Rome—The Midnight Mass in Many Lands
—Protestant Survivals of the Night Services—Christmas in the Greek Church—
The Eastern Epiphany and the Blessing of the Waters—The *Presepio* or Crib, its
Supposed Institution by St. Francis—Early Traces of the Crib—The Crib in
Germany, Tyrol, &c.—Cradle-rocking in Mediaeval Germany—Christmas Min-
strels in Italy and Sicily—The *Presepio* in Italy—Ceremonies with the *Culla* and
the *Bambino* in Rome—Christmas in Italian London—The Spanish Christmas—
Possible Survivals of the Crib in England.

FROM a study of Christmas as reflected in lyric poetry, we now
pass to other forms of devotion in which the Church has
welcomed the Redeemer at His birth. These are of two kinds—
liturgical and popular ; and they correspond in a large degree to
the successive ways of apprehending the meaning of Christmas
which we traced in the foregoing chapters. Strictly liturgical
devotions are little understood of the people : only the clergy
can fully join in them ; for the mass of the lay folk they are
mysterious rites in an unknown tongue, to be followed with
reverence, as far as may be, but remote and little penetrated with
humanity. Side by side with these, however, are popular devotions, full of vivid colour, highly anthropomorphic, bringing the
mysteries of religion within the reach of the simplest minds, and
warm with human feeling. The austere Latin hymns of the
earlier centuries belong to liturgy ; the vernacular Christmas
poetry of later ages is largely associated with popular devotion.

THE CHRISTIAN FEAST

Liturgiology is a vast and complicated, and except to the few, an unattractive, subject. To attempt here a survey of the liturgies in their relation to Christmas is obviously impossible; we must be content to dwell mainly upon the present-day Roman offices, which, in spite of various revisions, give some idea of the mediaeval services of Latin Christianity, and to cast a few glances at other western rites, and at those of the Greek Church.

Whatever may be his attitude towards Catholicism, or, indeed, Christianity, no one sensitive to the music of words, or the suggestions of poetic imagery, can read the Roman Breviary and Missal without profound admiration for the amazing skill with which the noblest passages of Hebrew poetry are chosen and fitted to the expression of Christian devotion, and the gold of psalmists, prophets, and apostles is welded into coronals for the Lord and His saints. The office-books of the Roman Church are, in one aspect, the greatest of anthologies.

Few parts of the Roman Breviary have more beauty than the Advent * offices, where the Church has brought together the majestic imagery of the Hebrew prophets, the fervent exhortation of the apostles, to prepare the minds of the faithful for the coming of the Christ, for the celebration of the Nativity.

Advent begins with a stirring call. If we turn to the opening service of the Christian Year, the First Vespers of the First Sunday in Advent, we shall find as the first words in the "Proper of the Season" the trumpet-notes of St. Paul: "Brethren, it is high time to awake out of sleep; for now is our salvation nearer than when we believed." This, the Little Chapter for the office, is followed by the ancient hymn, "Creator alme siderum," [1] chanting in awful tones the two comings of

---

* The first mention of a season corresponding to Advent is at the Council of Tours, about 567, when a fast for monks in December is vaguely indicated. At the Council of Mâcon (581) it is enjoined that from Martinmas the second, fourth, and sixth days of the week should be fasting days; and at the close of the sixth century Rome, under Gregory the Great, adopted the rule of the four Sundays in Advent. In the next century it became prevalent in the West. In the Greek Church, forty days of fasting are observed before Christmas; this custom appears to have been established in the thirteenth century. In the Roman Church the practice as to fasting varies: in the British Isles Wednesday and Friday are observed, but in some countries no distinction is made between Advent and ordinary weeks of the year.[2]

Christ, for redemption and for judgment; and then are sung the words that strike the keynote of the Advent services, and are heard again and again.

" *Rorate, coeli, desuper, et nubes pluant Justum*
  (Drop down, ye heavens, from above, and let the skies pour down the Righteous One).
  Aperiatur terra et germinet Salvatorem
  (Let the earth open, and let her bring forth the Saviour)."

Rorate, coeli, desuper—Advent is a time of longing expectancy. It is a season of waiting patiently for the Lord, whose coming in great humility is to be commemorated at Christmas, to whose coming again in His glorious majesty to judge both the quick and the dead the Christian looks forward with mingled hope and awe. There are four weeks in Advent, and an ancient symbolical explanation interprets these as typifying four comings of the Son of God: the first in the flesh, the second in the hearts of the faithful through the Holy Spirit, the third at the death of every man, and the fourth at the Judgment Day. The fourth week is never completed (Christmas Eve is regarded as not part of Advent), because the glory bestowed on the saints at the Last Coming will never end.

The great Eucharistic hymn, " Gloria in excelsis," is omitted in Advent, in order, say the symbolists, that on Christmas night, when it was first sung by the angels, it may be chanted with the greater eagerness and devotion. The " Te Deum " at Matins too is left unsaid, because Christ is regarded as not yet come. But " Alleluia " is not omitted, because Advent is only half a time of penitence: there is awe at the thought of the Coming for Judgment, but joy also in the hope of the Incarnation to be celebrated at Christmas, and the glory in store for the faithful.[3]

Looking forward is above all things the note of Advent; the Church seeks to share the mood of the Old Testament saints, and she draws more now than at any other season, perhaps, on the treasures of Hebrew prophecy for her lessons, antiphons, versicles, and responds. Looking for the glory that shall be revealed, she awaits, at this darkest time of the year, the rising of the Sun of Righteousness. *Rorate, coeli, desuper*—the mood comes at times to all idealists, and even those moderns who hope not for a supernatural Redeemer, but for the triumph of social justice on this earth, must be stirred by the poetry of the Advent offices.

It is at Vespers on the seven days before Christmas Eve that the Church's longing finds its noblest expression—in the antiphons known as the " Great O's," sung before and after the "Magnificat," one on each day. " O Sapientia," runs the first, " O Wisdom, which camest out of the mouth of the Most High, and reachest from one end to another, mightily and sweetly ordering all things : come and teach us the way of prudence." " O Adonai," " O Root of Jesse," " O Key of David," " O Day-spring, Brightness of Light Everlasting," " O King of the Nations," thus the Church calls to her Lord, " O Emmanuel, our King and Lawgiver, the Desire of all nations, and their Salvation : come and save us, O Lord our God."[4]

At last Christmas Eve is here, and at Vespers we feel the nearness of the great Coming. " Lift up your heads : behold your redemption draweth nigh," is the antiphon for the last psalm. " To-morrow shall be done away the iniquity of the earth," is the versicle after the Office Hymn. And before and after the " Magnificat " the Church sings : " When the sun shall have risen, ye shall see the King of kings coming forth from the Father, as a bridegroom out of his chamber."

Yet only with the night office of Matins does the glory of the festival begin. There is a special fitness at Christmas in the Church's keeping watch by night, like the shepherds of Bethlehem, and the office is full of the poetry of the season, full of exultant joy. To the "Venite, exultemus Domino" a Christmas note is added by the oft-repeated Invitatory, "Unto us the Christ is born : O come, let us adore Him." Psalms follow—among them the three retained by the Anglican Church in her Christmas Matins—and lessons from the Old and New Testaments and the homilies of the Fathers, interspersed with Responsories bringing home to the faithful the wonders of the Holy Night. Some are almost dramatic ; this, for instance :—

CHRISTMAS IN LITURGY

"Whom saw ye, O shepherds ? speak ; tell us who hath appeared
    on the earth.
We saw the new-born Child, and angels singing praise unto the
    Lord.
Speak, what saw ye ? and tell us of the birth of Christ.
We saw the new-born Child, and angels singing praise unto the
    Lord."

It is the wonder of the Incarnation, the marvel of the spotless
Birth, the song of the Angels, the coming down from heaven of
true peace, the daybreak of redemption and everlasting joy, the
glory of the Only-begotten, now beheld by men—the supernatural side, in fact, of the festival, that the Church sets forth in
her radiant words ; there is little thought of the purely human
side, the pathos of Bethlehem.

It was customary at certain places, in mediaeval times, to lay
on the altar three veils, and remove one at each nocturn of
Christmas Matins. The first was black, and symbolised the
time of darkness before the Mosaic Law ; the second white,
typifying, it would seem, the faith of those who lived under
that Law of partial revelation ; the third red, showing the love
of Christ's bride, the Church, in the time of grace flowing from
the Incarnation.[5]

A stately ceremony took place in England in the Middle Ages
at the end of Christmas Matins—the chanting of St. Matthew's
genealogy of Christ. The deacon, in his dalmatic, with acolytes
carrying tapers, with thurifer and cross-bearer, all in albs and
tunicles, went in procession to the pulpit or the rood-loft, to
sing this portion of the Gospel. If the bishop were present,
he it was who chanted it, and a rich candlestick was held to
light him.* Then followed the chanting of the " Te Deum."[6]
The ceremony does not appear in the ordinary Roman books,
but it is still performed by the Benedictines, as one may read
in the striking account of the monastic Christmas given by
Huysmans in " L'Oblat."[7]

---

* Anthony Beck, Bishop of Durham, bequeathed to his cathedral a Christmas
candlestick of silver-gilt, on the base of which was an image of St. Mary with
her Son lying in the crib.

THE CHRISTIAN FEAST

Where, as in religious communities, the offices of the Church are performed in their full order, there follows on Matins that custom peculiar to Christmas, the celebration of Midnight Mass. On Christmas morning every priest is permitted to say three Masses, which should in strictness be celebrated at midnight, at dawn, and in full daylight. Each has its own Collect, Epistle, and Gospel, each its own Introit, Gradual, and other anthems. In many countries the Midnight Mass is the distinctive Christmas service, a great and unique event in the year, something which by its strangeness gives to the feast of the Nativity a place by itself. Few Catholic rites are more impressive than this Midnight Mass, especially in country places; through the darkness and cold of the winter's night, often for long distances, the faithful journey to worship the Infant Saviour in the splendour of the lighted church. It is a re-enactment of the visit of the shepherds to the cave at Bethlehem, aglow with supernatural light.

Various symbolical explanations of the three Masses were given by mediaeval writers. The midnight celebration was supposed to represent mankind's condition before the Law of Moses, when thick darkness covered the earth; the second, at dawn, the time of the Law and the Prophets with its growing light; the third, in full daylight, the Christian era of light and grace. Another interpretation, adopted by St. Thomas Aquinas, is more mystical; the three Masses stand for the threefold birth of Christ, the first typifying the dark mystery of the eternal generation of the Son, the second the birth of Christ the morning-star within the hearts of men, the third the bodily birth of the Son of Mary.[8]

At the Christmas Masses the "Gloria in excelsis" resounds again. This song of the angels was at first chanted only at Christmas; it was introduced into Rome during the fifth century at Midnight Mass in imitation of the custom of the Church of Jerusalem.[9]

It is, indeed, from imitation of the services at Jerusalem and Bethlehem that the three Roman Masses of Christmas seem to have sprung. From a late fourth-century document known as

THE NATIVITY.

From Add. MS. 32454 in the British Museum (French, 15th century).

To face p. 94.

the "Peregrinatio Silviae," the narrative of a pilgrimage to the holy places of the east by a great lady from southern Gaul, it appears that at the feast of the Epiphany—when the Birth of Christ was commemorated in the Palestinian Church—two successive "stations" were held, one at Bethlehem, the other at Jerusalem. At Bethlehem the station was held at night on the eve of the feast, then a procession was made to the church of the Anastasis or Resurrection—where was the Holy Sepulchre—arriving "about the hour when one man begins to recognise another, *i.e.*, near daylight, but before the day has fully broken." There a psalm was sung, prayers were said, and the catechumens and faithful were blessed by the bishop. Later, Mass was celebrated at the Great Church at Golgotha, and the procession returned to the Anastasis, where another Mass was said.[10]

At Bethlehem at the present time impressive services are held on the Latin Christmas Day. The Patriarch comes from Jerusalem, with a troop of cavalry and Kavasses in gorgeous array. The office lasts from 10 o'clock on Christmas Eve until long after midnight. "At the reading of the Gospel the clergy and as many of the congregation as can follow leave the church, and proceed by a flight of steps and a tortuous rock-hewn passage to the Grotto of the Nativity, an irregular subterranean chamber, long and narrow. They carry with them a waxen image of an infant—the *bambino*—wrap it in swaddling bands and lay it on the site which is said to be that of the manger." [11]

The Midnight Mass appears to have been introduced into Rome in the first half of the fifth century. It was celebrated by the Pope in the church of Santa Maria Maggiore, while the second Mass was sung by him at Sant' Anastasia—perhaps because of the resemblance of the name to the Anastasis at Jerusalem—and the third at St. Peter's.[12] On Christmas Eve the Pope held a solemn "station" at Santa Maria Maggiore, and two Vespers were sung, the first very simple, the second, at which the Pope pontificated, with elaborate ceremonial. Before the second Vespers, in the twelfth century, a good meal had to be prepared for the papal household by the Cardinal-Bishop of Albano. After Matins and Midnight Mass at Santa Maria Maggiore, the Pope went in procession to Sant' Anastasia for Lauds and the Mass of the Dawn. The third Mass, at St. Peter's, was an event of great solemnity, and at it took place in the year 800 that profoundly significant event, the coronation of Charlemagne by Leo III.—a turning-point in European history.[13]

Later it became the custom for the Pope, instead of proceeding to St. Peter's, to return to Santa Maria Maggiore for the third Mass. On his arrival he was given a cane with a lighted candle affixed to it; with this he had to set fire to some tow placed on the capitals of the columns.[14] The ecclesiastical explanation of this strange ceremony was that it symbolised the end of the world by fire, but one may conjecture that some pagan custom lay at its root. Since 1870 the Pope, as "the prisoner of the Vatican," has of course ceased to celebrate at Santa Maria Maggiore or Sant' Anastasia. The Missal, however, still shows a trace of the papal visit to Sant' Anastasia in a commemoration of this saint which comes as a curious parenthesis in the Mass of the Dawn.

On Christmas Day in the Vatican the Pope blesses a hat and a sword, and these are sent as gifts to some prince. The practice is said to have arisen from the mediaeval custom for the Holy Roman Emperor or some other sovereign to read one of the lessons at Christmas Matins, in the papal chapel, with his sword drawn.[15]

Celebrated in countries as distant from one another, both geographically and in character, as Ireland and Sicily, Poland and South America, the Midnight Mass naturally varies greatly in its tone and setting. Sometimes it is little more than a fashionable function, sometimes the devotion of those who attend is shown by a tramp over miles of snow through the darkness and the bitter wind.

In some charming memories of the Christmas of her childhood, Madame Th. Bentzon thus describes the walk to the Midnight Mass in a French country place about sixty years ago :—

CHRISTMAS IN LITURGY

" I can see myself as a little girl, bundled up to the tip of my nose in furs and knitted shawls, tiny wooden shoes on my feet, a lantern in my hand, setting out with my parents for the Midnight Mass of Christmas Eve. . . . We started off, a number of us, together in a stream of light. . . . Our lanterns cast great shadows on the white road, crisp with frost. As our little group advanced it saw others on their way, people from the farm and from the mill, who joined us, and once on the Place de l'Église we found ourselves with all the parishioners in a body. No one spoke—the icy north wind cut short our breath ; but the voice of the chimes filled the silence. . . . We entered, accompanied by a gust of wind that swept into the porch at the same time we did ; and the splendours of the altar, studded with lights, green with pine and laurel branches, dazzled us from the threshold." [16]

In devout Tyrol, the scenes on Christmas Eve before the Midnight Mass are often extremely impressive, particularly in narrow valleys where the houses lie scattered on the mountain slopes. Long before midnight the torches lighting the faithful on their way to Mass begin to twinkle ; downward they move, now hidden in pine-woods and ravines, now reappearing on the open hill-side. More and more lights show themselves and throw ruddy flashes on the snow, until at last, the floor of the valley reached, they vanish, and only the church windows glow through the darkness, while the solemn strains of the organ and chanting break the silence of the night.[17]

Not everywhere has the great Mass been celebrated amid scenes so still and devotional. In Madrid, says a writer of the early nineteenth century, " the evening of the vigil is scarcely dark when numbers of men, women, and boys are seen traversing the streets with torches, and many of them supplied with tambourines, which they strike loudly as they move along in a kind of Bacchanal procession. There is a tradition here that the shepherds who visited Bethlehem on the day of the Nativity had instruments of this sort upon which they expressed the sentiment of joy that animated them when they received the intelligence that a Saviour was born." At the Midnight Mass crowds of people who, perhaps, had been traversing the streets the whole night, came into the church

G

with their tambourines and guitars, and accompanied the organ. The Mass over, they began to dance in the very body of the church.[18]   A later writer speaks of the Midnight Mass in Madrid as a fashionable function to which many gay young people went in order to meet one another.[19]   Such is the character of the service in the Spanish-American cities.   In Lima the streets on Christmas Eve are crowded with gaily dressed and noisy folks, many of them masked, and everybody goes to the Mass.[20] In Paris the elaborate music attracts enormous and often not very serious crowds. In Sicily there is sometimes extraordinary irreverence at the midnight services : people take provisions with them to eat in church, and from time to time go out to an inn for a drink, and between the offices they imitate the singing of birds.[21]   We may see in such things the licence of pagan festivals creeping within the very walls of the sanctuary.

In the Rhineland Midnight Mass has been abolished, because the conviviality of Christmas Eve led to unseemly behaviour at the solemn service, but Mass is still celebrated very early—at four or five—and great crowds of worshippers attend. It is a stirring thing, this first Mass of Christmas, in some ancient town, when from the piercing cold, the intense stillness of the early morning, one enters a great church thronged with people, bright with candles, warm with human fellowship, and hears the vast congregation break out into a slow solemn chorale, full of devout joy that

> " In Bethlehem geboren
> Ist uns ein Kindelein."

It is interesting to trace survivals of the nocturnal Christmas offices in Protestant countries. In German " Evangelical" churches, midnight or early morning services were common in the eighteenth century ; but they were forbidden in some places because of the riot and drunkenness which accompanied them. The people seem to have regarded them as a part of their Christmas revellings rather than as sacred functions ; one writer compares the congregation to a crowd of wild drunken sailors in a tavern, another gives disgusting particulars of disorders in a church where the only sober man was the preacher.[22]

In Sweden the Christmas service is performed very early in the morning, the chancel is lighted up with many candles, and the celebrant is vested in a white chasuble with golden orphreys.[23]

A Midnight Mass is now celebrated in many Anglican churches, but this is purely a modern revival. The most distinct British *survival* is to be found in Wales in the early service known as *Plygain* (dawn), sometimes a celebration of the Communion. At Tenby at four o'clock on Christmas morning it was customary for the young men of the town to escort the rector with lighted torches from his house to the church. Extinguishing their torches in the porch, they went in to the early service, and when it was ended the torches were relighted and the procession returned to the rectory. At St. Peter's Church, Carmarthen, an early service was held, to the light of coloured candles brought by the congregation. At St. Asaph, Caerwys, at 4 or 5 a.m., *Plygain*, consisting of carols sung round the church in procession, was held.[24] The *Plygain* continued in Welsh churches until about the eighteen-fifties, and, curiously enough, when the Established Church abandoned it, it was celebrated in Nonconformist chapels.[25]

In the Isle of Man on Christmas Eve, or *Oiel Verry* (Mary's Eve), "a number of persons used to assemble in each parish church and proceed to shout carols or 'Carvals.' There was no unison or concert about the chanting, but a single person would stand up with a lighted candle in his or her hand, and chant in a dismal monotone verse after verse of some old Manx 'Carval,' until the candle was burnt out. Then another person would start up and go through a similar performance. No fresh candles might be lighted after the clock had chimed midnight." [26]

One may conjecture that the common English practice of ringing bells until midnight on Christmas Eve has also some connection with the old-time Midnight Mass.

For the Greek Church Christmas is a comparatively unimportant festival by the side of the Epiphany, the celebration of

THE CHRISTIAN FEAST

Christ's Baptism; the Christmas offices are, however, full of fine poetry. There is far less restraint, far less adherence to the words of Scripture, far greater richness of original composition, in the Greek than in the Roman service-books, and while there is less poignancy there is more amplitude and splendour. Christmas Day, with the Greeks, is a commemoration of the coming of the Magi as well as of the Nativity and the adoration of the shepherds, and the Wise Men are very prominent in the services. The following hymn of St. Anatolius (fifth century), from the First Vespers of the feast, is fairly typical of the character of the Christmas offices :—

> "When Jesus our Lord was born of Her,
> The Holy Virgin, all the universe
> Became enlightened.
> For as the shepherds watched their flocks,
> And as the Magi came to pray,
> And as the Angels sang their hymn
> Herod was troubled ; for God in flesh appeared,
> The Saviour of our souls.
>
> Thy kingdom, Christ our God, the kingdom is
> Of all the worlds, and Thy dominion
> O'er every generation bears the sway,
> Incarnate of the Holy Ghost,
> Man of the Ever-Virgin Mary,
> By Thy presence, Christ our God,
> Thou hast shined a Light on us.
> Light of Light, the Brightness of the Father,
> Thou hast beamed on every creature.
> All that hath breath doth praise Thee,
> Image of the Father's glory.
> Thou who art, and wast before,
> God who shinedst from the Maid,
> Have mercy upon us.
>
> What gift shall we bring to Thee,
> O Christ, since Thou as Man on earth
> For us hast shewn Thyself ?

CHRISTMAS IN LITURGY

Since every creature made by Thee
Brings to Thee its thanksgiving.
　　The Angels bring their song,
　　The Heavens bring their star,
　　The Magi bring their gifts,
　　The Shepherds bring their awe,
Earth gives a cave, the wilderness a manger,
And we the Virgin-Mother bring.
God before all worlds, have mercy upon us ! " [27]

A beautiful rite called the " Peace of God " is performed in
Slavonic churches at the end of the " Liturgy " or Mass on
Christmas morning—the people kiss one another on both cheeks,
saying, " Christ is born ! " To this the answer is made, " Of a
truth He is born ! " and the kisses are returned. This is repeated
till everyone has kissed and been kissed by all present. [28]

We must pass rapidly over the feasts of saints within the
Octave of the western Christmas, St. Stephen (December 26),
St. John the Evangelist (December 27), the Holy Innocents
(December 28), and St. Sylvester (December 31). None of
these, except the feast of the Holy Innocents, have any special
connection with the Nativity or the Infancy, and the popular
customs connected with them will come up for consideration
in our Second Part.

The commemoration of the Circumcision ("when eight days
were accomplished for the circumcising of the child") falls
naturally on January 1, the Octave of Christmas. It is not of
Roman origin, and was not observed in Rome until it had long
been established in the Byzantine and Gallican Churches. [29] In
Gaul, as is shown by a decree of the Council of Tours in 567,
a solemn fast was held on the Circumcision and the two days
following it, in order to turn away the faithful from the pagan
festivities of the Kalends. [30]

The feast of the Epiphany on January 6, as we have seen, is
in the eastern Church a commemoration of the Baptism of Christ.
In the West it has become primarily the festival of the adoration

of the Magi, the manifestation of Christ to the Gentiles. Still in the Roman offices many traces of the baptismal commemoration remain, and the memory of yet another manifestation of Christ's glory appears in the antiphon at "Magnificat" at the Second Vespers of the feast :—

"We keep holy a day adorned by three wonders : to-day a star led the Magi to the manger ; to-day at the marriage water was made wine ; to-day for our salvation Christ was pleased to be baptized of John in Jordan. Alleluia."

On the Octave of the Epiphany at Matins the Baptism is the central idea, and the Gospel at Mass bears on the same subject. In Rome itself even the Blessing of the Waters, the distinctive ceremony of the eastern Epiphany rite, is performed in certain churches according to a Latin ritual.[31] At Sant' Andrea della Valle, Rome, during the Octave of the Epiphany a Solemn Mass is celebrated every morning according to the Latin rite, and afterwards, on each of the days from January 7–13, there follows a Mass according to one of the eastern rites : Greco-Slav, Armenian, Chaldean, Coptic, Greco-Ruthenian, Greco-Melchite, and Greek.[32] It is a week of great opportunities for the liturgiologist and the lover of strange ceremonial.

The Blessing of the Waters is an important event in all countries where the Greek Church prevails. In Greece the "Great Blessing," as it is called, is performed in various ways according to the locality ; sometimes the sea is blessed, sometimes a river or reservoir, sometimes merely water in a church. In seaport towns, where the people depend on the water for their living, the celebration has much pomp and elaborateness. At the Piraeus enormous and enthusiastic crowds gather, and there is a solemn procession of the bishop and clergy to the harbour, where the bishop throws a little wooden cross, held by a long blue ribbon, into the water, withdraws it dripping wet, and sprinkles the bystanders. This is done three times. At Nauplia and other places a curious custom prevails : the archbishop throws a wooden cross into the waters of the harbour, and the fishermen of the place dive in after it and struggle for its possession ; he who wins it has the right of visiting all the houses of the town and levying a collection, which often brings in a large sum. In Samos all the women send to the church a vessel full of water to be blessed by the priest ; with this water the fields and the trees are sprinkled.[33]

The sense attached to the ceremony by the Church is shown in this prayer :—

"Thou didst sanctify the streams of Jordan by sending from Heaven Thy Holy Spirit, and by breaking the heads of the dragons lurking there. Therefore, O King, Lover of men, be Thou Thyself present also now by the visitation of Thy Holy Spirit, and sanctify this water. Give also to it the grace of ransom, the blessing of Jordan : make it a fountain of incorruption ; a gift of sanctification ; a washing away of sins ; a warding off of diseases ; destruction to demons ; repulsion to the hostile powers ; filled with angelic strength ; that all who take and receive of it may have it for purification of souls and bodies, for healing of sicknesses, for sanctification of houses, and meet for every need." [34]

Though for the Church the immersion of the cross represents the Baptism of Christ, and the blessings springing from that event are supposed to be carried to the people by the sprinkling with the water, it is held by some students that the whole practice is a Christianization of a primitive rain-charm—a piece of sympathetic magic intended to produce rain by imitating the drenching which it gives. An Epiphany song from Imbros connects the blessing of rain with the Baptism of Christ, and another tells how at the river Jordan "a dove came down, white and feathery, and with its wings opened ; it sent rain down on the Lord, and again it rained and rained on our Lady, and again it rained and rained on its wings."[35]

The Blessing of the Waters is performed in the Greek church of St. Sophia, Bayswater, London, on the morning of the Epiphany, which, through the difference between the old and new "styles," falls on our 19th of January. All is done within the church ; the water to be blessed is placed on a table under the dome, and is sanctified by the immersion of a small cross; afterwards it is sprinkled on everyone present, and some is taken home by the faithful in little vessels.36

In Moscow and St. Petersburg the Blessing is a function of great magnificence, but it is perhaps even more interesting as performed in Russian country places. Whatever may be the orthodox significance of the rite, to the country people it is the chasing away of "forest demons, sprites, and fairies, once the gods the peasants worshipped, but now dethroned from their high estate," who in the long dark winter nights bewitch and vex the sons of men. A vivid and imaginative account of the ceremony and its meaning to the peasants is given by Mr. F. H. E. Palmer in his "Russian Life in Town and Country." The district in which he witnessed it was one of forests and of lakes frozen in winter. On one of these lakes had been erected "a huge cross, constructed of blocks of ice, that glittered like diamonds in the brilliant winter sunlight. . . . At length, far away could be heard the sound of human voices, singing a strange, wild melody. Presently there was a movement in the snow among the trees, and waving banners appeared as a procession approached, headed by the pope in his vestments, and surrounded by the village dignitaries, venerable, grey-bearded patriarchs." A wide space in the procession was left for "a strange and motley band of gnomes and sprites, fairies and wood-nymphs," who, as the peasants believed, had been caught by the holy singing and the sacred sign on the waving banner. The chanting still went on as the crowd formed a circle around the glittering cross, and all looked on with awe while half a dozen peasants with their axes cut a large hole in the ice. "And now the priest's voice is heard, deep and sonorous, as he pronounces the words of doom. Alas for the poor sprites! Into that yawning chasm they must leap, and sink deep, deep below the surface of that ice-cold water."37

Following these eastern Epiphany rites we have wandered far from the cycle of ideas generally associated with Christmas. We must now pass to those popular devotions to the Christ Child which, though they form no part of the Church's liturgy, she has permitted and encouraged. It is in the West that we shall find them; the Latin Church, as we have seen, makes far more of Christmas than the Greek.

Rome is often condemned for using in her liturgy the dead language of Latin, but it must not be forgotten that in every country she offers to the faithful a rich store of devotional literature in their own tongue, and that, supplementary to the liturgical offices, there is much public prayer and praise in the vernacular. Nor, in that which appeals to the eye, does she limit herself to the mysterious symbolism of the sacraments and the ritual which surrounds them; she gives to the people concrete, pictorial images to quicken their faith. How ritual grew in mediaeval times into full-fledged drama we shall see in the next chapter; here let us consider that cult of the Christ Child in which the scene of Bethlehem is represented not by living actors but in plastic art, often most simple and homely.

The use of the "crib" (French *crèche*, Italian *presepio*, German *krippe*) at Christmas is now universally diffused in the Roman Church. Most readers of this book must have seen one of these structures representing the stable at Bethlehem, with the Child in the manger, His mother and St. Joseph, the ox and the ass, and perhaps the shepherds, the three kings, or worshipping angels. They are the delight of children, who through the season of Christmas and Epiphany wander into the open churches at all times of day to gaze wide-eyed on the life-like scene and offer a prayer to their Little Brother. No one with anything of the child-spirit can fail to be touched by the charm of the Christmas crib. Faults of artistic taste there may often be, but these are wont to be softened down by the flicker of tapers, the glow of ruby lights, amidst the shades of some dim aisle or chapel, and the scene of tender humanity, gently, mysteriously radiant, as though with "bright shoots of everlastingness," is full of religious and poetic suggestions.

The institution of the *presepio* is often ascribed to St. Francis of Assisi, who in the year 1224 celebrated Christmas at Greccio

with a Bethlehem scene with a real ox and ass. About fifteen
days before the Nativity, according to Thomas of Celano, the
blessed Francis sent for a certain nobleman, John by name, and
said to him : "If thou wilt that we celebrate the present festival
of the Lord at Greccio, make haste to go before and diligently
prepare what I tell thee. For I would fain make memorial of
that Child who was born in Bethlehem, and in some sort behold
with bodily eyes His infant hardships ; how He lay in a manger
on the hay, with the ox and the ass standing by." The
good man prepared all that the Saint had commanded, and at
last the day of gladness drew nigh. The brethren were called
from many convents ; the men and women of the town prepared
tapers and torches to illuminate the night. Finding all things
ready, Francis beheld and rejoiced : the manger had been prepared, the hay was brought, and the ox and ass were led in.
"Thus Simplicity was honoured, Poverty exalted, Humility com-
mended, and of Greccio there was made as it were a new
Bethlehem. The night was lit up as the day, and was
delightsome to men and beasts. . . . The woodland rang with
voices, the rocks made answer to the jubilant throng." Francis
stood before the manger, "overcome with tenderness and
filled with wondrous joy"; Mass was celebrated, and he, in
deacon's vestments, chanted the Holy Gospel in an "earnest,
sweet, and loud-sounding voice." Then he preached to the
people of "the birth of the poor King and the little town of
Bethlehem." "Uttering the word 'Bethlehem' in the manner
of a sheep bleating, he filled his mouth with the sound," and in
naming the Child Jesus "he would, as it were, lick his lips,
relishing with happy palate and swallowing the sweetness of that
word." At length, the solemn vigil ended, each one returned
with joy to his own place.[38]

It has been suggested by Countess Martinengo [39] that this
beautiful ceremony was "the crystallization of haunting memories
carried away by St. Francis from the real Bethlehem"; for he
visited the east in 1219–20, and the Greccio celebration took
place in 1224. St. Francis and his followers may well have
helped greatly to popularize the use of the *presepio*, but it can be

traced back far earlier than their time. In the liturgical drama known as the " Officium Pastorum," which probably took shape in the eleventh century, we find a *praesepe* behind the altar as the centre of the action [40] ; but long before this something of the kind seems to have been in existence in the church of Santa Maria Maggiore in Rome—at one time called " Beata Maria ad praesepe." Here Pope Gregory III. (731–41) placed "a golden image of the Mother of God embracing God our Saviour, in various gems."[41] According to Usener's views this church was founded by Pope Liberius (352–66), and was intended to provide a special home for the new festival of Christmas introduced by him, while an important part of the early Christmas ritual there was the celebration of Mass over a " manger " in which the consecrated Host was laid, as once the body of the Holy Child in the crib at Bethlehem.[42] Further, an eastern homily of the late fourth century suggests that the preacher had before his eyes a representation of the Nativity. Such material representations, Usener conjectures, may have arisen from the devotions of the faithful at the supposed actual birthplace at Bethlehem, which would naturally be adorned with the sacred figures of the Holy Night.[43]

In the fourteenth and fifteenth centuries the crib can be traced at Milan, Parma, and Modena, and an Italian example carved in 1478 still exists.[44] The Bavarian National Museum at Munich has a fine collection of cribs of various periods and from various lands — Germany, Tyrol, Italy, and Sicily — showing what elaborate care has been bestowed upon the preparation of these models. Among them is a great erection made at Botzen in the first half of the nineteenth century, and large enough to fill a fair-sized room. It represents the central square of a town, with imposing buildings, including a great cathedral not unlike our St. Paul's. Figures of various sizes were provided to suit the perspective, and the crib itself was probably set up in the porch of the church, while processions of puppets were arranged on the wide open square. Another, made in Munich, shows the adoration of the shepherds in a sort of ruined castle, while others, from Naples, lay the scene among remains of classical temples. One Tyrolese crib has a wide landscape background with a village and mountains typical of the country. The figures are often numerous, and, as their makers generally dressed them in the costume of their contemporaries, are sometimes exceedingly quaint. An angel with a wasp-waist, in a powdered wig, a hat trimmed with big feathers, and a red velvet dress with heavy gold embroidery, seems comic to us moderns, yet this is how the Ursuline nuns of Innsbruck conceived the heavenly messenger. Many of the cribs and figures, however, are of fine artistic quality, especially those from Naples and Sicily, and to the student of costume the various types of dress are of great interest.45

The use of the Christmas crib is by no means confined to churches ; it is common in the home in many Catholic regions, and in at least one Protestant district, the Saxon Erzgebirge.46 In Germany the *krippe* is often combined with the Christmas-tree ; at Treves, for instance, the present writer saw a magnificent tree covered with glittering lights and ornaments, and underneath it the cave of the Nativity with little figures of the holy persons. Thus have pagan and Christian symbols met together.

There grew up in Germany, about the fourteenth century, the extremely popular Christmas custom of " cradle-rocking," a response to the people's need of a lifelike and homely presentation of Christianity. By the *Kindelwiegen* the lay-folk were brought into most intimate touch with the Christ Child ; the crib became a cradle (*wiege*) that could be rocked, and the worshippers were thus able to express in physical action their devotion to the newborn Babe. The cradle-rocking seems to have been done at first by priests, who impersonated the Virgin and St. Joseph, and sang over the Child a duet :—

> " Joseph, lieber neve mîn,
> Hilf mir wiegen daz kindelîn.
>
> Gerne, liebe muome mîn,
> Hilf ich dir wiegen dîn kindelîn." *

* " Joseph, dear nephew mine, help me to rock the Child." " Gladly, dear aunt, will I help thee to rock thy Child." (Note the curious words of relationship ; Joseph and Mary were both of the seed of David.)

Photo]   [Meisenbach, Riffarth & Co., Munich.

A NEAPOLITAN "PRESEPIO."

To face p. 108.

CHRISTMAS IN POPULAR DEVOTION

The choir and people took their part in the singing; and dancing, to the old Germans a natural accompaniment of festive song, became common around the cradle, which in time the people were allowed to rock with their own hands.47   "In dulci jubilo" has the character of a dance, and the same is true of another delightful old carol, "Lasst uns das Kindlein wiegen," still used, in a form modified by later editors, in the churches of the Rhineland.   The present writer has heard it sung, very slowly, in unison, by vast congregations, and very beautiful is its mingling of solemnity, festive joy, and tender sentiment :—

> "Lasst uns das Kindlein wiegen,
> Das Herz zum Krippelein biegen !
> Lasst uns den Geist erfreuen,
> Das Kindlein benedeien :
> O Jesulein süss ! O Jesulein süss !
>
> .   .   .   .   .
>
> Lasst uns sein Händel und Füsse,
> Sein feuriges Herzlein grüssen !
> Und ihn demütiglich eren
> Als unsern Gott und Herren !
> O Jesulein süss ! O Jesulein süss !" * 48

Two Latin hymns, "Resonet in laudibus" and "Quem pastores laudavere," 49 were also sung at the *Kindelwiegen*, and

---

* "Let us rock the Child and bow our hearts before the crib ! Let us delight our spirits and bless the Child : sweet little Jesu ! sweet little Jesu ! . . . Let us greet His little hands and feet, His little heart of fire, and reverence Him humbly as our Lord and God !   Sweet little Jesu ! sweet little Jesu !"

a charming and quite untranslatable German lullaby has come
down to us :—

> " Sausa ninne, gottes minne,
>   Nu sweig und ru !
>   Wen du wilt, so wellen wir deinen willen tun,
>   Hochgelobter edler furst, nu schweig und wein auch nicht,
>   Tûste das, so wiss wir, dass uns wol geschicht." [50]

It was by appeals like this *Kindelwiegen* to the natural, homely
instincts of the folk that the Church gained a real hold over the
masses, making Christianity during the fifteenth, sixteenth, and
seventeenth centuries a genuinely popular religion in Germany.
Dr. Alexander Tille, the best historian of the German Christmas,
has an interesting passage on the subject : " In the dancing and
jubilation around the cradle," he writes, " the religion of the
Cross, however much it might in its inmost character be opposed
to the nature of the German people and their essential healthiness,
was felt no longer as something alien. It had become naturalized,
but had lost in the process its very core. The preparation for a
life after death, which was its Alpha and Omega, had passed into
the background. It was not joy at the promised ' Redemption '
that expressed itself in the dance around the cradle ; for the
German has never learnt to feel himself utterly vile and sinful :
it was joy at the simple fact that a human being, a particular
human being in peculiar circumstances, was born into the
world. . . . The Middle Ages showed in the cradle-rocking ' a
true German and most lovable childlikeness.' The Christ Child
was the ' universal little brother of all children of earth,' and they
acted accordingly, they lulled Him to sleep, they fondled and
rocked Him, they danced before Him and leapt around Him *in
dulci jubilo*." [51] There is much here that is true of the cult of the
Christ Child in other countries than Germany, though perhaps
Dr. Tille underestimates the religious feeling that is often
joined to the human sentiment.

The fifteenth century was the great period for the *Kindelwiegen*,
the time when it appears to have been practised in all the
churches of Germany ; in the sixteenth it began to seem

irreverent to the stricter members of the clergy, and the figure of the infant Jesus was in many places no longer rocked in the cradle but enthroned on the altar.[52] This usage is described by Naogeorgus (1553) :—

"A woodden childe in clowtes is on the aultar set,
About the which both boyes and gyrles do daunce and trymly jet,
And Carrols sing in prayse of Christ, and, for to helpe them heare,
The organs aunswere every verse with sweete and solemne cheare.
The priestes do rore aloude ; and round about the parentes stande
To see the sport, and with their voyce do helpe them and their hande." [53]

The placing of a "Holy Child" above the altar at Christmas is still customary in many Roman Catholic churches.

Protestantism opposed the *Kindelwiegen,* on the grounds both of superstition and of the disorderly proceedings that accompanied it, but it was long before it was utterly extinguished even in the Lutheran churches. In Catholic churches the custom did not altogether die out, though the unseemly behaviour which often attended it—and the growth of a pseudo-classical taste—caused its abolition in most places.[54]

At Tübingen as late as 1830 at midnight on Christmas Eve an image of the Christ Child was rocked on the tower of the chief church in a small cradle surrounded with lights, while the spectators below sang a cradle-song.[55] According to a recent writer the "rocking" is still continued in the Upper Innthal.[56] In the Tyrolese cathedral city of Brixen it was once performed every day between Christmas and Candlemas by the sacristan or boy-acolytes. That the proceedings had a tendency to be disorderly is shown by an eighteenth-century instruction to the sacristan : "Be sure to take a stick or a thong of ox-hide, for the boys are often very ill-behaved." [57]

There are records of other curious ceremonies in German or Austrian churches. At St. Peter am Windberge in Mühlkreis in Upper Austria, during the service on Christmas night a life-sized wooden figure of the Holy Child was offered in a basket to the congregation; each person reverently kissed it and passed it on to his neighbour. This was done as late as 1883.[58] At Crimmitschau in Saxony a boy, dressed as an angel, used to be let down from the roof singing Luther's "Vom Himmel hoch," and the custom was only given up when the breaking of the rope which supported the singer had caused a serious accident.[59]

It is in Italy, probably, that the cult of the Christ Child is most ardently practised to-day. No people have a greater love of children than the Italians, none more of that dramatic instinct which such a form of worship demands. "Easter," says Countess Martinengo-Cesaresco, "is the great popular feast in the eastern Church, Christmas in the Latin—especially in Italy. One is the feast of the next world, and the other of this. Italians are fond of this world." [60] Christmas is for the poorer Italians a summing up of human birthdays, an occasion for pouring out on the *Bambino* parental and fraternal affection as well as religious worship.

In Rome, Christmas used to be heralded by the arrival, ten days before the end of Advent, of the Calabrian minstrels or *pifferari* with their sylvan pipes (*zampogne*), resembling the Scottish bagpipe, but less harsh in sound. These minstrels were to be seen in every street in Rome, playing their wild plaintive music before the shrines of the Madonna, under the traditional notion of charming away her labour-pains. Often they would stop at a carpenter's shop "per politezza al messer San Giuseppe."[61] Since 1870 the *pifferari* have become rare in Rome, but some were seen there by an English lady quite recently. At Naples, too, there are *zampognari* before Christmas, though far fewer than there used to be; for one *lira* they will pipe their rustic melodies before any householder's street Madonna through a whole *novena*.[62]

In Sicily, too, men come down from the mountains nine days before Christmas to sing a *novena* to a plaintive melody accompanied by 'cello and violin. "All day long," writes Signora Caico about Montedoro in Caltanissetta, "the melancholy dirge

Within the illustration: DITE AVE MARIA

CALABRIAN SHEPHERDS PLAYING IN ROME AT CHRISTMAS.

After an Etching by D. Allan.

From Hone's "Every-day Book" (London, 1826).

To face p. 112.

was sung round the village, house after house, always the same minor tune, the words being different every day, so that in nine days the whole song was sung out. . . . I often looked out of the window to see them at a short distance, grouped before a house, singing their stanzas, well muffled in shawls, for the air is cold in spite of the bright sunshine. . . . The flat, white houses all round, the pure sky overhead, gave an Oriental setting to the scene."

Another Christmas custom in the same place was the singing of a *novena* not outside but within some of the village houses before a kind of altar gaily decorated and bearing at the top a waxen image of the Child Jesus. " Close to it the orchestra was grouped—a 'cello, two violins, a guitar, and a tambourine. The kneeling women huddled in front of the altar. All had on their heads their black *mantelline*. They began at once singing the *novena* stanzas appointed for that day ; the tune was primitive and very odd : the first half of the stanza was quick and merry, the second half became a wailing dirge." A full translation of a long and very interesting and pathetic *novena* is given by Signora Caico.*[63]

The *presepio* both in Rome and at Naples is the special Christmas symbol in the home, just as the lighted tree is in Germany. In Rome the Piazza Navona is the great place for the sale of little clay figures of the holy persons. (Is there perchance a survival here of the *sigillaria*, the little clay dolls sold in Rome at the *Saturnalia* ?) These are bought in the market for two *soldi* each, and the *presepi* or " Bethlehems " are made at home with cardboard and moss.[64] The home-made *presepi* at Naples are well described by Matilde Serao ; they are pasteboard models of the landscape of Bethlehem—a hill with the sacred cave beneath it and two or three paths leading down to the grotto, a little tavern, a shepherd's hut, a few trees, sometimes a stream in glittering glass. The ground is made verdant with moss, and there is

---

* Turning for a moment from Sicilian domestic celebrations to a public and communal action, I may mention a strange ceremony that takes place at Messina in the dead of night ; at two o'clock on Christmas morning a naked *Bambino* is carried in procession from the church of Santa Lucia to the cathedral and back.[65]

straw within the cave for the repose of the infant Jesus ; singing angels are suspended by thin wires, and the star of the Wise Men hangs by an invisible thread. There is little attempt to realize the scenery of the East ; the Child is born and the Magi adore Him in a Campanian or Calabrian setting.[66]

Italian churches, as well as Italian homes, have their *presepi*. " Thither come the people, bearing humble gifts of chestnuts, apples, tomatoes, and the like, which they place as offerings in the hands of the figures. These are very often life-size. Mary is usually robed in blue satin, with crimson scarf and white head-dress. Joseph stands near her dressed in the ordinary working-garb. The onlookers are got up like Italian contadini. The Magi are always very prominent in their grand clothes, with satin trains borne by black slaves, jewelled turbans, and satin tunics all over jewels." [67]

In Rome the two great centres of Christmas devotion are the churches of Santa Maria Maggiore, where are preserved the relics of the cradle of Christ, and Ara Coeli, the home of the most famous *Bambino* in the world. A vivid picture of the scene at Santa Maria Maggiore in the early nineteenth century is given by Lady Morgan. She entered the church at midnight on Christmas Eve to wait for the procession of the *culla*, or cradle. " Its three ample naves, separated by rows of Ionic columns of white marble, produced a splendid vista. Thousands of wax tapers marked their form, and contrasted their shadows ; some blazed from golden candlesticks on the superb altars of the lateral chapels. . . . Draperies of gold and crimson decked the columns, and spread their shadows from the inter-columniations over the marble pavement. In the midst of this imposing display of church magnificence, sauntered or reposed a population which displayed the most squalid misery. The haggard natives of the mountains . . . were mixed with the whole mendicity of Rome. . . . Some of these terrific groups lay stretched in heaps on the ground, congregating for warmth ; and as their dark eyes scowled from beneath the mantle which half hid a sheepskin dress, they had the air of banditti awaiting their prey ; others with their wives and children knelt, half asleep,

ST. FRANCIS INSTITUTES THE " PRESEPIO " AT GRECCIO.

By Giotto.

(Upper Church of St Francis, Assissi).

To face p. 114.

round the chapel of the *Santa Croce*. . . . In the centre of the nave, multitudes of gay, gaudy, noisy persons, the petty shopkeepers, laquais, and *popolaccio* of the city, strolled and laughed, and talked loud." About three o'clock the service began, with a choral swell, blazing torches, and a crowded procession of priests of every rank and order. It lasted for two hours; then began the procession to the cell where the cradle lay, enshrined in a blaze of tapers and guarded by groups of devotees. Thence it was borne with solemn chants to the chapel of *Santa Croce*. A musical Mass followed, and the *culla* being at last deposited on the High Altar, the wearied spectators issued forth just as the dome of St. Peter's caught the first light of the morning.[68]

Still to-day the scene in the church at the five o'clock High Mass on Christmas morning is extraordinarily impressive, with the crowds of poor people, the countless lights at which the children gaze in open-eyed wonder, the many low Masses said in the side chapels, the imposing procession and the setting of the silver casket on the High Altar. The history of the relics of the *culla*—five long narrow pieces of wood—is obscure, but it is admitted even by some orthodox Roman Catholics that there is no sufficient evidence to connect them with Bethlehem.[69]

The famous *Bambino* at the Franciscan church of Ara Coeli on the citadel of Rome is "a fresh-coloured doll, tightly swathed in gold and silver tissue, crowned, and sparkling with jewels," no thing of beauty, but believed to have miraculous powers. An inscription in the sacristy of the church states that it was made by a devout Minorite of wood from the Mount of Olives, and given flesh-colour by the interposition of God Himself. It has its own servants and its own carriage in which it drives out to visit the sick. There is a strange story of a theft of the wonder-working image by a woman who feigned sickness, obtained permission to have the *Bambino* left with her, and then sent back to the friars another image dressed in its clothes. That night the Franciscans heard great ringing of bells and knockings at the church door, and found outside the true *Bambino*, naked in the wind and rain. Since then it has never been allowed out alone.[70]

THE CHRISTIAN FEAST

All through the Christmas and Epiphany season Ara Coeli is crowded with visitors to the *Bambino*. Before the *presepio*, where it lies, is erected a wooden platform on which small boys and girls of all ranks follow one another with little speeches— " preaching " it is called—in praise of the infant Lord. " They say their pieces," writes Countess Martinengo, " with an infinite charm that raises half a smile and half a tear." They have the vivid dramatic gift, the extraordinary absence of self-consciousness, typical of Italian children, and their " preaching " is anything but a wooden repetition of a lesson learned by heart. Nor is there any irksome constraint ; indeed to northerners the scene in the church might seem irreverent, for the children blow toy trumpets and their parents talk freely on all manner of subjects. The church is approached by one hundred and twenty-four steps, making an extraordinarily picturesque spectacle at this season, when they are thronged by people ascending and descending, and by vendors of all sorts of Christmas prints and images. On the Octave of the Epiphany there is a great procession, ending with the blessing of Rome by the Holy Child. The *Bambino* is carried out to the space at the top of the giddy flight of marble steps, and a priest raises it on high and solemnly blesses the Eternal City.[71]

A glimpse of the southern Christmas may be had in London in the Italian colony in and around Eyre Street Hill, off the Clerkenwell Road, a little town of poor Italians set down in the midst of the metropolis. The steep, narrow Eyre Street Hill, with its shops full of southern wares, is dingy enough by day, but after dark on Christmas Eve it looks like a bit of Naples. The windows are gay with lights and coloured festoons, there are lantern-decked sweetmeat stalls, one old man has a *presepio* in his room, other people have little altars or shrines with candles burning, and bright pictures of saints adorn the walls. It is a strangely pathetic sight, this *festa* of the children of the South, this attempt to keep an Italian Christmas amid the cold damp dreariness of a London slum. The colony has its own church, San Pietro, copied from some Renaissance basilica at Rome, a building half tawdry, half magnificent, which transports him who enters it far away to the South. Like every Italian church, it is

THE " BAMBINO " OF ARA COELI.

To face p. 116.

at once the Palace of the Great King and the refuge of the humblest—no other church in London is quite so intimately the home of the poor. Towards twelve o'clock on Christmas Eve the deep-toned bell of San Pietro booms out over the colony, and the people crowd to the Midnight Mass, and pay their devotions at a great *presepio* set up for the veneration of the faithful. When on the Octave of the Epiphany * the time comes to close the crib, an impressive and touching ceremony takes place. The afternoon Benediction over, the priest, with the acolytes, goes to the *presepio* and returns to the chancel with the *Bambino*. Holding it on his arm, he preaches in Italian on the story of the Christ Child. The sermon ended, the notes of " Adeste, fideles " are heard, and while the Latin words are sung the faithful kneel at the altar rails and reverently kiss the Holy Babe. It is their farewell to the *Bambino* till next Christmas.

A few details may here be given about the religious customs at Christmas in Spain. The Midnight Mass is there the great event of the festival. Something has already been said as to its celebration in Madrid. The scene at the midnight service in a small Andalusian country town is thus described by an English traveller :—" The church was full ; the service orderly ; the people of all classes. There were muleteers, wrapped in their blue and white checked rugs ; here, Spanish gentlemen, enveloped in their graceful capas, or capes . . . here, again, were crowds of the commonest people,—miners, fruitsellers, servants, and the like,— the women kneeling on the rush matting of the dimly-lit church, the men standing in dark masses behind, or clustering in groups round every pillar. . . . At last, from under the altar, the senior priest . . . took out the image of the Babe New-born, reverently and slowly, and held it up in his hands for adoration. Instantly every one crossed himself, and fell on his knees in silent worship." [72] The crib is very popular in Spanish homes and is the delight of children, as may be learnt from Fernan Caballero's interesting sketch of Christmas Eve in Spain, "La Noche de Navidad." [73]

* Or on the Sunday following the Octave, if the Octave itself is a week-day.

THE CHRISTIAN FEAST

In England the Christmas crib is to be found nowadays in most Roman, and a few Anglican, churches. In the latter it is of course an imitation, not a survival. It is, however, possible that the custom of carrying dolls about in a box at Advent or Christmas time, common in some parts of England in the nineteenth century, is a survival, from the Middle Ages, of something like the crib. The so-called "vessel-cup" was "a box containing two dolls, dressed up to represent the Virgin and the infant Christ, decorated with ribbons and surrounded by flowers and apples." The box had usually a glass lid, was covered by a white napkin, and was carried from door to door by a woman. [74] It was esteemed very unlucky for any household not to be visited by the "Advent images" before Christmas Eve, and the bearers sang the well-known carol of the "Joys of Mary." [75] In Yorkshire only one image was carried about. [76] At Gilmorton, Leicestershire, a friend of the present writer remembers that the children used to carry round what they called a "Christmas Vase," an open box without lid in which lay three dolls side by side, with oranges and sprigs of evergreen. Some people regarded these as images of the Virgin, the Christ Child, and Joseph.*

In this study of the feast of the Nativity as represented in liturgy and ceremonial we have already come close to what may strictly be called drama ; in the next chapter we shall cross the border line and consider the religious plays of the Middle Ages and the relics of or parallels to them found in later times.

---

* Tempting as it is to connect these dolls with the crib, it is possible that their origin should be sought rather in anthropomorphic representations of the spirits of vegetation, and that they are of the same nature as the images carried about with garlands in May and at other seasons. [77]

CHAPTER V

CHRISTMAS
DRAMA

CHAPTER V

CHRISTMAS DRAMA

Origins of the Mediaeval Drama—Dramatic Tendencies in the Liturgy—Latin Liturgical Plays—The Drama becomes Laicized—Characteristics of the Popular Drama—The Nativity in the English Miracle Cycles—Christmas Mysteries in France—Later French Survivals of Christmas Drama—German Christmas Plays—Mediaeval Italian Plays and Pageants—Spanish Nativity Plays—Modern Survivals in Various Countries—The Star-singers, &c.

In this chapter the Christian side only of the Christmas drama will be treated. Much folk-drama of pagan origin has gathered round the festival, but this we shall study in our Second Part. Our subject here is the dramatic representation of the story of the Nativity and the events immediately connected with it. The Christmas drama has passed through the same stages as the poetry of the Nativity. There is first a monastic and hieratic stage, when the drama is but an expansion of the liturgy, a piece of ceremonial performed by clerics with little attempt at verisimilitude and with Latin words drawn mainly from the Bible or the offices of the Church. Then, as the laity come to take a more personal interest in Christianity, we find fancy beginning to play around the subject, bringing out its human pathos and charm, until, after a transitional stage, the drama leaves the sanctuary, passes from Latin to the vulgar tongue, is played by lay performers in the streets and squares of the city, and, while its framework remains religious, takes into itself episodes of a more or less secular character. The Latin liturgical plays are to the "miracles" and "mysteries" of the later Middle Ages as a Romanesque church, solemn, oppressive, hieratic, to a Gothic cathedral, soaring, audacious, reflecting every phase of the popular life.

The mediaeval religious drama [1] was a natural development from the Catholic liturgy, not an imitation of classical models. The classical drama had expired at the break-up of the Roman Empire; its death was due largely, indeed, to the hostility of Christianity, but also to the rude indifference of the barbarian invaders. Whatever secular dramatic impulses remained in the Dark Ages showed themselves not in public and organized performances, but obscurely in the songs and mimicry of minstrels and in traditional folk-customs. Both of these classes of practices were strongly opposed by the Church, because of their connection with heathenism and the licence towards which they tended. Yet the dramatic instinct could not be suppressed. The folk-drama in such forms as the Feast of Fools found its way, as we shall see, even into the sanctuary, and—most remarkable fact of all—the Church's own services took on more and more a dramatic character.

While the secular stage decayed, the Church was building up a stately system of ritual. It is needless to dwell upon the dramatic elements in Catholic worship. The central act of Christian devotion, the Eucharist, is in its essence a drama, a representation of the death of the Redeemer and the participation of the faithful in its benefits, and around this has gathered in the Mass a multitude of dramatic actions expressing different aspects of the Redemption. Nor, of course, is there merely symbolic *action*; the offices of the Church are in great part *dialogues* between priest and people, or between two sets of singers. It was from this antiphonal song, this alternation of versicle and respond, that the religious drama of the Middle Ages took its rise. In the ninth century the "Antiphonarium" traditionally ascribed to Pope Gregory the Great had become insufficient for ambitious choirs, and the practice grew up of supplementing it by new melodies and words inserted at the beginning or end or even in the middle of the old antiphons. The new texts were called "tropes," and from the ninth to the thirteenth century many were written. An interesting Christmas example is the following ninth-century trope ascribed to Tutilo of St. Gall :—

"Hodie cantandus est nobis puer, quem gignebat ineffabiliter ante tempora pater, et eundem sub tempore generavit inclyta mater. (To-day must we sing of a Child, whom in unspeakable wise His Father begat before all times, and whom, within time, a glorious mother brought forth.)
Int[errogatio].
Quis est iste puer quem tam magnis praeconiis dignum vociferatis? Dicite nobis ut collaudatores esse possimus. (Who is this Child whom ye proclaim worthy of so great laudations ? Tell us that we also may praise Him.)
Resp[onsio].
Hic enim est quem praesagus et electus symmista Dei ad terram venturum praevidens longe ante praenotavit, sicque praedixit. (This is He whose coming to earth the prophetic and chosen initiate into the mysteries of God foresaw and pointed out long before, and thus foretold.)"

Here followed at once the Introit for the third Mass of Christmas Day, "Puer natus est nobis, et filius datus est nobis, &c. (Unto us a child is born, unto us a son is given.)" The question and answer were no doubt sung by different choirs.[2]

One can well imagine that this might develop into a regular little drama. As a matter of fact, however, it was from an Easter trope in the same manuscript, the "Quem quaeritis," a dialogue between the three Maries and the angel at the sepulchre, that the liturgical drama sprang. The trope became very popular, and was gradually elaborated into a short symbolic drama, and its popularity led to the composition of similar pieces for Christmas and Ascensiontide. Here is the Christmas trope from a St. Gall manuscript :—

"*On the Nativity of the Lord at Mass let there be ready two deacons having on dalmatics, behind the altar, saying :*

Quem quaeritis in praesepe, pastores, dicite ? (Whom seek ye in the manger, say, ye shepherds ?)

THE CHRISTIAN FEAST

Let two cantors in the choir answer :

Salvatorem Christum Dominum, infantem pannis involutum, secundum sermonem angelicum. (The Saviour, Christ the Lord, a child wrapped in swaddling clothes, according to the angelic word.)

And the deacons :

Adest hic parvulus cum Maria, matre sua, de qua, vaticinando, Isaias Propheta : ecce virgo concipiet et pariet filium ; et nuntiantes dicite quia natus est. (Present here is the little one with Mary, His Mother, of whom Isaiah the prophet foretold : Behold, a virgin shall conceive, and shall bring forth a son ; and do ye say and announce that He is born.)

Then let the cantor lift up his voice and say :

Alleluia, alleluia, jam vere scimus Christum natum in terris, de quo canite, omnes, cum Propheta dicentes : Puer natus est ! (Alleluia, alleluia. Now we know indeed that Christ is born on earth, of whom sing ye all, saying with the Prophet : Unto us a child is born.) " [3]

The dramatic character of this is very marked. A comparison with later liturgical plays suggests that the two deacons in their broad vestments were meant to represent the midwives mentioned in the apocryphal Gospel of St. James, and the cantors the shepherds.

A development from this trope, apparently, was the " Office of the Shepherds," which probably took shape in the eleventh century, though it is first given in a Rouen manuscript of the thirteenth. It must have been an impressive ceremony as performed in the great cathedral, dimly lit with candles, and full of mysterious black recesses and hints of infinity. Behind the high altar a *praesepe* or " crib " was prepared, with an image of the Virgin. After the " Te Deum " had been sung five canons or their vicars, clad in albs and amices, entered by the great door of the choir, and proceeded towards the apse. These were the shepherds. Suddenly from high above them came a clear boy's voice : " Fear not, behold I bring you good tidings of great joy," and the rest of the angelic message. The " multitude of the heavenly host " was represented by other boys stationed probably in the triforium galleries, who broke out into the exultant " Gloria in excelsis." Singing a hymn, " Pax in terris nunciatur," the shepherds advanced towards the crib where two priests—the midwives—awaited them. These addressed to the shepherds the question " Whom seek ye in the manger ? " and then came the rest of the " Quem quaeritis " which we already know, a hymn to the Virgin being sung while the shepherds adored the Infant. Mass followed immediately, the little drama being merely a prelude.4

More important than this Office of the Shepherds is an Epiphany play called by various names, " Stella," " Tres Reges," " Magi," or " Herodes," and found in different forms at Limoges, Rouen, Laon, Compiègne, Strasburg, Le Mans, Freising in Bavaria, and other places. Mr. E. K. Chambers suggests that its kernel is a dramatized Offertory. It was a custom for Christian kings to present gold, frankincense, and myrrh at the Epiphany—the offering is still made by proxy at the Chapel Royal, St. James's—and Mr. Chambers takes " the play to have served as a substitute for this ceremony, when no king actually regnant was present." 5 Its most essential features were the appearance of the Star of Bethlehem to the Magi, and their offering of the mystic gifts. The star, bright with candles, hung from the roof of the church, and was sometimes made to move.

In the Rouen version of the play it is ordered that on the day of the Epiphany, Terce having been sung, three clerics, robed as kings, shall come from the east, north, and south, and meet before the altar, with their servants bearing the offerings of the Magi. The king from the east, pointing to the star with his stick, exclaims :—

" Stella fulgore nimio rutilat. (The star glows with exceeding brightness.) "

The second monarch answers :

" Quae regem regum natum demonstrat. (Which shows the birth of the King of Kings.) "

And the third :

" Quem venturum olim prophetiae signaverant. (To whose coming
the prophecies of old had pointed.) "

Then the Magi kiss one another and together sing :

" Eamus ergo et inquiramus eum, offerentes ei munera : aurum, thus,
et myrrham. (Let us therefore go and seek Him, offering unto Him
gifts : gold, frankincense, and myrrh.) "

Antiphons are sung, a procession is formed, and the Magi go to
a certain altar above which an image of the Virgin has been
placed with a lighted star before it. Two priests in dalmatics—
apparently the midwives—standing on either side of the altar,
inquire who the Magi are, and receiving their answer, draw aside
a curtain and bid them approach to worship the Child, "for He is
the redemption of the world." The three kings do adoration,
and offer their gifts, each with a few pregnant words :—

" Suscipe, rex, aurum. (Receive, O King, gold.) "
" Tolle thus, tu vere Deus. (Accept incense, Thou very God.) "
" Myrrham, signum sepulturae. (Myrrh, the sign of burial.) "

The clergy and people then make their offerings, while the
Magi fall asleep and are warned by an angel to return home
another way. This they do symbolically by proceeding back to
the choir by a side aisle.[6]

In its later forms the Epiphany play includes the appearance of
Herod, who is destined to fill a very important place in the
mediaeval drama. Hamlet's saying " he out-Herods Herod "
sufficiently suggests the raging tyrant whom the playwrights of the
Middle Ages loved. His appearance marks perhaps the first introduction into the Christian religious play of the evil principle so
necessary to dramatic effect. At first Herod holds merely a mild
conversation with the Magi, begging them to tell him when they
have found the new-born King ; in later versions of the play,
however, his wrath is shown on learning that the Wise Men have

departed home by another way; he breaks out into bloodthirsty tirades, orders the slaying of the Innocents, and in one form takes a sword and brandishes it in the air. He becomes in fact the outstanding figure in the drama, and one can understand why it was sometimes named after him.

In the Laon " Stella " the actual murder of the Innocents was represented, the symbolical figure of Rachel weeping over her children being introduced. The plaint and consolation of Rachel, it should be noted, seem at first to have formed an independent little piece performed probably on Holy Innocents' Day.[7] This later coalesced with the " Stella," as did also the play of the shepherds, and, at a still later date, another liturgical drama which we must now consider—the " Prophetae."

This had its origin in a sermon (wrongly ascribed to St. Augustine) against Jews, Pagans, and Arians, a portion of which was used in many churches as a Christmas lesson. It begins with a rhetorical appeal to the Jews who refuse to accept Jesus as the Messiah in spite of the witness of their own prophets. Ten prophets are made to give their testimony, and then three Pagans are called upon, Virgil, Nebuchadnezzar and the Erythraean Sibyl. The sermon has a strongly dramatic character, and when chanted in church the parts of the preacher and the prophets were possibly distributed among different choristers. In time it developed into a regular drama, and more prophets were brought in. It was, indeed, the germ of the great Old Testament cycles of the later Middle Ages.[8]

An extension of the " Prophetae " was the Norman or Anglo-Norman play of " Adam," which began with the Fall, continued with Cain and Abel, and ended with the witness of the prophets. In the other direction the " Prophetae " was extended by the addition of the " Stella." It so happens that there is no text of a Latin drama containing both these extensions at the same time, but such a play probably existed. From the mid-thirteenth to the mid-fourteenth century, indeed, there was a tendency for the plays to run together into cycles and become too long and too elaborate for performance in church. In the eleventh century, even, they had begun to pass out into the churchyard or the market-place, and to be played not only by the clergy but by laymen. This change had extremely important effects on their character. In the first place the vulgar tongue crept in. As early, possibly, as the twelfth century are the Norman "Adam" and the Spanish "Misterio de los Reyes Magos," the former, as we have seen, an extended vernacular "Prophetae," the latter, a fragment of a highly developed vernacular "Stella." They are the first of the popular as distinguished from the liturgical plays ; they were meant, as their language shows, for the instruction and delight of the folk ; they were not to be listened to, like the mysterious Latin of the liturgy, in uncomprehending reverence, but were to be understanded of the people.

The thirteenth and fourteenth centuries saw a progressive supplanting of Latin by the common speech, until, in the great cycles, only a few scraps of the church language were left to tell of the liturgical origin of the drama. The process of popularization, the development of the plays from religious ceremonial to lively drama, was probably greatly helped by the *goliards* or vagabond scholars, young, poor, and fond of amusement, who wandered over Europe from teacher to teacher, from monastery to monastery, in search of learning. Their influence is shown not merely in the broadening of the drama, but also in its passing from the Latin of the monasteries to the language of the common folk.

A consequence of the outdoor performance of the plays was that Christmas, in the northern countries at all events, was found an unsuitable time for them. The summer was naturally preferred, and we find comparatively few mentions of plays at Christmas in the later Middle Ages. Whitsuntide and Corpus Christi became more popular dates, especially in England, and the pieces then performed were vast cosmic cycles, like the York, Chester, Towneley, and "Coventry" plays, in which the Christmas and Epiphany episodes formed but links in an immense chain extending from the Creation to the Last Judgment, and representing the whole scheme of salvation. It is in these Nativity scenes, however, that we have the only English renderings of the Christmas story in drama,[9] and though they were actually performed not at the winter festival * but in the summer, they give in so striking a way the feelings, the point of view, of our mediaeval forefathers in regard to the Nativity that we are justified in dealing with them here at some length.

As the drama became laicized, it came to reflect that strange medley of conflicting elements, pagan and Christian, materialistic and spiritual, which was the actual religion of the folk, as distinguished from the philosophical theology of the doctors and councils and the mysticism of the ascetics. The popularizing of Christianity had reached its climax in most countries of western Europe in the fifteenth century, approximately the period of the great " mysteries." However little the ethical teaching of Jesus may have been acted upon, the Christian religion on its external side had been thoroughly appropriated by the people and wrought into a many-coloured polytheism, a true reflection of their minds.

The figures of the drama are contemporaries of the spectators both in garb and character ; they are not Orientals of ancient times, but Europeans of the end of the Middle Ages. Bethlehem is a "faier borow," Herod a "mody king," like unto some haughty, capricious, and violent monarch of the time, the shepherds are rustics of England or Germany or France or Italy, the Magi mighty potentates with gorgeous trains, and the Child Himself is a little being subject to all the pains and necessities of infancy, but delighted with sweet and pleasant things like a bob of cherries or a ball. The realism of the writers is sometimes astounding, and comic elements often appear—to the people of the Middle Ages religion was so real and natural a thing that they could laugh at it without ceasing to believe in or to love it.

The English mediaeval playwrights, it may safely be said, are surpassed by no foreigners in their treatment of Christmas subjects. To illustrate their way of handling the scenes I may

---

* Though no texts are extant of religious plays in English acted at Christmastide, there are occasional records of such performances :—at Tintinhull for instance in 1451 and at Dublin in 1528, while at Aberdeen a processional "Nativity" was performed at Candlemas. And the "Stella," whether in English or Latin it is uncertain, is found at various places between 1462 and 1579.[10]

gather from the four great cycles a few of the most interesting passages.

From the so-called "Ludus Coventriae" I take the arrival of Joseph and Mary at Bethlehem; they ask a man in the street where they may find an inn :—

"*Joseph*.   Heyl, wurchepful sere, and good day !
A ceteceyn of this cytë ye seme to be ;
Of herborwe * ffor spowse and me I yow pray,
ffor trewly this woman is fful werë,
And fayn at reste, sere, wold she be ;

We wolde ffulffylle the byddynge of oure emperoure,
ffor to pay tribute, as right is oure,
And to kepe oureselfe ffrom dolowre,
We are come to this cytë.

Cives.   Sere, ostage in this towne know I non,
Thin wyff and thou in for to slepe ;
This cetë is besett with pepyl every won,
And yett thei ly withowte fful every strete.

Withinne no walle, man, comyst thou nowth,
Be thou onys † withinne the cytë gate ;
Onethys ‡ in the strete a place may be sowth,
Theron to reste, withowte debate.

Joseph.   Nay, sere, debate that wyl I nowth ;
Alle suche thyngys passyn my powere :
But yitt my care and alle my thought
Is for Mary, my derlynge dere.

A ! swete wyff, wat xal we do ?
Wher xal we logge this nyght ?
Onto the ffadyr of heffne pray we so,
Us to kepe ffrom every wykkyd whyt.

Cives.   Good man, o word I wyl the sey,
If thou wylt do by the counsel of me ;
Yondyr is an hous of haras § that stant be the wey,
Amonge the bestys herboryd may ye be.

---

* Lodging.   ‡ Scarcely.
† Once.   § Horses. Hous of haras = stable.

CHRISTMAS DRAMA

Maria. Now the fadyr of hefne he mut yow yelde !
  His sone in my wombe forsothe he is ;
He kepe the and thi good be fryth and ffelde !
  Go we hens, husbond, for now tyme it is." [11]

The scene immediately after the Nativity is delicately and reverently presented in the York cycle. The Virgin worships the Child, saluting Him thus :—

"Hayle my lord God ! hayle prince of pees !
 Hayle my fadir, and hayle my sone !
 Hayle souereyne sege all synnes to sesse !
 Hayle God and man in erth to wonne ! *
                Hayle ! thurgh whos myht
 All this worlde was first be-gonne,
                merkness † and light.

 Sone, as I am sympill sugett of thyne,
 Vowchesaffe, swete sone I pray the,
 That I myght the take in the[r] armys of mine,
 And in this poure wede to arraie the ;
                Graunte me thi blisse !
 As I am thy modir chosen to be
                in sothfastnesse."

Joseph, who has gone out to get a light, returns, and this dialogue follows :—

"*Joseph.* Say, Marie doghtir, what chere with the ?
 Mary. Right goode, Joseph, as has been ay.
 Joseph. O Marie ! what swete thyng is that on thy kne ?
 Mary. It is my sone, the soth to saye,
                that is so gud.
 Joseph. Wel is me I bade this day,
                to se this foode ! ‡
 Me merueles mekill of this light
 That thus-gates shynes in this place,
 For suth it is a selcouth § sight !

---

* Dwell.   ‡ Being.
† Darkness.   § Wonderful.

131

THE CHRISTIAN FEAST

Mary. This hase he ordand of his grace,
my sone so ying,
A starne to be schynyng a space
at his bering

   .   .   .   .

Joseph. Nowe welcome, floure fairest of hewe,
I shall the menske * with mayne and myght.
Hayle ! my maker, hayle Crist Jesu !
Hayle, riall king, roote of all right !
Hayle, saueour.
Hayle, my lorde, lemer † of light,
Hayle, blessid floure !
Mary. Nowe lord ! that all this worlde schall wynne,
To the my sone is that I saye,
Here is no bedde to laye the inne,
Therfore my dere sone, I the praye
sen it is soo,
Here in this cribbe I myght the lay
betwene ther bestis two.
And I sall happe ‡ the, myn owne dere childe,
With such clothes as we haue here.
Joseph. O Marie ! beholde thes beestis mylde,
They make louyng in ther manere
as thei wer men.
For-sothe it semes wele be ther chere
thare lord thei ken.
Mary. Ther lorde thai kenne, that wate I wele,
They worshippe hym with myght and mayne ;
The wedir is colde, as ye may feele,
To halde hym warme thei are full fayne,
with thare warme breth." [12]

The playwrights are at their best in the shepherd scenes ; indeed these are the most original parts of the cycles, for here the writers found little to help them in theological tradition, and were thrown upon their own wit. In humorous dialogue and naïve sentiment the lusty burgesses of the fifteenth century were thoroughly at home, and the comedy and pathos of these scenes must have been as welcome a relief to the spectators, from the

---

* Worship.　　　　† Shedder.　　　　‡ Wrap.

long-winded solemnity of many of the plays, as they are to modern readers. In the York mysteries the shepherds make uncouth exclamations at the song of the angels and ludicrously try to imitate it. The Chester shepherds talk in a very natural way of such things as the diseases of sheep, sit down with much relish to a meal of " ale of Halton," sour milk, onions, garlick and leeks, green cheese, a sheep's head soused in ale, and other items ; then they call their lad Trowle, who grumbles because his wages have not been paid, refuses to eat, wrestles with his masters and throws them all. They sit down discomfited ; then the Star of Bethlehem appears, filling them with wonder, which grows when they hear the angels' song of " Gloria in excelsis." They discuss what the words were—" glore, glare with a glee," or, " glori, glory, glorious," or, " glory, glory, with a glo." At length they go to Bethlehem, and arrived at the stable, the first shepherd exclaims :—

> " Sym, Sym, sickerlye
> Heare I see Marye,
> And Jesus Christe faste by,
> Lapped in haye." [13]

Joseph is strangely described :—

> "Whatever this oulde man that heare is,
> Take heede howe his head is whore,
> His beirde is like a buske of breyers,
> With a pound of heaire about his mouth and more." [14]

Their gifts to the Infant are a bell, a flask, a spoon to eat pottage with, and a cape. Trowle the servant has nought to offer but a pair of his wife's old hose ; four boys follow with presents of a bottle, a hood, a pipe, and a nut-hook. Quaint are the words of the last two givers :—

> " *The Thirde Boye.*
> O, noble childe of thee !
> Alas ! what have I for thee,
> Save only my pipe ?

THE CHRISTIAN FEAST

Elles trewly nothinge,
Were I in the rockes or in,
I coulde make this pippe
That all this woode should ringe,
And quiver, as yt were.

The Fourth Boye.

Nowe, childe, although thou be comon from God,
And be God thy selfe in thy manhoode,
Yet I knowe that in thy childehoode
Thou wylte for sweete meate loke,
To pull downe aples, peares, and plumes,
Oulde Joseph shall not nede to hurte his thombes,
Because thou hast not pleintie of crombes,
I geve thee heare my nutthocke." [15]

Let no one deem this irreverent; the spirit of this adoration
of the shepherds is intensely devout; they go away longing to
tell all the world the wonder they have seen; one will become a
pilgrim; even the rough Trowle exclaims that he will forsake
the shepherd's craft and will betake himself to an anchorite's
hard by, in prayers to "wache and wake."

More famous than this Chester "Pastores" are the two
shepherd plays in the Towneley cycle.[16] The first begins with
racy talk, leading to a wrangle between two of the shepherds
about some imaginary sheep; then a third arrives and makes fun
of them both; a feast follows, with much homely detail; they
go to sleep and are awakened by the angelic message; after
much debate over its meaning and over the foretellings of the
prophets—one of them, strangely enough, quotes a Latin passage
from Virgil—they go to Bethlehem and present to the Child a
"lytyll spruce cofer," a ball, and a gourd-bottle.

The second play surpasses in humour anything else in the
mediaeval drama of any country. We find the shepherds first
complaining of the cold and their hard lot; they are "al lappyd
in sorow." They talk, almost like modern Socialists, of the
oppressions of the rich :—

"For the tylthe of our landys lyys falow as the floore,
As ye ken.

134

THE ADORATION OF THE SHEPHERDS.

From Broadside No. 305 in the Collection of the Society of Antiquaries at Burlington House
(by permission).

(Photo lent by Mr. F. Sidgwick, who has published the print on a modern Christmas broadside.)

To face p. 134.

CHRISTMAS DRAMA

We ar so hamyd,*
For-taxed and ramyd,†
We ar mayde hand-tamyd,
    With thyse gentlery men.

Thus thay refe ‡ us our rest, Our Lady theym wary ! §
These men that ar lord-fest,‖ they cause the ploghe tary."

To these shepherds joins himself Mak, a thieving neighbour.
Going to sleep, they make him lie between them, for they doubt
his honesty. But for all their precautions he manages to steal
a sheep, and carries it home to his wife. She thinks of an
ingenious plan for concealing it from the shepherds if they visit
the cottage seeking their lost property : she will pretend that she
is in child-bed and that the sheep is the new-born infant. So it
is wrapped up and laid in a cradle, and Mak sings a lullaby.
The shepherds do suspect Mak, and come to search his house ;
his wife upbraids them and keeps them from the cradle. They
depart, but suddenly an idea comes to one of them :—

"*The First Shepherd.* Gaf ye the chyld any thyng?
The Second. I trow not oone farthyng.
The Third. Fast agane will I flyng,
    Abyde ye me there. [*He goes back.*]
Mak, take it to no grefe, if I com to thi barne."

Mak tries to put him off, but the shepherd will have
his way :—

"Gyf me lefe hym to kys, and lyft up the clowtt.
What the devill is this? he has a long snowte."

So the secret is out. Mak's wife gives a desperate explanation :—

"He was takyn with an elfe,
    I saw it myself.
When the clok stroke twelf
    Was he forshapyn."

---

* Crippled.   ‡ Deprive of.   ‖ Strong in lordliness.
† Overreached.   § Curse.

135

Naturally this avails nothing, and her husband is given a good tossing by the shepherds until they are tired out and lie down to rest. Then comes the "Gloria in excelsis" and the call of the angel :—

> "Ryse, hyrd men heynd! for now is he borne
> That shall take fro the feynd that Adam had lorne :
> That warloo* to sheynd,† this nyght is he borne,
> God is made youre freynd : now at this morne
>   He behestys,
>   At Bedlem go se,
>   Ther lygys that fre‡
> In a cryb fulle poorely,
>   Betwyx two bestys."

The shepherds wonder at the song, and one of them tries to imitate it ; then they go even unto Bethlehem, and there follows the quaintest and most delightful of Christmas carols :—

> "*Primus Pastor.*
>
> Hail, comly and clene,
>   Hail, yong child !
> Hail, maker, as I meene,
>   Of a maden so milde !
> Thou has warëd,§ I weene,
>   The warlo ‖ so wilde ;
> The fals giler of teen,¶
>   Now goes he begilde.
>   Lo ! he merys,**
> Lo ! he laghës, my sweting.
> A welfare meting !
> I have holden my heting.††
>   Have a bob of cherys !
>
> *Secundus Pastor.*
>
> Hail, sufferan Savioure,
>   For thou has us soght !
> Hail, frely ‡‡ foyde §§ and floure,
>   That all thing has wroght !

* Wizard.	† Noble being.	‖ Warlock.	** Grows merry.
† Shame.	§ Cursed.	¶ Sorrow.	†† Promise.
	‡‡ Noble.	§§ Child.	

CHRISTMAS DRAMA

Hail, full of favoure,
  That made all of noght!
Hail, I kneel and I cowre.
  A bird have I broght
    To my barne.
Hail, litel tinë mop!*
Of oure crede thou art crop ; †
I wold drink on thy cop,
    Litel day starne.

Tertius Pastor.

Hail, derling dere,
  Full of godhede!
I pray thee be nere
  When that I have nede.
Hail! swete is thy chere ; ‡
  My hart woldë blede
To see thee sitt here
  In so poorë wede,
    With no pennys.
Hail! Put forth thy dall! §
I bring thee bot a ball ;
Have and play thee with all,
    And go to the tenis!" [17]

The charm of this will be felt by every reader ; it lies in a curious incongruity—extreme homeliness joined to awe ; the Infinite is contained within the narrowest human bounds ; God Himself, the Creator and Sustainer of the universe, a weak, helpless child. But a step more, and all would have been irreverence ; as it is we have devotion, human, naïve, and touching.

It would be interesting to show how other scenes connected with Christmas are handled in the English miracle-plays : how Octavian (Caesar Augustus) sent out the decree that all the world should be taxed, and learned from the Sibyl the birth of Christ ; how the Magi were led by the star and offered their symbolic gifts ; how the raging of the boastful tyrant Herod, the

---

* Baby.   † Head.   ‡ Face.   § Hand.

137

Slaughter of the Innocents, and the Flight into Egypt are treated ; but these scenes, though full of colour, are on the whole less remarkable than the shepherd and Nativity pieces, and space forbids us to dwell upon them. They contain many curious anachronisms, as when Herod invokes Mahounde, and talks about his princes, prelates, barons, baronets and burgesses.*

The religious play in England did not long survive the Reformation. Under the influence of Protestantism, with its vigilant dread of profanity and superstition, the cycles were shorn of many of their scenes, the performances became irregular, and by the end of the sixteenth century they had mostly ceased to be. Not sacred story, but the play of human character, was henceforth the material of the drama. The rich, variegated religion of the people, communal in its expression, tinged everywhere with human colour, gave place to a sterner, colder, more individual faith, fearful of contamination by the use of the outward and visible.

There is little or no trace in the vernacular Christmas plays of direct translation from one language into another, though there was some borrowing of motives. Thus the Christmas drama of each nation has its own special flavour.

If we turn to France, we find a remarkable fifteenth-century cycle that belongs purely to the winter festival, and shows the strictly Christmas drama at its fullest development. This great mystery of the " Incarnacion et nativité de nostre saulveur et redempteur Jesuchrist" was performed out-of-doors at Rouen in 1474, an exceptional event for a northern city in winter-time. The twenty-four *establies* or "mansions" set up for the various scenes reached across the market-place from the " Axe and Crown" Inn to the "Angel."

---

* Besides the Nativity plays in the four great cycles there exists a "Shearmen and Tailors' Play" which undoubtedly belongs to Coventry, unlike the "Ludus Coventriae," whose connection with that town is, to say the least, highly doubtful. It opens with a prologue by the prophet Isaiah, and in a small space presents the events connected with the Incarnation from the Annunciation to the Murder of the Innocents. The Nativity and shepherd scenes have less character and interest than those in the great cycles, and need not be dealt with here.[18]

CHRISTMAS DRAMA

After a prologue briefly explaining its purpose, the mystery begins, like the old liturgical plays, with the witness of the prophets ; then follows a scene in Limbo where Adam is shown lamenting his fate, and another in Heaven where the Redemption of mankind is discussed and the Incarnation decided upon. With the Annunciation and the Visitation of the Virgin the first day closed. The second day opened with the ordering by Octavian of the world-census. The edict is addressed :—

> "A tous roys, marquis, ducs et contes,
> Connestables, bailifs, vicomtes
> Et tous autres generalment
> Qui sont desoubz le firmament."

Joseph, in order to fulfil the command of Cyrenius, governor of Syria, leaves Nazareth for Bethlehem. A comic shepherds' scene follows, with a rustic song :—

> " Joyeusement, la garenlo,
> Chantons en venant a la veille,
> Puisque nous avons la bouteille
> Nous y berons jusques a bo."

When Joseph and Mary reach the stable where the Nativity is to take place, there is a charming dialogue. Joseph laments over the meanness of the stable, Mary accepts it with calm resignation.

Joseph.

> Las ! vecy bien povre merrien
> Pour edifier un hostel
> Et logis a ung seigneur tel.
> Il naistra en bien povre place.

Marie.

> Il plait a Dieu qu'ainsy se face.

.   .   .   .

Joseph.

> Ou sont ces chambres tant fournies
> De Sarges, de Tapiceries

Batus d'or, ou luyt mainte pierre,
Et nates mises sur la terre,
Affin que le froit ne mefface ?

Marie.
Il plait a Dieu qu'ainsy se face.

.   .   .   .   .

Joseph.
Helas ! cy gerra povrement
Le createur du firmament
Celui qui fait le soleil luire,
Qui fait la terre fruis produire,
Qui tient la mer en son espace.

Marie.
Il plait a Dieu qu'ainsy se face."

At last Christ is born, welcomed by the song of the angels, adored by His mother. In the heathen temples the idols fall ; Hell mouth opens and shows the rage of the demons, who make a hideous noise ; fire issues from the nostrils and eyes and ears of Hell, which shuts up with the devils within it. And then the angels in the stable worship the Child Jesus. The adoration of the shepherds was shown with many naïve details for the delight of the people, and the performance ended with the offering of a sacrifice in Rome by the Emperor Octavian to an image of the Blessed Virgin.[19]

The French playwrights, quite as much as the English, love comic shepherd scenes with plenty of eating and drinking and brawling. A traditional figure is the shepherd Rifflart, always a laughable type. In the strictly mediaeval plays the shepherds are true French rustics, but with the progress of the Renaissance classical elements creep into the pastoral scenes; in a mystery printed in 1507 Orpheus with the Nymphs and Oreads is introduced. As might be expected, anachronisms often occur ; a peculiarly piquant instance is found in the S. Geneviève mystery, where Caesar Augustus gets a piece of Latin translated into French for his convenience.

THE SHEPHERDS OF BETHLEHEM.

From "Le grant Kalendrier compost des Bergiers" (N. le Rouge, Troyes, 152¹).

(Reproduced from a modern broadside published by Mr. F. Sidgwick.)

To face p. 140.

Late examples of French Christmas mysteries are the so-called " comedies " of the Nativity, Adoration of the Kings, Massacre of the Innocents, and Flight into Egypt contained in the " Marguerites " (published in 1547) of Marguerite, Queen of Navarre, sister of François I. Intermingled with the traditional figures treated more or less in the traditional way are personified abstractions like Philosophy, Tribulation, Inspiration, Divine Intelligence, and Contemplation, which largely rob the plays of dramatic effect. There is some true poetry in these pieces, but too much theological learning and too little simplicity, and in one place the ideas of Calvin seem to show themselves.[20]

The French mystery began to fall into decay about the middle of the sixteenth century. It was attacked on every side : by the new poets of the Renaissance, who preferred classical to Christian subjects ; by the Protestants, who deemed the religious drama a trifling with the solemn truths of Scripture ; and even by the Catholic clergy, who, roused to greater strictness by the challenge of Protestantism, found the comic elements in the plays offensive and dangerous, and perhaps feared that too great familiarity with the Bible as represented in the mysteries might lead the people into heresy.[21] Yet we hear occasionally of Christmas dramas in France in the seventeenth, eighteenth, and nineteenth centuries. In the neighbourhood of Nantes, for instance, a play of the Nativity by Claude Macée, hermit, probably written in the seventeenth century, was commonly performed in the first half of the nineteenth.[22] At Clermont the adoration of the shepherds was still performed in 1718, and some kind of representation of the scene continued in the diocese of Cambrai until 1834, when it was forbidden by the bishop. In the south, especially at Marseilles, " pastorals " were played towards the end of the nineteenth century ; they had, however, largely lost their sacred character, and had become a kind of review of the events of the year.[23] At Dinan, in Brittany, some sort of Herod play was performed, though it was dying out, in 1886. It was acted by young men on the Epiphany, and there was an " innocent " whose throat they pretended to cut with a wooden sword.[24]

THE CHRISTIAN FEAST

An interesting summary of a very full Nativity play performed in the churches of Upper Gascony on Christmas Eve is given by Countess Martinengo-Cesaresco.[25] It ranges from the arrival of Joseph and Mary at Bethlehem to the Flight into Egypt and the Murder of the Innocents, but perhaps the most interesting parts are the shepherd scenes. After the message of the angel—a child in a surplice, with wings fastened to his shoulders, seated on a chair drawn up to the ceiling and supported by ropes—the shepherds leave the church, the whole of which is now regarded as the stable of the Divine Birth. They knock for admittance, and Joseph, regretting that the chamber is "so badly lighted," lets them in. They fall down before the manger, and so do the shepherdesses, who "deposit on the altar steps a banner covered with flowers and greenery, from which hang strings of small birds, apples, nuts, chestnuts, and other fruits. It is their Christmas offering to the curé; the shepherds have already placed a whole sheep before the altar, in a like spirit." The play is not mere dumb-show, but has a full libretto.

A rather similar piece of dramatic ceremonial is described by Barthélemy in his edition of Durandus,[26] as customary in the eighteenth century at La Villeneuve-en-Chevrie, near Mantes. At the Midnight Mass a *crèche* with a wax figure of the Holy Child was placed in the choir, with tapers burning about it. After the "Te Deum" had been sung, the celebrant, accompanied by his attendants, censed the *crèche*, to the sound of violins, double-basses, and other instruments. A shepherd then prostrated himself before the crib, holding a sheep with a sort of little saddle bearing sixteen lighted candles. He was followed by two shepherdesses in white with distaffs and tapers. A second shepherd, between two shepherdesses, carried a laurel branch, to which were fastened oranges, lemons, biscuits, and sweetmeats. Two others brought great *pains-bénits* and lighted candles; then came four shepherdesses, who made their adoration, and lastly twenty-six more shepherds, two by two, bearing in one hand a candle and in the other a festooned crook. The same ceremonial was practised at the Offertory and after the close of the Mass. All was done, it is said, with such piety and edification that

CHRISTMAS DRAMA

St. Luke's words about the Bethlehem shepherds were true of these French swains—they "returned glorifying and praising God for all the things they had heard and seen."

In German there remain very few Christmas plays earlier than the fifteenth century. Later periods, however, have produced a multitude, and dramatic performances at Christmas have continued down to quite modern times in German-speaking parts.

At Oberufer near Pressburg—a German Protestant village in Hungary—some fifty years ago, a Christmas play was performed under the direction of an old farmer, whose office as instructor had descended from father to son. The play took place at intervals of from three to ten years and was acted on all Sundays and festivals from Advent to the Epiphany. Great care was taken to ensure the strictest piety and morality in the actors, and no secular music was allowed in the place during the season for the performances. The practices began as early as October. On the first Sunday in Advent there was a solemn procession to the hall hired for the play. First went a man bearing a gigantic star—he was called the "Master Singer"—and another carrying a Christmas-tree decked with ribbons and apples; then came all the actors, singing hymns. There was no scenery and no theatrical apparatus beyond a straw-seated chair and a wooden stool. When the first was used, the scene was understood to be Jerusalem, when the second, Bethlehem. The Christmas drama, immediately preceded by an Adam and Eve play, and succeeded by a Shrove Tuesday one, followed mediaeval lines, and included the wanderings of Joseph and Mary round the inns of Bethlehem, the angelic tidings to the shepherds, their visit to the manger, the adoration of the Three Kings, and various Herod scenes. Protestant influence was shown by the introduction of Luther's "Vom Himmel hoch," but the general character was very much that of the old mysteries, and the dialogue was full of quaint naïveté.[27]

At Brixlegg, in Tyrol, as late as 1872 a long Christmas play was acted under Catholic auspices; some of its dialogue was in the Tyrolese *patois* and racy and humorous, other parts, and particularly the speeches of Mary and Joseph—out of respect for these holy personages—had been rewritten in the eighteenth century in a very stilted and undramatic style. Some simple shepherd plays are said to be still presented in the churches of the Saxon Erzgebirge.[28]

The German language is perhaps richer in real Christmas plays, as distinguished from Nativity and Epiphany episodes in great cosmic cycles, than any other. There are some examples in mediaeval manuscripts, but the most interesting are shorter pieces performed in country places in comparatively recent times, and probably largely traditional in substance. Christianity by the fourteenth century had at last gained a real hold upon the German people, or perhaps one should rather say the German people had laid a strong hold upon Christianity, moulding it into something very human and concrete, materialistic often, yet not without spiritual significance. In cradle-rocking and religious dancing at Christmas the instincts of a lusty, kindly race expressed themselves, and the same character is shown in the short popular Christmas dramas collected by Weinhold and others.[29] Many of the little pieces—some are rather duets than plays—were sung or acted in church or by the fireside in the nineteenth century, and perhaps even now may linger in remote places. They are in dialect, and the rusticity of their language harmonizes well with their naïve, homely sentiment. In them we behold the scenes of Bethlehem as realized by peasants, and their mixture of rough humour and tender feeling is thoroughly in keeping with the subject.

One is made to feel very vividly the amazement of the shepherds at the wondrous and sudden apparition of the angels :—

> *"Riepl.* Woas is das für a Getümmel,
> 1 versteh mi nit in d'Welt.
> *Jörgl.* Is den heunt eingfalln der Himmel,
> Fleugn d'Engeln auf unserm Feld ?
> *R.* Thuen Sprüng macha
> *J.* Von oben acha !

> *R.* I turft das Ding nit noacha thoan,
> that mir brechn Hals und Boan." * 30

The cold is keenly brought home to us when they come to the manger :—

> "*J.* Mei Kind, kanst kei Herberg finden ?
> Muest so viel Frost leiden schoan.
> *R.* Ligst du under kalden Windeln !
> Lägts ihm doch a Gwandl oan !
> *J.* Machts ihm d'Füess ein,
> Hüllts in zue fein !" † 31

Very homely are their presents to the Child :—

> "Ein drei Eier und ein Butter
> Bringen wir auch, nemt es an !
> Einen Han zu einer Suppen,
> Wanns die Mutter kochen kann.
> Giessts ein Schmalz drein, wirds wol guet sein.
> Weil wir sonsten gar nix han,
> Sind wir selber arme Hirten,
> Nemts den guten Willen an." ‡ 32

One of the dialogues ends with a curious piece of ordinary human kindliness, as if the Divine nature of the Infant were quite forgotten for the moment :—

> "*J.* Bleib halt fein gsund, mein kloans Liebl,
> Wannst woas brauchst, so komm ze mir.

> .   .   .   .   .

> *J.* Pfüet di Gôt halt !

* "*Riepl.* What a noise there is. Everything seems so strange to me !
Jörgl. Have the heavens fallen to-day ; are the angels flying over our field ?
R. They are leaping
J. Down from above.
R. I couldn't do the thing ; 'twould break my neck and legs."
† "*J.* My child, canst find no lodging ? Must Thou bear such frost and cold ?
R. Thou liest in cold swaddling-clothes ! Come, put a garment about Him !
J. Cover His feet up ; wrap Him up delicately !"
‡ "Three eggs and some butter we bring, too ; deign to accept it ! A fowl to make some broth if Thy mother can cook it—put some dripping in, and 'twill be good Because we've nothing else—we are but poor shepherds—accept our goodwill."

R. Wär fein gross bald!
J. Kannst in mein Dienst stehen ein,
Wann darzu wirst gross gnue sein." * 33

Far more interesting in their realism and naturalness are these little plays of the common folk than the elaborate Christmas dramas of more learned German writers, Catholic and Lutheran, who in the sixteenth and seventeenth centuries became increasingly stilted and bombastic.

The Italian religious drama 34 evolved somewhat differently from that of the northern countries. The later thirteenth century saw the outbreak of the fanaticism of the Flagellants or *Battuti,* vast crowds of people of all classes who went in procession from church to church, from city to city, scourging their naked bodies in terror and repentance till the blood flowed. When the wild enthusiasm of this movement subsided it left enduring traces in the foundation of lay communities throughout the land, continuing in a more sober way the penitential practices of the Flagellants. One of their aids to devotion was the singing or reciting of vernacular poetry, less formal than the Latin hymns of the liturgy, and known as *laude.*† These *laude* developed a more or less dramatic form, which gained the name of *divozioni.*‡ They were, perhaps (though not certainly, for there seems to have been another tradition derived from the regular liturgical drama), the source from which sprang the gorgeously produced *sacre rappresentazioni* of the fifteenth century.

The *sacre rappresentazioni* corresponded, though with considerable differences, to the miracle-plays of England and France. Their great period was the fifty years from 1470 to 1520, and

---

* " *J.* The best of health to thee ever, my little dear ; when thou wantest anything, come to me.

J. God keep thee ever!

R. Grow up fine and tall soon!

J. I'll take thee into service when thou'rt big enough."

† Jacopone da Todi, whose Christmas songs we have already considered, was probably connected with the movement.

‡ An interesting and pathetic Christmas example is given by Signor D'Ancona in his " Origini del Teatro in Italia." 35

they were performed, like the *divozioni*, by confraternities of religious laymen. The actors were boys belonging to the brotherhoods, and the plays were intended to be edifying for youth. They are more refined than the northern religious dramas, but only too often fall into insipidity.

Among the texts given by D'Ancona in his collection of *sacre rappresentazioni* is a Tuscan " Natività," [36] opening with a pastoral scene resembling those in the northern mysteries, but far less vigorous. It cannot compare, for character and humour, with the Towneley plays. Still the shepherds, whose names are Bobi del Farucchio, Nencio di Pucchio, Randello, Nencietto, Giordano, and Falconcello, are at least meant to have a certain rusticity, as they feast on bread and cheese and wine, play to the Saviour on bagpipe or whistle, and offer humble presents like apples and cheese. The scenes which follow, the coming of the Magi and the Murder of the Innocents, are not intrinsically of great interest.

It is possible that this play may have been the spectacle performed in Florence in 1466, as recorded by Machiavelli, "to give men something to take away their thoughts from affairs of state." It "represented the coming of the three Magi Kings from the East, following the star which showed the Nativity of Christ, and it was of so great pomp and magnificence that it kept the whole city busy for several months in arranging and preparing it." [37]

An earlier record of an Italian pageant of the Magi is this account by the chronicler Galvano Flamma of what took place at Milan in 1336 :—

"There were three kings crowned, on great horses, . . . and an exceeding great train. And there was a golden star running through the air, which went before these three kings, and they came to the columns of San Lorenzo, where was King Herod in effigy, with the scribes and wise men. And they were seen to ask King Herod where Christ was born, and having turned over many books they answered, that He should be born in the city of David distant five miles from Jerusalem. And having heard this, those three kings, crowned with golden crowns, holding in their hands golden cups with gold, incense, and myrrh, came to the church of Sant' Eustorgio, the star preceding them through the air, . . . and a wonderful train, with resounding trumpets and horns going before them, with apes, baboons, and diverse kinds of animals, and a marvellous tumult of people. There at the side of the high altar was a manger with ox and ass, and in the manger was the little Christ in the arms of the Virgin Mother. And those kings offered gifts unto Christ ; then they were seen to sleep, and a winged angel said to them that they should not return by the region of San Lorenzo but by the Porta Romana ; which also was done. There was so great a concourse of the people and soldiers and ladies and clerics that scarce anything like it was ever beheld. And it was ordered that every year this festal show should be performed." [38]

How suggestive this is of the Magi pictures of the fifteenth century, with their gorgeous eastern monarchs and retinues of countless servants and strange animals. No other story in the New Testament gives such opportunity for pageantry as the Magi scene. All the wonder, richness, and romance of the East, all the splendour of western Renaissance princes could lawfully be introduced into the train of the Three Kings. With Gentile da Fabriano and Benozzo Gozzoli it has become a magnificent procession ; there are trumpeters, pages, jesters, dwarfs, exotic beasts—all the motley, gorgeous retinue of the monarchs of the time, while the kings themselves are romantic figures in richest attire, velvet, brocade, wrought gold, and jewels. It may be that much of this splendour was suggested to the painters by dramatic spectacles which actually passed before their eyes.

I have already alluded to the Spanish "Mystery of the Magi Kings," a mere fragment, but of peculiar interest to the historian of the drama as one of the two earliest religious plays in a modern European language. Though plays are known to have been performed in Spain at Christmas and Easter in the Middle Ages, [39] we have no further texts until the very short "Representation of the Birth of Our Lord," by Gómez Manrique, Señor de Villazopeque (1412–91), acted at the convent at Calabazanos, of which the author's sister was Superior. The characters introduced are the Virgin, St. Joseph, St. Gabriel, St. Michael, St. Raphael, another angel, and three shepherds.[40]

Touched by the spirit of the Renaissance, and particularly by the influence of Virgil, is Juan del Encina of Salamanca (1469–1534), court poet to the Duke of Alba, and author of two Christmas eclogues.[41] The first introduces four shepherds who bear the names of the Evangelists, Matthew, Mark, Luke, and John, and are curiously mixed personages, their words being half what might be expected from the shepherds of Bethlehem and half sayings proper only to the authors of the Gospels. It ends with a *villancico* or carol. The second eclogue is far more realistic, and indeed resembles the English and French pastoral scenes. The shepherds grumble about the weather — it has been raining for two months, the floods are terrible, and no fords or bridges are left; they talk of the death of a sacristan, a fine singer; and they play a game with chestnuts; then comes the angel—whom one of them calls a "smartly dressed lad" (*garzon replcado*)—to tell them of the Birth, and they go to adore the Child, taking Him a kid, butter-cakes, eggs, and other presents.

Infinitely more ambitious is "The Birth of Christ"[42] by the great Lope de Vega (1562–1635). It opens in Paradise, immediately after the Creation, and ends with the adoration of the Three Kings. Full of allegorical conceits and personified qualities, it will hardly please the taste of modern minds. Another work of Lope's, "The Shepherds of Bethlehem," a long pastoral in prose and verse, published in 1612, contains, amid many incongruities, some of the best of his shorter poems; one lullaby, sung by the Virgin in a palm-grove while her Child sleeps, has been thus translated by Ticknor:—

> "Holy angels and blest,
>   Through these palms as ye sweep,
> Hold their branches at rest,
>   For my babe is asleep.
>
> And ye Bethlehem palm-trees,
>   As stormy winds rush

THE CHRISTIAN FEAST

In tempest and fury,
   Your angry noise hush ;
Move gently, move gently,
   Restrain your wild sweep ;
Hold your branches at rest,
   My babe is asleep.

My babe all divine,
   With earth's sorrows oppressed,
Seeks in slumber an instant
   His grievings to rest ;
He slumbers, he slumbers,
   O, hush, then, and keep
Your branches all still,
   My babe is asleep ! " [43]

.   .   .   .   .

Apart from such modern revivals of the Christmas drama as Mr. Laurence Housman's "Bethlehem," Miss Buckton's "Eager Heart," Mrs. Percy Dearmer's "The Soul of the World," and similar experiments in Germany and France, a genuine tradition has lingered on in some parts of Europe into modern times. We have already noticed some French and German instances ; to these may be added a few from other countries.

In Naples there is no Christmas without the "Cantata dei pastori" ; it is looked forward to no less than the Midnight Mass. Two or three theatres compete for the public favour in the performance of this play in rude verse. It begins with Adam and Eve and ends with the birth of Jesus and the adoration of the shepherds. Many devils are brought on the stage, their arms and legs laden with brass chains that rattle horribly. Awful are their names, Lucifero, Satanasso, Belfegor, Belzebù, &c. They not only tempt Adam and Eve, but annoy the Virgin and St. Joseph, until an angel comes and frightens them away. Two non-Biblical figures are introduced, Razzullo and Sarchiapone, who are tempted by devils and aided by angels.[44] In Sicily too the Christmas play still lingers under the name of *Pastorale*.[45]

CHRISTMAS DRAMA

A nineteenth-century Spanish survival of the "Stella" is described in Fernan Caballero's sketch, "La Noche de Navidad." [46] At the foot of the altar of the village church, according to this account, images of the Virgin and St. Joseph were placed, with the Holy Child between them, lying on straw. On either side knelt a small boy dressed as an angel. Solemnly there entered the church a number of men attired as shepherds, bearing their offerings to the Child; afterwards they danced with slow and dignified movements before the altar. The shepherds were followed by the richest men of the village dressed as the Magi Kings, mounted on horseback, and followed by their train. Before them went a shining star. On reaching the church they dismounted; the first, representing a majestic old man with white hair, offered incense to the Babe; the others, Caspar and Melchior, myrrh and gold respectively. This was done on the feast of the Epiphany.

A remnant possibly of the "Stella" is to be found in a Christmas custom extremely widespread in Europe and surviving even in some Protestant lands—the carrying about of a star in memory of the Star of Bethlehem. It is generally borne by a company of boys, who sing some sort of carol, and expect a gift in return.

The practice is—or was—found as far north as Sweden. All through the Christmas season the "star youths" go about from house to house. Three are dressed up as the Magi Kings, a fourth carries on a stick a paper lantern in the form of a six-pointed star, made to revolve and lighted by candles. There are also a Judas, who bears the purse for the collection, and, occasionally, a King Herod. A doggerel rhyme is sung, telling the story of the Nativity and offering good wishes.[47] In Norway and Denmark processions of a like character were formerly known.[48]

In Normandy at Christmas children used to go singing through the village streets, carrying a lantern of coloured paper on a long osier rod.[49] At Pleudihen in Brittany three young men representing the Magi sang carols in the cottages, dressed in their holiday clothes covered with ribbons.[50]

151

THE CHRISTIAN FEAST

In England there appears to be no trace of the custom, which is however found in Germany, Austria, Holland, Italy, Bohemia, Roumania, Poland, and Russia.[51]

In Thuringia a curious carol used to be sung, telling how Herod tried to tempt the Wise Men—

> " 'Oh, good Wise Men, come in and dine ;
> I will give you both beer and wine,
> And hay and straw to make your bed,
> And nought of payment shall be said.' "

But they answer :—

> " 'Oh, no ! oh, no ! we must away,
> We seek a little Child to-day,
> A little Child, a mighty King,
> Him who created everything.' " [52]

In Tyrol the "star-singing" is very much alive at the present day. In the Upper Innthal three boys in white robes, with blackened faces and gold paper crowns, go to every house on Epiphany Eve, one of them carrying a golden star on a pole. They sing a carol, half religious, half comic—almost a little drama—and are given money, cake, and drink. In the Ilsethal the boys come on Christmas Eve, and presents are given them by well-to-do people. In some parts there is but one singer, an old man with a white beard and a turban, who twirls a revolving star. A remarkable point about the Tyrolese star-singers is that before anything is given them they are told to stamp on the snowy fields outside the houses, in order to promote the growth of the crops in summer.[53]

In Little Russia the "star" is made of pasteboard and has a transparent centre with a picture of Christ through which the light of a candle shines. One boy carries the star and another twirls the points.[54] In Roumania it is made of wood and adorned with frills and little bells. A representation of the "manger," illuminated from behind, forms the centre, and the star also shows pictures of Adam and Eve and angels.[55]

CHRISTMAS DRAMA

A curious traditional drama, in which pagan elements seem to have mingled with the Herod story, is still performed by the Roumanians during the Christmas festival. It is called in Wallachia "Vicleim" (from Bethlehem), in Moldavia and Transylvania "Irozi" (plural from *Irod*=Herod). At least ten persons figure in it : "Emperor" Herod, an old grumbling monarch who speaks in harsh tones to his followers ; an officer and two soldiers in Roman attire ; the three Magi, in Oriental garb, a child, and "two comical figures—the *paiaţa* (the clown) and the *moşul*, or old man, the former in harlequin accoutrement, the latter with a mask on his face, a long beard, a hunch on his back, and dressed in a sheepskin with the wool on the outside. The plot of the play is quite simple. The officer brings the news that three strange men have been caught, going to Bethlehem to adore the new-born Messiah ; Herod orders them to be shown in : they enter singing in a choir. Long dialogues ensue between them and Herod, who at last orders them to be taken to prison. But then they address the Heavenly Father, and shout imprecations on Herod, invoking celestial punishment on him, at which unaccountable noises are heard, seeming to announce the fulfilment of the curse. Herod falters, begs the Wise Men's forgiveness, putting off his anger till more opportune times. The Wise Men retire. . . . Then a child is introduced, who goes on his knees before Herod, with his hands on his breast, asking pity. He gives clever answers to various questions and foretells the Christ's future career, at which Herod stabs him. The whole troupe now strikes up a tune of reproach to Herod, who falls on his knees in deep repentance." The play is sometimes performed by puppets instead of living actors.[56]

Christmas plays performed by puppets are found in other countries too. In Poland " during the week between Christmas and New Year is shown the *Jaselki* or manger, a travelling series of scenes from the life of Christ or even of modern peasants, a small travelling puppet-theatre, gorgeous with tinsel and candles, and something like our 'Punch and Judy' show. The market-place of Cracow, especially at night, is a very pretty spectacle, its sidewalks all lined with these glittering Jaselki." [57] In Madrid at the Epiphany a puppet-play was common, in which the events of the Nativity and the Infancy were mimed by wooden figures,[58] and in Provence, in the mid-nineteenth century, the Christmas scenes were represented in the same way.[59]

Last may be mentioned a curious Mexican mixture of religion and amusement, a sort of drama called the "Posadas," described by Madame Calderon de la Barca in her "Life in Mexico" (1843).[60] The custom was based upon the wanderings of the Virgin and St. Joseph in Bethlehem in search of repose. For eight days these wanderings of the holy pair to the different *posadas* were represented. On Christmas Eve, says the narrator, "a lighted candle was put into the hand of each lady [this was at a sort of party], and a procession was formed, two by two, which marched all through the house . . . the whole party singing the Litanies. . . . A group of little children, dressed as angels, joined the procession. . . . At last the procession drew up before a door, and a shower of fireworks was sent flying over our heads, I suppose to represent the descent of the angels ; for a group of ladies appeared, dressed to represent the shepherds. . . . Then voices, supposed to be those of Mary and Joseph, struck up a hymn, in which they begged for admittance, saying that the night was cold and dark, that the wind blew hard, and that they prayed for a night's shelter. A chorus of voices from within refused admittance. Again those without entreated shelter, and at length declared that she at the door, who thus wandered in the night, and had not where to lay her head, was the Queen of Heaven ! At this name the doors were thrown wide open, and the Holy Family entered singing. The scene within was very pretty : a *nacimiento*. . . . One of the angels held a waxen baby in her arms. . . . A padre took the baby from the angel and placed it in the cradle, and the *posada* was completed. We then returned to the drawing-room—angels, shepherds, and all, and danced till supper-time." [60] Here the religious drama has sunk to little more than a "Society" game.

THE ADORATION OF THE MAGI. MASACCIO

(Berlin: Kaiser Friedrich Museum)

POSTSCRIPT

Before we pass on to the pagan aspects of Christmas, let us gather up our thoughts in an attempt to realize the peculiar appeal of the Feast of the Nativity, as it has been felt in the past, as it is felt to-day even by moderns who have no belief in the historical truth of the story it commemorates.

This appeal of Christmas seems to lie in the union of two modes of feeling which may be called the *carol spirit* and the *mystical spirit*. The *carol spirit*—by this we may understand the simple, human joyousness, the tender and graceful imagination, the kindly, intimate affection, which have gathered round the cradle of the Christ Child. The folk-tune, the secular song adapted to a sacred theme—such is the carol. What a sense of kindliness, not of sentimentality, but of genuine human feeling, these old songs give us, as though the folk who first sang them were more truly comrades, more closely knit together than we under modern industrialism.

One element in the carol spirit is the rustic note that finds its sanction as regards Christmas in St. Luke's story of the shepherds keeping watch over their flocks by night. One thinks of the stillness over the fields, of the hinds with their rough talk, " simply chatting in a rustic row," of the keen air, and the great burst of light and song that dazes their simple wits, of their journey to Bethlehem where " the heaven-born Child all meanly wrapt in the rude manger lies," of the ox and ass linking the beasts of the field to the Christmas adoration of mankind.*

For many people, indeed, the charm of Christmas is inseparably associated with the country ; it is lost in London—the city is too vast, too modern, too sophisticated. It is bound up with the thought of frosty fields, of bells heard far away, of bare trees

---

* Though the ox and ass are not mentioned by St. Luke, it is an easy transition to them from the idea of the manger. Early Christian writers found a Scriptural sanction for them in two passages in the prophets : Isaiah i. 3, " The ox knoweth his owner and the ass his master's crib," and Habakkuk iii. 2 (a mistranslation), " In the midst of two beasts shalt Thou be known."

against the starlit sky, of carols sung not by trained choirs but by rustic folk with rough accent, irregular time, and tunes learnt by ear and not by book.

Again, without the idea of winter half the charm of Christmas would be gone. Transplanted in the imagination of western Christendom from an undefined season in the hot East to Europe at midwinter, the Nativity scenes have taken on a new pathos with the thought of the bitter cold to which the great Little One lay exposed in the rough stable, with the contrast between the cold and darkness of the night and the fire of love veiled beneath that infant form. *Lux in tenebris* is one of the strongest notes of Christmas : in the bleak midwinter a light shines through the darkness ; when all is cold and gloom, the sky bursts into splendour, and in the dark cave is born the Light of the World.

There is the idea of royalty too, with all it stands for of colour and magnificence, though not so much in literature as in painting is this side of the Christmas story represented. The Epiphany is the great opportunity for imaginative development of the regal idea. Then is seen the union of utter poverty with highest kingship ; the monarchs of the East come to bow before the humble Infant for whom the world has found no room in the inn. How suggestive by their long, slow syllables are the Italian names of the Magi. Gasparre, Baldassarre, Melchiorre—we picture Oriental monarchs in robes mysteriously gorgeous, wrought with strange patterns, heavy with gold and precious stones. With slow processional motion they advance, bearing to the King of Kings their symbolic gifts, gold for His crowning, incense for His worship, myrrh for His mortality, and with them come the mystery, colour, and perfume of the East, the occult wisdom which bows itself before the revelation in the Child.

Above all, as the foregoing pages have shown, it is the *childhood* of the Redeemer that has won the heart of Europe for Christmas; it is the appeal to the parental instinct, the love for the tender, weak, helpless, yet all-potential babe, that has given the Church's festival its strongest hold. And this side of Christmas is penetrated often by the *mystical spirit*—that sense of the Infinite in the finite without which the highest human life is impossible.

POSTSCRIPT

The feeling for Christmas varies from mere delight in the Christ Child as a representative symbol on which to lavish affection, as a child delights in a doll, to the mystical philosophy of Eckhart, in whose Christmas sermons the Nativity is viewed as a type of the Birth of God in the depths of man's being. Yet even the least spiritual forms of the cult of the Child are seldom without some hint of the supersensual, the Infinite, and even in Eckhart there is a love of concrete symbolism. Christmas stands peculiarly for the sacramental principle that the outward and visible is a sign and shadow of the inward and spiritual. It means the seeing of common, earthly things shot through by the glory of the Infinite. " Its note," as has been said of a stage of the mystic consciousness, the Illuminative Way, " is sacramental not ascetic. It entails . . . the discovery of the Perfect One ablaze in the Many, not the forsaking of the Many in order to find the One . . . an ineffable radiance, a beauty and a reality never before suspected, are perceived by a sort of clairvoyance shining in the meanest things." [1] Christmas is the festival of the Divine Immanence, and it is natural that it should have been beloved by the saint and mystic whose life was the supreme manifestation of the *Via Illuminativa*, Francis of Assisi.

Christmas is the most human and lovable of the Church's feasts. Easter and Ascensiontide speak of the rising and exaltation of a glorious being, clothed in a spiritual body refined beyond all comparison with our natural flesh ; Whitsuntide tells of the coming of a mysterious, intangible Power—like the wind, we cannot tell whence It cometh and whither It goeth ; Trinity offers for contemplation an ineffable paradox of Pure Being. But the God of Christmas is no ethereal form, no mere spiritual essence, but a very human child, feeling the cold and the roughness of the straw, needing to be warmed and fed and cherished. Christmas is the festival of the natural body, of this world ; it means the consecration of the ordinary things of life, affection and comradeship, eating and drinking and merry-making ; and in some degree the memory of the Incarnation has been able to blend with the pagan joyance of the New Year.

Part II—Pagan Survivals

CHAPTER VI

PRE-CHRISTIAN
WINTER FESTIVALS

CHAPTER VI

PRE-CHRISTIAN WINTER FESTIVALS

The Church and Superstition—Nature of Pagan Survivals—Racial Origins—Roman Festivals of the *Saturnalia* and Kalends—Was there a Teutonic Midwinter Festival ?—The Teutonic, Celtic, and Slav New Year—Customs attracted to Christmas or January 1—The Winter Cycle of Festivals—*Rationale* of Festival Ritual : (*a*) Sacrifice and Sacrament, (*b*) the Cult of the Dead, (*c*) Omens and Charms for the New Year—Compromise in the Later Middle Ages—The Puritans and Christmas—Decay of Old Traditions.

WE have now to leave the commemoration of the Nativity of Christ, and to turn to the other side of Christmas—its many traditional observances which, though sometimes coloured by Christianity, have nothing to do with the Birth of the Redeemer. This class of customs has often, especially in the first millennium of our era, been the object of condemnations by ecclesiastics, and represents the old paganism which Christianity failed to extinguish. The Church has played a double part, a part of sheer antagonism, forcing heathen customs into the shade, into a more or less surreptitious and unprogressive life, and a part of adaptation, baptizing them into Christ, giving them a Christian name and interpretation, and often modifying their form. The general effect of Christianity upon pagan usages is well suggested by Dr. Karl Pearson :—

"What the missionary could he repressed, the more as his church grew in strength ; what he could not repress he adopted or simply left unregarded. . . . What the missionary tried to repress became mediaeval witchcraft ; what he judiciously disregarded survives to this day in peasant weddings and in the folk-festivals at the great changes of season." [1]

We find then many pagan practices concealed beneath a superficial Christianity—often under the mantle of some saint—but side by side with these are many usages never Christianized even in appearance, and obviously identical with heathen customs against which the Church thundered in the days of her youth. Grown old and tolerant—except of novelties—she has long since ceased to attack them, and they have themselves mostly lost all definite religious meaning. As the old pagan faith decayed, they tended to become in a literal sense "superstition," something standing over, like shells from which the living occupant has gone. They are now often mere "survivals" in the technical folk-lore sense, pieces of custom separated from the beliefs that once gave them meaning, performed only because in a vague sort of way they are supposed to bring good luck. In many cases those who practise them would be quite unable to explain how or why they work for good.

Mental inertia, the instinct to do and believe what has always been done and believed, has sometimes preserved the animating faith as well as the external form of these practices, but often all serious significance has departed. What was once religious or magical ritual, upon the due observance of which the welfare of the community was believed to depend, has become mere pageantry and amusement, often a mere children's game. [2]

Sometimes the spirit of a later age has worked upon these pagan customs, revivifying and transforming them, giving them charm. Often, however, one does not find in them the poetry, the warm humanity, the humour, which mark the creations of popular Catholicism. They are fossils and their interest is that of the fossil : they are records of a vanished world and help us to an imaginative reconstruction of it. But further, just as on a stratum of rock rich in fossils there may be fair meadows and gardens and groves, depending for their life on the denudation of the rock beneath, so have these ancient religious products largely supplied the soil in which more spiritual and more beautiful things have flourished. Amid these, as has been well said, " they still emerge, unchanged and unchanging, like the quaint outcrops of some ancient rock formation amid rich vegetation and fragrant flowers." 3

The survivals of pagan religion at Christian festivals relate not so much to the worship of definite divinities—against this the missionaries made their most determined efforts, and the names of the old gods have practically disappeared—as to cults which preceded the development of anthropomorphic gods with names and attributes. These cults, paid to less personally conceived spirits, were of older standing and no doubt had deeper roots in the popular mind. Fundamentally associated with agricultural and pastoral life, they have in many cases been preserved by the most conservative element in the population, the peasantry.

Many of the customs we shall meet with are magical, rather than religious in the proper sense ; they are not directed to the conciliation of spiritual beings, but spring from primitive man's belief "that in order to produce the great phenomena of nature on which his life depended he had only to imitate them." 4 Even when they have a definitely religious character, and are connected with some spirit, magical elements are often found in them.

Before we consider these customs in detail it will be necessary to survey the pagan festivals briefly alluded to in Chapter I., to note the various ideas and practices that characterized them, and to study the attitude of the Church towards survivals of such practices while the conversion of Europe was in progress, and also during the Middle Ages.

The development of religious custom and belief in Europe is a matter of such vast complexity that I cannot in a book of this kind attempt more than the roughest outline of the probable origins of the observances, purely pagan or half-Christianized, clustering round Christmas. It is difficult, in the present state of knowledge, to discern clearly the contributions of different peoples to the traditional customs of Europe, and even, in many cases, to say whether a given custom is " Aryan " or pre-Aryan. The proportion of the Aryan military aristocracy to the peoples whom they conquered was not uniform in all countries, and probably was often small. While the families of the conquerors succeeded in imposing their languages, it by no means necessarily follows that the folk-practices of countries now Aryan in speech came entirely or even chiefly from Aryan sources. Religious tradition has a marvellous power of persistence, and it must be remembered that the lands conquered by men of Aryan speech had been previously occupied for immense periods.5 Similarly, in countries like our own, which have been successively invaded by Celts, Romans, Anglo-Saxons, Danes, and Normans, it is often extraordinarily hard to say even to what *national* source a given custom should be assigned.

It is but tentatively and with uncertain hands that scholars are trying to separate the racial strains in the folk-traditions of Europe, and here I can hardly do more than point out three formative elements in Christian customs : the ecclesiastical, the classical (Greek and Roman), and the barbarian, taking the last broadly and without a minute racial analysis. So far, indeed, as ritual, apart from mythology, is concerned, there seems to be a broad common ground of tradition among the Aryan-speaking peoples. How far this is due to a common derivation we need not here attempt to decide. The folk-lore of the whole world, it is to be noted, " reveals for the same stages of civilization a wonderful uniformity and homogeneity. . . . This uniformity is not, however, due to necessary uniformity of origin, but to a great extent to the fact that it represents the state of equilibrium arrived at between minds at a certain level and their environment." [6]

The scientific study of primitive religion is still almost in its infancy, and a large amount of conjecture must necessarily enter into any explanations of popular ritual that can be offered. In attempting to account for Christmas customs we must be mindful, therefore, of the tentative nature of the theories put forward. Again, it is important to remember that ritual practices are far more enduring than the explanations given to them. " The antique religions," to quote the words of Robertson Smith, " had for the most part no creed ; they consisted entirely of institutions and practices . . . as a rule we find that while the practice was rigorously fixed, the meaning attached to it was extremely vague, and the same rite was explained by different people in different ways." 7

Thus if we can arrive at the significance of a rite at a given period, it by no means follows that those who began it meant the same thing. At the time of the conflict of the heathen religions with Christianity elaborate structures of mythology had grown up around their traditional ceremonial, assigning to it meanings that had often little to do with its original purpose. Often, too, when the purpose was changed, new ceremonies were added, so that a rite may look very unlike what it was at first.

With these cautions and reservations we must now try to trace the connection between present-day or recent goings-on about Christmas-time and the festival practices of pre-Christian Europe.

Christmas, as we saw in Chapter I., has taken the date of the *Natalis Invicti*. We need not linger over this feast, for it was not attended by folk-customs, and there is nothing to connect it with modern survivals. The Roman festivals that really count for our present purpose are the Kalends of January and, probably, the *Saturnalia*. The influence of the Kalends is strongest naturally in the Latin countries, but is found also all over Europe. The influence of the *Saturnalia* is less certain ; the festival is not mentioned in ecclesiastical condemnations after the institution of Christmas, and possibly its popularity was not so widespread as that of the Kalends. There are, however, some curiously interesting Christmas parallels to its usages.

The strictly religious feast of the *Saturnalia* 8 was held on December 17, but the festal customs were kept up for seven days, thus lasting until the day before our Christmas Eve. Among them was a fair called the *sigillariorum celebritas*, for the sale of little images of clay or paste which were given away as presents.* Candles seem also to have been given away, perhaps

* With this may be compared the fair still held in Rome in the Piazza Navona just before Christmas, at which booths are hung with little clay figures for use in *presepi* (see p. 113). One cannot help being reminded too, though probably there is no direct connection, of the biscuits in human shapes to be seen in German markets and

as symbols of, or even charms to ensure, the return of the sun's
power after the solstice. The most remarkable and typical
feature, however, of the *Saturnalia* was the mingling of all
classes in a common jollity. Something of the character of
the celebration (in a Hellenized form) may be gathered from
the "Cronia" or "Saturnalia" of Lucian, a dialogue between
Cronus or Saturn and his priest. We learn from it that the
festivities were marked by "drinking and being drunk, noise
and games and dice, appointing of kings and feasting of slaves,
singing naked, clapping of tremulous hands, an occasional ducking
of corked faces in icy water," and that slaves had licence to revile
their lords.9

The spirit of the season may be judged from the legislation
which Lucian attributes to Cronosolon, priest and prophet of
Cronus, much as a modern writer might make Father Christmas
or Santa Klaus lay down rules for the due observance of Yule.
Here are some of the laws :—

*"All business, be it public or private, is forbidden during the feast days,
save such as tends to sport and solace and delight. Let none follow their
avocations saving cooks and bakers.*

All men shall be equal, slave and free, rich and poor, one with another.

Anger, resentment, threats, are contrary to law.

*No discourse shall be either composed or delivered, except it be witty and
lusty, conducing to mirth and jollity."*

There follow directions as to the sending of presents of money,
clothing, or vessels, by rich men to poor friends, and as to poor
men's gifts in return. If the poor man have learning, his return
gift is to be "an ancient book, but of good omen and festive
humour, or a writing of his own after his ability. . . . For the
unlearned, let him send a garland or grains of frankincense."
The "Cronosolon" closes with "Laws of the Board," of which
the following are a few :—

*"Every man shall take place as chance may direct ; dignities and birth and
wealth shall give no precedence.*

shops at Christmas, and of the paste images which English bakers used to make at this
season.10

PRE-CHRISTIAN WINTER FESTIVALS

All shall be served with the same wine. . . . Every man's portion of meat shall be alike.

When the rich man shall feast his slaves, let his friends serve with him." [11]

Over the whole festival brooded the thought of a golden age in the distant past, when Saturn ruled, a just and kindly monarch, when all men were good and all men were happy.

A striking feature of the *Saturnalia* was the choosing by lot of a mock king, to preside over the revels. His word was law, and he was able to lay ridiculous commands upon the guests ; " one," says Lucian, " must shout out a libel on himself, another dance naked, or pick up the flute-girl and carry her thrice round the house."[12] This king may have been originally the representative of the god Saturn himself. In the days of the classical writers he is a mere " Lord of Misrule," but Dr. Frazer has propounded the very interesting theory that this time of privilege and gaiety was once but the prelude to a grim sacrifice in which he had to die in the character of the god, giving his life for the world.[13] Dr. Frazer's theory, dependent for its evidence upon the narrative of the martyrdom of a fourth-century saint, Dasius by name, has been keenly criticized by Dr. Warde Fowler. He holds that there is nothing whatever to show that the " Saturn " who in the fourth century, according to the story, was sacrificed by soldiers on the Danube, had anything to do with the customs of ancient Rome.[14] Still, in whatever way the king of the *Saturnalia* may be explained, it is interesting to note his existence and compare him with the merry monarchs whom we shall meet at Christmas and Twelfth Night.

How far the Saturnalian customs in general were of old Latin origin it is difficult to say ; the name Saturnus (connected with the root of *serere*, to sow) and the date point to a real Roman festival of the sowing of the crops, but this was heavily overlaid with Greek ideas and practice.[15] It is especially important to bear this in mind in considering Lucian's statements.

The same is true of the festival of the January Kalends, a few days after the *Saturnalia*. On January 1, the Roman New

167

Year's Day, the new consuls were inducted into office, and for at least three days high festival was kept. The houses were decorated with lights and greenery—these, we shall find, may be partly responsible for the modern Christmas-tree. As at the *Saturnalia* masters drank and gambled with slaves. *Vota*, or solemn wishes of prosperity for the Emperor during the New Year, were customary, and the people and the Senate were even expected to present gifts of money to him. The Emperor Caligula excited much disgust by publishing an edict requiring these gifts and by standing in the porch of his palace to receive them in person. Such gifts, not only presented to the Emperor, but frequently exchanged between private persons, were called *strenae*, a name still surviving in the French *étrennes* (New Year's presents).[16]

An interesting and very full account of the Kalends celebrations is given in two discourses of Libanius, the famous Greek sophist of the fourth century :—

"The festival of the Kalends," he says, "is celebrated everywhere as far as the limits of the Roman Empire extend. . . . Everywhere may be seen carousals and well-laden tables ; luxurious abundance is found in the houses of the rich, but also in the houses of the poor better food than usual is put upon the table. The impulse to spend seizes everyone. He who the whole year through has taken pleasure in saving and piling up his pence, becomes suddenly extravagant. He who erstwhile was accustomed and preferred to live poorly, now at this feast enjoys himself as much as his means will allow. . . . People are not only generous towards themselves, but also towards their fellow-men. A stream of presents pours itself out on all sides. . . . The highroads and footpaths are covered with whole processions of laden men and beasts. . . . As the thousand flowers which burst forth everywhere are the adornment of Spring, so are the thousand presents poured out on all sides, the decoration of the Kalends feast. It may justly be said that it is the fairest time of the year. . . . The Kalends festival banishes all that is connected with toil, and allows men to give themselves up to undisturbed enjoyment. From the minds of young people it removes two kinds of dread : the dread of the schoolmaster and the dread of the stern pedagogue. The slave also it allows, so far as possible, to breathe the air of freedom. . . .

Another great quality of the festival is that it teaches men not to hold too fast to their money, but to part with it and let it pass into other hands." [17]

The resemblances here to modern Christmas customs are very striking. In another discourse Libanius speaks of processions on the Eve of the festival. Few people, he says, go to bed ; most go about the streets with singing and leaping and all sorts of mockery. The severest moralist utters no blame on this occasion. When morning begins to dawn they decorate their houses with laurels and other greenery, and at daybreak may go to bed to sleep off their intoxication, for many deem it necessary at this feast to follow the flowing bowl. On the 1st of January money is distributed to the populace ; on the 2nd no more presents are given : it is customary to stay at home playing dice, masters and slaves together. On the 3rd there is racing ; on the 4th the festivities begin to decline, but they are not altogether over on the 5th.[18]

Another feature of the Kalends, recorded not in the pages of classical writers but in ecclesiastical condemnations, was the custom of dressing up in the hides of animals, in women's clothes, and in masks of various kinds.[19] Dr. Tille [20] regards this as Italian in origin, but it seems likely that it was a native custom in Greece, Gaul, Germany, and other countries conquered by the Romans. In Greece the skin-clad mummers may have belonged to the winter festivals of Dionysus supplanted by the *Kalendae*.[21]

The Church's denunciations of pagan festal practices in the winter season are mainly directed against the Kalends celebrations, and show into how many regions the keeping of the feast had spread. Complaints of its continued observance abound in the writings of churchmen and the decrees of councils. In the second volume of his " Mediaeval Stage " [22] Mr. Chambers has made an interesting collection of forty excerpts from such denunciations, ranging in date from the fourth century to the eleventh, and coming from Spain, Italy, Antioch, northern Africa, Constantinople, Germany, England, and various districts of what is now France.

PAGAN SURVIVALS

As a specimen I may translate a passage describing at some length the practices condemned. It is from a sermon often ascribed to St. Augustine of Hippo, but probably composed in the sixth century, very likely by Caesarius of Arles in southern Gaul :—

"On those days," says the preacher, speaking of the Kalends of January, "the heathen, reversing the order of all things, dress themselves up in indecent deformities. . . . These miserable men, and what is worse, some who have been baptized, put on counterfeit forms and monstrous faces, at which one should rather be ashamed and sad. For what reasonable man would believe that any men in their senses would by making a stag (*cervulum*) turn themselves into the appearance of animals ? Some are clothed in the hides of cattle ; others put on the heads of beasts, rejoicing and exulting that they have so transformed themselves into the shapes of animals that they no longer appear to be men. . . . How vile, further, it is that those who have been born men are clothed in women's dresses, and by the vilest change effeminate their manly strength by taking on the forms of girls, blushing not to clothe their warlike arms in women's garments ; they have bearded faces, and yet they wish to appear women. . . . There are some who on the Kalends of January practise auguries, and do not allow fire out of their houses or any other favour to anyone who asks. Also they both receive and give diabolical presents (*strenas*). Some country people, moreover, lay tables with plenty of things necessary for eating . . . thinking that thus the Kalends of January will be a warranty that all through the year their feasting will be in like measure abundant. Now as for them who on those days observe any heathen customs, it is to be feared that the name of Christian will avail them nought. And therefore our holy fathers of old, considering that the majority of men on those days became slaves to gluttony and riotous living and raved in drunkenness and impious dancing, determined for the whole world that throughout the Churches a public fast should be proclaimed. . . . Let us therefore fast, beloved brethren, on those days. . . . For he who on the Kalends shows any civility to foolish men who are wantonly sporting, is undoubtedly a partaker of their sin." [23]

There are several points to be noted here. First, the zeal of the Church against the Kalends celebrations as impious relics of heathenism : to root them out she even made the first three days of the year a solemn fast with litanies.24 Next, the particular offences should be observed. These are : first, the dressing up of men in the hides of animals and the clothes of women ; next, the New Year auguries and the superstition about fire, the giving of presents, and the laying of tables with good things ; and last, drunkenness and riot in general. All these we shall find fully represented in modern Christmas customs.

That Roman customs either spread to Germany, or were paralleled there, is shown by a curious letter written in 742 by St. Boniface to Pope Zacharias. The saint complained that certain Alamanni, Bavarians, and Franks refused to give up various heathen practices because they had seen such things done in the sacred city of Rome, close to St. Peter's, and, as they deemed, with the sanction of the clergy. On New Year's Eve, it was alleged, processions went through the streets of Rome, with impious songs and heathen cries ; tables of fortune were set up, and at that time no one would lend fire or iron or any other article to his neighbour. The Pope replied that these things were odious to him, and should be so to all Christians ; and next year all such practices at the January Kalends were formally forbidden by the Council of Rome.25

So much for Roman customs ; if indeed such practices as beast-masking are Roman, and not derived from the religion of peoples conquered by the imperial legions. We must now turn to the winter festivals of the barbarians with whom the Church began to come into contact soon after the establishment of Christmas.

Much attention has been bestowed upon a supposed midwinter festival of the ancient Germans. In the mid-nineteenth century it was customary to speak of Christmas and the Twelve Nights as a continuation of the holy season kept by our forefathers at the winter solstice. The festive fires of Christmas were regarded as symbols of the sun, who then began his upward journey in the heavens, while the name Yule was traced back to the Anglo-Saxon word *hwéol* (wheel), and connected with the circular course of the sun through the wheeling-points of the solstices and equinoxes. More recent research, however, has thrown the gravest doubts upon the existence of any Teutonic festival at the winter solstice.* It appears from philology and the study of surviving customs that the Teutonic peoples had no knowledge of the solstices and equinoxes, and until the introduction of the Roman Calendar divided their year not into four parts but into two, three, and six, holding their New Year's Day with its attendant festivities not at the end of December or beginning of January, but towards the middle of November. At that time in Central Europe the first snowfall usually occurred and the pastures were closed to the flocks. A great slaughter of cattle would then take place, it being impossible to keep the beasts in stall throughout the winter, and this time of slaughter would naturally be a a season of feasting and sacrifice and religious observances.† [26]

The Celtic year, like the Teutonic, appears to have begun in November with the feast of *Samhain*—a name that may mean either " summer-end " or " assembly." It appears to have been in origin a " pastoral and agricultural festival, which in time came to be looked upon as affording assistance to the powers of growth in their conflict with the powers of blight," and to have had many features in common with the Teutonic feast at the same season, for instance animal sacrifice, commemoration of the dead, and omens and charms for the New Year. [27]

. There is some reason also to believe that the New Year

---

* Among the Scandinavians, who were late in their conversion, a pre-Christian Yule feast seems to have been held in the ninth century, but it appears to have taken place not in December but about the middle of January, and to have been transferred to December 25 by the Christian king Hakon the Good of Norway (940–63). [28]

† It is only right to mention here Professor G. Bilfinger's monograph "Das germanische Julfest" (Stuttgart, 1901), where it is maintained that the only festivals from which the Christmas customs of the Teutonic peoples have sprung are the January Kalends of the Roman Empire and the Christian feast of the Nativity. Bilfinger holds that there is no evidence either of a November beginning-of-winter festival or of an ancient Teutonic midwinter feast. Bilfinger's is the most systematic of existing treatises on Christmas origins, but the considerations brought forward in Tille's " Yule and Christmas " in favour of the November festival are not lightly to be set aside, and while recognizing that its celebration must be regarded rather as a probable hypothesis than an established fact, I shall here follow in general the suggestions of Tille and try to show the contributions of this northern New Year feast to Christmas customs.

festival of the Slavs took place in the autumn and that its usages have been transferred to the feast of the Nativity.[29] A description based on contemporary documents cannot be given of these barbarian festivals ; we have, rather, to reconstruct them from survivals in popular custom. At the close of this book, when such relics have been studied, we may have gained some idea of what went on upon these pre-Christian holy-days. It is the Teutonic customs that have been most fully recorded and discussed by scholars, and these will loom largest in our review ; at the same time Celtic and Slav practices will be considered, and we shall find that they often closely resemble those current in Teutonic lands.

The customs of the old New Year feasts have frequently wandered from their original November date, and to this fact we owe whatever elements of northern paganism are to be found in Christmas. Some practices seem to have been put forward to Michaelmas ; one side of the festivals, the cult of the dead, is represented especially by All Saints' and All Souls' days (November 1 and 2). St. Martin's Day (November 11) probably marks as nearly as possible the old Teutonic date, and is still in Germany an important folk-feast attended by many customs derived from the beginning-of-winter festival. Other practices are found strewn over various holy-days between Martinmas and Epiphany, and concentrated above all on the Church's feast of the Nativity and the Roman New Year's Day, January 1, both of which had naturally great power of attraction.[30]

The progress of agriculture, as Dr. Tille points out,[31] tended to destroy the mid-November celebration. In the Carolingian period an improvement took place in the cultivation of meadows, and the increased quantity of hay made it possible to keep the animals fattening in stall, instead of slaughtering them as soon as the pastures were closed. Thus the killing-time, with its festivities, became later and later. St. Andrew's Day (November 30) and St. Nicholas's (December 6) may mark stages in its progress into the winter. In St. Nicholas's Day, indeed, we find a feast that closely resembles Martinmas, and seems to be the same folk-festival transferred to a later date. Again, as regards England we must remember the difference between its climate and that of Central Europe. Mid-November would here not be a date beyond which pasturing was impossible, and thus the slaughter and feast held then by Angles and Saxons in their old German home would tend to be delayed.[32]

Christmas, as will be gathered from the foregoing, cannot on its pagan side be separated from the folk-feasts of November and December. The meaning of the term will therefore here be so extended as to cover the whole period between All Saints' Day and Epiphany. That this is not too violent a proceeding will be seen later on.

For the purposes of this book it seems best to treat the winter festivals calendarially, so to speak : to start at the beginning of November, and show them in procession, suggesting, as far as may be, the probable origins of the customs observed. Thus we may avoid the dismemberment caused by taking out certain practices from various festivals and grouping them under their probable origins, a method which would, moreover, be perilous in view of the very conjectural nature of the theories offered.

Before we pass to our procession of festivals, something must be said about the general nature and *rationale* of the customs associated with them. For convenience these customs may be divided into three groups :—

    I. *Sacrificial or Sacramental Practices.*
    II. *Customs connected with the Cult of the Dead and the Family Hearth.*
    III. *Omens and Charms for the New Year.*

Though these three classes overlap and it is sometimes difficult to place a given practice exclusively in one of them, they will form a useful framework for a brief account of the primitive ritual which survives at the winter festivals.

I. Sacrificial and Sacramental Practices.

To most people, probably, the word " sacrifice " suggests an offering, something presented to a divinity in order to obtain his favour. Such seems to have been the meaning generally given to sacrificial rites in Europe when Christianity came into conflict with paganism. It is, however, held by many scholars that the original purpose of sacrifice was sacramental—the partaking by the worshipper of the divine life, conceived of as present in the victim, rather than the offering of a gift to a divinity.33

The whole subject of sacred animals is obscure, and in regard, especially, to totemism—defined by Dr. Frazer 34 as " belief in the kinship of certain families with certain species of animals " and practices based upon that belief—the most divergent views are held by scholars. The religious significance which some have seen in totemistic customs is denied by others, while there is much disagreement as to the probability of their having been widespread in Europe. Still, whatever may be the truth about totemism, there is much that points to the sometime existence in Europe of sacrifices that were not offerings, but solemn feasts of communion in the flesh and blood of a worshipful animal.35 That the idea of sacrificial communion preceded the sacrifice-gift is suggested by the fact that in many customs which appear to be sacrificial survivals the body of the victim has some kind of sacramental efficacy ; it conveys a blessing to that which is brought into contact with it. The actual eating and drinking of the flesh and blood is the most perfect mode of contact, but the same end seems to have been aimed at in such customs as the sprinkling of worshippers with blood, the carrying of the victim in procession from house to house, the burying of flesh in furrows to make the crops grow, and the wearing of hides, heads, or horns of sacrificed beasts.36 We shall meet, during the Christmas season, with various practices that seem to have originated either in a sacrificial feast or in some such sacramental rites as have just been described. So peculiarly prominent are animal masks, apparently derived from hide-, head-, and horn-wearing, that we may dwell upon them a little at this point.

We have already seen how much trouble the Kalends custom of beast-masking gave the ecclesiastics. Its probable origin is thus suggested by Robertson Smith :—

" It is . . . appropriate that the worshipper should dress himself in the skin of a victim, and so, as it were, envelop himself in its sanctity. To rude nations dress is not merely a physical comfort, but a fixed part of social religion, a thing by which a man constantly bears on his body the token of his religion, and which is itself a charm and a means of divine protection. . . . When the dress of sacrificial skin, which at once declared a man's religion and his sacred kindred, ceased to be used in ordinary life, it was still retained in holy and especially in piacular functions ; . . . examples are afforded by the Dionysiac mysteries and other Greek rites, and by almost every rude religion ; while in later cults the old rite survives at least in the religious use of animal masks." * 37

If we accept the animal-worship and sacrificial communion theory, many a Christmas custom will carry us back in thought to a stage of religion far earlier than the Greek and Roman classics or the Celtic and Teutonic mythology of the conversion period : we shall be taken back to a time before men had come to have anthropomorphic gods, when they were not conscious of their superiority to the beasts of the field, but regarded these beings, mysterious in their actions, extraordinary in their powers, as incarnations of potent spirits. At this stage of thought, it would seem, there were as yet no definite divinities with personal names and characters, but the world was full of spirits immanent in animal or plant or chosen human being, and able to pass from one incarnation to another. Or indeed it may be that animal sacrifice originated at a stage of religion before the idea of definite "spirits" had arisen, when man was conscious rather of a vague force like the Melanesian *mana*, in himself and in almost everything, and "constantly trembling on the verge of personality." 38 "*Mana*" better than "god" or "spirit" may express that with which the partaker in the communal feast originally sought contact. "When you sacrifice," to quote some words of Miss Jane Harrison, "you build as it were a bridge between your *mana*, your will, your desire, which is weak and impotent, and

* Accounts of such maskings are to be found in innumerable books of travel. In *Folk-Lore*, June 30, 1911, Professor Edward Westermarck gives a particularly full and interesting description of Moroccan customs of this sort. He describes at length various masquerades in the skins and heads of beasts, accompanied often by the dressing-up of men as women and by gross obscenities.

NEW YEAR MUMMERS IN MANCHURIA.

An Asiatic example of animal masks.

To face p. 176.

that unseen outside *mana* which you believe to be strong and efficacious. In the fruits of the earth which grow by some unseen power there is much *mana* ; you want that *mana*. In the loud-roaring bull and the thunder is much *mana* ; you want that *mana*. It would be well to get some, to eat a piece of that bull raw, but it is dangerous, not a thing to do unawares alone ; so you consecrate the first-fruits, you sacrifice the bull and then in safety you—communicate." 39 "Sanctity"—the quality of awfulness and mystery—rather than divinity or personality, may have been what primitive man saw in the beasts and birds which he venerated in "their silent, aloof, goings, in the perfection of their limited doings." 40 When we use the word "spirit" in connection with the pagan sacramental practices of Christmastide, it is well to bear in mind the possibility that at the origin of these customs there may have been no notion of communion with strictly personal beings, but rather some such *mana* idea as has been suggested above.

It is probable that animal-cults had their origin at a stage of human life preceding agriculture, when man lived not upon cultivated plants or tamed beasts, but upon roots and fruits and the products of the chase. Some scholars, indeed, hold that the domestication of animals for practical use was an outcome of the sacred, inviolable character of certain creatures : they may originally have been spared not for reasons of convenience but because it was deemed a crime to kill them—except upon certain solemn occasions—and may have become friendly towards man through living by his side.41 On the other hand it is possible that totems were originally staple articles of food, that they were sacred because they were eaten with satisfaction, and that the very awe and respect attached to them because of their life-giving powers tended to remove them from common use and limit their consumption to rare ceremonial occasions.

Closely akin to the worship of animals is that of plants, and especially trees, and there is much evidence pointing to sacramental cults in connection with the plant-world.42 Some cakes and special vegetable dishes eaten on festal days may be survivals of sacramental feasts parallel to those upon the flesh and blood of an animal victim. Benediction by external contact, again, is suggested by the widespread use in various ways of branches or sprigs or whole trees. The Christmas-tree and evergreen decorations are the most obvious examples; we shall see others in the course of our survey, and in connection with plants as well as with animals we shall meet with processions intended to convey a blessing to every house by carrying about the sacred elements— to borrow a term from Christian theology. Even the familiar practice of going carol-singing may be a Christianized form of some such perambulation.

It is possible that men and women had originally separate cults. The cult of animals, according to a theory set forth by Mr. Chambers, would at first belong to the men, who as hunters worshipped the beasts they slew, apologizing to them, as some primitive people do to-day, for the slaughter they were obliged to commit. Other animals, apparently, were held too sacred to be slain, except upon rare and solemn occasions, and hence, as we have seen, may have arisen domestication and the pastoral life which, with its religious rites, was the affair of the men. To women, on the other hand, belonged agriculture; the cult of Mother Earth and the vegetation-spirits seems to have been originally theirs. Later the two cults would coalesce, but a hint of the time when certain rites were practised only by women may be found in that dressing up of men in female garments which appears not merely in the old Kalends customs but in some modern survivals.* 43

Apart from any special theory of the origin of sacrifice, we may note the association at Christmas of physical feasting with religious rejoicing. In this the modern European is the heir of an agelong tradition. "Everywhere," says Robertson Smith,

---

* Another suggested explanation connects the change of clothes with rites of initiation at the passage from boyhood to manhood. "Manhood, among primitive peoples, seems to be envisaged as ceasing to be a woman. . . . Man is born of woman, reared of woman. When he passes to manhood, he ceases to be a woman-thing, and begins to exercise functions other and alien. That moment is one naturally of extreme peril ; he at once emphasizes it and disguises it. He wears woman's clothes." From initiation rites, according to this theory, the custom spread to other occasions when it was desirable to "change the luck." 44

"we find that a sacrifice ordinarily involves a feast, and that a feast cannot be provided without a sacrifice. For a feast is not complete without flesh, and in early times the rule that all slaughter is sacrifice was not confined to the Semites. The identity of religious occasions and festal seasons may indeed be taken as the determining characteristic of the type of ancient religion generally ; when men meet their god they feast and are glad together, and whenever they feast and are glad they desire that the god should be of the party." 45   To the paganism that preceded Christianity we must look for the origin of that Christmas feasting which has not seldom been a matter of scandal for the severer type of churchman.

A letter addressed in 601 by Pope Gregory the Great to Abbot Mellitus, giving him instructions to be handed on to Augustine of Canterbury, throws a vivid light on the process by which heathen sacrificial feasts were turned into Christian festivals. "Because," the Pope says of the Anglo-Saxons, "they are wont to slay many oxen in sacrifices to demons, some solemnity should be put in the place of this, so that on the day of the dedication of the churches, or the nativities of the holy martyrs whose relics are placed there, they may make for themselves tabernacles of branches of trees around those churches which have been changed from heathen temples, and may celebrate the solemnity with religious feasting. Nor let them now sacrifice animals to the Devil, but to the praise of God kill animals for their own eating, and render thanks to the Giver of all for their abundance ; so that while some outward joys are retained for them, they may more readily respond to inward joys. For from obdurate minds it is undoubtedly impossible to cut off everything at once, because he who strives to ascend to the highest place rises by degrees or steps and not by leaps." 46

We see here very plainly the mind of the ecclesiastical compromiser. Direct sacrifice to heathen gods the Church of course could not dream of tolerating ; it had been the very centre of her attack since the days of St. Paul, and refusal to take part in it had cost the martyrs their lives. Yet the festivity and merrymaking to which it gave occasion were to be left to the people, for a time at all events. The policy had its advantages, it made the Church festivals popular; but it had also its dangers, it encouraged the intrusion of a pagan fleshly element into their austere and chastened joys. A certain orgiastic licence crept in, an unbridling of the physical appetites, which has ever been a source of sorrow and anger to the most earnest Christians and even led the Puritans of the seventeenth century to condemn all festivals as diabolical.

Before we leave the subject of sacrificial survivals, it must be added that certain Christmas customs may come, little as those who practise them suspect it, from that darkest of religious rites, human sacrifice. Reference has already been made to Dr. Frazer's view of the Saturnalian king and his awful origin. We shall meet with various similar figures during the Christmas season—the " King of the Bean," for instance, and the " Bishop of Fools." If the theories about human sacrifice set forth in " The Golden Bough " be accepted, we may regard these personages as having once been mock kings chosen to suffer instead of the real kings, who had at first to perish by a violent death in order to preserve from the decay of age the divine life incarnate in them. Such mock monarchs, according to Dr. Frazer, were exalted for a brief season to the glory and luxury of kingship ere their doom fell upon them; [47] in the Christmas "kings" the splendour alone has survived, the dark side is forgotten.

II. The Cult of the Dead and the Family Hearth.

Round the winter festival cluster certain customs apparently connected with distinctively domestic religion, rather than with such public and communal cults as we have considered under the heading of Sacrifice and Sacrament. A festival of the family— that is, perhaps, what Christmas most prominently is to-day: it is the great season for gatherings "round the old fireside "; it is a joyous time for the children of the house, and the memory or the departed is vivid then, if unexpressed. Further, by the Yule log customs and certain other ceremonies still practised in the remoter corners of Europe, we are carried back to a stage of thought at which the dead were conceived as hovering about or visiting the abodes of the living. Ancestral spirits, it seems, were once believed to be immanent in the fire that burned on the hearth, and had to be propitiated with libations, while elsewhere the souls of the dead were thought to return to their old homes at the New Year, and meat and drink had to be set out for them. The Church's establishment of All Souls' Day did much to keep practices of tendance of the departed to early November, but sometimes these have wandered to later dates and especially to Christmas. In folk-practices directed towards the dead two tendencies are to be found : on the one hand affection or at all events consideration for the departed persists, and efforts are made to make them comfortable ; on the other, they are regarded with dread, and the sight of them is avoided by the living.

In the passage quoted from Caesarius of Arles there was mention of the laying of tables with abundance of food at the Kalends. The same practice is condemned by St. Jerome in the fifth century, and is by him specially connected with Egypt.48 He, like Caesarius and others, regards it as a kind of charm to ensure abundance during the coming year, but it is very possible that its real purpose was different, that the food was an offering to supernatural beings, the guardians and representatives of the dead.49 Burchardus of Worms in the early eleventh century says definitely that in his time tables were laid with food and drink and three knives for "those three Sisters whom the ancients in their folly called *Parcae*."50 The *Parcae* were apparently identified with the three " weird" Sisters known in England and in other Teutonic regions, and seem to have some connection with the fairies. As we shall see later on, it is still in some places the custom to lay out tables for supernatural beings, whether, as at All Souls' tide, explicitly for the dead, or for Frau Perchta, or for the Virgin or some other Christian figure. Possibly the name *Modranicht* (night of mothers), which Bede gives to Christmas Eve,51 may be connected with this practice.

Not remote, probably, in origin from a belief in "ghosts" is the driving away of spirits that sometimes takes place about

Christmas-time. Many peoples, as Dr. Frazer has shown, have
an annual expulsion of goblins, ghosts, devils, witches, and evil
influences, commonly at the end of the Old or beginning of the
New Year. Sometimes the beings so driven away are definitely
the spirits of the departed. An appalling racket and a great flare
of torches are common features of these expulsions, and we shall
meet with similar customs during the Christmas season. Such
purifications, according to Dr. Frazer, are often preceded or
followed by periods of licence, for when the burden of evil is
about to be, or has just been, removed, it is felt that a little
temporary freedom from moral restraints may be allowed with
impunity.[52] Hence possibly, in part, the licence which has often
attended the Christmas season.

III. Omens and Charms for the New Year.

Customs of augury are to be met with at various dates, which
may mark the gradual shifting of the New Year festival from
early November to January 1, while actual charms to secure
prosperity are commonest at Christmas itself or at the modern
New Year. Magical rather than religious in character, they are
attempts to discover or influence the future by a sort of crude
scientific method based on supposed analogies. Beneath the
charms lie the primitive ideas that like produces like and that
things which have once been in contact continue to act upon one
another after they are separated in space.[53] The same ideas
obviously underlie many of the sacramental practices alluded to a
few pages back, and these are often of the nature of charms.
Probably, too, among New Year charms should be included such
institutions as the bonfires on Hallowe'en in Celtic countries, on
Guy Fawkes Day in England, and at Martinmas in Germany,
for it would seem that they are intended to secure by imitation
a due supply of sunshine.[54] The principle that " well begun
is well ended "—or, as the Germans have it, " *Anfang gut, alles
gut* "—is fundamental in New Year practices : hence the custom
of giving presents as auguries of wealth during the coming year ;
hence perhaps partly the heavy eating and drinking—a kind of
charm to ensure abundance.

PRE-CHRISTIAN WINTER FESTIVALS

Enough has already been said about the attitude of the early Church towards traditional folk-customs. Of the position taken up by the later mediaeval clergy we get an interesting glimpse in the "Largum Sero" of a certain monk Alsso of Brěvnov, an account of Christmas practices in Bohemia written about the year 1400. It supplies a link between modern customs and the Kalends prohibitions of the Dark Ages. Alsso tells of a number of laudable Christmas Eve practices, gives elaborate Christian interpretations of them, and contrasts them with things done by bad Catholics with ungodly intention. Here are some of his complaints :—

Presents, instead of being given, as they should be, in memory of God's great Gift to man, are sent because he who does not give freely will be unlucky in the coming year. Money, instead of being given to the poor, as is seemly, is laid on the table to augur wealth, and people open their purses that luck may enter. Instead of using fruit as a symbol of Christ the Precious Fruit, men cut it open to predict the future [probably from the pips]. It is a laudable custom to make great white loaves at Christmas as symbols of the True Bread, but evil men set out such loaves that the gods may eat of them.

Alsso's assumption is that the bad Catholics are diabolically perverting venerable Christmas customs, but there can be little doubt that precisely the opposite was really the case—the Christian symbolism was merely a gloss upon pagan practices. In one instance Alsso admits that the Church had adopted and transformed a heathen usage : the old *calendisationes* or processions with an idol Bel had been changed into processions of clergy and choir-boys with the crucifix. Round the villages on the Eve and during the Octave of Christmas went these messengers of God, robed in white raiment as befitted the servants of the Lord of purity ; they would chant joyful anthems of the Nativity, and receive in return some money from the people—they were, in fact, carol-singers. Moreover with their incense they would drive out the Devil from every corner.55

Alsso's attitude is one of compromise, or at least many of the old heathen customs are allowed by him, when reinterpreted in a

Christian sense. Such seems to have been the general tendency of the later Catholic Church, and also of Anglicanism in so far as it continued the Catholic tradition. It will be seen, however, from what has already been said, that the English Puritans were but following early Christian precedents when they attacked the paganism that manifested itself at Christmas.

A strong Puritan onslaught is to be found in the "Anatomie of Abuses" by the Calvinist, Philip Stubbes, first published in 1583. "Especially," he says, "in Christmas tyme there is nothing els vsed but cardes, dice, tables, maskyng, mumming, bowling, and suche like fooleries; and the reason is, that they think they haue a commission and prerogatiue that tyme to doe what they list, and to followe what vanitie they will. But (alas!) doe they thinke that they are preuiledged at that time to doe euill? The holier the time is (if one time were holier than an other, as it is not), the holier ought their exercises to bee. Can any tyme dispence with them, or giue them libertie to sinne? No, no; the soule which sinneth shall dye, at what tyme soeuer it offendeth. . . . Notwithstandyng, who knoweth not that more mischeef is that tyme committed than in all the yere besides?" [56]

When the Puritans had gained the upper hand they proceeded to the suppression not only of abuses, but of the festival itself. An excellent opportunity for turning the feast into a fast—as the early Church had done, it will be remembered, with the Kalends festival—came in 1644. In that year Christmas Day happened to fall upon the last Wednesday of the month, a day appointed by the Lords and Commons for a Fast and Humiliation. In its zeal against carnal pleasures Parliament published the following "Ordinance for the better observation of the Feast of the Nativity of Christ" :—

"Whereas some doubts have been raised whether the next Fast shall be celebrated, because it falleth on the day which, heretofore, was usually called the Feast of the Nativity of our Saviour; the lords and commons do order and ordain that public notice be given, that the Fast appointed to be kept on the last Wednesday in every month, ought to be observed until it be otherwise ordered by both houses;

and that this day particularly is to be kept with the more solemn humiliation because it may call to remembrance our sins and the sins of our forefathers, who have turned this Feast, pretending the memory of Christ, into an extreme forgetfulness of him, by giving liberty to carnal and sensual delights ; being contrary to the life which Christ himself led here upon earth, and to the spiritual life of Christ in our souls ; for the sanctifying and saving whereof Christ was pleased both to take a human life, and to lay it down again."[57]

But the English people's love of Christmas could not be destroyed. "These poor simple creatures are made after superstitious festivals, after unholy holidays," said a speaker in the House of Commons. "I have known some that have preferred Christmas Day before the Lord's Day," said Calamy in a sermon to the Lords in Westminster Abbey, "I have known those that would be sure to receive the Sacrament on Christmas Day though they did not receive it all the year after. This was the superstition of this day, and the profaneness was as great. There were some that did not play cards all the year long, yet they must play at Christmas." Various protests were made against the suppression of the festival. Though Parliament sat every Christmas Day from 1644 to 1656, the shops in London in 1644 were all shut, and in 1646 the people who opened their shops were so roughly used that next year they petitioned Parliament to protect them in future. In 1647 the shops were indeed all closed, but evergreen decorations were put up in the City, and the Lord Mayor and City Marshal had to ride about setting fire to them. There were even riots in country places, notably at Canterbury. With the Restoration Christmas naturally came back to full recognition, though it may be doubted whether it has ever been quite the same thing since the Puritan Revolution.[58]

Protestantism, in proportion to its thoroughness and the strength of its Puritan elements, has everywhere tended to destroy old pagan traditions and the festivals to which they cling. Calvinism has naturally been more destructive than Lutheranism, which in the Scandinavian countries has left standing many of the externals of Catholicism and also many Christmas customs that are purely pagan, while in Germany it has tolerated and even hallowed the ritual of the Christmas-tree. But more powerful than religious influences, in rooting out the old customs, have been modern education and the growth of modern industry, breaking up the old traditional country life, and putting in its place the mobile, restless life of the great town. Many of the customs we shall have to consider belong essentially to the country, and have no relation to the life of the modern city. When communal in their character, a man could not perform them in separation from his rustic neighbours. Practices domestic in their purpose may indeed be transferred to the modern city, but it is the experience of folk-lorists that they seldom descend to the second generation.

It is in regions like Bavaria, Tyrol, Styria, or the Slav parts of the Austrian Empire, or Roumania and Servia, that the richest store of festival customs is to be found nowadays. Here the old agricultural life has been less interfered with, and at the same time the Church, whether Roman or Greek, has succeeded in keeping modern ideas away from the people and in maintaining a popular piety that is largely polytheistic in its worship of the saints, and embodies a great amount of traditional paganism. In our half-suburbanized England but little now remains of these vestiges of primitive religion and magic whose interest and importance were only realized by students in the later nineteenth century, when the wave of "progress" was fast sweeping them away.

Old traditions have a way of turning up unexpectedly in remote corners, and it is hard to say for certain that any custom is altogether extinct ; every year, however, does its work of destruction, and it may well be that some of the practices here described in the present tense have passed into the Limbo of discarded things.

CHAPTER VII

ALL HALLOW TIDE
TO MARTINMAS

CHAPTER VII

ALL HALLOW TIDE TO MARTINMAS

All Saints' and All Souls' Days, their Relation to a New Year Festival—All Souls' Eve and Tendance of the Departed—Soul Cakes in England and on the Continent—Pagan Parallels of All Souls'—Hallowe'en Charms and Omens—Hallowe'en Fires—Guy Fawkes Day—" Old Hob," the *Schimmelreiter,* and other Animal Masks—Martinmas and its Slaughter—Martinmas Drinking—St. Martin's Fires in Germany—Winter Visitors in the Low Countries and Germany—St. Martin as Gift-bringer—St. Martin's Rod.

All Saints' and All Souls' Days.

In the reign of Charles I. the young gentlemen of the Middle Temple were accustomed to reckon All Hallow Tide (November 1) the beginning of Christmas.[1] We may here do likewise and start our survey of winter festivals with November, in the earlier half of which, apparently, fell the Celtic and Teutonic New Year's Days. It is impossible to fix precise dates, but there is reason for thinking that the Celtic year began about November 1,*[2] and the Teutonic about November 11.[3]

On November 1 falls one of the greater festivals of the western Church, All Saints'—or, to give it its old English name, All Hallows'—and on the morrow is the solemn commemoration of the departed—All Souls'. In these two anniversaries the Church has

* According to Sir John Rhys, in the Isle of Man *Hollantide* (November 1, Old Style, therefore November 12) is still to-day the beginning of a new year. But the ordinary calendar is gaining ground, and some of the associations of the old New Year's Day are being transferred to January 1, the Roman date. "In Wales this must have been decidedly helped by the influence of Roman rule and Roman ideas ; but even there the adjuncts of the Winter Calends have never been wholly transferred to the Calends of January."[4]

preserved at or near the original date one part of the old beginning-of-winter festival—the part concerned with the cult of the dead. Some of the practices belonging to this side of the feast have been transferred to the season of Christmas and the Twelve Days, but these have often lost their original meaning, and it is to All Souls' Day that we must look for the most conscious survivals of that care for the departed which is so marked a feature of primitive religion. Early November, when the leaves are falling, and all around speaks of mortality, is a fitting time for the commemoration of the dead.

The first clear testimony to All Souls' Day is found at the end of the tenth century, and in France. All Saints' Day, however, was certainly observed in England, France, and Germany in the eighth century,[5] and probably represents an attempt on the part of the Church to turn the minds of the faithful away from the pagan belief in and tendance of " ghosts " to the contemplation of the saints in the glory of Paradise. It would seem that this attempt failed, that the people needed a way of actually doing something for their own dead, and that All Souls' Day with its solemn Mass and prayers for the departed was intended to supply this need and replace the traditional practices.[6] Here again the attempt was only partly successful, for side by side with the Church's rites there survived a number of usages related not to any Christian doctrine of the after-life, but to the pagan idea, widespread among many peoples, that on one day or night of the year the souls of the dead return to their old homes and must be entertained.

All Souls' Day then appeals to instincts older than Christianity. How strong is the hold of ancient custom even upon the sceptical and irreligious is shown very strikingly in Roman Catholic countries : even those who never go to church visit the graves of their relations on All Souls' Eve to deck them with flowers.

The special liturgical features of the Church's celebration are the Vespers, Matins, and Lauds of the Dead on the evening of November 1, and the solemn Requiem Mass on November 2, with the majestic " Dies irae " and the oft-recurrent versicle, " Requiem aeternam dona eis, Domine, et lux perpetua luceat eis," that most beautiful of prayers. The priest and altar are vested in black, and a catafalque with burning tapers round it stands in the body of the church. For the popular customs on the Eve we may quote Dr. Tylor's general description :—

> " In Italy the day is given to feasting and drinking in honour of the dead, while skulls and skeletons in sugar and paste form appropriate children's toys. In Tyrol, the poor souls released from purgatory fire for the night may come and smear their burns with the melted fat of the ' soul light ' on the hearth, or cakes are left for them on the table, and the room is kept warm for their comfort. Even in Paris the souls of the departed come to partake of the food of the living. In Brittany the crowd pours into the churchyard at evening, to kneel barefoot at the grave of dead kinsfolk, to fill the hollow of the tombstone with holy water, or to pour libations of milk upon it. All night the church bells clang, and sometimes a solemn procession of the clergy goes round to bless the graves. In no household that night is the cloth removed, for the supper must be left for the souls to come and take their part, nor must the fire be put out, where they will come to warm themselves. And at last, as the inmates retire to rest, there is heard at the door a doleful chant—it is the souls, who, borrowing the voices of the parish poor, have come to ask the prayers of the living." [7]

To this may be added some further accounts of All Souls' Eve as the one night in the year when the spirits of the departed are thought to revisit their old homes.

In the Vosges mountains while the bells are ringing in All Souls' Eve it is a custom to uncover the beds and open the windows in order that the poor souls may enter and rest. Prayer is made for the dead until late in the night, and when the last " De profundis " has been said " the head of the family gently covers up the beds, sprinkles them with holy water, and shuts the windows." [8]

The Esthonians on All Souls' Day provide a meal for the dead and invite them by name. The souls arrive at the first cock-crow and depart at the second, being lighted out of the house by the head of the family, who waves a white cloth after them and bids them come again next year. [9]

In Brittany, as we have seen, the dead are thought to return at

this season. It is believed that on the night between All Saints'
and All Souls' the church is lighted up and the departed attend a
nocturnal Mass celebrated by a phantom priest. All through the
week, in one district, people are afraid to go out after nightfall lest
they should see some dead person.[10] In Tyrol it is believed that
the " poor souls " are present in the howling winds that often blow
at this time.[11]

In the Abruzzi on All Souls' Eve " before people go to sleep
they place on the table a lighted lamp or candle and a frugal meal
of bread and water. The dead issue from their graves and stalk
in procession through every street of the village. . . . First pass
the souls of the good, and then the souls of the murdered and
the damned." [12]

In Sicily a strange belief is connected with All Souls' Day
(*jornu di li morti*) : the family dead are supposed, like Santa
Klaus in the North, to bring presents to children ; the dead
relations have become the good fairies of the little ones. On the
night between November 1 and 2 little Sicilians believe that the
departed leave their dread abode and come to town to steal from
rich shopkeepers sweets and toys and new clothes. These they
give to their child relations who have been " good " and have
prayed on their behalf. Often they are clothed in white and
wear silken shoes, to elude the vigilance of the shopkeepers.
They do not always enter the houses ; sometimes the presents are
left in the children's shoes put outside doors and windows. In the
morning the pretty gifts are attributed by the children to the
morti in whose coming their parents have taught them to
believe.[13]

A very widespread custom at this season is to burn candles,
perhaps in order to lighten the darkness for the poor souls. In
Catholic Ireland candles shine in the windows on the Vigil
of All Souls',[14] in Belgium a holy candle is burnt all night,
or people walk in procession with lighted tapers, while in
many Roman Catholic countries, and even in the Protestant
villages of Baden, the graves are decked with lights as well as
flowers.[15]

Another practice on All Saints' and All Souls' Days, curiously common formerly in Protestant England, is that of making and giving "soul-cakes." These and the quest of them by children were customary in various English counties and in Scotland.[16] The youngsters would beg not only for the cakes but also sometimes for such things as "apples and strong beer," presumably to make a "wassail-bowl" of "lambswool," hot spiced ale with roast apples in it.[17] Here is a curious rhyme which they sang in Shropshire as they went round to their neighbours, collecting contributions :—

> "Soul ! soul ! for a soul-cake !
> I pray, good missis, a soul-cake !
> An apple or pear, a plum or a cherry,
> Any good thing to make us merry.
> One for Peter, two for Paul,
> Three for Him who made us all.
> Up with the kettle, and down with the pan,
> Give us good alms, and we'll be gone."[18]

Shropshire is a county peculiarly rich in "souling" traditions, and one old lady had cakes made to give away to the souling-children up to the time of her death in 1884. At that period the custom of "souling" had greatly declined in the county, and where it still existed the rewards were usually apples or money. Grown men, as well as children, sometimes went round, and the ditties sung often contained verses of good-wishes for the household practically identical with those sung by wassailers at Christmas.[19]

The name "soul-cake" of course suggests that the cakes were in some way associated with the departed, whether given as a reward for prayers for souls in Purgatory, or as a charity for the benefit of the "poor souls," or baked that the dead might feast upon them.* It seems most probable that they were relics of a feast once laid out for the souls. On the other hand it is just possible that they were originally a sacrament of the corn-spirit.

* In Burne and Jackson's "Shropshire Folk-Lore" (p. 305 f.) there are details about cakes and other doles given to the poor at funerals. These probably had the same origin as the November "soul-cakes."

PAGAN SURVIVALS

A North Welsh tradition recorded by Pennant may conceivably have preserved a vague memory of some agricultural connection : he tells us that on receiving soul-cakes the poor people used to pray to God to bless the next crop of wheat.[20]

Not in Great Britain alone are soul-cakes found ; they are met with in Belgium, southern Germany, and Austria. In western Flanders children set up on All Souls' Eve little street altars, putting a crucifix or Madonna with candles on a chair or stool, and begging passers-by for money "for cakes for the souls in Purgatory." On All Souls' morning it is customary, all over the Flemish part of Belgium, to bake little cakes of finest white flour, called "soul-bread." They are eaten hot, and a prayer is said at the same time for the souls in Purgatory. It is believed that a soul is delivered for every cake eaten. At Antwerp the cakes are coloured yellow with saffron to suggest the Purgatorial flames. In southern Germany and Austria little white loaves of a special kind are baked ; they are generally oval in form, and are usually called by some name into which the word "soul" enters. In Tyrol they are given to children by their godparents ; those for the boys have the shape of horses or hares, those for the girls, of hens. In Tyrol the cakes left over at supper remain on the table and are said to "belong to the poor souls."[21]

In Friuli in the north-east of Italy there is a custom closely corresponding to our "soul-cakes." On All Souls' Day every family gives away a quantity of bread. This is not regarded as a charity ; all the people of the village come to receive it and before eating it pray for the departed of the donor's family. The most prosperous people are not ashamed to knock at the door and ask for this *pane dei morti*.[22]

In Tyrol All Souls' is a day of licensed begging, which has become a serious abuse. A noisy rabble of ragged and disorderly folk, with bags and baskets to receive gifts, wanders from village to village, claiming as a right the presents of provisions that were originally a freewill offering for the benefit of the departed, and angrily abusing those who refuse to give.[23]

The New Year is the time for a festival of the dead in many parts of the world.[24] I may quote Dr. Frazer's account of what goes on in Tonquin ; it shows a remarkable likeness to some European customs * :—

"In Tonquin, as in Sumba, the dead revisit their kinsfolk and their old homes at the New Year. From the hour of midnight, when the New Year begins, no one dares to shut the door of his house for fear of excluding the ghosts, who begin to arrive at that time. Preparations have been made to welcome and refresh them after their long journey. Beds and mats are ready for their weary bodies to repose upon, water to wash their dusty feet, slippers to comfort them, and canes to support their feeble steps."[25]

In Lithuania, the last country in Europe to be converted to Christianity, heathen traditions lingered long, and sixteenth-and seventeenth-century travellers give accounts of a pagan New Year's feast which has great interest. In October, according to one account, on November 2, according to another, the whole family met together, strewed the tables with straw and put sacks on the straw. Bread and two jugs of beer were then placed on the table, and one of every kind of domestic animal was roasted before the fire after a prayer to the god Zimiennik (possibly an ancestral spirit), asking for protection through the year and offering the animals. Portions were thrown to the corners of the room with the words "Accept our burnt sacrifice, O Zimiennik, and kindly partake thereof." Then followed a great feast. Further, the spirits of the dead were invited to leave their graves and visit the bath-house, where platters of food were spread out and left for three days. At the end of this time the remains of the repast were set out over the graves and libations poured.[26]

The beginning of November is not solely a time of memory of the dead ; customs of other sorts linger, or until lately used to linger, about it, especially in Scotland, northern England, Ireland, Cornwall, Wales, and the West Midlands. One may conjecture that these are survivals from the Celtic New Year's Day, for most of them are of the nature of omens or charms. Apples and nuts are prominent on Hallowe'en, the Eve of All

* Cf. pp. 191–2 and 235–6 of this volume.

Saints ;* they may be regarded either as a kind of sacrament or
the vegetation-spirit, or as simply intended by homoeopathic magic
to bring fulness and fruitfulness to their recipients. A custom
once common in the north of England [27] and in Wales [28] was to
catch at apples with the mouth, the fruit being suspended on a
string, or on one end of a large transverse beam with a lighted
candle at the other end. In the north apples and nuts were the
feature of the evening feast, hence the name " Nutcrack night." [29]

Again, at St. Ives in Cornwall every child is given a big apple
on Allhallows' Eve—" Allan Day " as it is called. [30] Nuts and
apples were also used as means of forecasting the future. In
Scotland for instance nuts were put into the fire and named
after particular lads and lasses. " As they burn quietly together
or start from beside one another, the course and issue of the
courtship will be." [31] On Hallowe'en in Nottinghamshire if a
girl had two lovers and wanted to know which would be the
more constant, she took two apple-pips, stuck one on each cheek
(naming them after her lovers) and waited for one to fall off.
The poet Gay alludes to this custom :—

> " See from the core two kernels now I take,
>   This on my cheek for Lubberkin is worn,
>   And Booby Clod on t'other side is borne ;
>   But Booby Clod soon falls upon the ground,
>   A certain token that his love's unsound ;
>   While Lubberkin sticks firmly to the last ;
>   Oh ! were his lips to mine but joined so fast." [32]

In Nottinghamshire apples are roasted and the parings thrown
over the left shoulder. " Notice is taken of the shapes which the
parings assume when they fall to the ground. Whatever letter
a paring resembles will be the initial letter of the Christian name
of the man or woman whom you will marry." [33]

* The prominence of " Eves " in festival customs is a point specially to be noticed ;
it is often to them rather than to the actual feast days that old practices cling. This
is perhaps connected with the ancient Celtic and Teutonic habit of reckoning by nights
instead of days—a trace of this is left in our word "fortnight "—but it must be
remembered that the Church encouraged the same tendency by her solemn services on
the Eves of festivals, and that the Jewish Sabbath begins on Friday evening.

HALLOWE'EN

Hallowe'en is indeed in the British Isles the favourite time for forecasting the future, and various methods are employed for this purpose.

A girl may cross her shoes upon her bedroom floor in the shape of a **T** and say these lines :—

> "I cross my shoes in the shape of a **T**,
> Hoping this night my true love to see,
> Not in his best or worst array,
> But in the clothes of every day."

Then let her get into bed backwards without speaking any more that night, and she will see her future husband in her dreams.[34]

"On All Hallowe'en or New Year's Eve," says Mr. W. Henderson, "a Border maiden may wash her sark, and hang it over a chair to dry, taking care to tell no one what she is about. If she lie awake long enough, she will see the form of her future spouse enter the room and turn the sark. We are told of one young girl who, after fulfilling this rite, looked out of bed and saw a coffin behind the sark ; it remained visible for some time and then disappeared. The girl rose up in agony and told her family what had occurred, and the next morning she heard of her lover's death." [35]

In Scotland [36] and Ireland [37] other methods of foreseeing the future are practised on Hallowe'en ; we need not consider them here, for we shall have quite enough of such auguries later on. (Some Scottish customs are introduced by Burns into his poem "Hallowe'en.") I may, however, allude to the custom formerly prevalent in Wales for women to congregate in the church on this "Night of the Winter Kalends," in order to discover who of the parishioners would die during the year.[38] East of the Welsh border, at Dorstone in Herefordshire, there was a belief that on All Hallows' Eve at midnight those who were bold enough to look through the windows would see the church lighted with an unearthly glow, and Satan in monk's habit fulminating anathemas from the pulpit and calling out the names of those who were to render up their souls.[39]

PAGAN SURVIVALS

Again, there are numerous Hallowe'en fire customs, probably sun-charms for the New Year, a kind of homoeopathic magic intended to assist the sun in his struggle with the powers of darkness. To this day great bonfires are kindled in the Highlands, and formerly brands were carried about and the new fire was lit in each house.[40] It would seem that the Yule log customs (see Chapter X.) are connected with this new lighting of the house-fire, transferred to Christmas.

In Ireland fire was lighted at this time at a place called Tlachtga, from which all the hearths in Ireland are said to have been annually supplied.[41] In Wales the habit of lighting bonfires on the hills is perhaps not yet extinct.[42] Within living memory when the flames were out somebody would raise the cry, " May the tailless black sow seize the hindmost," and everyone present would run for his life.[43] This may point to a former human sacrifice, possibly of a victim laden with the accumulated evils of the past year.[44]

In North Wales, according to another account, each family used to make a great bonfire in a conspicuous place near the house. Every person threw into the ashes a white stone, marked ; the stones were searched for in the morning, and if any one were missing the person who had thrown it in would die, it was believed, during the year.[45] The same belief and practice were found at Callander in Perthshire.[46]

Though, probably, the Hallowe'en fire rites had originally some connection with the sun, the conscious intention of those who practised them in modern times was often to ward off witchcraft. With this object in one place the master of the family used to carry a bunch of burning straw about the corn, in Scotland the red end of a fiery stick was waved in the air, in Lancashire a lighted candle was borne about the fells, and in the Isle of Man fires were kindled.[47]

GUY FAWKES DAY.

Probably the burning of Guy Fawkes on November 5 is a survival of a New Year bonfire. There is every reason to think that the commemoration of the deliverance from " gunpowder treason and plot" is but a modern meaning attached to an ancient traditional practice, for the burning of the effigy has many parallels in folk-custom. Dr. Frazer [48] regards such effigies as representatives of the spirit of vegetation—by burning them in a fire that represented the sun men thought they secured sunshine for trees and crops. Later, when the ideas on which the custom was based had faded away, people came to identify these images with persons whom they regarded with aversion, such as Judas Iscariot, Luther (in Catholic Tyrol), and, apparently, Guy Fawkes in England. At Ludlow in Shropshire, it is interesting to note, if any well-known local man had aroused the enmity of the populace his effigy was substituted for, or added to, that of Guy Fawkes. Bonfire Day at Ludlow is marked by a torchlight procession and a huge conflagration.[49] At Hampstead the Guy Fawkes fire and procession are still in great force. The thing has become a regular carnival, and on a foggy November night the procession along the steep curving Heath Street, with the glare of the torches lighting up the faces of dense crowds, is a strangely picturesque spectacle.*

ANIMAL MASKS.

On All Souls' Day in Cheshire there began to be carried about a curious construction called "Old Hob," a horse's head enveloped in a sheet ; it was taken from door to door, and accompanied by the singing of begging rhymes.[50] Old Hob, who continued to appear until Christmas, is an English parallel to the German *Schimmel* or white horse. We have here to do with one of those strange animal forms which are apparently relics of sacrificial customs. They come on various days in the winter festival season, and also at other times, and may as well be considered at this point. In some cases they are definitely imitations of animals, and may have replaced real sacrificial beasts taken about in procession, in others they are simply men wearing the head, horn, hide, or tail of a beast, like the worshippers at many

---

* Attempts are being made to suppress the November carnival at Hampstead, and perhaps the 1911 celebration may prove to have been the last.

a heathen sacrifice to-day. (Of the *rationale* of masking something has already been said in Chapter VI.)

The mingling of Roman and non-Roman customs makes it very hard to separate the different elements in the winter festivals. In regard particularly to animal masks it is difficult to pronounce in favour of one racial origin rather than another ; we may, however, infer with some probability that when a custom is attached not to Christmas or the January Kalends but to one of the November or early December feasts, it is not of Roman origin. For, as the centuries have passed, Christmas and the Kalends— the Roman festivals ecclesiastical and secular—have increasingly tended to supplant the old northern festal times, and a transference of, for instance, a Teutonic custom from Martinmas to Christmas or January 1, is far more conceivable than the attraction of a Roman practice to one of the earlier and waning festivals.

Let us take first the horse-forms, seemingly connected with that sacrificial use of the horse among the Teutons to which Tacitus and other writers testify.[51] "Old Hob" is doubtless one form of the hobby horse, so familiar in old English festival customs. His German parallel, the *Schimmel*, is mostly formed thus in the north : a sieve with a long pole to whose end a horse's head is fastened, is tied beneath the chest of a young man, who goes on all fours, and some white cloths are thrown over the whole. In Silesia the *Schimmel* is formed by three or four youths. The rider is generally veiled, and often wears on his head a pot with glowing coals shining forth through openings that represent eyes and a mouth.[52] In Pomerania the thing is called simply *Schimmel*,[53] in other parts emphasis is laid upon the rider, and the name *Schimmelreiter* is given. Some mythologists have seen in this rider on a white horse an impersonation of Woden on his great charger ; but it is more likely that the practice simply originated in the taking round of a real sacrificial horse.[54] The *Schimmelreiter* is often accompanied by a "bear," a youth dressed in straw who plays the part of a bear tied to a pole.[55] He may be connected with some such veneration of the animal as is suggested by the custom still surviving at Berne, of keeping bears at the public expense.

To return to Great Britain, here is an account of a so-called

ANIMAL MASKS

"hodening" ceremony once performed at Christmas-time at Ramsgate : "A party of young people procure the head of a dead horse, which is affixed to a pole about four feet in length, a string is tied to the lower jaw, a horse-cloth is then attached to the whole, under which one of the party gets, and by frequently pulling the string keeps up a loud snapping noise and is accompanied by the rest of the party grotesquely habited and ringing hand-bells. They thus proceed from house to house, sounding their bells and singing carols and songs." [56]

Again, in Wales a creature called "the Mari Llwyd" was known at Christmas. A horse's skull is "dressed up with ribbons, and supported on a pole by a man who is concealed under a large white cloth. There is a contrivance for opening and shutting the jaws, and the figure pursues and bites everybody it can lay hold of, and does not release them except on payment of a fine." [57] The movable jaws here give the thing a likeness to certain Continental figures representing other kinds of animals and probably witnessing to their former sacrificial use. On the island of Usedom appears the *Klapperbock*, a youth who carries a pole with the hide of a buck thrown over it and a wooden head at the end. The lower jaw moves up and down and clatters, and he charges at children who do not know their prayers by heart. [58] In Upper Styria we meet the *Habergaiss*. Four men hold on to one another and are covered with white blankets. The foremost one holds up a wooden goat's head with a movable lower jaw that rattles, and he butts children. [59] At Ilsenburg in the Harz is found the *Habersack*, formed by a person taking a pole ending in a fork, and putting a broom between the prongs so that the appearance of a head with horns is obtained. The carrier is concealed by a sheet. [60]

In connection with horns we must not forget the "horndance" at Abbots Bromley in Staffordshire, held now in September, but formerly at Christmas. Six of the performers wear sets of horns kept from year to year in the church. [61] Plot, in his "Natural History of Staffordshire" (1686, p. 434) calls it a "*Hobby-horse Dance* from a person who carried the image of a horse between his legs, made of thin boards." [62]

PAGAN SURVIVALS

In Denmark, Sweden, and Norway creatures resembling both the *Schimmelreiter* and the *Klapperbock* are or were to be met with at Christmas. The name *Julebuk* (yule buck) is used for various objects : sometimes for a person dressed up in hide and horns, or with a buck's head, who " goes for " little boys and girls ; sometimes for a straw puppet set up or tossed about from hand to hand ; sometimes for a cake in the form of a buck. People seem to have had a bad conscience about these things, for there are stories connecting them with the Devil. A girl, for instance, who danced at midnight with a straw *Julebuk*, found that her partner was no puppet but the Evil One himself. Again, a fellow who had dressed himself in black and put horns on his head, claws on his hands, and fiery tow in his mouth, was carried off by the Prince of Darkness whose form he had mimicked.[63] The association of animal maskings with the infernal powers is doubtless the work of the Church. To the zealous missionary the old heathen ritual was no mere foolish superstition but a service of intensely real and awful beings, the very devils of hell, and one may even conjecture that the traditional Christian devil-type, half animal half human, was indirectly derived from skin-clad worshippers at pagan festivals.

MARTINMAS.

Between All Souls' Day and Martinmas (November 11) there are no folk-festivals of great importance, though on St. Hubert's Day, November 3, in Flemish Belgium special little cakes are made, adorned with the horn of the saint, the patron of hunting, and are eaten not only by human beings but by dogs, cats, and other domestic animals.[64] The English Guy Fawkes Day has already been considered, while November 9, Lord Mayor's Day, the beginning of the municipal year, may remind us of the old Teutonic New Year.

Round Martinmas popular customs cluster thickly, as might be expected, since it marks as nearly as possible the date of the old beginning-of-winter festival, the feast perhaps at which Germanicus surprised the Marsi in A.D. 14.[65]

The most obvious feature of Martinmas is its physical feasting.

MARTINMAS

Economic causes, as we saw in Chapter VI., must have made the middle of November a great killing season among the old Germans, for the snow which then began rendered it impossible longer to pasture the beasts, and there was not fodder enough to keep the whole herd through the winter. Thus it was a time of feasting on flesh, and of animal sacrifices, as is suggested by the Anglo-Saxon name given to November by Bede, *Blot-monath*, sacrifice-month.[66]

Christmas does not seem to have quickly superseded the middle of November as a popular feast in Teutonic countries ; rather one finds an outcome of the conciliatory policy pursued by Gregory the Great (see Chapter VI.) in the development of Martinmas. Founded in the fifth century, it was made a great Church festival by Pope Martin I. (649–654),[67] and it may well have been intended to absorb and Christianize the New Year festivities of the Teutonic peoples. The veneration of St. Martin spread rapidly in the churches of northern Europe, and he came to be regarded as one of the very chief of the saints.[68] His day is no longer a Church feast of high rank, but its importance as a folk festival is great.

The tradition of slaughter is preserved in the British custom of killing cattle on St. Martin's Day—" Martlemas beef " [69]—and in the German eating of St. Martin's geese and swine.[70] The St. Martin's goose, indeed, is in Germany as much a feature of the festival as the English Michaelmas goose is of the September feast of the angels.

In Denmark too a goose is eaten at Martinmas, and from its breast-bone the character of the coming winter can be foreseen. The white in it is a sign of snow, the brown of very great cold. Similar ideas can be traced in Germany, though there is not always agreement as to what the white and the brown betoken.[71]

At St. Peter's, Athlone, Ireland, a very obviously sacrificial custom lasted on into the nineteenth century. Every household would kill an animal of some kind, and sprinkle the threshold with its blood. A cow or sheep, a goose or turkey, or merely a cock or hen, was used according to the means of the family.[72] It seems that the animal was actually offered to St. Martin, apparently as the successor of some god, and bad luck came if the custom were not observed.   Probably these rites were transferred to Martinmas from the old Celtic festival of *Samhain*.   Again, in a strange Irish legend the saint himself is said to have been cut up and eaten in the form of an ox.73

In the wine-producing regions of Germany Martinmas was the day for the first drinking of the new wine, and the feasting in general on his day gave the saint the reputation of a guzzler and a glutton ; it even became customary to speak of a person who had squandered his substance in riotous living as a *Martinsmann*.74 As we have seen survivals of sacrifice in the Martinmas slaughter, so we may regard the *Martinsminne* or toast as originating in a sacrifice of liquor.75   In the Böhmerwald it is believed that wine taken at Martinmas brings strength and beauty, and the lads and girls gather in the inns to drink, while a common German proverb runs :—

> " Heb an Martini,
> Trink Wein per circulum anni." * 76

Here, by the way, is a faint suggestion that Martinmas is regarded as the beginning of the year ; as such it certainly appears in a number of legal customs, English, French, and German, which existed in the Middle Ages and in some cases in quite recent times.   It was often at Martinmas that leases ended, rents had to be paid, and farm-servants changed their places.77

There is a survival, perhaps, of a cereal sacrifice or sacrament in the so-called " Martin's horns," horseshoe pastries given at Martinmas in many parts of Germany.78   Another kind of sacrifice is suggested by a Dutch custom of throwing baskets of fruit into Martinmas bonfires, and by a German custom of casting in empty fruit-baskets.79   In Venetia the peasants keep over from the vintage a few grapes to form part of their Martinmas supper, and as far south as Sicily it is considered essential to taste the new wine at this festival.80

Bonfires appear at Martinmas in Germany, as at All Hallows tide in the British Isles.   On St. Martin's Eve in the Rhine

---

* " Raise the glass at Martinmas, drink wine all through the year."

MARTINMAS

Valley between Cologne and Coblentz, numbers of little fires burn on the heights and by the river-bank,[81] the young people leap through the flames and dance about them, and the ashes are strewn on the fields to make them fertile.[82] Survivals of fire-customs are found also in other regions. In Belgium, Holland, and north-west Germany processions of children with paper or turnip lanterns take place on St. Martin's Eve. In the Eichsfeld district the little river Geislede glows with the light of candles placed in floating nutshells. Even the practice of leaping through the fire survives in a modified form, for in northern Germany it is not uncommon for people on St. Martin's Day or Eve to jump over lighted candles set on the parlour floor.[83] In the fifteenth century the Martinmas fires were so many that the festival actually got the name of *Funkentag* (Spark Day).[84]

On St. Martin's Eve in Germany and the Low Countries we begin to meet those winter visitors, bright saints and angels on the one hand, mock-terrible bogeys and monsters on the other, who add so much to the romance and mystery of the children's Christmas. Such visitors are to be found in many countries, but it is in the lands of German speech that they take on the most vivid and picturesque forms. St. Martin, St. Nicholas, Christ-kind, Knecht Ruprecht, and the rest are very real and personal beings to the children, and are awaited with pleasant expectation or mild dread. Often they are beheld not merely with the imagination but with the bodily eye, when father or friend is wondrously transformed into a supernatural figure.

What are the origins of these holy or monstrous beings? It is hard to say with certainty, for many elements, pagan and Christian, seem here to be closely blended. It is pretty clear, however, that the grotesque half-animal shapes are direct relics of heathendom, and it is highly probable that the forms of saints or angels—even, perhaps, of the Christ Child Himself—represent attempts of the Church to transform and sanctify alien things which she could not suppress. What some of these may have been we shall tentatively guess as we go along. Though no grown-up person would take the mimic Martin or Nicholas

205

seriously nowadays, there seem to be at the root of them things once regarded as of vital moment. Just as fairy-tales, originally serious attempts to explain natural facts, have now become reading for children, so ritual practices which our ancestors deemed of vast importance for human welfare have become mere games to amuse the young.

On St. Martin's Eve, to come back from speculation to the facts of popular custom, the saint appears in the nurseries of Antwerp and other Flemish towns. He is a man dressed up as a bishop, with a pastoral staff in his hand. His business is to ask if the children have been " good," and if the result of his inquiries is satisfactory he throws down apples, nuts, and cakes. If not, it is rods that he leaves behind. At Ypres he does not visibly appear, but children hang up stockings filled with hay, and next morning find presents in them, left by the saint in gratitude for the fodder provided for his horse. He is there imagined as a rider on a white horse, and the same conception prevails in Austrian Silesia, where he brings the " Martin's horns " already mentioned.[85] In Silesia when it snows at Martinmas people say that the saint is coming on his white horse, and there, it may be noted, the *Schimmelreiter* appears at the same season.[86] In certain respects, it has been suggested, St. Martin may have taken the place of Woden.[87] It is perhaps not without significance that, like the god, he is a military hero, and conceived as a rider on horseback. At Düsseldorf he used to be represented in his festival procession by a man riding on another fellow's back.[88]

At Mechlin and other places children go round from house to house, singing and collecting gifts. Often four boys with paper caps on their heads, dressed as Turks, carry a sort of litter whereon St. Martin sits. He has a long white beard of flax and a paper mitre and stole, and holds a large wooden spoon to receive apples and other eatables that are given to the children, as well as a leather purse for offerings of money.[89]

In the Ansbach region a different type of being used to appear —Pelzmärten (Skin Martin) by name ; he ran about and frightened the children, before he threw them their apples and nuts. In several places in Swabia, too, Pelzmärte was known ;

he had a black face, a cow-bell hung on his person, and he distributed blows as well as nuts and apples.[90] In him there is obviously more of the pagan mummer than the Christian bishop.

In Belgium St. Martin is chiefly known as the bringer of apples and nuts for children ; in Bavaria and Austria he has a different aspect : a *gerte* or rod, supposed to promote fruitfulness among cattle and prosperity in general, is connected with his day. The rods are taken round by the neatherds to the farmers, and one is given to each—two to rich proprietors ; they are to be used, when spring comes, to drive out the cattle for the first time. In Bavaria they are formed by a birch-bough with all the leaves and twigs stripped off—except at the top, to which oak-leaves and juniper-twigs are fastened. At Etzendorf a curious old rhyme shows that the herdsman with the rod is regarded as the representative of St. Martin.[91]

Can we connect this custom with the saint who brings presents to youngsters ? * There seems to be a point of contact when we note that at Antwerp St. Martin throws down rods for naughty children as well as nuts and apples for good ones, and that Pelzmärte in Swabia has blows to bestow as well as gifts. St. Martin's main functions—and, as we shall see, St. Nicholas has the same—are to beat the bad children and reward the good with apples, nuts, and cakes. Can it be that the ethical distinction is of comparatively recent origin, an invention perhaps for children when the customs came to be performed solely for their benefit, and that the beating and the gifts were originally shared by all alike and were of a sacramental character ? We shall meet with more whipping customs later on, they are common enough in folk-ritual, and are not punishments, but kindly services ; their purpose is to drive away evil influences, and to bring to the flogged one the life-giving virtues of the tree from which the twigs or boughs are taken.[92] Both the flogging and the eating of fruit may, indeed, be means of contact with the vegetation-spirit, the one in

---

* It is interesting to note that in the Italian province of Venetia, as well as in more northerly regions, Martinmas is especially a children's feast. In the sweetshops are sold little sugar images of the saint on horseback with a long sword, and in Venice itself children go about singing, playing on tambourines, and begging for money.[93]

an external, the other in a more internal way. Or possibly the rod and the fruit may once have been conjoined, the beating being performed with fruit-laden boughs in order to produce prosperity. It is noteworthy that at Etzendorf so many head of cattle and loads of hay are augured for the farmer as there are juniper-*berries* and twigs on St. Martin's *gerte*.94

Attempts to account for the figures of SS. Martin and Nicholas in northern folk-customs have been made along various lines. Some scholars regard them as Christianizations of the pagan god Woden ; but they might also be taken as akin to the "first-foots" whom we shall meet on January 1—visitors who bring good luck—or as maskers connected with animal sacrifices (Pelzmärte suggests this), or again as related to the Boy Bishop, the Lord of Misrule and the Twelfth Night King. May I suggest that some at least of their aspects could be explained on the supposition that they represent administrants of primitive vegetation sacraments, and that these administrants, once ordinary human beings, have taken on the name and attributes of the saint who under the Christian dispensation presides over the festival ? In any case it is a strange irony of history that around the festival of Martin of Tours, the zealous soldier of Christ and deadly foe of heathenism, should have gathered so much that is unmistakably pagan.

CHAPTER VIII

ST. CLEMENT TO
ST. THOMAS

CHAPTER VIII

ST. CLEMENT TO ST. THOMAS

St. Clement's Day.

The next folk-feast after Martinmas is St. Clement's Day, November 23, once reckoned the first day of winter in England.[1] It marks apparently one of the stages in the progress of the winter feast towards its present solstitial date. In England some interesting popular customs existed on this day. In Staffordshire children used to go round to the village houses begging for gifts, with rhymes resembling in many ways the " souling " verses I have already quoted. Here is one of the Staffordshire " clemencing " songs :—

> "Clemany! Clemany! Clemany mine!
> A good red apple and a pint of wine,
> Some of your mutton and some of your veal,
> If it is good, pray give me a deal ;
> If it is not, pray give me some salt.
> Butler, butler, fill your bowl ;
> If thou fill'st it of the best,
> The Lord'll send your soul to rest ;
> If thou fill'st it of the small,
> Down goes butler, bowl and all,

PAGAN SURVIVALS

Pray, good mistress, send to me
One for Peter, one for Paul,
One for Him who made us all ;
Apple, pear, plum, or cherry,
Any good thing to make us merry ;
A bouncing buck and a velvet chair,
Clement comes but once a year ;
Off with the pot and on with the pan,
A good red apple and I'll be gone." [2]

In Worcestershire on St. Clement's Day the boys chanted
similar rhymes, and at the close of their collection they would
roast the apples received and throw them into ale or cider.[3]   In
the north of England men used to go about begging drink, and at
Ripon Minster the choristers went round the church offering
everyone a rosy apple with a sprig of box on it.[4]   The Cambridge bakers held their annual supper on this day,[5] at Tenby
the fishermen were given a supper,[6] while the blacksmiths'
apprentices at Woolwich had a remarkable ceremony, akin perhaps
to the Boy Bishop customs.   One of their number was chosen
to play the part of " Old Clem," was attired in a great coat,
and wore a mask, a long white beard, and an oakum wig.   Seated
in a large wooden chair, and surrounded by attendants bearing
banners, torches, and weapons, he was borne about the town
on the shoulders of six men, visiting numerous public-houses
and the blacksmiths and officers of the dockyard.   Before him he
had a wooden anvil, and in his hands a pair of tongs and a wooden
hammer, the insignia of the blacksmith's trade.[7]

St. Catherine's Day.

November 25 is St. Catherine's Day, and at Woolwich Arsenal
a similar ceremony was then performed : a man was dressed in
female attire, with a large wheel by his side to represent the saint,
and was taken round the town [8] in a wooden chair.   At Chatham
there was a torchlight procession on St. Catherine's Day, and a
woman in white muslin with a gilt crown was carried about in a
chair.   She was said to represent not the saint, but Queen
Catherine.[9]

ST. CATHERINE'S DAY

St. Catherine's Day was formerly a festival for the lacemakers of Northamptonshire, Buckinghamshire, and Bedfordshire. She was the patroness of spinsters in the literal as well as the modern sense of the word, and at Peterborough the workhouse girls used to go in procession round the city on her day, dressed in white with coloured ribbons; the tallest was chosen as Queen and bore a crown and sceptre. As they went to beg money of the chief inhabitants they sang a quaint ballad which begins thus :—

> "Here comes Queen Catherine, as fine as any queen,
> With a coach and six horses a-coming to be seen,
> And a-spinning we will go, will go, will go,
> And a-spinning we will go." [10]

We may perhaps see in this Saint or Queen Catherine a female counterpart of the Boy Bishop, who began his career on St. Nicholas's Day. Catherine, it must be remembered, is the patron saint of girls as Nicholas is of boys. In Belgium her day is still a festival for the "young person" both in schools and in families.[11] Even in modern Paris the dressmaker-girls celebrate it, and in a very charming way, too.

"At midday the girls of every workroom present little mob-caps trimmed with yellow ribbons to those of their number who are over twenty-five and still unmarried. Then they themselves put on becoming little caps with yellow flowers and yellow ribbons and a sprig of orange blossom on them, and out they go arm-in-arm to parade the streets and collect a tribute of flowers from every man they meet. . . . Instead of working all the afternoon, the midinettes entertain all their friends (no men admitted, though, for it is the day of St. Catherine) to concerts and even to dramatic performances in the workrooms, where the work-tables are turned into stages, and the employers provide supper." [12]

St. Andrew's Day.

The last day of November is the feast of St. Andrew. Of English customs on this day the most interesting perhaps are those connected with the " Tander " or " Tandrew " merry-makings of the Northamptonshire lacemakers. A day of general licence used to end in masquerading. Women went about in male attire and men and boys in female dress.[13] In Kent and Sussex squirrel-hunting was practised on this day [14]—a survival apparently of some old sacrificial custom comparable with the hunting of the wren at Christmas (see Chapter XII.).

In Germany St. Andrew's Eve is a great occasion for prognostications of the future. Indeed, like Hallowe'en in Great Britain, *Andreasabend* in Germany seems to have preserved the customs of augury connected with the old November New Year festival.[15] To a large extent the practices are performed by girls anxious to know what sort of husband they will get. Many and various are the methods.

Sometimes it suffices to repeat some such rhyme as the following before going to sleep, and the future husband will appear in a dream :—

> " St. Andrew's Eve is to-day,
> Sleep all people,
> Sleep all children of men,
> Who are between heaven and earth,
> Except this only man,
> Who may be mine in marriage." [16]

Again, at nightfall let a girl shut herself up naked in her bedroom, take two beakers, and into one pour clear water, into the other wine. These let her place on the table, which is to be covered with white, and let the following words be said :—

> " My dear St. Andrew !
> Let now appear before me
> My heart's most dearly beloved.
> If he shall be rich,
> He will pour a cup of wine ;
> If he is to be poor,
> Let him pour a cup of water."

This done, the form of the future husband will enter and drink of one of the cups. If he is poor, he will take the water ; if rich, the wine.[17]

One of the most common practices is to pour molten lead or tin through a key into cold water, and to discover the calling of the future husband by the form it takes, which will represent the tools of his trade. The white of an egg is sometimes used for the same purpose.[18] Another very wide-spread custom is to put nutshells to float on water with little candles burning in them. There are twice as many shells as there are girls present ; each girl has her shell, and to the others the names of possible suitors are given. The man and the girl whose shells come together will marry one another. Sometimes the same method is practised with little cups of silver foil.[19]

On the border of Saxony and Bohemia, a maiden who wishes to know the bodily build of her future husband goes in the darkness to a stack of wood and draws out a piece. If the wood is smooth and straight the man will be slim and well built ; if it is crooked, or knotted, he will be ill-developed or even a hunchback.[20]

These are but a few of the many ways in which girls seek to peer into the future and learn something about the most important event in their lives. Far less numerous, but not altogether absent on this night, are other kinds of prognostication. A person, for instance, who wishes to know whether he will die in the coming year, must on St. Andrew's Eve before going to bed make on the table a little pointed heap of flour. If by the morning it has fallen asunder, the maker will die.[21]

The association of St. Andrew's Eve with the foreseeing of the future is not confined to the German race ; it is found also on Slavonic and Roumanian ground. In Croatia he who fasts then will behold his future wife in a dream,[22] and among the Roumanians mothers anxious about their children's luck break small sprays from fruit-trees, bind them together in bunches, one for each child, and put them in a glass of water. The branch of the lucky one will blossom.[23]

In Roumania St. Andrew's Eve is a creepy time, for on it vampires are supposed to rise from their graves, and with coffins on their heads walk about the houses in which they once lived. Before nightfall every woman takes some garlic and anoints with it the door locks and window casements ; this will keep away the vampires. At the cross-roads there is a great fight of these loathsome beings until the first cock crows ; and not only the dead take part in this, but also some living men who are vampires from their birth. Sometimes it is only the souls of these living vampires that join in the fight ; the soul comes out through the mouth in the form of a bluish flame, takes the shape of an animal, and runs to the crossway. If the body meanwhile is moved from its place the person dies, for the soul cannot find its way back.[24]

St. Andrew's Day is sometimes the last, sometimes the first important festival of the western Church's year. It is regarded in parts of Germany as the beginning of winter, as witness the saying :—

> " Sünten-Dres-Misse,
> es de Winter gewisse." * [25]

The nights are now almost at their longest, and as November passes away, giving place to the last month of the year, Christmas is felt to be near at hand.

In northern Bohemia it is customary for peasant girls to keep for themselves all the yarn they spin on St. Andrew's Eve, and the *Hausfrau* gives them also some flax and a little money. With this they buy coffee and other refreshments for the lads who come to visit the parlours where in the long winter evenings the women sit spinning. These evenings, when many gather together in a brightly lighted room and sing songs and tell stories while they spin, are cheerful enough, and spice is added by the visits of the village lads, who in some places come to see the girls home.[26]

THE KLÖPFELNÄCHTE.

On the Thursday nights in Advent it is customary in southern Germany for children or grown-up people to go from house

* " At St. Andrew's Mass winter is certain."

to house, singing hymns and knocking on the doors with rods
or little hammers, or throwing peas, lentils, and the like against
the windows. Hence these evenings have gained the name of
Klöpfel or *Knöpflinsnächte* (Knocking Nights).[27] The practice is
described by Naogeorgus in the sixteenth century :—

> "Three weekes before the day whereon was borne the Lord ot
>> Grace,
> And on the Thursdaye Boyes and Girles do runne in every
>> place,
> And bounce and beate at every doore, with blowes and lustie snaps,
> And crie, the Advent of the Lorde not borne as yet perhaps.
> And wishing to the neighbours all, that in the houses dwell,
> A happie yeare, and every thing to spring and prosper well :
> Here have they peares, and plumbs, and pence, ech man gives
>> willinglee,
> For these three nightes are alwayes thought, unfortunate to bee ;
> Wherein they are afrayde of sprites and cankred witches' spight,
> And dreadfull devils blacke and grim, that then have chiefest
>> might." [28]

With it may be compared the Macedonian custom for village
boys to go in parties at nightfall on Christmas Eve, knocking at
the cottage doors with sticks, shouting *Kolianda ! Kolianda !* and
receiving presents,[29] and also one in vogue in Holland between
Christmas and the Epiphany. There "the children go out in
couples, each boy carrying an earthenware pot, over which a
bladder is stretched, with a piece of stick tied in the middle.
When this stick is twirled about, a not very melodious grumbling
sound proceeds from the contrivance, which is known by the
name of 'Rommelpot.' By going about in this manner the
children are able to collect some few pence." [30]

Can such practices have originated in attempts to drive out evil
spirits from the houses by noise ? Similar methods are used for
that purpose by various European and other peoples.[31] Anyhow
something mysterious hangs about the *Klöpfelnächte*. They are
occasions for girls to learn about their future husbands, and
upon them in Swabia goes about Pelzmärte, whom we already
know.[32]

PAGAN SURVIVALS

In Tyrol curious mummeries are then performed. At Piller-see in the Lower Innthal two youths combine to form a mimic ass, upon which a third rides, and they are followed by a motley train. The ass falls sick and has to be cured by a "vet," and all kinds of satirical jokes are made about things that have happened in the parish during the year. Elsewhere two men dress up in straw as husband and wife, and go out with a masked company. The pair wrangle with one another and carry on a play of wits with the peasants whose house they are visiting. Sometimes the satire is so cutting that permanent enmities ensue, and for this reason the practice is gradually being dropped.33

St. Nicholas's Day.

On December 6 we reach the most distinctive children's festival of the whole year, St. Nicholas's Day. In England it has gone out of mind, and in the flat north of Germany Protestantism has largely rooted it out, as savouring too much of saint-worship, and transferred its festivities to the more Evangelical season of Christmas.34 In western and southern Germany, however, and in Austria, Switzerland, and the Low Countries, it is still a day of joy for children, though in some regions even there its radiance tends to pale before the greater glory of the Christmas-tree.

It is not easy either to get at the historic facts about St. Nicholas, the fourth-century bishop of Myra in Asia Minor, or to ascertain why he became the patron saint of boys. The legends of his infant piety and his later wondrous works for the benefit of young people may either have given rise, or be them-selves due to, his connection with children.35 In eastern Europe and southern Italy he is above all things the saint of seafaring men, and among the Greeks his cult has perhaps replaced that of Artemis as a sea divinity.36 This aspect of him does not, how-ever, appear in the German festival customs with which we are here chiefly concerned.

It has already been hinted that in some respects St. Nicholas is a duplicate of St. Martin. His feast, indeed, is probably a later beginning-of-winter festival, dating from the period when improved methods of agriculture and other causes made early December, rather than mid-November, the time for the great annual slaughter and its attendant rejoicings. Like St. Martin he brings sweet things for the good children and rods for the bad.

St. Nicholas's Eve is a time of festive stir in Holland and Belgium ; the shops are full of pleasant little gifts : many-shaped biscuits, gilt gingerbreads, sometimes representing the saint, sugar images, toys, and other trifles. In many places, when evening comes on, people dress up as St. Nicholas, with mitre and pastoral staff, enquire about the behaviour of the children, and if it has been good pronounce a benediction and promise them a reward next morning. Before they go to bed the children put out their shoes, with hay, straw, or a carrot in them for the saint's white horse or ass. When they wake in the morning, if they have been " good " the fodder is gone and sweet things or toys are in its place ; if they have misbehaved themselves the provender is untouched and no gift but a rod is there.37

In various parts of Germany, Switzerland, and Austria St. Nicholas is mimed by a man dressed up as a bishop.38 In Tyrol children pray to the saint on his Eve and leave out hay for his white horse and a glass of *schnaps* for his servant. And he comes in all the splendour of a church-image, a reverend grey-haired figure with flowing beard, gold-broidered cope, glittering mitre, and pastoral staff. Children who know their catechism are rewarded with sweet things out of the basket carried by his servant ; those who cannot answer are reproved, and St. Nicholas points to a terrible form that stands behind him with a rod—the hideous Klaubauf, a shaggy monster with horns, black face, fiery eyes, long red tongue, and chains that clank as he moves.39

In Lower Austria the saint is followed by a similar figure called Krampus or Grampus ;40 in Styria this horrible attendant is named Bartel ; 41 all are no doubt related to such monsters as the *Klapperbock* (see Chapter VII.). Their heathen origin is evident though it is difficult to trace their exact pedigree. Sometimes St. Nicholas himself appears in a non-churchly form like Pelzmärte, with a bell,42 or with a sack of ashes which gains him the name of Aschenklas.43

PAGAN SURVIVALS

Not only by hideous figures is St. Nicholas attended. Sometimes, as at Warnsdorf near Rumburg, there come with him the forms of Christ Himself, St. Peter, an angel, and the famous Knecht Ruprecht, whom we shall meet again on Christmas Eve. They are represented by children, and a little drama is performed, one personage coming in after the other and calling for the next in the manner of the English mummers' play. St. Nicholas, St. Peter, and Ruprecht accuse the children of all kinds of naughtiness, the "Heiliger Christ" intercedes and at last throws nuts down and receives money from the parents.44 In Tyrol there are St. Nicholas plays of a more comic nature, performed publicly by large companies of players and introducing a number of humorous characters and much rude popular wit.45

Sometimes a female bogey used to appear: Budelfrau in Lower Austria, Berchtel in Swabia, Buzebergt in the neighbourhood of Augsburg.46 The last two are plainly variants of Berchte, who is specially connected with the Epiphany. Berchtel used to punish the naughty children with a rod, and reward the good with nuts and apples; Buzebergt wore black rags, had her face blackened and her hair hanging unkempt, and carried a pot of starch which she smeared upon people's faces.47

As Santa Klaus St. Nicholas is of course known to every English child, but rather as a sort of incarnation of Christmas than as a saint with a day of his own. Santa Klaus, probably, has come to us *viâ* the United States, whither the Dutch took him, and where he has still immense popularity.

In the Middle Ages in England as elsewhere the Eve of St. Nicholas was a day of great excitement for boys. It was then that the small choristers and servers in cathedral and other churches generally elected their "Boy Bishop" or "Nicholas."48 He had in some places to officiate at First Vespers and at the services on the festival itself. As a rule, however, the feast of the Holy Innocents, December 28, was probably the most important day in the Boy Bishop's career, and we may therefore postpone our consideration of him. We will here only note his connection with the festival of the patron saint of boys, a connection perhaps implying a common origin for him and for the St. Nicholases who in bishops' vestments make their present-giving rounds.

The festival of St. Nicholas is naturally celebrated with most splendour at the place where his body lies, the seaport of Bari in south-eastern Italy. The holy bones are preserved in a sepulchre beneath a crypt of rich Saracenic architecture, above which rises a magnificent church. Legend relates that in the eleventh century they were stolen by certain merchants of Bari from the saint's own cathedral at Myra in Asia Minor. The tomb of St. Nicholas is a famous centre for pilgrimages, and on the 6th of December many thousands of the faithful, bearing staves bound with olive and pine, visit it. An interesting ceremony on the festival is the taking of the saint's image out to sea by the sailors of the port. They return with it at nightfall, and a great procession escorts it back to the cathedral with torches and fireworks and chanting.49 Here may be seen the other, the seafaring, aspect of St. Nicholas ; by this mariners' cult we are taken far away from the present-giving saint who delights the small children of the North.

St. Lucia's Day.

The only folk-festivals of note between St. Nicholas's Day and Christmas are those of St. Lucia (December 13) and St. Thomas the Apostle (December 21).

In Sweden St. Lucia's Day was formerly marked by some interesting practices. It was, so to speak, the entrance to the Christmas festival, and was called "little Yule." 50 At the first cock-crow, between 1 and 4 a.m., the prettiest girl in the house used to go among the sleeping folk, dressed in a white robe, a red sash, and a wire crown covered with whortleberry-twigs and having nine lighted candles fastened in it. She awakened the sleepers and regaled them with a sweet drink or with coffee,* sang a special song, and was named "Lussi" or "Lussibruden" (Lucy bride). When everyone was dressed, breakfast was taken, the room being lighted by many candles. The domestic animals

---

* This custom may be compared with the Scotch eating of sowans in bed on Christmas morning (see Chapter XII.).

were not forgotten on this day, but were given special portions. A peculiar feature of the Swedish custom is the presence of lights on Lussi's crown.   Lights indeed are the special mark of the festival ; it was customary to shoot and fish on St. Lucy's Day by torchlight, the parlours, as has been said, were brilliantly illuminated in the early morning, in West Gothland Lussi went round the village preceded by torchbearers, and in one parish she was represented by a cow with a crown of lights on her head. In schools the day was celebrated with illuminations.[51]

What is the explanation of this feast of lights ? There is nothing in the legend of the saint to account for it ; her name, however, at once suggests *lux*—light. It is possible, as Dr. Feilberg supposes, that the name gave rise to the special use of lights among the Latin-learned monks who brought Christianity to Sweden, and that the custom spread from them to the common people. A peculiar fitness would be found in it because St. Lucia's Day according to the Old Style was the shortest day of the year, the turning-point of the sun's light.[52]

In Sicily also St. Lucia's festival is a feast of lights. After sunset on the Eve a long procession of men, lads, and children, each flourishing a thick bunch of long straws all afire, rushes wildly down the streets of the mountain village of Montedoro, as if fleeing from some danger, and shouting hoarsely. " The darkness of the night," says an eye-witness, " was lighted up by this savage procession of dancing, flaming torches, whilst bonfires in all the side streets gave the illusion that the whole village was burning." At the end of the procession came the image of Santa Lucia, holding a dish which contained her eyes.* In the midst of the *piazza* a great mountain of straw had been prepared ; on this everyone threw his own burning torch, and the saint was placed in a spot from which she could survey the vast bonfire.[53]

In central Europe we see St. Lucia in other aspects. In the Böhmerwald she goes round the village in the form of a nanny-goat with horns, gives fruit to the good children, and threatens to rip open the belly of the naughty. Here she is evidently related

---

* In a legend of the saint she is said to have plucked out her own eyes when their beauty caused a prince to seek to ravish her away from her convent.[54]

to the pagan monsters already described. In Tyrol she plays a more graceful part : she brings presents for girls, an office which St. Nicholas is there supposed to perform for boys only.55

In Lower Austria St. Lucia's Eve is a time when special danger from witchcraft is feared and must be averted by prayer and incense. A procession is made through each house to cense every room. On this evening, too, girls are afraid to spin lest in the morning they should find their distaffs twisted, the threads broken, and the yarn in confusion. (We shall meet with like superstitions during the Twelve Nights.) At midnight the girls practise a strange ceremony: they go to a willow-bordered brook, cut the bark of a tree partly away, without detaching it, make with a knife a cross on the inner side of the cut bark, moisten it with water, and carefully close up the opening. On New Year's Day the cutting is opened, and the future is augured from the markings found. The lads, on the other hand, look out at midnight for a mysterious light, the *Luzieschein*, the forms of which indicate coming events.56

In Denmark, too, St. Lucia's Eve is a time for seeing the future. Here is a prayer of Danish maids : " Sweet St. Lucy let me know : whose cloth I shall lay, whose bed I shall make, whose child I shall bear, whose darling I shall be, whose arms I shall sleep in." 57

St. Thomas's Day.

Many and various are the customs and beliefs associated with the feast of St. Thomas (December 21). In Denmark it was formerly a great children's day, unique in the year, and rather resembling the mediaeval Boy Bishop festival. It was the breaking-up day for schools ; the children used to bring their master an offering of candles and money, and in return he gave them a feast. In some places it had an even more delightful side: for this one day in the year the children were allowed the mastery in the school. Testimonials to their scholarship and industry were made out, and elaborate titles were added to their names, as exalted sometimes as " Pope," " Emperor," or " Empress." Poor children used to go about showing these documents and collecting money. Games and larks of all sorts went on in the schools without a word of reproof, and the children were wont to burn their master's rod.[58]

In the neighbourhood of Antwerp children go early to school on St. Thomas's Day, and lock the master out, until he promises to treat them with ale or other drink. After this they buy a cock and hen, which are allowed to escape and have to be caught by the boys or the girls respectively. The girl who catches the hen is called "queen," the boy who gets the cock, "king." Elsewhere in Belgium children lock out their parents, and servants their masters, while schoolboys bind their teacher to his chair and carry him over to the inn. There he has to buy back his liberty by treating his scholars with punch and cakes. Instead of the chase for the fowls, it was up to 1850 the custom in the Ardennes for the teacher to give the children hens and let them chop the heads off.[59] Some pagan sacrifice no doubt lies at the root of this barbarous practice, which has many parallels in the folk-lore of western and southern Europe.[60]

As for schoolboys' larks with their teachers, the custom of "barring out the master" existed in England, and was practised before Christmas[61] as well as at other times of the year, notably Shrove Tuesday. At Bromfield in Cumberland on Shrove Tuesday there was a regular siege, the school doors were strongly barricaded within, and the boy-defenders were armed with popguns. If the master won, heavy tasks were imposed, but if, as more often happened, he was defeated in his efforts to regain his authority, he had to make terms with the boys as to the hours of work and play.[62]

St. Thomas's Eve is in certain regions one of the uncanniest nights in the year. In some Bohemian villages the saint is believed to drive about at midnight in a chariot of fire. In the churchyard there await him all the dead men whose name is Thomas; they help him to alight and accompany him to the churchyard cross, which glows red with supernatural radiance. There St. Thomas kneels and prays, and then rises to bless his namesakes. This done, he vanishes beneath the cross, and each Thomas returns to his grave. The saint here seems to have taken over the character of some pagan god, who, like the Teutonic Odin or Woden, ruled the souls of the departed. In the houses the people listen with awe for the sound of his chariot, and when it is heard make anxious prayer to him for protection from all ill. Before retiring to rest the house-father goes to the cowhouse with holy water and consecrated salt, asperges it from without, and then entering, sprinkles every cow. Salt is also thrown on the head of each animal with the words, "St. Thomas preserve thee from all sickness." In the Böhmerwald the cattle are fed on this night with consecrated bayberries, bread, and salt, in order to avert disease.[63]

In Upper and Lower Austria St. Thomas's Eve is reckoned as one of the so-called *Rauchnächte* (smoke-nights) when houses and farm-buildings must be sanctified with incense and holy water, the other nights being the Eves of Christmas, the New Year, and the Epiphany.[64]

In Germany St. Thomas's, like St. Andrew's Eve, is a time for forecasting the future, and the methods already described are sometimes employed by girls who wish to behold their future husbands. A widely diffused custom is that of throwing shoes backwards over the shoulders. If the points are found turned towards the door the thrower is destined to leave the house during the year; if they are turned away from it another year will be spent there. In Westphalia a belief prevails that you must eat and drink heartily on this night in order to avert scarcity.[65]

In Lower Austria it is supposed that sluggards can cure themselves of oversleeping by saying a special prayer before they go to bed on St. Thomas's Eve, and in Westphalia in the mid-nineteenth century the same association of the day with slumber was shown by the schoolchildren's custom of calling the child who arrived last at school *Domesesel* (Thomas ass). In Holland, again, the person who lies longest in bed on St. Thomas's Day is greeted with shouts of "lazybones." Probably the fact that December 21 is the shortest day is enough to account for this.[66]

In England there was divination by means of "St. Thomas's onion." Girls used to peel an onion, wrap it in a handkerchief and put it under their heads at night, with a prayer to the saint

to show them their true love in a dream.[67]   The most notable
English custom on this day, however, was the peregrinations of
poor people begging for money or provisions for Christmas.   Going
" a-gooding," or " a-Thomassin,' " or " a-mumping," this was
called.   Sometimes in return for the charity bestowed a sprig of
holly or mistletoe was given.[68]   Possibly the sprig was originally
a sacrament of the healthful spirit of growth : it may be compared
with the olive- or cornel-branches carried about on New Year's
Eve by Macedonian boys,[69] and also with the St. Martin's rod
(see last chapter).

One more English custom on December 21 must be mentioned
—it points to a sometime sacrifice—the bull-baiting practised until
1821 at Wokingham in Berkshire.   Its abolition in 1822 caused
great resentment among the populace, although the flesh continued
to be duly distributed.[70]

We are now four days from the feast of the Nativity, and many
things commonly regarded as distinctive of Christmas have already
come under notice.   We have met, for instance, with several kinds
of present-giving, with auguries for the New Year, with processions
of carol-singers and well-wishers, with ceremonial feasting that
anticipates the Christmas eating and drinking, and with various
figures, saintly or monstrous, mimed or merely imagined, which
we shall find reappearing at the greatest of winter festivals.   These
things would seem to have been attracted from earlier dates to the
feast of the Nativity, and the probability that Christmas has borrowed much from an old November festival gradually shifted into
December, is our justification for having dwelt so long upon the
feasts that precede the Twelve Days.

CHAPTER IX

CHRISTMAS EVE AND THE TWELVE DAYS

CHRISTMAS EVE IN DEVONSHIRE—THE MUMMERS COMING IN.

To face p 229.

CHAPTER IX

CHRISTMAS EVE AND THE TWELVE DAYS

Christkind, Santa Klaus, and Knecht Ruprecht—Talking Animals and other Wonders of Christmas Eve—Scandinavian Beliefs about Trolls and the Return of the Dead—Traditional Christmas Songs in Eastern Europe—The Twelve Days, their Christian Origin and Pagan Superstitions—The Raging Host—Hints of Supernatural Visitors in England—The German *Frauen*—The Greek *Kallikantzaroi*.

CHRISTMAS EVE.

CHRISTMAS in the narrowest sense must be reckoned as beginning on the evening of December 24. Though Christmas Eve is not much observed in modern England, throughout the rest of Europe its importance so far as popular customs are concerned is far greater than that of the Day itself. Then in Germany the Christmas-tree is manifested in its glory; then, as in the England of the past, the Yule log is solemnly lighted in many lands; then often the most distinctive Christmas meal takes place.

We shall consider these and other institutions later; though they appear first on Christmas Eve, they belong more or less to the Twelve Days as a whole. Let us look first at the supernatural visitors, mimed by human beings, who delight the minds of children, especially in Germany, on the evening of December 24, and at the beliefs that hang around this most solemn night of the year.

First of all, the activities of St. Nicholas are not confined to his own festival; he often appears on Christmas Eve. We have already seen how he is attended by various companions, including

Christ Himself, and how he comes now vested as a bishop, now as a masked and shaggy figure. The names and attributes of the Christmas and Advent visitors are rather confused, but on the whole it may be said that in Protestant north Germany the episcopal St. Nicholas and his Eve have been replaced by Christmas Eve and the Christ Child, while the name Klas has become attached to various unsaintly forms appearing at or shortly before Christmas.

We can trace a deliberate substitution of the Christ Child for St. Nicholas as the bringer of gifts. In the early seventeenth century a Protestant pastor is found complaining that parents put presents in their children's beds and tell them that St. Nicholas has brought them. "This," he says, "is a bad custom, because it points children to the saint, while yet we know that not St. Nicholas but the holy Christ Child gives us all good things for body and soul, and He alone it is whom we ought to call upon." [1]

The ways in which the figure, or at all events the name, of Christ Himself, is introduced into German Christmas customs, are often surprising. The Christ Child, "Christkind," so familiar to German children, has now become a sort of mythical figure, a product of sentiment and imagination working so freely as almost to forget the sacred character of the original. Christkind bears little resemblance to the Infant of Bethlehem ; he is quite a tall child, and is often represented by a girl dressed in white, with long fair hair. He hovers, indeed, between the character of the Divine Infant and that of an angel, and is regarded more as a kind of good fairy than as anything else.

In Alsace the girl who represents Christkind has her face "made up" with flour, wears a crown of gold paper with lighted candles in it—a parallel to the headgear of the Swedish Lussi ; in one hand she holds a silver bell, in the other, a basket of sweetmeats. She is followed by the terrible Hans Trapp, dressed in a bearskin, with blackened face, long beard, and threatening rod. He "goes for" the naughty children, who are only saved by the intercession of Christkind.[2]

In the Mittelmark the name of *de hêle* (holy) *Christ* is strangely given to a skin- or straw-clad man, elsewhere called **Knecht** Ruprecht, Klas, or Joseph.3   In the Ruppin district a man dresses up in white with ribbons, carries a large pouch, and is called *Christmann* or *Christpuppe*.   He is accompanied by a *Schimmelreiter* and by other fellows who are attired as women, have blackened faces, and are named *Feien* (we may see in them a likeness to the Kalends maskers condemned by the early Church).   The procession goes round from house to house.   The *Schimmelreiter* as he enters has to jump over a chair ; this done, the *Christpuppe* is admitted.   The girls present begin to sing, and the *Schimmelreiter* dances with one of them.   Meanwhile the *Christpuppe* makes the children repeat some verse of Scripture or a hymn ; if they know it well, he rewards them with gingerbreads from his wallet ; if not, he beats them with a bundle filled with ashes. Then both he and the *Schimmelreiter* dance and pass on.   Only when they are gone are the *Feien* allowed to enter ; they jump wildly about and frighten the children.4

Knecht Ruprecht, to whom allusion has already been made, is a prominent figure in the German Christmas.   On Christmas Eve in the north he goes about clad in skins or straw and examines children ; if they can say their prayers perfectly he rewards them with apples, nuts and gingerbreads; if not, he punishes them.   In the Mittelmark, as we have seen, a personage corresponding to him is sometimes called " the holy Christ " ; in Mecklenburg he is "rû Klas" (rough Nicholas—note his identification with the saint) ; in Brunswick, Hanover, and Holstein " Klas," " Klawes," " Klas Bûr " and " Bullerklas " ; and in Silesia " Joseph."   Sometimes he wears bells and carries a long staff with a bag of ashes at the end — hence the name " Aschenklas " occasionally given to him.5   An ingenious theory connects this aspect of him with the *polaznik* of the Slavs, who on Christmas Day in Crivoscian farms goes to the hearth, takes up the ashes of the Yule log and dashes them against the cauldron-hook above so that sparks fly (see Chapter X.).6   As for the name " Ruprecht " the older mythologists interpreted it as meaning "shining with glory," *hruodperaht*, and identified its owner with the god Woden.7   Dr. Tille, however, regards him as dating only from the seventeenth century.⁸ It can hardly be said that any satisfactory account has as yet been given of the origins of this personage, or of his relation to St. Nicholas, Pelzmärte, and monstrous creatures like the *Klapperbock*.

In the south-western part of Lower Austria, both St. Nicholas— a proper bishop with mitre, staff, and ring—and Ruprecht appear on Christmas Eve, and there is quite an elaborate ceremonial. The children welcome the saint with a hymn ; then he goes to a table and makes each child repeat a prayer and show his lesson-books. Meanwhile Ruprecht in a hide, with glowing eyes and a long red tongue, stands at the door to overawe the young people. Each child next kneels before the saint and kisses his ring, whereupon Nicholas bids him put his shoes out-of-doors and look in them when the clock strikes ten. After this the saint lays on the table a rod dipped in lime, solemnly blesses the children, sprinkling them with holy water, and noiselessly departs. The children steal out into the garden, clear a space in the snow, and set out their shoes ; when the last stroke of ten has sounded they find them filled with nuts and apples and all kinds of sweet things.⁹

In the Troppau district of Austrian Silesia, three figures go round on Christmas Eve—Christkindel, the archangel Gabriel, and St. Peter—and perform a little play before the presents they bring are given. Christkindel announces that he has gifts for the good children, but the bad shall feel the rod. St. Peter complains of the naughtiness of the youngsters: they play about in the streets instead of going straight to school; they tear up their lesson-books and do many other wicked things. However, the children's mother pleads for them, and St. Peter relents and gives out the presents.¹⁰

In the Erzgebirge appear St. Peter and Ruprecht, who is clad in skin and straw, has a mask over his face, a rod, a chain round his body, and a sack with apples, nuts, and other gifts; and a somewhat similar performance is gone through.¹¹

If we go as far east as Russia we find a parallel to the girl Christkind in Kolyáda, a white-robed maiden driven about in a sledge from house to house on Christmas Eve. The young people who attended her sang carols, and presents were given them in return. *Kolydda* is the name for Christmas and appears to be derived from *Kalendae*, which probably entered the Slavonic languages by way of Byzantium. The maiden is one of those beings who, like the Italian Befana, have taken their names from the festival at which they appear.[12]

No time in all the Twelve Nights and Days is so charged with the supernatural as Christmas Eve. Doubtless this is due to the fact that the Church has hallowed the night of December 24–5 above all others in the year. It was to the shepherds keeping watch over their flocks *by night* that, according to the Third Evangelist, came the angelic message of the Birth, and in harmony with this is the unique Midnight Mass of the Roman Church, lending a peculiar sanctity to the hour of its celebration. And yet many of the beliefs associated with this night show a large admixture of paganism.

First, there is the idea that at midnight on Christmas Eve animals have the power of speech. This superstition exists in various parts of Europe, and no one can hear the beasts talk with impunity. The idea has given rise to some curious and rather grim tales. Here is one from Brittany :—

" Once upon a time there was a woman who starved her cat and dog. At midnight on Christmas Eve she heard the dog say to the cat, ' It is quite time we lost our mistress ; she is a regular miser. To-night burglars are coming to steal her money ; and if she cries out they will break her head.' ' 'Twill be a good deed,' the cat replied. The woman in terror got up to go to a neighbour's house ; as she went out the burglars opened the door, and when she shouted for help they broke her head." [13]

Again a story is told of a farm servant in the German Alps who did not believe that the beasts could speak, and hid in a stable on Christmas Eve to learn what went on. At midnight he heard surprising things. " We shall have hard work to do this day week," said one horse. " Yes, the farmer's servant is heavy," answered the other. " And the way to the churchyard is long and steep," said the first. The servant was buried that day week.[14]

PAGAN SURVIVALS

It may well have been the traditional association of the ox and ass with the Nativity that fixed this superstition to Christmas Eve, but the conception of the talking animals is probably pagan.

Related to this idea, but more Christian in form, is the belief that at midnight all cattle rise in their stalls or kneel and adore the new-born King. Readers of Mr. Hardy's " Tess " will remember how this is brought into a delightful story told by a Wessex peasant. The idea is widespread in England and on the Continent,[15] and has reached even the North American Indians. Howison, in his " Sketches of Upper Canada," relates that an Indian told him that " on Christmas night all deer kneel and look up to Great Spirit." [16] A somewhat similar belief about bees was held in the north of England : they were said to assemble on Christmas Eve and hum a Christmas hymn.[17] Bees seem in folk-lore in general to be specially near to humanity in their feelings.

It is a widespread idea that at midnight on Christmas Eve all water turns to wine. A Guernsey woman once determined to test this ; at midnight she drew a bucket from the well. Then came a voice :—

> "Toute l'eau se tourne en vin,
> Et tu es proche de ta fin."

She fell down with a mortal disease, and died before the end of the year. In Sark the superstition is that the water in streams and wells turns into blood, and if you go to look you will die within the year.[18]

There is also a French belief that on Christmas Eve, while the genealogy of Christ is being chanted at the Midnight Mass, hidden treasures are revealed.[19] In Russia all sorts of buried treasures are supposed to be revealed on the evenings between Christmas and the Epiphany, and on the eves of these festivals the heavens are opened, and the waters of springs and rivers turn into wine.[20]

Another instance of the supernatural character of the night is found in a Breton story of a blacksmith who went on working after the sacring bell had rung at the Midnight Mass. To him came a tall, stooping man with a scythe, who begged him to put in a nail. He did so ; and the visitor in return bade him send for a priest, for this work would be his last. The figure disappeared, the blacksmith felt his limbs fail him, and at cock-crow he died. He had mended the scythe of the *Ankou*—Death the reaper.[21]

In the Scandinavian countries simple folk have a vivid sense of the nearness of the supernatural on Christmas Eve. On Yule night no one should go out, for he may meet uncanny beings of all kinds. In Sweden the Trolls are believed to celebrate Christmas Eve with dancing and revelry. " On the heaths witches and little Trolls ride, one on a wolf, another on a broom or a shovel, to their assemblies, where they dance under their stones. . . . In the mount are then to be heard mirth and music, dancing and drinking. On Christmas morn, during the time between cock-crowing and daybreak, it is highly dangerous to be abroad." [22]

Christmas Eve is also in Scandinavian folk-belief the time when the dead revisit their old homes, as on All Souls' Eve in Roman Catholic lands. The living prepare for their coming with mingled dread and desire to make them welcome. When the Christmas Eve festivities are over, and everyone has gone to rest, the parlour is left tidy and adorned, with a great fire burning, candles lighted, the table covered with a festive cloth and plentifully spread with food, and a jug of Yule ale ready. Sometimes before going to bed people wipe the chairs with a clean white towel ; in the morning they are wiped again, and, if earth is found, some kinsman, fresh from the grave, has sat there. Consideration for the dead even leads people to prepare a warm bath in the belief that, like living folks, the kinsmen will want a wash before their festal meal.* Or again beds were made ready for them while the living slept on straw. Not always is it consciously the dead for whom these preparations are made, sometimes they are said to be for the Trolls and sometimes even for

* The bath-house in the old-fashioned Swedish farm is a separate building to which everyone repairs on Christmas Eve, but which is, or was, seldom used except on this one night of the year.[23]

the Saviour and His angels.[24]   (We may compare with this
Christian idea the Tyrolese custom of leaving some milk for the
Christ Child and His Mother[25] at the hour of Midnight Mass,
and a Breton practice of leaving food all through Christmas night
in case the Virgin should come.[26])

It is difficult to say how far the other supernatural beings—
their name is legion—who in Norway, Sweden, Denmark, and
Iceland are believed to come out of their underground hiding-places
during the long dark Christmas nights, were originally ghosts of
the dead.   Twenty years ago many students would have accounted
for them all in this way, but the tendency now is strongly against
the derivation of all supernatural beings from ancestor-worship.
Elves, trolls, dwarfs, witches, and other uncanny folk—the beliefs
about their Christmas doings are too many to be treated here ;
readers of Danish will find a long and very interesting chapter
on this subject in Dr. Feilberg's " Jul." [27]   I may mention just
one familiar figure of the Scandinavian Yule, Tomte Gubbe, a
sort of genius of the house corresponding very much to the
"drudging goblin" of Milton's "L'Allegro," for whom the
cream-bowl must be duly set.   He may perhaps be the spirit of
the founder of the family.   At all events on Christmas Eve
Yule porridge and new milk are set out for him, sometimes
with other things, such as a suit of small clothes, spirits, or
even tobacco.   Thus must his goodwill be won for the coming
year.[28]

In one part of Norway it used to be believed that on Christmas
Eve, at rare intervals, the old Norse gods made war on Christians, coming down from the mountains with great blasts of wind
and wild shouts, and carrying off any human being who might
be about.   In one place the memory of such a visitation was
preserved in the nineteenth century.   The people were preparing
for their festivities, when suddenly from the mountains came the
warning sounds.   "In a second the air became black, peals of
thunder echoed among the hills, lightning danced about the
buildings, and the inhabitants in the darkened rooms heard the
clatter of hoofs and the weird shrieks of the hosts of the
gods." [29]

CHRISTMAS EVE

The Scandinavian countries, Protestant though they are, have retained many of the outward forms of Catholicism, and the sign of the cross is often used as a protection against uncanny visitors. The cross—perhaps the symbol was originally Thor's hammer—is marked with chalk or tar or fire upon doors and gates, is formed of straw or other material and put in stables and cowhouses, or is smeared with the remains of the Yule candle on the udders of the beasts—it is in fact displayed at every point open to attack by a spirit of darkness.[30]

Christmas Eve is in Germany a time for auguries. Some of the methods already noted on other days are practised upon it—for instance the pouring of molten lead into water, the flinging of shoes, the pulling out of pieces of wood, and the floating of nut-shells—and there are various others which it might be tedious to describe.[31]

Among the southern Slavs if a girl wants to know what sort of husband she will get, she covers the table on Christmas Eve, puts on it a white loaf, a plate, and a knife, spoon, and fork, and goes to bed. At midnight the spirit of her future husband will appear and fling the knife at her. If it falls without injuring her she will get a good husband and be happy, but if she is hurt she will die early. There is a similar mode of divination for a young fellow. On Christmas Eve, when everybody else has gone to church, he must, naked and in darkness, sift ashes through a sieve. His future bride will then appear, pull him thrice by the nose, and go away.[32]

In eastern Europe Christmas, and especially Christmas Eve, is the time for the singing of carols called in Russian *Kolyádki*, and in other Slav countries by similar names derived from *Kalendae*.[33] More often than not these are without connection with the Nativity; sometimes they have a Christian form and tell of the doings of God, the Virgin and the saints, but frequently they are of an entirely secular or even pagan character. Into some the sun, moon, and stars and other natural objects are introduced, and they seem to be based on myths to which a Christian appearance has been given by a sprinkling of names of holy persons of the

Church.   Here for instance is a fragment from a Carpathian song :—

>"A golden plough goes ploughing,
>   And behind that plough is the Lord Himself.
>   The holy Peter helps Him to drive,
>   And the Mother of God carries the seed corn,
>   Carries the seed corn, prays to the Lord God,
>   'Make, O Lord, the strong wheat to grow,
>   The strong wheat and the vigorous corn !
>   The stalks then shall be like reeds !'" [34]

Often they contain wishes for the prosperity of the household and end with the words, "for many years, for many years." The Roumanian songs are frequently very long, and a typical, oft-recurring refrain is :—

>"This evening is a great evening,
>   White flowers ;
>   Great evening of Christmas,
>   White flowers." [35]

Sometimes they are ballads of the national life.

In Russia a carol beginning "Glory be to God in heaven, Glory !" and calling down blessings on the Tsar and his people, is one of the most prominent among the *Kolyádki*, and opens the singing of the songs called *Podblyudnuiya*. "At the Christmas festival a table is covered with a cloth, and on it is set a dish or bowl (*blyudo*) containing water. The young people drop rings or other trinkets into the dish, which is afterwards covered with a cloth, and then the *Podblyudnuiya* Songs commence. At the end of each song one of the trinkets is drawn at random, and its owner deduces an omen from the nature of the words which have just been sung." [36]

The Twelve Days.

Whatever the limits fixed for the beginning and end of the Christmas festival, its core is always the period between Christmas

THE TWELVE DAYS

Eve and the Epiphany—the "Twelve Days."* A cycle of feasts falls within this time, and the customs peculiar to each day will be treated in calendarial order. First, however, it will be well to glance at the character of the Twelve Days as a whole, and at the superstitions which hang about the season. So many are these superstitions, so "bewitched" is the time, that the older mythologists not unnaturally saw in it a Teutonic festal season, dating from pre-Christian days. In point of fact it appears to be simply a creation of the Church, a natural linking together of Christmas and Epiphany. It is first mentioned as a festal tide by the eastern Father, Ephraem Syrus, at the end of the fourth century, and was declared to be such by the western Council of Tours in 567.[37]

While Christmas Eve is the night *par excellence* of the supernatural, the whole season of the Twelve Days is charged with it. It is hard to see whence Shakespeare could have got the idea which he puts into the mouth of Marcellus in "Hamlet":—

> "Some say that ever 'gainst that season comes
> Wherein our Saviour's birth is celebrated,
> The bird of dawning singeth all night long ;
> And then, they say, no spirit dare stir abroad ;
> The nights are wholesome ; then no planets strike,
> No fairy takes, nor witch hath power to charm,
> So hallow'd and so gracious is the time." [38]

Against this is the fact that in folk-lore Christmas is a quite peculiarly uncanny time. Not unnatural is it that at this midwinter season of darkness, howling winds, and raging storms, men should have thought to see and hear the mysterious shapes and voices of dread beings whom the living shun.

Throughout the Teutonic world one finds the belief in a "raging

* Sometimes Christmas is reckoned as one of the Twelve Days, sometimes not. In the former case, of course, the Epiphany is the thirteenth day. In England we call the Epiphany Twelfth Day, in Germany it is generally called Thirteenth ; in Belgium and Holland it is Thirteenth ; in Sweden it varies, but is usually Thirteenth. Sometimes then the Twelve Days are spoken of, sometimes the Thirteen. "The Twelve Nights," in accordance with the old Teutonic mode of reckoning by nights, is a natural and correct term.[39]

host" or "wild hunt" of spirits, rushing howling through the air on stormy nights. In North Devon its name is "Yeth (heathen) hounds";[40] elsewhere in the west of England it is called the "Wish hounds." [41] It is the train of the unhappy souls of those who died unbaptized, or by violent hands, or under a curse, and often Woden is their leader.[42] At least since the seventeenth century this "raging host" (*das wüthende Heer*) has been particularly associated with Christmas in German folk-lore,[43] and in Iceland it goes by the name of the "Yule host." [44]

In Guernsey the powers of darkness are supposed to be more than usually active between St. Thomas's Day and New Year's Eve, and it is dangerous to be out after nightfall. People are led astray then by Will o' the Wisp, or are preceded or followed by large black dogs, or find their path beset by white rabbits that go hopping along just under their feet. [45]

In England there are signs that supernatural visitors were formerly looked for during the Twelve Days. First there was a custom of cleansing the house and its implements with peculiar care. In Shropshire, for instance, "the pewter and brazen vessels had to be made so bright that the maids could see to put their caps on in them—otherwise the fairies would pinch them, but if all was perfect, the worker would find a coin in her shoe." Again in Shropshire special care was taken to put away any suds or "back-lee" for washing purposes, and no spinning might be done during the Twelve Days.[46] It was said elsewhere that if any flax were left on the distaff, the Devil would come and cut it.[47]

The prohibition of spinning may be due to the Church's hallowing of the season and the idea that all work then was wrong. This churchly hallowing may lie also at the root of the Danish tradition that from Christmas till New Year's Day nothing that runs round should be set in motion,[48] and of the German idea that no thrashing must be done during the Twelve Days, or all the corn within hearing will spoil. The expectation of uncanny visitors in the English traditions calls, however, for special attention ; it is perhaps because of their coming that the house must be left spotlessly clean and with as little as possible about on which they can work mischief.[49] Though I know of no distinct English belief in the return of the family dead at Christmas, it may be that the fairies expected in Shropshire were originally ancestral ghosts. Such a derivation of the elves and brownies that haunt the hearth is very probable.[50]

The belief about the Devil cutting flax left on the distaff links the English superstitions to the mysterious *Frau* with various names, who in Germany is supposed to go her rounds during the Twelve Nights. She has a special relation to spinning, often punishing girls who leave their flax unspun. In central Germany and in parts of Austria she is called Frau Holle or Holda, in southern Germany and Tyrol Frau Berchta or Perchta, in the north down to the Harz Mountains Frau Freen or Frick, or Fru Gode or Fru Harke, and there are other names too.[51] Attempts have been made to dispute her claim to the rank of an old Teutonic goddess and to prove her a creation of the Middle Ages, a representative of the crowd of ghosts supposed to be specially near to the living at Christmastide.[52] It is questionable whether she can be thus explained away, and at the back of the varying names, and much overlaid no doubt with later superstitions, there may be a traditional goddess corresponding to that old divinity Frigg to whom we owe the name of Friday. The connection of Frick with Frigg is very probable, and Frick shares characteristics with the other *Frauen*.[53]

All are connected with spinning and spinsters (in the literal sense). Fru Frick or Freen in the Uckermark and the northern Harz permits no spinning during the time when she goes her rounds, and if there are lazy spinsters she soils the unspun flax on their distaff. In like manner do Holda, Harke, Berchta, and Gode punish lazy girls.[54]

The characters of the *Frauen* can best be shown by the things told of them in different regions. They are more dreaded than loved, but if severe in their chastisements they are also generous in rewarding those who do them service.

Frau Gaude (also called Gode, Gaue, or Wode) is said in Mecklenburg to love to drive through the village streets on the Twelve Nights with a train of dogs. Wherever she finds a street-door open she sends a little dog in. Next morning he wags his tail at the inmates and whines, and will not be driven away. If killed, he turns into a stone by day; this, though it may be thrown away, always returns and is a dog again by night. All through the year he whines and brings ill luck upon the house; so people are careful to keep their street-doors shut during the Twelve Nights.[55]

Good luck, however, befalls those who do Frau Gaude a service. A man who put a new pole to her carriage was brilliantly repaid—the chips that fell from the pole turned to glittering gold. Similar stories of golden chips are told about Holda and Berchta.[56]

A train of dogs belongs not only to Frau Gaude but also to Frau Harke; with these howling beasts they go raging through the air by night.[57] The *Frauen* in certain aspects are, indeed, the leaders of the " Wild Host."

Holda and Perchta, as some strange stories show, are the guides and guardians of the *heimchen* or souls of children who have died unbaptized. In the valley of the Saale, so runs a tale, Perchta, queen of the *heimchen*, had her dwelling of old, and at her command the children watered the fields, while she worked with her plough. But the people of the place were ungrateful, and she resolved to leave their land. One night a ferryman beheld on the bank of the Saale a tall, stately lady with a crowd of weeping children. She demanded to be ferried across, and the children dragged a plough into the boat, crying bitterly. As a reward for the ferrying, Perchta, mending her plough, pointed to the chips. The man grumblingly took three, and in the morning they had turned to gold-pieces.[58]

Holda, whose name means " the kindly one," is the most friendly of the *Frauen*. In Saxony she brings rewards for diligent spinsters, and on every New Year's Eve, between nine and ten o'clock, she drives in a carriage full of presents through villages where respect has been shown to her. At the crack of her whip the people come out to receive her gifts. In Hesse and Thuringia she is imagined as a beautiful woman clad in white with long golden hair, and, when it snows hard, people say, " Frau Holle is shaking her featherbed."[59]

THE TWELVE DAYS

More of a bugbear on the whole is Berchte or Perchte (the name is variously spelt). She is particularly connected with the Eve of the Epiphany, and it is possible that her name comes from the old German *giper(c)hta Na(c)ht*, the bright or shining night, referring to the manifestation of Christ's glory.[60] In Carinthia the Epiphany is still called *Berchtentag*.[61]

Berchte is sometimes a bogey to frighten children. In the mountains round Traunstein children are told on Epiphany Eve that if they are naughty she will come and cut their stomachs open.[62] In Upper Austria the girls must finish their spinning by Christmas ; if Frau Berch finds flax still on their distaffs she will be angered and send them bad luck.[63]

In the Orlagau (between the Saale and the Orle) on the night before Twelfth Day, Perchta examines the spinning-rooms and brings the spinners empty reels with directions to spin them full within a very brief time ; if this is not done she punishes them by tangling and befouling the flax. She also cuts open the body of any one who has not eaten *zemmede* (fasting fare made of flour and milk and water) that day, takes out any other food he has had, fills the empty space with straw and bricks, and sews him up again.[64] And yet, as we have seen, she has a kindly side—at any rate she rewards those who serve her—and in Styria at Christmas she even plays the part of Santa Klaus, hearing children repeat their prayers and rewarding them with nuts and apples.[65]

There is a charming Tyrolese story about her. At midnight on Epiphany Eve a peasant—not too sober—suddenly heard behind him "a sound of many voices, which came on nearer and nearer, and then the Berchtl, in her white clothing, her broken ploughshare in her hand, and all her train of little people, swept clattering and chattering close past him. The least was the last, and it wore a long shirt which got in the way of its little bare feet, and kept tripping it up. The peasant had sense enough left to feel compassion, so he took his garter off and bound it for a girdle round the infant, and then set it again on its way. When the Berchtl saw what he had done, she turned back and thanked him, and told him that in return for his compassion his children should never come to want." [66]

PAGAN SURVIVALS

In Tyrol, by the way, it is often said that the Perchtl is Pontius Pilate's wife, Procula.[67] In the Italian dialects of south Tyrol the German Frau Berchta has been turned into *la donna Berta*.[68] If one goes further south, into Italy itself, one meets with a similar being, the Befana, whose name is plainly nothing but a corruption of *Epiphania*. She is so distinctly a part of the Epiphany festival that we may leave her to be considered later.

Of all supernatural Christmas visitors, the most vividly realized and believed in at the present day are probably the Greek *Kallikantzaroi* or *Karkantzaroi*.[69] They are the terror of the Greek peasant during the Twelve Days; in the soil of his imagination they flourish luxuriantly, and to him they are a very real and living nuisance.

Traditions about the *Kallikantzaroi* vary from region to region, but in general they are half-animal, half-human monsters, black, hairy, with huge heads, glaring red eyes, goats' or asses' ears, blood-red tongues hanging out, ferocious tusks, monkeys' arms, and long curved nails, and commonly they have the foot of some beast. " From dawn till sunset they hide themselves in dark and dank places . . . but at night they issue forth and run wildly to and fro, rending and crushing those who cross their path. Destruction and waste, greed and lust mark their course." When a house is not prepared against their coming, " by chimney and door alike they swarm in, and make havoc of the home; in sheer wanton mischief they overturn and break all the furniture, devour the Christmas pork, befoul all the water and wine and food which remains, and leave the occupants half dead with fright or violence." Many like or far worse pranks do they play, until at the crowing of the third cock they get them away to their dens. The signal for their final departure does not come until the Epiphany, when, as we saw in Chapter IV., the " Blessing of the Waters " takes place. Some of the hallowed water is put into vessels, and with these and with incense the priests sometimes make a round of the village, sprinkling the people and their houses. The fear of the

244

Kallikantzaroi at this purification is expressed in the following lines :—

> " Quick, begone ! we must begone,
> Here comes the pot-bellied priest,
> With his censer in his hand
> And his sprinkling-vessel too ;
> He has purified the streams
> And he has polluted us."

Besides this ecclesiastical purification there are various Christian precautions against the *Kallikantzaroi*—*e.g.*, to mark the house-door with a black cross on Christmas Eve, the burning of incense and the invocation of the Trinity—and a number of other means of aversion : the lighting of the Yule log, the burning of something that smells strong, and—perhaps as a peace-offering—the hanging of pork-bones, sweetmeats, or sausages in the chimney.

Just as men are sometimes believed to become vampires temporarily during their lifetime, so, according to one stream of tradition, do living men become *Kallikantzaroi*. In Greece children born at Christmas are thought likely to have this objectionable characteristic as a punishment for their mothers' sin in bearing them at a time sacred to the Mother of God. In Macedonia [70] people who have a " light " guardian angel undergo the hideous transformation.

Many attempts have been made to account for the *Kallikantzaroi*. Perhaps the most plausible explanation of the outward form, at least, of the uncanny creatures, is the theory connecting them with the masquerades that formed part of the winter festival of Dionysus and are still to be found in Greece at Christmastide. The hideous bestial shapes, the noise and riot, may well have seemed demoniacal to simple people slightly " elevated," perhaps, by Christmas feasting, while the human nature of the maskers was not altogether forgotten.[71] Another theory of an even more prosaic character has been propounded—" that the Kallikantzaroi are nothing more than established nightmares, limited like indigestion to the twelve days of feasting. This view is taken by Allatius, who says that a Kallikantzaros has all the characteristics of nightmare, rampaging abroad and jumping on men's shoulders, then leaving them half senseless on the ground." [72]

Such theories are ingenious and suggestive, and may be true to a certain degree, but they hardly cover all the facts. It is possible that the *Kallikantzaroi* may have some connection with the departed ; they certainly appear akin to the modern Greek and Slavonic vampire, " a corpse imbued with a kind of half-life," and with eyes gleaming like live coals.[73] They are, however, even more closely related to the werewolf, a man who is supposed to change into a wolf and go about ravening. It is to be noted that " man-wolves " (λυκάνθρωποι) is the very name given to the *Kallikantzaroi* in southern Greece, and that the word *Kallikantzaros* itself has been conjecturally derived by Bernhard Schmidt from two Turkish words meaning " black " and " werewolf." [74] The connection between Christmas and werewolves is not confined to Greece. According to a belief not yet extinct in the north and east of Germany, even where the real animals have long ago been extirpated, children born during the Twelve Nights become were-wolves, while in Livonia and Poland that period is the special season for the werewolf's ravenings.[75]

Perhaps on no question connected with primitive religion is there more uncertainty than on the ideas of early man about the nature of animals and their relation to himself and the world. When we meet with half-animal, half-human beings we must be prepared to find much that is obscure.

With the *Kallikantzaroi* may be compared some goblins of the Celtic imagination ; especially like is the Manx *Fynnodderee* (lit. " the hairy-dun one "), " something between a man and a beast, being covered with black shaggy hair and having fiery eyes," and prodigiously strong.[76] The Russian *Domovy* or house-spirit is also a hirsute creature,[77] and the Russian *Ljeschi*, goat-footed woodland sprites, are, like the *Kallikantzaroi*, supposed to be got rid of by the "Blessing of the Waters " at the Epiphany.[78] Some of the monstrous German figures already dealt with here bear strong resemblances to the Greek demons. And, of course, on Greek ground one cannot help thinking of Pan and the Satyrs and Centaurs.*

* Those who wish to pursue further the study of the *Kallikantzaroi* should read the elaborate and fascinating, if not altogether convincing, theories of Mr. J. C. Lawson in his "Modern Greek Folklore and Ancient Greek Religion." He distinguishes two classes of *Kallikantzaroi*, one of which he identifies with ordinary werewolves, while the other is the type of hairy, clawed demons above described. He sets forth a most ingenious hypothesis connecting them with the Centaurs.

CHAPTER X
THE YULE LOG

CHAPTER X

THE YULE LOG

THE peoples of Europe have various centres for their Christmas rejoicing. In Spain and Italy the crib is often the focus of the festival in the home as well as the church. In England— after the old tradition—, in rural France, and among the southern Slavs, the centre is the great log solemnly brought in and kindled on the hearth, while in Germany, one need hardly say, the light-laden tree is the supreme symbol of Christmas. The crib has already been treated in our First Part, the Yule log and the Christmas-tree will be considered in this chapter and the next.

The log placed on the fire on the Vigil of the Nativity no longer forms an important part of the English Christmas. Yet within the memory of many it was a very essential element in the celebration of the festival, not merely as giving out welcome warmth in the midwinter cold, but as possessing occult, magical properties. In some remote corners of England it probably lingers yet. We shall return to the traditional English Yule log after a study of some Continental customs of the same kind.

First, we may travel to a part of eastern Europe where the log ceremonies are found in their most elaborate form. Among the Serbs and Croats on Christmas Eve two or three young oaks are felled for every house, and, as twilight comes on, are brought in and laid on the fire. (Sometimes there is one for each male member of the family, but one large log is the centre of the ritual.) The felling takes place in some districts before sunrise, corn being thrown upon the trees with the words, "Good morning, Christmas!" At Risano and other places in Lower Dalmatia the women and girls wind red silk and gold wire round the oak trunks, and adorn them with leaves and flowers. While they are being carried into the house lighted tapers are held on either side of the door. As the house-father crosses the threshold in the twilight with the first log, corn—or in some places wine—is thrown over him by one of the family. The log or *badnjak* is then placed on the fire. At Ragusa the house-father sprinkles corn and wine upon the *badnjak*, saying, as the flame shoots up, "Goodly be thy birth!" In the mountains above Risano he not only pours corn and wine but afterwards takes a bowl of corn, an orange, and a ploughshare, and places them on the upper end of the log in order that the corn may grow well and the beasts be healthy during the year. In Montenegro, instead of throwing corn, he more usually breaks a piece of unleavened bread, places it upon the log, and pours over it a libation of wine.[1]

The first visit on Christmas Day is considered important—we may compare this with "first-footing" in the British Isles on January 1—and in order that the right sort of person may come, some one is specially chosen to be the so-called *polaznik*. No outsider but this *polaznik* may enter a house on Christmas Day, where the rites are strictly observed. He appears in the early morning, carries corn in his glove and shakes it out before the threshold with the words, "Christ is born," whereupon some member of the household sprinkles him with corn in return, answering, "He is born indeed." Afterwards the *polaznik* goes to the fire and makes sparks fly from the remains of the *badnjak*, at the same time uttering a wish for the good luck of the house-father and his household and farm. Money and sometimes an orange are then placed on the *badnjak*. It is not allowed to burn quite away; the last remains of the fire are extinguished and the embers are laid between the branches of young fruit-trees to promote their growth.[2]

How shall we interpret these practices? Mannhardt regards the log as an embodiment of the vegetation-spirit, and its burning as an efficacious symbol of sunshine, meant to secure the genial vitalizing influence of the sun during the coming year.3 It is, however, possible to connect it with a different circle of ideas and to see in its burning the solemn annual rekindling of the sacred hearth-fire, the centre of the family life and the dwelling-place of the ancestors. Primitive peoples in many parts of the world are accustomed to associate fire with human generation,4 and it is a general belief among Aryan and other peoples that ancestral spirits have their seat in the hearth. In Russia, for instance, "in the Nijegorod Government it is still forbidden to break up the smouldering faggots in a stove, because to do so might cause the ancestors to fall through into hell. And when a Russian family moves from one house to another, the fire is conveyed to the new one, where it is received with the words, 'Welcome, grandfather, to the new home!'"5

Sir Arthur Evans in three articles in *Macmillan's Magazine* for 18816 gave a minute account of the Christmas customs of the Serbian highlanders above Risano, who practise the log-rites with elaborate ceremonial, and explained them as connected in one way or other with ancestor-worship, though the people themselves attach a Christian meaning to many of them. He pointed to the following facts as showing that the Serbian Christmas is at bottom a feast of the dead :—(1) It is said on Christmas Eve, "To-night Earth is blended with Paradise" [*Raj*, the abode of the dead among the heathen Slavs]. (2) There is talk of unchristened folk beneath the threshold wailing "for a wax-light and offerings to be brought them ; when that is done they lie still enough "—here there may be a modified survival of the idea that ancestral spirits dwell beneath the doorway. (3) The food must on no account be cleared away after the Christmas meal, but is left for three days, apparently for the house-spirits. (4) Blessings are invoked upon the "Absent Ones," which seems to mean the departed, and (5) a toast is drunk and a bread-cake broken in memory of "the Patron Namegiver of all house-fathers," ostensibly Christ but perhaps originally the founder of the family. Some of these customs resemble those we have noted on All Souls' Eve and— in Scandinavia—on Christmas Eve ; other parallels we shall meet with later. Among the Slav races the old organization of the family under an elective house-elder and holding things in common has been faithfully preserved, and we might expect to find among the remote Serbian highlanders specially clear traces of the old religion of the hearth. One remarkable point noted by Sir Arthur Evans was that in the Crivoscian cottage where he stayed the fire-irons, the table, and the stools were removed to an obscure corner before the logs were brought in and the Christmas rites began—an indication apparently of the extreme antiquity of the celebration, as dating from a time when such implements were unknown.7

If we take the view that ancestral spirits are the centre of the *badnjak* observances, we may regard the libations upon the fire as intended for their benefit. On the sun and vegetation hypothesis, however, the libations would be meant to secure, by homoeopathic magic, that sunshine should alternate with the rain necessary for the welfare of plants.* 8 The fertilizing powers possessed by the sparks and ashes of the Christmas log appear frequently in folk-lore, and may be explained either by the connection of fire with human generation already noted, or, on the other theory, by the burning log being a sort of sacrament of sunshine. It is not perhaps necessary to exclude the idea of the log's connection with the vegetation-spirit even on the ancestral cult hypothesis, for the tree which furnished the fuel may have been regarded as the source of the life of the race.9 The Serbian rites certainly suggest very strongly some sort of veneration for the log itself as well as for the fire that it feeds.

We may now return to western Europe. In France the Christmas log or *souche de Noël* is common in the less modernized places, particularly in the south. In Dauphiné it is called *chalen-*

---

* It is to be borne in mind that the oak was a sacred tree among the heathen Slavs ; it was connected with the thunder-god Perun, the counterpart of Jupiter, and a fire of oak burned night and day in his honour. The neighbours of the Slavs, the Lithuanians, had the same god, whom they called Perkunas ; they too kept up a perpetual oak-fire in his honour, and in time of drought they used to pour beer on the flames, praying to Perkunas to send showers.10 The libations of wine on the Yule log may conceivably have had a similar purpose.

dal, in Provence *calignaou* (from *Kalendae*, of course) or *tréfoir*, in Orne *tréfouet*. On Christmas Eve in Provence the whole family goes solemnly out to bring in the log. A carol meanwhile is sung praying for blessings on the house, that the women may bear children, the nanny-goats kids, and the ewes lambs, that corn and flour may abound, and the cask be full of wine. Then the youngest child in the family pours wine on the log in the name of the Father, Son, and Holy Ghost. The log is then thrown upon the fire, and the charcoal is kept all the year and used as a remedy for various ills.[11]

Another account is given in his Memoirs by Frédéric Mistral, the Provençal poet. On Christmas Eve everyone, he says, speaking of his boyhood, sallied forth to fetch the Yule log, which had to be cut from a fruit-tree :—

" Walking in line we bore it home, headed by the oldest at one end, and I, the last born, bringing up the rear. Three times we made the tour of the kitchen, then, arrived at the flagstones of the hearth, my father solemnly poured over the log a glass of wine, with the dedicatory words :

' Joy, joy. May God shower joy upon us, my dear children. Christmas brings us all good things. God give us grace to see the New Year, and if we do not increase in numbers may we at all events not decrease.'

In chorus we responded :

' Joy, joy, joy ! ' and lifted the log on the fire dogs. Then as the first flame leapt up my father would cross himself, saying, 'Burn the log, O fire,' and with that we all sat down to the table."[12]

In some places the *tréfoir* or *tison de Noël* is burnt every evening during the Thirteen Nights. If put under the bed its charcoal protects the house all the year round from lightning ; contact with it preserves people from chilblains and animals from various diseases ; mixed with fodder it makes cows calve ; its brands thrown into the soil keep the corn healthy. In Périgord the portion which has not been burnt is used to form part of a plough, and is believed to make the seed prosper ; women also keep some fragments until Epiphany that their poultry may thrive.[13] In

Brittany the *tison* is a protection against lightning and its ashes are put in wells to keep the water good.[14]

In northern Italy also the *ceppo* or log is (or was) known—the Piedmontese call it *suc*—and in Tuscany Christmas is called after it *Festa di Ceppo*. In the Val di Chiana on Christmas Eve the family gathers, a great log is set on the fire, the children are blindfolded and have to beat it with tongs, and an *Ave Maria del Ceppo* is sung.[15] Under the name in Lombardy of *zocco*, in Tuscany of *ciocco, di Natale*, the Yule log was in olden times common in Italian cities ; the custom can there be traced back to the eleventh century. A little book probably printed in Milan at the end of the fifteenth century gives minute particulars of the ritual observed, and we learn that on Christmas Eve the father, or the head of the household, used to call all the family together and with great devotion, in the name of the Holy Trinity, take the log and place it on the fire. Juniper was put under it, and on the top money was placed, afterwards to be given to the servants. Wine in abundance was poured three times on the fire when the head of the house had drunk and given drink to all present. It was an old Italian custom to preserve the ashes of the *zocco* as a protection against hail. A modern superstition is to keep some splinters of the wood and burn them in the fires made for the benefit of silkworms ; so burnt, they are supposed to keep ills away from the creatures.[16]

In many parts of Germany Yule log customs can be traced. In Hesse and Westphalia, for instance, it was the custom on Christmas Eve or Day to lay a large block of wood on the fire and, as soon as it was charred a little, to take it off and preserve it. When a storm threatened, it was kindled again as a protection against lightning. It was called the *Christbrand*.[17] In Thuringia a *Christklotz* (Christ log) is put on the fire before people go to bed, so that it may burn all through the night. Its remains are kept to protect the house from fire and ill-luck. In parts of Thuringia and in Mecklenburg, Pomerania, East Prussia, Saxony, and Bohemia, the fire is kept up all night on Christmas or New Year's Eve, and the ashes are used to rid cattle of vermin and protect plants and fruit-trees from insects, while in the country between the Sieg and Lahn the powdered ashes of an oaken log are strewn during the Thirteen Nights on the fields, to increase their fertility.[18]   In Sweden, too, some form of Yule log was known,[19] and in Greece, as we have seen, the burning of a log is still supposed to be a protection against *Kallikantzaroi*.

As for the English customs, they can hardly be better introduced than in Herrick's words :—

> " Come, bring, with a noise,
>   My merry, merry boys,
> The Christmas Log to the firing :
>   While my good Dame she
>   Bids ye all be free,
> And drink to your hearts' desiring.
>
>   With the last year's Brand
>   Light the new Block, and
> For good success in his spending,
>   On your psaltries play,
>   That sweet luck may
> Come while the log is a-teending." * [20]

We may note especially that the block must be kindled with last year's brand ; here there is a distinct suggestion that the lighting of the log at Christmas is a shrunken remnant of the keeping up of a perpetual fire, the continuity being to some extent preserved by the use of a brand from last year's blaze.

Another tradition and its origin are thus described by Sir Laurence Gomme :—

" From there being an ever-burning fire, it has come to be that the fire must not be allowed to be extinguished on the last day of the old year, so that the old year's fire may last into the new year.   In Lanarkshire it is considered unlucky to give out a light to any one on the morning of the new year, and therefore if the house-fire has been allowed to become extinguished recourse must be had to the embers of

* Kindling.

the village pile [for on New Year's Eve a great public bonfire is made]. In some places the self-extinction of the yule-log at Christmas is portentous of evil." [21]

In the north of England in the days of tinder-boxes, if any one could not get a light it was useless to ask a neighbour for one, so frightfully unlucky was it to allow any light to leave the house between Christmas Eve and New Year's Day.[22] The idea of the unluckiness of giving out fire at the Kalends of January can be traced back to the eighth century when, as we saw in Chapter VI., St. Boniface alluded to this superstition among the people of Rome.

In Shropshire the idea is extended even to ashes, which must not be thrown out of the house on Christmas Day, "for fear of throwing them in Our Saviour's face." Perhaps such superstitions may originally have had to do with dread that the "luck" of the family, the household spirit, might be carried away with the gift of fire from the hearth.[23]

When Miss Burne wrote in the eighties there were still many West Shropshire people who could remember seeing the "Christmas Brand" drawn by horses to the farmhouse door, and placed at the back of the wide open hearth, where the flame was made up in front of it. "The embers," says one informant, "were raked up to it every night, and it was carefully tended that it might not go out during the whole season, during which time no light might either be struck, given, or borrowed." At Cleobury Mortimer in the south-east of the county the silence of the curfew bell during "the Christmas" points to a time when fires might not be extinguished during that season.[24]

The place of the Yule log in Devonshire is taken by the "ashen [sometimes "ashton"] faggot," still burnt in many a farm on Christmas Eve. The sticks of ash are fastened together by ashen bands, and the traditional custom is for a quart of cider to be called for and served to the merrymaking company, as each band bursts in the flames.[25]

In England the Yule log was often supplemented or replaced

by a great candle. At Ripon in the eighteenth century the
chandlers sent their customers large candles on Christmas Eve,
and the coopers, logs of wood.[26] Hampson, writing in 1841,
says :—

"In some places candles are made of a particular kind, because the
candle that is lighted on Christmas Day must be so large as to burn
from the time of its ignition to the close of the day, otherwise it will
portend evil to the family for the ensuing year. The poor were wont
to present the rich with wax tapers, and yule candles are still in the
north of Scotland given by merchants to their customers. At one
time children at the village schools in Lancashire were required to
bring each a mould candle before the *parting* or separation for the
Christmas holidays." * [27]

In the Scandinavian countries the Yule candle is, or was, very
prominent indeed. In West Jutland (Denmark) two great
tallow candles stood on the festive board. No one dared to touch
or extinguish them, and if by any mischance one went out it was
a portent of death. They stood for the husband and wife, and
that one of the wedded pair whose candle burnt the longer would
outlive the other.[28]

In Norway also two lights were placed on the table.[29] All
over the Scandinavian lands the Yule candle had to burn throughout the night ; it was not to be extinguished till the sun rose o r
—as was said elsewhere—till the beginning of service on
Christmas Day. Sometimes the putting-out had to be done by
the oldest member of the family or the father of the household.
In Norway the candle was lighted every evening until New
Year's Day. While it foreshadowed death if it went out, so long
as it duly burned it shed a blessing with its light, and, in order to
secure abundance of good things, money, clothes, food, and drink
were spread out that its rays might fall upon them. The remains
of the candle were used in various ways to benefit man and beast.
Sometimes a cross was branded with them upon the animals on
Christmas morning ; in Sweden the plough was smeared with

* The custom referred to in the last sentence may be compared with the Danish
St. Thomas's Day practice (see Chapter VIII.).

the tallow, when used for the first time in spring. Or again the tallow was given to the fowls ; and, lastly, in Denmark the ends were preserved and burnt in thundery weather to protect the house from lightning.[30] There is an analogy here with the use of the Christmas log, and also of the candles of the Purification (see Chapter XVI.).

CHAPTER XI

THE CHRISTMAS-TREE, DECORATIONS, AND GIFTS

CHAPTER XI

THE CHRISTMAS-TREE, DECORATIONS, AND GIFTS

THE CHRISTMAS-TREE

THE most widespread, and to children the most delightful, of all festal institutions is the Christmas-tree. Its picturesqueness and gay charm have made it spread rapidly all over Europe without roots in national tradition, for, as most people know, it is a German creation, and even in Germany it attained its present immense popularity only in the nineteenth century. To Germany, of course, one should go to see the tree in all its glory. Many people, indeed, maintain that no other Christmas can compare with the German *Weihnacht*. "It is," writes Miss I. A. R. Wylie, " that childish, open-hearted simplicity which, so it seems to me, makes Christmas essentially German, or at any rate explains why it is that nowhere else in the world does it find so pure an expression. The German is himself simple, warm-hearted, unpretentious, with something at the bottom of him which is child-like in the best sense. He is the last ' Naturmensch' in civiliza-tion." Christmas suits him " as well as a play suits an actor for whose character and temperament it has been especially written." [1]

PAGAN SURVIVAL

In Germany the Christmas-tree is not a luxury for well-to-do people as in England, but a necessity, the very centre of the festival ; no one is too poor or too lonely to have one. There is something about a German *Weihnachtsbaum*—a romance and a wonder—that English Christmas-trees do not possess. For one thing, perhaps, in a land of forests the tree seems more in place ; it is a kind of sacrament linking mankind to the mysteries of the woodland. Again the German tree is simply a thing of beauty and radiance ; no utilitarian presents hang from its boughs—they are laid apart on a table—and the tree is purely splendour for splendour's sake. However tawdry it may look by day, at night it is a true thing of wonder, shining with countless lights and glittering ornaments, with fruit of gold and shimmering festoons of silver. Then there is the solemnity with which it is surrounded ; the long secret preparations behind the closed doors, and, when Christmas Eve arrives, the sudden revelation of hidden glory. The Germans have quite a religious feeling for their *Weihnachtsbaum*, coming down, one may fancy, from some dim ancestral worship of the trees of the wood.

As Christmas draws near the market-place in a German town is filled with a miniature forest of firs ; the trees are sold by old women in quaint costumes, and the shop-windows are full of candles and ornaments to deck them. Mrs. Alfred Sidgwick in her " Home Life in Germany " gives a delightful picture of such a Christmas market in " one of the old German cities in the hill country, when the streets and the open places are covered with crisp clean snow, and the mountains are white with it. . . . The air is cold and still, and heavy with the scent of the Christmas-trees brought from the forest for the pleasure of the children. Day by day you see the rows of them growing thinner, and if you go to the market on Christmas Eve itself you will find only a few trees left out in the cold. The market is empty, the peasants are harnessing their horses or their oxen, the women are packing up their unsold goods. In every home in the city one of the trees that scented the open air a week ago is shining now with lights and little gilded nuts and apples, and is helping to make that Christmas smell, all compact of the pine forest, wax candles, cakes and painted toys, you must associate so long as you live with Christmas in Germany." 2

Even in London one may get a glimpse of the Teutonic Christmas in the half-German streets round Fitzroy Square. They are bald and drab enough, but at Christmas here and there a window shines with a lighted tree, and the very prosaic Lutheran church in Cleveland Street has an unwonted sight to show—two great fir-trees decked with white candles, standing one on each side of the pulpit. The church of the German Catholics, too, St. Boniface's, Whitechapel, has in its sanctuary two Christmas-trees strangely gay with coloured glistening balls and long strands of gold and silver *engelshaar*. The candles are lit at Benediction during the festival, and between the shining trees the solemn ritual is performed by the priest and a crowd of serving boys in scarlet and white with tapers and incense.

There is a pretty story about the institution of the *Weihnachtsbaum* by Martin Luther : how, after wandering one Christmas Eve under the clear winter sky lit by a thousand stars, he set up for his children a tree with countless candles, an image of the starry heaven whence Christ came down. This, however, belongs to the region of legend ; the first historical mention of the Christmas-tree is found in the notes of a certain Strasburg citizen of unknown name, written in the year 1605. "At Christmas," he writes, "they set up fir-trees in the parlours at Strasburg and hang thereon roses cut out of many-coloured paper, apples, wafers, gold-foil, sweets, &c." 3

We next meet with the tree in a hostile allusion by a distinguished Strasburg theologian, Dr. Johann Konrad Dannhauer, Professor and Preacher at the Cathedral. In his book, "The Milk of the Catechism," published about the middle of the seventeenth century, he speaks of "the Christmas- or fir-tree, which people set up in their houses, hang with dolls and sweets, and afterwards shake and deflower." "Whence comes the custom," he says, "I know not ; it is child's play. . . . Far better were it to point the children to the spiritual cedar-tree, Jesus Christ."4

In neither of these references is there any mention of candles—

the most fascinating feature of the modern tree.   These appear, however, in a Latin work on Christmas presents by Karl Gott-fried Kissling of the University of Wittenberg, written in 1737. He tells how a certain country lady of his acquaintance set up a little tree for each of her sons and daughters, lit candles on or around the trees, laid out presents beneath them, and called her children one by one into the room to take the trees and gifts intended for them.5

With the advance of the eighteenth-century notices of the *Weihnachtsbaum* become more frequent : Jung Stilling, Goethe, Schiller, and others mention it, and about the end of the century its use seems to have been fairly general in Germany.6 In many places, however, it was not common till well on in the eighteen hundreds : it was a Protestant rather than a Catholic institution, and it made its way but slowly in regions where the older faith was held.7   Well-to-do townspeople welcomed it first, and the peasantry were slow to adopt it.   In Old Bavaria, for instance, in 1855 it was quite unknown in country places, and even to-day it is not very common there, except in the towns.8 " It is more in vogue on the whole," wrote Dr. Tille in 1893, " in the Protestant north than in the Catholic south," 9 but its popularity was rapidly growing at that time.

A common substitute for the Christmas-tree in Saxony during the nineteenth century, and one still found in country places, was the so-called " pyramid," a wooden erection adorned with many-coloured paper and with lights.   These pyramids were very popular among the smaller *bourgeoisie* and artisans, and were kept from one Christmas to another.10   In Berlin, too, the pyramid was once very common.   It was there adorned with green twigs as well as with candles and coloured paper, and had more resem-blance to the Christmas-tree.11   Tieck refers to it in his story, " Weihnacht-Abend " (1805).12

Pyramids, without lights apparently, were known in England before 1840.   In Hertfordshire they were formed of gilt ever-greens, apples, and nuts, and were carried about just before Christmas for presents.   In Herefordshire they were known at the New Year.13

THE GERMAN CHRISTMAS-TREE IN THE EIGHTEENTH CENTURY.

From an engraving by Joseph Kellner.

To face p. 266.

THE CHRISTMAS-TREE

The Christmas-tree was introduced into France in 1840, when Princess Helene of Mecklenburg brought it to Paris. In 1890 between thirty and thirty-five thousand of the trees are said to have been sold in Paris.[14]

In England it is alluded to in 1789,[15] but its use did not become at all general until about the eighteen-forties. In 1840 Queen Victoria and Prince Albert had a Christmas-tree, and the fashion spread until it became completely naturalized.[16] In Denmark and Norway it was known in 1830, and in Sweden in 1863 (among the Swedish population on the coast of Finland it seems to have been in use in 1800).[17] In Bohemia it is mentioned in 1862.[18] It is also found in Russia, the United States, Spain, Italy, and Holland,[19] and of course in Switzerland and Austria, so largely German in language and customs. In non-German countries it is rather a thing for the well-to-do classes than for the masses of the people.

The Christmas-tree is essentially a domestic institution. It has, however, found its way into Protestant churches in Germany and from them into Catholic churches. Even the Swiss Zwinglians, with all their Puritanism, do not exclude it from their bare, white-washed fanes. In the Münsterthal, for instance, a valley of Romonsch speech, off the Lower Engadine, a tree decked with candles, festoons, presents, and serpent-squibs, stands in church at Christmas, and it is difficult for the minister to conduct service, for all the time, except during the prayers, the people are letting off fireworks. On one day between Christmas Eve and New Year there is a great present-giving in church.[20]

In Munich, and doubtless elsewhere, the tree appears not only in the church and in the home, but in the cemetery. The graves of the dead are decked on Christmas Eve with holly and mistletoe and a little Christmas-tree with gleaming lights, a touching token of remembrance, an attempt, perhaps, to give the departed a share in the brightness of the festival.[21]

The question of the origin of Christmas-trees is of great interest. Though their affinity to other sacraments of the vegetation-spirit is evident, it is difficult to be certain of their exact ancestry. Dr. Tille regards them as coming from a union of two elements : the old Roman custom of decking houses with laurels and green trees at the Kalends of January, and the popular belief that every Christmas Eve apple and other trees blossomed and bore fruit.[22]

Before the advent of the Christmas-tree proper—a fir with lights and ornaments often imitating and always suggesting flowers and fruit—it was customary to put trees like cherry or hawthorn into water or into pots indoors, so that they might bud and blossom at New Year or Christmas.[23] Even to-day the practice of picking boughs in order that they may blossom at Christmas is to be found in some parts of Austria. In Carinthia girls on St. Lucia's Day (December 13) stick a cherry-branch into wet sand; if it blooms at Christmas their wishes will be fulfilled. In other parts the branches—pear as well as cherry— are picked on St. Barbara's Day (December 4), and in South Tyrol cherry-trees are manured with lime on the first Thursday in Advent so that they may blossom at Christmas.[24] The custom may have had to do with legendary lore about the marvellous transformation of Nature on the night of Christ's birth, when the rivers ran wine instead of water and trees stood in full blossom in spite of ice and snow.[25]

In England there was an old belief in trees blossoming at Christmas, connected with the well-known legend of St. Joseph of Arimathea. When the saint settled at Glastonbury he planted his staff in the earth and it put forth leaves ; moreover it blossomed every Christmas Eve. Not only the original thorn at Glastonbury but trees of the same species in other parts of England had this characteristic. When in 1752 the New Style was substituted for the Old, making Christmas fall twelve days earlier, folks were curious to see what the thorns would do. At Quainton in Buckinghamshire two thousand people, it is said, went out on the new Christmas Eve to view a blackthorn which had the Christmas blossoming habit. As no sign of buds was visible they agreed that the new Christmas could not be right, and refused to keep it. At Glastonbury itself nothing happened on December 24, but on January 5, the right day according to the Old Style, the thorn blossomed as usual.* 26

Let us turn to the customs of the Roman Empire which may be in part responsible for the German Christmas-tree. The practice of adorning houses with evergreens at the January Kalends was common throughout the Empire, as we learn from Libanius, Tertullian, and Chrysostom. A grim denunciation of such decorations and the lights which accompanied them may be quoted from Tertullian ; it makes a pregnant contrast of pagan and Christian. " Let them," he says of the heathen, " kindle lamps, they who have no light ; let them fix on the doorposts laurels which shall afterwards be burnt, they for whom fire is close at hand ; meet for them are testimonies of darkness and auguries of punishment. But thou," he says to the Christian, " art a light of the world and a tree that is ever green ; if thou hast renounced temples, make not a temple of thy own house-door." 27

That these New Year practices of the Empire had to do with the *Weihnachtsbaum* is very possible, but on the other hand it has closer parallels in certain folk-customs that in no way suggest Roman or Greek influence. Not only at Christmas are cere-monial "trees" to be found in Germany. In the Erzgebirge there is dancing at the summer solstice round "St. John's tree," a pyramid decked with garlands and flowers, and lit up at night by candles.28 At midsummer "in the towns of the Upper Harz Mountains tall fir-trees, with the bark peeled off their lower trunks, were set up in open places and decked with flowers and eggs, which were painted yellow and red. Round these trees the young folk danced by day and the old folk in the evening " ; 29 while on Dutch ground in Gelderland and Limburg at the beginning of May trees were adorned with lights.30

Nearer to Christmas is a New Year's custom found in some

* At Wormesley in Herefordshire there is a Holy Thorn which is still believed to blossom exactly at twelve o'clock on Twelfth Night. "The blossoms are thought to open at midnight, and drop off about an hour afterwards. A piece of thorn gathered at thi hour brings luck, if kept for the rest of the year." As recently as 1908 about forty people went to see the thorn blossom at this time (see E. M. Leather, "The Folk-Lore of Herefordshire" [London, 1912], 17).

Alsatian villages : the adorning of the fountain with a " May."
The girls who visit the fountain procure a small fir-tree or holly-
bush, and deck it with ribbons, egg-shells, and little figures representing a shepherd or a man beating his wife. This is set up
above the fountain on New Year's Eve. On the evening of the
next day the snow is carefully cleared away and the girls dance
and sing around the fountain. The lads may only take part in
the dance by permission of the girls. The tree is kept all through
the year as a protection to those who have set it up.[31]

In Sweden, before the advent of the German type of tree, it
was customary to place young pines, divested of bark and branches,
outside the houses at Christmastide.[32] An English parallel which
does not suggest any borrowing from Germany, was formerly to
be found at Brough in Westmoreland on Twelfth Night. A
holly-tree with torches attached to its branches was carried through
the town in procession. It was finally thrown among the populace, who divided into two parties, one of which endeavoured to
take the tree to one inn, and the other, to a rival hostelry.[33] We
have here pretty plainly a struggle of two factions—perhaps of
two quarters of a town that were once separate villages—for the
possession of a sacred object.*

We may find parallels, lastly, in two remote corners of Europe.
In the island of Chios—here we are on Greek ground—tenants
are wont to offer to their landlords on Christmas morning a
rhamna, a pole with wreaths of myrtle, olive, and orange leaves
bound around it ; " to these are fixed any flowers that may be
found—geraniums, anemones, and the like, and, by way of
further decoration, oranges, lemons, and strips of gold and coloured
paper." † [34] Secondly, among the Circassians in the early half of the
nineteenth century, a young pear-tree used to be carried into each
house at an autumn festival, to the sound of music and joyous cries.
It was covered with candles, and a cheese was fastened to its top.
Round about it they ate, drank, and sang. Afterwards it was

---

* Compare the struggle for the " Haxey hood," described in Chapter XVI., p. 347.

† This may be compared with the ancient Greek *Eiresione*, "a portable May-pole, a
branch hung about with wool, acorns, figs, cakes, fruits of all sorts and sometimes
wine-jars." [35]

removed to the courtyard, where it remained for the rest of the year.[36]

Though there is no recorded instance of the use of a tree at Christmas in Germany before the seventeenth century, the *Weihnachtsbaum* may well be a descendant of some sacred tree carried about or set up at the beginning-of-winter festival. All things considered, it seems to belong to a class of primitive sacraments of which the example most familiar to English peoples is the Maypole. This is, of course, an early summer institution, but in France and Germany a Harvest May is also known—a large branch or a whole tree, which is decked with ears of corn, brought home on the last waggon from the harvest field, and fastened to the roof of farmhouse or barn, where it remains for a year.[37] Mannhardt has shown that such sacraments embody the tree-spirit conceived as the spirit of vegetation in general, and are believed to convey its life-giving, fructifying influences. Probably the idea of contact with the spirit of growth lay also beneath the Roman evergreen decorations, so that whether or not we connect the Christmas-tree with these, the principle at the bottom is the same.

Certain Christian ideas, finally, besides that of trees blossoming on the night of the Nativity, may have affected the fortunes of the Christmas-tree. December 24 was in old Church calendars the day of Adam and Eve, the idea being that Christ the second Adam had repaired by His Incarnation the loss caused by the sin of the first. A legend grew up that Adam when he left Paradise took with him an apple or sprout from the Tree of Knowledge, and that from this sprang the tree from which the Cross was made. Or it was said that on Adam's grave grew a sprig from the Tree of Life, and that from it Christ plucked the fruit of redemption. The Cross in early Christian poetry was conceived as the Tree of Life planted anew, bearing the glorious fruit of Christ's body, and repairing the mischief wrought by the misuse of the first tree. We may recall a verse from the "Pange, lingua" of Passiontide :—

> "Faithful Cross! above all other,
> One and only noble tree!

PAGAN SURVIVALS

> None in foliage, none in blossom,
> None in fruit thy peer may be :
> Sweetest wood and sweetest iron !
> Sweetest weight is hung on thee."

In the religious Christmas plays the tree of Paradise was some-times shown to the people. At Oberufer, for instance, it was a fine juniper-tree, adorned with apples and ribbons. Sometimes Christ Himself was regarded as the tree of Paradise.[38] The thought of Him as both the Light of the World and the Tree of Life may at least have given a Christian meaning to the light-bearing tree, and helped to establish its popularity among pious folk.

CHRISTMAS DECORATIONS.

We have seen that the Christmas-tree may be a development, partly at least, from the custom of decorating buildings with evergreens at the New Year, and that such decorations were common throughout the Roman Empire.* Some further con-sideration may now be given to the subject of Christmas decora-tions in various lands. In winter, when all is brown and dead, the evergreens are manifestations of the abiding life within the plant-world, and they may well have been used as sacramental means of contact with the spirit of growth and fertility, threatened by the powers of blight. Particularly precious would be plants like the holly, the ivy, and the mistletoe, which actually bore fruit in the winter-time.[39]

In spite of ecclesiastical condemnations of Kalends decorations —as late as the sixth century the *capitula* of Bishop Martin of Braga forbid the adorning of houses with laurels and green trees [40] —the custom has found its way even into churches, and nowhere more than in England. At least as far back as the fifteenth century, according to Stow's "Survay of London," it was the custom at Christmas for "every man's house, as also the parish churches," to be "decked with holm, ivy, bays, and whatsoever the season of the year afforded to be green. The conduits and

---

* It by no means necessarily follows, of course, that they were exclusively Roman in origin.

standards in the streets were likewise garnished." [41]   Many people of the last generation will remember the old English mode of decoration—how sprigs of holly and yew, stuck into holes in the high pews, used to make the churches into miniature forests. Only upon the mistletoe does a trace of the ecclesiastical taboo remain, and even that is not universal, for at York Minster, for instance, some was laid upon the altar. [42]

English popular custom has connected particular plants with the winter festival in a peculiarly delightful way ; at the mere mention of holly or mistletoe the picture of Christmas with its country charm rises to the mind—we think of snowy fields and distant bells, of warm hearths and kindly merrymaking.

It is no wonder that the mistletoe has a special place in Christmas decorations, for it is associated with both Teutonic myth and Celtic ritual.   It was with mistletoe that the beloved Balder was shot, and the plant played an important part in a Druidic ceremony described by Pliny.   A white-robed Druid climbed a sacred oak and cut the mistletoe with a golden sickle.   As it fell it was caught in a white cloth, and two white bulls were then sacrificed, with prayer.   The mistletoe was called "all-healer" and was believed to be a remedy against poison and to make barren animals fruitful. [43] The significance of the ritual is not easy to find.   Pliny's account, Dr. MacCulloch has suggested, may be incomplete, and the cutting of the mistletoe may have been a preliminary to some other ceremony—perhaps the felling of the tree on which it grew, whose soul was supposed to be in it, or perhaps the slaying of a representative of the tree-spirit ; while the white oxen of Pliny's time may have replaced a human victim. [44]

It is interesting to find that the name "all-healer" is still given to the mistletoe in Celtic speech,* [45] and that in various European countries it is believed to possess marvellous powers of healing sickness or averting misfortune. [46]

* In Welsh it has also the name of "the tree of pure gold," a rather surprising title for a plant with green leaves and white berries.   Dr. Frazer has sought to explain this name by the theory that in a roundabout way the sun's golden fire was believed to be an emanation from the mistletoe, in which the life of the oak, whence fire was kindled, was held to reside. [47]

PAGAN SURVIVALS

It is hard to say exactly what is the origin of the English "kissing under the mistletoe," but the practice would appear to be due to an imagined relation between the love of the sexes and the spirit of fertility embodied in the sacred bough, and it may be a vestige of the licence often permitted at folk-festivals. According to one form of the English custom the young men plucked, each time they kissed a girl, a berry from the bough. When the berries were all picked, the privilege ceased.[48]

Sometimes a curious form, reminding one both of the German Christmas-tree and of the *Krippe*, is taken by the "kissing bunch." Here is an account from Derbyshire :—

"The 'kissing bunch' is always an elaborate affair. The size depends upon the couple of hoops—one thrust through the other—which form its skeleton. Each of the ribs is garlanded with holly, ivy, and sprigs of other greens, with bits of coloured ribbons and paper roses, rosy-cheeked apples, specially reserved for this occasion, and oranges. Three small dolls are also prepared, often with much taste, and these represent our Saviour, the mother of Jesus, and Joseph. These dolls generally hang within the kissing bunch by strings from the top, and are surrounded by apples, oranges tied to strings, and various brightly coloured ornaments. Occasionally, however, the dolls are arranged in the kissing bunch to represent a manger-scene. . . . Mistletoe is not very plentiful in Derbyshire ; but, generally, a bit is obtainable, and this is carefully tied to the bottom of the kissing bunch, which is then hung in the middle of the house-place, the centre of attention during Christmastide." [49]

Kissing under the mistletoe seems to be distinctively English. There is, however, a New Year's Eve custom in Lower Austria and the Rhaetian Alps that somewhat resembles our mistletoe bough practices. People linger late in the inns, the walls and windows of which are decorated with green pine-twigs. In the centre of the inn-parlour hangs from a roof-beam a wreath of the same greenery, and in a dark corner hides a masked figure known as "Sylvester," old and ugly, with a flaxen beard and *a wreath of mistletoe*. If a youth or maiden happens to pass under the pine wreath Sylvester springs out and imprints a rough kiss. When midnight comes he is driven out as the representative of the old year.[50]

CHRISTMAS DECORATIONS

There are traces in Britain of the sacredness of holly as well as mistletoe. In Northumberland it is used for divination : nine leaves are taken and tied with nine knots into a handkerchief, and put under the pillow by a person who desires prophetic dreams.[51] For this purpose smooth leaves (without prickles) must be employed, and it is to be noted that at Burford in Shropshire smooth holly only was used for the Christmas decorations.[52] Holly is hated by witches,[53] but perhaps this may be due not to any pre-Christian sanctity attached to it but to the association of its thorns and blood-red berries with the Passion— an association to which it owes its Danish name, *Kristdorn*.

In some old English Christmas carols holly and ivy are put into a curious antagonism, apparently connected with a contest of the sexes. Holly is the men's plant, ivy the women's, and the carols are debates as to the respective merits of each. Possibly some sort of rude drama may once have been performed.[54] Here is a fifteenth-century example of these carols :—

> "Holly and Ivy made a great party,
> Who should have the mastery,
>   In landës where they go.
>
> Then spoke Holly, 'I am free and jolly,
> I will have the mastery,
>   In landës where we go.'
>
> Then spake Ivy, 'I am lov'd and prov'd,
> And I will have the mastery,
>   In landës where we go.'
>
> Then spake Holly, and set him down on his knee,
> 'I pray thee, gentle Ivy,
> Say me no villainy,
>   In landës where we go.'" [55]

The sanctity of Christmas house-decorations in England is shown by the care taken in disposing of them when removed from the walls. In Shropshire old-fashioned people never threw them away, for fear of misfortune, but either burnt them or gave them to the cows ; it was very unlucky to let a piece fall to the ground. The Shropshire custom was to leave the holly and ivy up until Candlemas, while the mistletoe-bough was carefully preserved until the time came for a new one next year. West Shropshire tradition, by the way, connects the mistletoe with the New Year rather than with Christmas ; the bough ought not to be put up until New Year's Eve.[56]

In Sweden green boughs, apparently, are not used for decoration, but the floor of the parlour is strewn with sprigs of fragrant juniper or spruce-pine, or with rye-straw.[57] The straw was probably intended originally to bring to the house, by means of sacramental contact, the wholesome influences of the corn-spirit, though the common people connect it with the stable at Bethlehem. The practice of laying straw and the same Christian explanation are found also in Poland [58] and in Crivoscia.[59] In Poland before the cloth is laid on Christmas Eve the table is covered with a layer of hay or straw, and a sheaf stands in the corner. Years ago straw was also spread on the floor. Sometimes it is given to the cattle as a charm and sometimes it is used to tie up fruit-trees.[60]

Dr. Frazer conjectures that the Swedish Yule straw comes in part at least from the last sheaf at harvest, to which, as embodying the corn-spirit, a peculiar significance is attached. The Swedish, like the Polish, Yule straw has sundry virtues ; scattered on the ground it will make a barren field productive ; and it is used to bind trees and make them fruitful.[61] Again the peasant at Christmas will sit on a log and throw up Yule straws one by one to the roof ; as many as lodge in the rafters, so many will be the sheaves of rye at harvest.[62]

CHRISTMAS AND NEW YEAR GIFTS.

We have come across presents of various kinds at the pre-Christmas festivals ; now that we have reached Christmastide itself we may dwell a little upon the festival as the great present-giving season of the year, and try to get at the origins of the custom.

The Roman *strenae* offered to the Emperor or exchanged between private citizens at the January Kalends have already been noted. According to tradition they were originally merely branches plucked from the grove of the goddess Strenia, and the purpose of these may well have been akin to that of the greenery used for decorations, viz., to secure contact with a vegetation-spirit. In the time of the Empire, however, the *strenae* were of a more attractive character, "men gave honeyed things, that the year of the recipient might be full of sweetness, lamps that it might be full of light, copper and silver and gold that wealth might flow in amain." [63] Such presents were obviously a kind of charm for the New Year, based on the principle that as the beginning was, so would the rest of the year be.

With the adoption of the Roman New Year's Day its present-giving customs appear to have spread far and wide. In France, where the Latin spirit is still strong, January 1 is even now the great day for presents, and they are actually called *étrennes*, a name obviously derived from *strenae*. In Paris boxes of sweets are then given by bachelors to friends who have entertained them at their houses during the year—a survival perhaps of the "honeyed things" given in Roman times.

In many countries, however, present-giving is attached to the ecclesiastical festival of Christmas. This is doubtless largely due to attraction from the Roman New Year's Day to the feast hallowed by the Church, but readers of the foregoing pages will have seen that Christmas has also drawn to itself many practices of a November festival, and it is probable that German Christmas presents, at least, are connected as much with the apples and nuts of St. Martin and St. Nicholas* as with the Roman *strenae*. It has already been pointed out that the German St. Nicholas as present-giver appears to be a duplicate of St. Martin, and that St. Nicholas himself has often wandered from his own day to Christmas, or has been replaced by the Christ Child. We have also noted the rod associated with the two saints, and seen reason for thinking that its original purpose was not disciplinary but health-giving.

* In the neighbourhood of Reichenberg children hang up their stockings at the windows on St. Andrew's Eve, and in the morning find them filled with apples and nuts [64]—a parallel to Martinmas and St. Nicholas customs, at a date intermediate between the two festivals.

It is interesting to find that while, if we may trust tradition, the Roman *strenae* were originally twigs, Christmas gifts in sixteenth-century Germany showed a connection with the twigs or rods of St. Martin and St. Nicholas. The presents were tied together in a bundle, and a twig was added to them.[65] This was regarded by the pedagogic mind of the period not as a lucky twig but as a rod in the sinister sense. In some Protestant sermons of the latter half of the century there are curious detailed references to Christmas presents. These are supposed to be brought to children by the Saviour Himself, strangely called the *Haus-Christ*. Among the gifts mentioned as contained in the "Christ-bundles" are pleasant things like money, sugar-plums, cakes, apples, nuts, dolls; useful things like clothes; and also things "that belong to teaching, obedience, chastisement, and discipline, as A.B.C. tablets, Bibles and handsome books, writing materials, paper, &c., *and the ' Christ-rod.'* " [66]

A common gift to German children at Christmas or the New Year was an apple with a coin in it; the coin may conceivably be a Roman survival,[67] while the apple may be connected with those brought by St. Nicholas.

The Christ Child is still supposed to bring presents in Germany; in France, too, it is sometimes *le petit Jésus* who bears the welcome gifts.[68] In Italy we shall find that the great time for children's presents is Epiphany Eve, when the Befana comes, though in the northern provinces Santa Lucia is sometimes a gift-bringer.[69] In Sicily the days for gifts and the supposed bringers vary; sometimes, as we have already seen, it is the dead who bring them, on All Souls' Eve; sometimes it is *la Vecchia di Natali*—the Christmas old woman—who comes with them on Christmas Eve; sometimes they are brought by the old woman Strina—note the derivation from *strenae*—at the New Year; sometimes by the Befana at the Epiphany.[70]

A curious mode of giving presents on Christmas Eve belongs particularly to Sweden, though it is also found—perhaps borrowed—in Mecklenburg, Pomerania, and other parts of Germany. The so-called *Julklapp* is a gift wrapped up in innumerable coverings. The person who brings it raps noisily at

CHRISTMAS MORNING IN LOWER AUSTRIA.

By Ferdinand Waldmüller (b. 1793).

From Dr. E. M. Kronfeld's " Der Weihnachtsbaum."

To face p. 278.

the door, and throws or pushes the *Julklapp* into the room. It is essential that he should arrive quite unexpectedly, and come and go like lightning without revealing his identity. Great efforts are made to conceal the gift so that the recipient after much trouble in undoing the covering may have to search and search again to find it. Sometimes in Sweden a thin gold ring is hidden away in a great heavy box, or a little gold heart is put in a Christmas cake. Occasionally a man contrives to hide in the *Julklapp* and thus offer himself as a Christmas present to the lady whom he loves. The gift is often accompanied by some satirical rhyme, or takes a form intended to tease the recipient.[71]

Another custom, sometimes found in " better-class " Swedish households, is for the Christmas presents to be given by two masked figures, an old man and an old woman. The old man holds a bell in his hand and rings it, the old woman carries a basket full of sealed packets, which she delivers to the addressees.[72]

There is nothing specially interesting in modern English modes of present-giving. We may, however, perhaps see in the custom of Christmas boxes, inexorably demanded and not always willingly bestowed, a degeneration of what was once friendly entertainment given in return for the good wishes and the luck brought by wassailers. Instances of gifts to calling neighbours have already come before our notice at several pre-Christmas festivals, notably All Souls', St. Clement's, and St. Thomas's. As for the name " Christmas box," it would seem to have come from the receptacles used for the gifts. According to one account apprentices, journeymen, and servants used to carry about earthen boxes with a slit in them, and when the time for collecting was over, broke them to obtain the contents.[73]

The Christmas card, a sort of attenuated present, seems to be of quite modern origin. It is apparently a descendant of the "school pieces " or " Christmas pieces " popular in England in the first half of the nineteenth century—sheets of writing-paper with designs in pen and ink or copper-plate headings. The first Christmas card proper appears to have been issued in 1846, but it was not till about 1862 that the custom of card-sending obtained any foothold.[74]

CHAPTER XII

CHRISTMAS FEASTING AND
SACRIFICIAL SURVIVALS

CHRISTMAS FEASTING AND SACRIFICIAL SURVIVALS

Prominence of Eating in the English Christmas—The Boar's Head, the Goose, and other Christmas Fare—Frumenty, Sowens, Yule Cakes, and the Wassail Bowl—Continental Christmas Dishes, their Possible Origins—French and German Cakes—The Animals' Christmas Feast—Cakes in Eastern Europe—Relics of Animal Sacrifice—Hunting the Wren—Various Games of Sacrificial Origin.

FEASTING CUSTOMS.

In the mind of the average sensual Englishman perhaps the most vivid images called up by the word Christmas are those connected with eating and drinking. " Ha più di fare che i forni di Natale in Inghilterra," * an Italian proverb used of a very busy person, sufficiently suggests the character of our Christmas. †
It may be that the Christmas dinner looms larger among the English than among most other peoples, but in every country a distinctive meal of some kind is associated with the season. We have already seen how this illustrates the immemorial connection between material feasting and religious rejoicing.

Let us note some forms of " Christmas fare " and try to get an idea of their origin. First we may look at English feasting customs, though, as they have been pretty fully described by

* " He has more to do than the ovens in England at Christmas."
† The following quotation from an ancient account book is tersely suggestive of the English Christmas :—

					s.	d.
" Item payd to the preacher	...	...	...	...	... vi	ij
Item payd to the minstrell	...	...	...	...	... xii	o
Item payd to the coke	...	...	...	...	... xv	o "

previous writers, no very elaborate account of them need be given.

The gross eating and drinking in former days at Christmas, of which our present mild gluttony is but a pale reflection, would seem to be connected with the old November feast, though transferred to the season hallowed by Christ's birth. The show of slaughtered beasts, adorned with green garlands, in an English town just before Christmas, reminds one strongly of the old November killing. In displays of this kind the pig's head is specially conspicuous, and points to the time when the swine was a favourite sacrificial animal.[1] We may recall here the traditional carol sung at Queen's College, Oxford, as the boar's head is solemnly brought in at Christmas, and found elsewhere in other forms :—

> "The boar's head in hand bear I,
> Bedeck'd with bays and rosemary ;
> And I pray you, my masters, be merry,
>   *Quot estis in convivio.*
>   *Caput apri defero,*
>   *Reddens laudes Domino.*"[2]

The Christmas bird provided by the familiar "goose club" may be compared with the German Martinmas goose. The more luxurious turkey must be relatively an innovation, for that bird seems not to have been introduced into England until the sixteenth century.[3]

Cakes and pies, partly or wholly of vegetable origin, are, of course, as conspicuous at the English Christmas as animal food. The peculiar "luckiness" attached to some of them (as when mince-pies, eaten in different houses during the Twelve Days, bring a happy month each) makes one suspect some more serious original purpose than mere gratification of the appetite. A sacrificial or sacramental origin is probable, at least in certain cases ; a cake made of flour, for instance, may well have been regarded as embodying the spirit immanent in the corn.[4] Whether any mystic significance ever belonged to the plum-pudding it is hard to say, though the sprig of holly stuck into its top recalls the lucky green boughs we have so often come across, and a resemblance to the libations upon the Christmas log might be seen in the burning brandy.

A dish once prominent at Christmas was "frumenty" or "furmety" (variously spelt, and derived from the Latin *frumentum*, corn). It was made of hulled wheat boiled in milk and seasoned with cinnamon, sugar, &c.[5] This too may have been a cereal sacrament. In Yorkshire it was the first thing eaten on Christmas morning, just as ale posset was the last thing drunk on Christmas Eve. Ale posset was a mixture of beer and milk, and each member of the family in turn had to take a "sup," as also a piece of a large apple-pie.[6]

In the Highlands of Scotland, among those who observed Christmas, a characteristic dish was new sowens (the husks and siftings of oatmeal), given to the family early on Christmas Day in their beds. They were boiled into the consistence of molasses and were poured into as many bickers as there were people to partake of them. Everyone on despatching his bicker jumped out of bed.[7] Here, as in the case of the Yorkshire frumenty, the eating has a distinctly ceremonial character.

In the East Riding of Yorkshire a special Yule cake was eaten on Christmas Eve, "made of flour, barm, large cooking raisins, currants, lemon-peel, and nutmeg," and about as large as a dinner-plate.[8] In Shropshire "wigs" or caraway buns dipped in ale were eaten on Christmas Eve.[9] Again elsewhere there were Yule Doughs or Dows, little images of paste, presented by bakers to their customers.[10] We shall see plenty of parallels to these on the Continent. When they are in animal or even human form they may in some cases have taken the place of actual sacrificial victims.[11]

In Nottinghamshire the Christmas cake was associated with the wassail-bowl in a manner which may be compared with the Macedonian custom described later ; it was broken up and put into the bowl, hot ale was poured over it, and so it was eaten.[12]

The wassail-bowl—one cannot leave the subject of English Yuletide feasting without a few words upon this beloved beaker of hot spiced ale and toasted apples ("lambswool"). *Wassail* is derived from the Anglo-Saxon *wes hál* = be whole, and wassailing is in its essence the wishing of a person's very good health. The origin of drinking healths is not obvious ; perhaps it may be sacramental : the draught may have been at first a means of communion with some divinity, and then its consumption may have come to be regarded not only as benefiting the partaker, but as a rite that could be performed for the welfare of another person. Apart from such speculations, we may note the frequent mention of wassailing in old English carols of the less ecclesiastical type ; the singers carried with them a bowl or cup which they expected their wealthier neighbours to fill with drink.[13] Sometimes the bowl was adorned with ribbons and had a golden apple at the top,[14] and it is a noteworthy fact that the box with the Christmas images, mentioned in Chapter IV. (p. 118), is sometimes called " the Vessel [Wassail] Cup."[15]

The various Christmas dishes of Europe would form an interesting subject for exhaustive study. To suggest a religious origin for each would be going too far, for merely economic considerations must have had much to do with the matter, but it is very probable that in some cases they are relics of sacrifices or sacraments.

The pig is a favourite food animal at Christmas in other countries than our own, a fact probably connected with sacrificial customs. In Denmark and Sweden a pig's head was one of the principal articles of the great Christmas Eve repast.[16] In Germany it is a fairly wide-spread custom to kill a pig shortly before Christmas and partake of it on Christmas Day ; its entrails and bones and the straw which has been in contact with it are supposed to have fertilizing powers.[17] In Roumania a pig is the Christmas animal *par excellence*,[18] in Russia pigs' trotters are a favourite dish at the New Year,[19] and in every Servian house roast pig is the principal Christmas dish.[20]

In Upper Bavaria there is a custom which almost certainly has at its root a sacrifice : a number of poor people club together at Christmas-time and buy a cow to be killed and eaten at a common feast.[21]

More doubtful is the sacrificial origin of the dishes of certain

special kinds of fish on Christmas Eve. In Saxony and Thuringia herring salad is eaten—he who bakes it will have money
all the year—and in many parts of Germany and also in Styria
carp is then consumed.[22]   Round Ercé in Brittany the family
dish is cod.[23]   In Italy the *cenone* or great supper held on
Christmas Eve has fish for its animal basis, and stewed eels are
particularly popular.   It is to be remembered that in Catholic
countries the Vigil of the Nativity is a fast, and meat is not
allowed upon it ; this alone would account for the prominence of
fish on Christmas Eve.

We have already come across peculiar cakes eaten at various
pre-Christmas festivals ; at Christmas itself special kinds of bread,
pastry, and cakes abound on the Continent, and in some cases at
least may have a religious origin.

In France various sorts of cakes and loaves are known at the
season of *Noël*.   In Berry on Christmas morning loaves called
cornabœux, made in the shape of horns or a crescent, are distributed to the poor.   In Lorraine people give one another *cognés*
or *cogneux*, a kind of pastry in the shape of two crescents back
to back, or else long and narrow in form and with a crescent
at either end.   In some parts of France the *cornabœux* are known
as *hôlais*, and ploughmen give to the poor as many of these
loaves as they possess oxen and horses.[24]   These horns may be
substitutes for a sacrifice of oxen.

Sometimes the French Christmas cakes have the form of
complete oxen or horses—such were the thin unleavened cakes
sold in the early nineteenth century at La Châtre (Indre).   In
the neighbourhood of Chartres there are *cochenilles* and *coquelins*
in animal and human shapes.   Little cakes called *naulets* are sold
by French bakers, and actually represent the Holy Child.   With
them may be compared the *coignoles* of French Flanders, cakes of
oblong form adorned with the figure of the infant Jesus in
sugar.[25]   Sometimes the Christmas loaf or cake in France has
healing properties ; a certain kind of cake in Berry and Limousin
is kept all through the year, and a piece eaten in sickness has
marvellous powers.[26]

Cortet gives an extraordinary account of a French custom

connected with eating and drinking. At Mouthe (Doubs) there used to be brought to the church at Christmas pies, cakes, and other eatables, and wine of the best. They were called the "De fructu," and when at Vespers the verse "De fructu ventris tui ponam super sedem tuam" was reached, all the congregation made a rush for these refreshments, contended for them, and carried them off with singing and shouting.[27]

The most remarkable of Christmas cakes or loaves is the Swedish and Danish "Yule Boar," a loaf in the form of a boar-pig, which stands on the table throughout the festal season. It is often made from the corn of the last sheaf of the harvest, and in it Dr. Frazer finds a clear expression of the idea of the corn-spirit as embodied in pig form. "Often it is kept till sowing-time in spring, when part of it is mixed with the seed corn and part given to the ploughman and plough-horses or plough-oxen to eat, in the expectation of a good harvest." In some parts of the Esthonian island of Oesel the cake has not the form of a boar, but bears the same name, and on New Year's Day is given to the cattle. In other parts of the island the "Yule Boar" is actually a little pig, roasted on Christmas Eve and set up on the table.[28]

In Germany, besides *stollen*—a sort of plum-loaf—biscuits, often of animal or human shape, are very conspicuous on Christmas Eve. Any one who has witnessed a German Christmas will remember the extraordinary variety of them, *lebkuchen*, *pfeffernüsse*, *printen*, *spekulatius* biscuits, &c. In Berlin a great pile of biscuits heaped up on your plate is an important part of the Christmas Eve supper. These of course are nowadays mere luxuries, but they may well have had some sort of sacrificial origin. An admirable and exhaustive study of Teutonic Christmas cakes and biscuits has been made, with infinite pains, by an Austrian professor, Dr. Höfler, who reproduces some curious old biscuits, stamped with highly artistic patterns, preserved in museums.[29]

Among unsophisticated German peasants there is a belief in magical powers possessed by bread baked at Christmas, particularly when moistened by Christmas dew. (This dew is held to be peculiarly sacred, perhaps on account of the words "Rorate, coeli, desuper " used at the Advent Masses.) In Franconia such bread, thrown into a dangerous fire, stills the flames; in the north of Germany, if put during the Twelve Days into the fodder of the cattle, it makes them prolific and healthy throughout the year.[30]

It is pleasant to note that animals are often specially cared for at Christmas. Up till the early nineteenth century the cattle in Shropshire were always better fed at Christmas than at other times, and Miss Burne tells of an old gentleman in Cheshire who used then to give his poultry a double portion of grain, for, he said, " all creation should rejoice at Christmas, and the dumb creatures had no other manner of doing so." [31] The saying reminds one of that lover of Christmas and the animals, St. Francis of Assisi. It will be remembered how he wished that oxen and asses should have extra corn and hay at Christmas, " for reverence of the Son of God, whom on such a night the most Blessed Virgin Mary did lay down in the stall betwixt the ox and the ass." [32] It was a gracious thought, and no doubt with St. Francis, as with the old Cheshireman, it was a purely Christian one ; very possibly, however, the original object of such attention to the dumb creatures was to bring to the animals, by means of the corn, the influence of the spirit of fertility.

In Silesia on Christmas night all the beasts are given wheat to make them thrive, and it is believed that if wheat be kept in the pocket during the Christmas service and then given to fowls, it will make them grow fat and lay many eggs.[33] In Sweden on Christmas Eve the cattle are given the best forage the house can afford, and afterwards a mess of all the viands of which their masters have partaken ; the horses are given the choicest hay and, later on, ale ; and the other animals are treated to good things.[34]

At Loblang in Hungary the last sheat at harvest is kept, and given on New Year's morning to the wild birds.[35] In southern Germany corn is put on the roof for them on Christmas Eve, or,[36] as also in Sweden,[37] an unthreshed sheaf is set on a pole. In these cases it is possible that the food was originally an offering to ancestral or other spirits.

Revenons à nos gâteaux. In Rome and elsewhere in Italy an important article of Christmas food is the *panettone*, a currant loaf.

Such loaves are sent as presents to friends. In eastern Europe, too, Christmas loaves or cakes are very conspicuous. The *chesnitza* and *kolatch* cakes among the southern Slavs are flat and wheel-like, with a circular hole in the middle and a number of lines radiating from it. In the central hole is sometimes placed a lighted taper or a small Christmas-tree hung with ribbons, tinsel, and sweetmeats. These cakes, made with elaborate ceremonial early in the morning, are solemnly broken by the house-father on Christmas Day, and a small piece is eaten by each member of the family. In some places one is fixed on the horn of the " eldest ox," and if he throws it off it is a good sign.38 The last practice may be compared with a Herefordshire custom which we shall meet with on Twelfth Night (p. 346).

In southern Greece a special kind of flat loaves with a cross on the top is made on Christmas Eve. The name given is " Christ's Loaves." " The cloth is not removed from the table ; but everything is left as it is in the belief that ' Christ will come and eat' during the night." 39 Probably Christ has here taken the place of ancestral spirits.

In Tyrol peasants eat at Christmastide the so-called *zelten*, a kind of pie filled with dried pear-slices, nuts, figs, raisins, and the like. It is baked on the Eve of St. Thomas, and its filling is as important an event for the whole family as was the plum-pudding and mincemeat making in old-fashioned English households. When the *zelten* is filled the sign of the cross is made upon it and it is sprinkled with holy water and put in the oven. When baked and cooled, it is laid in the family stock of rye and is not eaten until St. Stephen's Day or Epiphany. Its cutting by the father of the family is a matter of considerable solemnity. Smaller pies are made at the same time for the maid-servants, and a curious custom is connected with them. It is usual for the maids to visit their relations during the Christmas holidays and share with them their *zelten*. A young man who wishes to be engaged to a maid should offer to carry her pie for her. This is his declaration of love, and if she accepts the offer she signifies her approval of him. To him falls the duty or privilege of cutting the *zelten*.40

FEASTING CUSTOMS

Other cake customs are associated with the Epiphany, and will be considered in connection with that festival. We may here in conclusion notice a few further articles of Christmas good cheer.

In Italy and Spain[41] a sort of nougat known as *torrone* or *turron* is eaten at Christmas. You may buy it even in London in the Italian quarter; in Eyre Street Hill it is sold on Christmas Eve on little gaily-decked street stalls. Its use may well be a survival of the Roman custom of giving sweet things at the Kalends in order that the year might be full of sweetness.

Some Little Russian feasting customs are probably pagan in origin, but have received a curious Christian interpretation. All Little Russians sit down to honey and porridge on Christmas Eve. They call it *koutia*, and cherish the custom as something that distinguishes them from Great and White Russians. Each dish is said to represent the Holy Crib. First porridge is put in, which is like putting straw in the manger; then each person helps himself to honey and fruit, and that symbolizes the Babe. A place is made in the porridge, and then the honey and fruit are poured in; the fruit stands for the body, the honey for the spirit or the blood.[42]

Something like this is the special dish eaten in every Roumanian peasant household on Christmas Eve—the *turte*. It is made up of a pile of thin dry leaves of dough, with melted sugar or honey, or powdered walnut, or the juice of the hemp-seed. The *turte* are traditionally said to represent the swaddling clothes of the Holy Child.[43]

In Poland a few weeks before Christmas monks bring round small packages of wafers made of flour and water, blessed by a priest, and with figures stamped upon them. No Polish family is without these *oplatki*; they are sent in letters to relations and friends, as we send Christmas cards. When the first star appears on Christmas Eve the whole family, beginning with the eldest member, break one of these wafers between themselves, at the same time exchanging good wishes. Afterwards the master and mistress go to the servants' quarters to divide the wafer there.[44]

PAGAN SURVIVALS

We have noted a connection, partial at least, between Christmas good cheer and sacrifice ; let us now glance at a few customs of a different character but seemingly of sacrificial origin.

Traces of sacrifices of cats and dogs are to be found in Germany and Bohemia. In Lauenburg and Mecklenburg on Christmas morning, before the cattle are watered, a dog is thrown into their drinking water, in order that they may not suffer from the mange. In the Uckermark a cat may be substituted for the dog. In Bohemia a black cat is caught, boiled, and buried by night under a tree, to keep evil spirits from injuring the fields.45

A strange Christmas custom is the "hunting of the wren," once wide-spread in England and France and still practised in Ireland. In the Isle of Man very early on Christmas morning, when the church bells had rung out midnight, servants went out to hunt the wren. They killed the bird, fastened it to the top of a long pole, and carried it in procession to every house, chanting these words :—

> "We hunted the wren for Robin the Bobbin,
>   We hunted the wren for Jack of the Can,
>   We hunted the wren for Robin the Bobbin,
>   We hunted the wren for every one."

At each house they sought to collect money. At last, when all had been visited, they laid the wren on a bier, carried it to the churchyard, and buried it with the utmost solemnity, singing Manx dirges. Another account, from the mid-nineteenth century, describes how on St. Stephen's Day Manx boys went from door to door with a wren suspended by the legs in the centre of two hoops crossing one another at right angles and decorated with evergreens and ribbons. In exchange for a small coin they would give a feather of the wren, which was carefully kept as a preservative against shipwreck during the year.* 46

* In County Louth, Ireland, boys used to carry about a thorn-bush decked with streamers of coloured paper and with a wren tied to one of the branches.47

292

There are also traces of a Manx custom of boiling and eating the bird.[48]

The wren is popularly called "the king of birds," and it is supposed to be highly unlucky to kill one at ordinary times. Probably it was once regarded as sacred, and the Christmas "hunting" is the survival of an annual custom of slaying the divine animal, such as is found among primitive peoples.[49] The carrying of its body from door to door is apparently intended to convey to each house a portion of its virtues, while the actual eating of the bird would be a sort of communion feast. Perhaps the custom, in a Cornish village, of eating blackbird pie on Twelfth Day should be explained in the same way.[50]

I can here hardly do more than allude to the many games[51] that were traditional in England at Christmas—hoodman-blind, shoe the wild mare, hot cockles, steal the white loaf, snap-dragon, and the rest. To attempt to describe and explain them would lead me too far, but it is highly probable that some at least might be traced to an origin in sacrificial ritual. The degeneration of religious rites into mere play is, indeed, as we have seen, a process illustrated by the whole history of Christmas.

Only two British Christmas games can be discussed in this book : blindman's buff and football. An account of a remarkable Christmas football match will be found in the chapter on Epiphany customs, where it is brought into connection with that closely related game, the "Haxey hood."

As for blindman's buff, it is distinctly a Christmas sport, and it is known nearly all over Europe by names derived from animals, *e.g.*, "blind cow" and "blind mouse." Mr. N. W. Thomas has suggested that "the explanation of these names is that the players originally wore masks ; the game is known in some cases as the 'blinde Mumm,' or blind mask. . . . The player who is 'it' seems to be the sacrificer ; he bears the same name as the victim, just as in agricultural customs the reaper of the last corn bears the same name as the last sheaf."[52]

The Scandinavian countries are very rich in Christmas games and dances,[53] of which it would be interesting to attempt explanations if space allowed. One Swedish song and dance game—

it may be related to the sword-dance (see Chapter XIII.)—is obviously sacrificial. Several youths, with blackened faces and persons disguised, are the performers. One of them is put to death with a knife by a woman in hideous attire. Afterwards, with gross gestures, she dances with the victim.[54] According to another account, from Gothland, the victim sits clad in a skin, holding in his mouth a wisp of straw cut sharp at the ends and standing out. It has been conjectured that this is meant to resemble a swine's bristles, and that the man represents a hog sacrificed to Frey.[55]

Lastly a Russian game may be mentioned, though it has no sacrificial suggestion. During the Christmas season girls play at what is called "the Burial of the Gold." They form a circle, with one girl standing in the centre, and pass from hand to hand a gold ring, which the maiden inside tries to detect. Meanwhile a song is sung, "Gold I bury, gold I bury." Some imaginative mythologists interpret the ring as representing the sun, buried by the clouds of winter.[56]

CHAPTER XIII

MASKING, THE MUMMERS' PLAY,
THE FEAST OF FOOLS,
AND THE BOY BISHOP

CHAPTER XIII

MASKING, THE MUMMERS' PLAY, THE FEAST OF FOOLS, AND THE BOY BISHOP

English Court Masking—"The Lord of Misrule"—The Mummers' Play, the Sword-Dance, and the Morris Dance—Origin of St. George and other Characters—Mumming in Eastern Europe—The Feast of Fools, its History and Suppression—The Boy Bishop, his Functions and Sermons—Modern Survivals of the Boy Bishop.

WE have already seen a good deal of masking in connection with St. Nicholas, Knecht Ruprecht, and other figures of the German Christmas ; we may next give some attention to English customs of the same sort during the Twelve Days, and then pass on to the strange burlesque ceremonies of the Feast of Fools and the Boy Bishop, ceremonies which show an intrusion of pagan mummery into the sanctuary itself.

CHRISTMAS MASKING.

The custom of Christmas masking, "mumming," or "disguising" can be traced at the English court as early as the reign of Edward III. It is in all probability connected with that wearing of beasts' heads and skins ot which we have already noted various examples—its origin in folk-custom seems to have been the coming of a band of worshippers clad in this uncouth but auspicious garb to bring good luck to a house.[1] The most direct English survival is found in the village mummers who still call themselves "guisers" or "geese-dancers" and claim the right to enter every house. These will be dealt with shortly, after a consideration of more courtly customs of the same kind.

PAGAN SURVIVALS

In the sixteenth and early seventeenth centuries the English court masque reached its greatest developments ; the fundamental idea was then generally overlaid with splendid trappings, the dresses and the arrangements were often extremely elaborate, and the introduction of dialogued speech made these " disguises " regular dramatic performances. A notable example is Ben Jonson's " Masque of Christmas." [2] Shakespeare, however, gives us in " Henry VIII."[3] an example of a simpler impromptu form : the king and a party dressed up as shepherds break in upon a banquet of Wolsey's.

In this volume we are more concerned with the popular Christmas than with the festivities of kings and courts and grandees. Mention must, however, be made of a personage who played an important part in the Christmas of the Tudor court and appeared also in colleges, Inns of Court, and the houses of the nobility—the " Lord of Misrule." [4] He was annually elected to preside over the revels, had a retinue of courtiers, and was surrounded by elaborate ceremonial. He seems to be the equivalent and was probably the direct descendant of the " Abbot " or " Bishop " of the Feast of Fools, who will be noticed later in this chapter. Sometimes indeed he is actually called " Abbot of Misrule." A parallel to him is the Twelfth Night "king," and he appears to be a courtly example of the temporary monarch of folk-custom, though his name is sometimes extended to " kings " of quite vulgar origin elected not by court or gentry but by the common people. The "Lord of Misrule" was among the relics of paganism most violently attacked by Puritan writers like Stubbes and Prynne, and the Great Rebellion seems to have been the death of him.

MUMMERS' PLAYS AND MORRIS DANCES.

Let us turn now to the rustic Christmas mummers, to-day fast disappearing, but common enough in the mid-nineteenth century. Their goings-on are really far more interesting, because more traditional, than the elaborate shows and dressings-up of the court. Their names vary : " mummers " and " guisers " are the commonest ; in Sussex they are " tipteerers," perhaps because of

the perquisites they collect, in Cornwall " geese-dancers "
(" geese " no doubt comes from " disguise "), in Shropshire
" morris "—or " merry "—" dancers." 5 It is to be noted that
they are unbidden guests, and enter your house as of right.6
Sometimes they merely dance, sing, and feast, but commonly
they perform a rude drama.7

The plays acted by the mummers 8 vary so much that it is
difficult to describe them in general terms. There is no reason
to suppose that the words are of great antiquity—the earliest
form may perhaps date from the seventeenth century ; they
appear to be the result of a crude dramatic and literary instinct
working upon the remains of traditional ritual, and manipulating
it for purposes of entertainment. The central figure is St.
George (occasionally he is called Sir, King, or Prince George),
and the main dramatic substance, after a prologue and introduction of the characters, is a fight and the arrival of a doctor to
bring back the slain to life. At the close comes a *quête* for
money. The name George is found in all the Christmas plays,
but the other characters have a bewildering variety of names
ranging from Hector and Alexander to Bonaparte and Nelson.

Mr. Chambers in two very interesting and elaborately docu-
mented chapters has traced a connection between these St.
George players and the sword-dancers found at Christmas or
other festivals in Germany, Spain, France, Italy, Sweden, and
Great Britain. The sword-dance in its simplest form is described
by Tacitus in his " Germania " : " they have," he says of the Germans, " but one kind of public show : in every gathering it is the
same. Naked youths, who profess this sport, fling themselves in
dance among swords and levelled lances." 9 In certain forms of
the dance there are figures in which the swords are brought
together on the heads of performers, or a pretence is made to cut
at heads and feet, or the swords are put in a ring round a person's
neck. This strongly suggests that an execution, probably a
sacrifice, lies at the bottom of the dances. In several cases,
moreover, they are accompanied by sets of verses containing the
incident of a quarrel and the violent death of one of the
performers. The likeness to the central feature of the St.

George play—the slaying—will be noticed. In one of the dances, too, there is even a doctor who revives the victim.

In England the sword-dance is found chiefly in the north, but with it appear to be identical the morris-dances—characterized by the wearing of jingling bells—which are commoner in the southern counties. Blackened faces are common in both, and both have the same grotesque figures, a man and a woman, often called Tommy and Bessy in the sword-dance and "the fool" and Maid Marian in the morris. Moreover the morris-dancers in England sometimes use swords, and in one case the performers of an undoubted sword-dance were called "morrice" dancers in the eighteenth century. Bells too, so characteristic of the morris, are mentioned in some Continental accounts of the sword-dance.*

Intermediate between these dances and the fully developed St. George dramas are the plays performed on Plough Monday in Lincolnshire and the East Midlands. They all contain a good deal of dancing, a violent death and a revival, and grotesques found both in the dances and in the Christmas plays.

The sword-dance thus passes by a gradual transition, the dancing diminishing, the dramatic elements increasing, into the mummers' plays of St. George. The central motive, death and revival, Mr. Chambers regards as a symbol of the resurrection of the year or the spirit of vegetation,† like the Thuringian custom of executing a "wild man" covered with leaves, whom a doctor brings to life again by bleeding. This piece of ritual has apparently been attracted to Christmas from an early feast of spring, and Plough Monday, when the East Midland plays take place, is just such an early spring feast. Again, in some places the St.

---

* Dancing is, as everyone knows, a common and indeed a central feature of primitive festivals ; and such dancing is wont to take a dramatic form, to be mimetic, whether re-enacting some past event or *pre*-doing something with magical intent to produce it.[10] The Greek tragedy itself probably sprang from a primitive dance of a dramatic and magical character, centred in a death and re-birth.[11]

† In Thessaly and Macedonia at Carnival time folk-plays of a somewhat similar character are performed, including a quarrel, a death, and a miraculous restoration to life—evidently originating in magical ritual intended to promote the fertility of vegetation.[12] Parallels can be found in the Carnival customs of other countries.

YORKSHIRE SWORD-ACTORS : ST. GEORGE IN COMBAT WITH ST. PETER.

From an article by Mr. T. M. Fallow in *The Antiquary*, May, 1895.

(By permission of Messrs. Elliot Stock.)

To face p. 300.

George play is performed at Easter, a date alluded to in the title, "Pace-eggers'" or "Pasque-eggers'" play.[13]

Two grotesque figures appear with varying degrees of clearness and with various names in the dances and in the plays—the "fool" (Tommy) who wears the skin and tail of a fox or other animal, and a man dressed in woman's clothes (Bessy). In these we may recognize the skin-clad mummer and the man aping a woman whom we meet in the old Kalends denunciations. Sometimes the two are combined, while a hobby-horse also not unfrequently appears.[14]

How exactly St. George came to be the central figure of the Christmas plays is uncertain ; possibly they may be a development of a dance in which appeared the "Seven Champions," the English national heroes—of whom Richard Johnson wrote a history in 1596—with St. George at their head. It is more probable, however, that the saint came in from the mediaeval pageants held on his day in many English towns.[15]

Can it be that the German St. Nicholas plays are more Christianized and sophisticated forms of folk-dramas like in origin to those we have been discussing ? They certainly resemble the English plays in the manner in which one actor calls in another by name; while the grotesque figures introduced have some likeness to the "fool" of the morris.

Christmas mumming, it may be added, is found in eastern as well as western Europe. In Greece, where ecclesiastical condemnations of such things can be traced with remarkable clearness from early times to the twelfth century, it takes sundry forms. "At Pharsala," writes Mr. J. C. Lawson, "there is a sort of play at the Epiphany, in which the mummers represent bride, bridegroom, and 'Arab' ; the Arab tries to carry off the bride, and the bridegroom defends her. . . . Formerly also at 'Kozane and in many other parts of Greece,' according to a Greek writer in the early part of the nineteenth century, throughout the Twelve Days boys carrying bells used to go round the houses, singing songs and having 'one or more of their company dressed up with masks and bells and foxes' brushes and other such things to give them a weird and monstrous look.'" [16]

PAGAN SURVIVALS

In Russia, too, mummers used to go about at Christmastide, visiting houses, dancing, and performing all kinds of antics. "Prominent parts were always played by human representatives of a goat and a bear. Some of the party would be disguised as 'Lazaruses,' that is, as blind beggars." A certain number of the mummers were generally supposed to play the part of thieves anxious to break in.[17] Readers of Tolstoy's "War and Peace" may remember a description of some such maskings in the year 1810.

THE FEAST OF FOOLS.

So far, in this Second Part, we have been considering customs practised chiefly in houses, streets, and fields. We must now turn to certain festivities following hard upon Christmas Day, which, though pagan in origin and sometimes even blasphemous, found their way in the Middle Ages within the walls of the church.

Shortly after Christmas a group of *tripudia* or revels was held by the various inferior clergy and ministrants of cathedrals and other churches. These festivals, of which the best known are the Feast of Fools and the Boy Bishop ceremonies, have been so fully described by other writers, and my space here is so limited, that I need but treat them in outline, and for detail refer the reader to such admirable accounts as are to be found in Chapters XIII., XIV., and XV. of Mr. Chambers's "The Mediaeval Stage."[18]

Johannes Belethus, Rector of Theology at Paris towards the end of the twelfth century, speaks of four *tripudia* held after Christmas :—those of the deacons on St. Stephen's Day, the priests on St. John's, the choir-boys on Holy Innocents', and the sub-deacons on the Circumcision, the Epiphany, or the Octave of the Epiphany. The feast of subdeacons, says Belethus, "we call that of fools." It is this feast which, though not apparently the earliest in origin of the four, was the most riotous and disorderly, and shows most clearly its pagan character. Belethus' mention of it is the first clear notice, though disorderly revels of the same kind seem to have existed at Constantinople as early as the ninth century. At first confined to the subdeacons, the Feast of Fools became in its later developments a festival not only of that order but of the

302

THE FEAST OF FOOLS

inferior clergy in general, of the vicars choral, the chaplains, and the choir-clerks, as distinguished from the canons. For this rabble of poor and low-class clergy it was no doubt a welcome relaxation, and one can hardly wonder that they let themselves go in burlesquing the sacred but often wearisome rites at which it was their business to be present through many long hours, or that they delighted to usurp for once in a way the functions ordinarily performed by their superiors. The putting down of the mighty from their seat and the exalting of them of low degree was the keynote of the festival. While "Deposuit potentes de sede : et exaltavit humiles" was being sung at the "Magnificat," it would appear that the precentor's *baculus* or staff was handed over to the clerk who was to be "lord of the feast" for the year, and throughout the services of the day the inferior clergy predominated, under the leadership of this chosen "lord." He was usually given some title of ecclesiastical dignity, "bishop," "prelate," "archbishop," "cardinal," or even "pope," was vested in full pontificals, and in some cases sat on the real bishop's throne, gave benedictions, and issued indulgences.

These lower clergy, it must be remembered, belonged to the peasant or small *bourgeois* class and were probably for the most part but ill-educated. They were likely to bring with them into the Church the superstitions floating about among the people, and the Feast of Fools may be regarded as a recoil of paganism upon Christianity in its very sanctuary. "An ebullition of the natural lout beneath the cassock" it has been called by Mr. Chambers, and many of its usages may be explained by the reaction of coarse natures freed for once from restraint. It brought to light, however, not merely personal vulgarity, but a whole range of traditional customs, derived probably from a fusion of the Roman feast of the Kalends of January with Teutonic or Celtic heathen festivities.

A general account of its usages is given in a letter addressed in 1445 by the Paris Faculty of Theology to the bishops and chapters of France :—

"Priests and clerks may be seen wearing masks and monstrous visages at the hours of office. They dance in the choir dressed as women, panders or minstrels. They sing wanton songs. They eat black puddings at the horn of the altar while the celebrant is saying Mass. They play at dice there. They cense with stinking smoke from the soles of old shoes. They run and leap through the church, without a blush at their own shame. Finally they drive about the town and its theatres in shabby traps and carts, and rouse the laughter of their fellows and the bystanders in infamous performances, with indecent gesture and verses scurrilous and unchaste." [19]

The letter also speaks of "bishops" or "archbishops" of Fools, who wore mitres and held pastoral staffs. We here see clearly, besides mere irreverence, an outcrop of pagan practices. Topsy-turvydom, the temporary exaltation of inferiors, was itself a characteristic of the Kalends celebrations, and a still more remarkable feature of them was, as we have seen, the wearing of beast-masks and the dressing up of men in women's clothes. And what is the "bishop" or "archbishop" but a parallel to, and, we may well believe, an example of, the mock king whom Dr. Frazer has traced in so many a folk-festival, and who is found at the *Saturnalia*?

One more feature of the Feast of Fools must be considered, the Ass who gave to it the not uncommon title of *asinaria festa*. At Bourges, Sens, and Beauvais, a curious half-comic hymn was sung in church, the so-called "Prose of the Ass." It begins as follows :—

> "Orientis partibus
> Adventavit Asinus,
> Pulcher et fortissimus,
> Sarcinis aptissimus.
> Hez, Sir Asnes, car chantez,
> Belle bouche rechignez,
> Vous aurez du foin assez
> Et de l'avoine a plantez."

And after eight verses in praise of the beast, with some mention of his connection with Bethlehem and the Wise Men, it closes thus :—

> "Amen dicas, Asine,
> Iam satur de gramine,

THE FEAST OF FOOLS

> Amen, Amen, itera,
> Aspernare vetera.
> Hez va, hez va ! hez va, hez !
> Bialx Sire Asnes, car allez :
> Belle bouche, car chantez." [20]

An ass, it would seem, was actually brought into church, at Beauvais at all events, during the singing of this song on the feast of the Circumcision. On January 14 an extraordinary ceremony took place there. A girl with a child in her arms rode upon an ass into St. Stephen's church, to represent the Flight into Egypt. The Introit, " Kyrie," " Gloria," and " Credo " at Mass ended in a bray, and at the close of the service the priest instead of saying " Ite, missa est," had to bray three times, and the people to respond in like manner. Mr. Chambers's theory is that the ass was a descendant of the *cervulus* or hobby-buck who figures so largely in ecclesiastical condemnations of Kalends customs.

The country *par excellence* of the Feast of the Fools was France. It can also be traced in Germany and Bohemia, while in England too there are notices of it, though far fewer than in France. Its abuses were the subject of frequent denunciations by Church reformers from the twelfth to the fifteenth century. The feast was prohibited at various times, and notably by the Council of Basle in 1435, but it was too popular to be quickly suppressed, and it took a century and a half to die out after this condemnation by a general council of the Church. In one cathedral, Amiens, it even lingered until 1721.

When in the fifteenth century and later the Feast of Fools was expelled from the churches of France, associations of laymen sprang up to carry on its traditions outside. It was indeed a form of entertainment which the townsfolk as well as the lower clergy thoroughly appreciated, and they were by no means willing to let it die. A *Prince des Sots* took the place of the " bishop," and was chosen by *sociétés joyeuses* organized by the youth of the cities for New Year merry-making. Gradually their activities grew, and their celebrations came to take place at other festive times beside the Christmas season. The *sots* had a distinctive dress, its most characteristic feature being a hood with asses' ears, probably a relic of the primitive days when the heads of sacrificed animals were worn by festal worshippers.[21]

The Boy Bishop.

Of older standing than the Feast of Fools were the Christmas revels of the deacons, the priests, and the choir-boys. They can be traced back to the early tenth century, and may have originated at the great song-school of St. Gall near Constance. The most important of the three feasts was that of the boys on Holy Innocents' Day, a theoretically appropriate date. Corresponding to the "lord" of the Feast of Fools was the famous " Boy Bishop," a choir-boy chosen by the lads themselves, who was vested in cope and mitre, held a pastoral staff, and gave the benediction. Other boys too usurped the dignities of their elders, and were attired as dean, archdeacons, and canons. Offices for the festival, in which the Boy Bishop figures largely, are to be found in English, French, and German service-books, the best known in this country being those in the Sarum Processional and Breviary. In England these ceremonies were far more popular and lasting than the Feast of Fools, and, unlike it, they were recognized and approved by authority, probably because boys were more amenable to discipline than men, and objectionable features could be pruned away with comparative ease. The festivities must have formed a delightful break in the year of the mediaeval schoolboy, for whom holidays, as distinguished from holy-days for church-going, scarcely existed. The feast, as we shall see, was by no means confined within the church walls; there was plenty of merry-making and money-making outside.

Minute details have been preserved of the Boy Bishop customs at St. Paul's Cathedral in the thirteenth century. It had apparently been usual for the "bishop" to make the cathedral dignitaries act as taper- and incense-bearers, thus reversing matters so that the great performed the functions of the lowly. In 1263 this was forbidden, and only clerks of lower rank might be chosen for these offices. But the "bishop" had the right to demand after Compline on the Eve of the Innocents a supper for himself and his train from the Dean or one of his canons. The number of his following must, however, be limited ; if he went to the Dean's he might take with him a train of fifteen : two chaplains, two taper-bearers, five clerks, two vergers, and four residentiary canons ; if to a lesser dignitary his attendants were to be fewer.

On Innocents' Day he was given a dinner, after which came a cavalcade through the city, that the " bishop " might bless the people. He had also to preach a sermon—no doubt written for him.

Examples of such discourses are still extant,[22] and are not without quaint touches. For instance the bidding prayer before one of them alludes to " the ryghte reverende fader and worshypfull lorde my broder Bysshopp of London, your dyoceasan," and " my worshypfull broder [the] Deane of this cathedrall chirche," [23] while in another the preacher remarks, speaking of the choristers and children of the song-school, " Yt is not so long sens I was one of them myself." [24]

In some places it appears, though this is by no means certain, that the boy actually sang Mass. The " bishop's " office was a very desirable one not merely because of the feasting, but because he had usually the right to levy contributions on the faithful, and the amounts collected were often very large. At York, for instance, in 1396 the " bishop " pocketed about £77, all expenses paid.

The general parallelism of the Boy Bishop customs and the Feast of Fools is obvious, and no doubt they had much the same folk-origin. One point, already mentioned, should specially be noticed : the election of the Boy Bishop generally took place on December 5, the Eve of St. Nicholas, patron of children ; he was often called " Nicholas bishop " ; and sometimes, as at Eton and Mayence, he exercised episcopal functions at divine service on the eve and the feast itself. It is possible, as Mr. Chambers suggests, that St. Nicholas's Day was an older date for the boys' festival than Holy Innocents', and that from the connection with St. Nicholas, the bishop saint *par excellence* (he was said to have been consecrated by divine command when still a mere layman), sprang the custom of giving the title "bishop" to the "lord" first of the boys' feast and later of the Feast of Fools.

In the late Middle Ages the Boy Bishop was found not merely in cathedral, monastic, and collegiate churches but in many parish churches throughout England and Scotland. Various inventories of the vestments and ornaments provided for him still exist. With the beginnings of the Reformation came his suppression : a proclamation of Henry VIII., dated July 22, 1541, commands "that from henceforth all suche superstitions be loste and clyerlye extinguisshed throughowte all this his realmes and dominions, forasmoche as the same doo resemble rather the unlawfull superstition of gentilitie [paganism], than the pure and sincere religion of Christe." 25   In Mary's reign the Boy Bishop reappeared, along with other "Popish" usages, but after Elizabeth's accession he naturally fell into oblivion. A few traces of him lingered in the seventeenth century.   "The Schoole-boies in the west," says Aubrey, "still religiously observe St. Nicholas day (Decemb. 6th), he was the Patron of the Schooleboies.   At Curry-Yeovill in Somersetshire, where there is a Howschole (or schole) in the Church, they have annually at that time a Barrell of good Ale brought into the church ; and that night they have the priviledge to breake open their Masters Cellar-dore." 26

In France he seems to have gradually vanished, as, after the Reformation, the Catholic Church grew more and more "respectable," but traces of him are to be found in the eighteenth century at Lyons and Rheims ; and at Sens, even in the nineteenth, the choir-boys used to play at being bishops on Innocents' Day and call their "archbishop" *âne*—a memory this of the old *asinaria festa*.27   In Denmark a vague trace of him was retained in the nineteenth century in a children's game.   A boy was dressed up in a white shirt, and seated on a chair, and the children sang a verse beginning, "Here we consecrate a Yule-bishop," and offered him nuts and apples.28

CHAPTER XIV

ST. STEPHEN'S,
ST. JOHN'S, AND
HOLY INNOCENTS' DAYS

CHAPTER XIV

ST. STEPHEN'S, ST. JOHN'S, AND HOLY INNOCENTS' DAYS

Horse Customs of St. Stephen's Day—The Swedish St. Stephen—St. John's Wine—
Childermas and its Beatings.

THE three saints' days immediately following Christmas—St. Stephen's (December 26), St. John the Evangelist's (December 27), and the Holy Innocents' (December 28)—have still various folk-customs associated with them, in some cases purely secular, in others hallowed by the Church.

ST. STEPHEN'S DAY.

In Tyrolese churches early in the morning of St. Stephen's Day there takes place a consecration of water and of salt brought by the people. The water is used by the peasants to sprinkle food, barns, and fields in order to avert the influence of witches and evil spirits, and bread soaked in it is given to the cattle when they are driven out to pasture on Whit Monday. The salt, too, is given to the beasts, and the peasants themselves partake of it before any important journey like a pilgrimage. Moreover when a storm is threatening some is thrown into the fire as a protection against hail.[1]

The most striking thing about St. Stephen's Day, however, is its connection with horses. St. Stephen is their patron; in England in former times they were bled on his festival in the belief that it would benefit them,[2] and the custom is still continued in some parts of Austria.[3] In Tyrol it is the custom not only to

311

bleed horses on St. Stephen's Day, but also to give them consecrated salt and bread or oats and barley.4

In some of the Carinthian valleys where horse-breeding is
specially carried on, the young men ride into the village on their
unsaddled steeds, and a race is run four or five times round the
church, while the priest blesses the animals, sprinkling them with
holy water and exorcizing them.5

Similar customs are or were found in various parts of Germany.
In Munich, formerly, during the services on St. Stephen's Day
more than two hundred men on horseback used to ride three
times round the interior of a church. The horses were decorated
with many-coloured ribbons, and the practice was not abolished
till 1876.6 At Backnang in Swabia horses were ridden out, as
fast as possible, to protect them from the influence of witches,
and in the Hohenlohe region men-servants were permitted by their
masters to ride in companies to neighbouring places, where much
drinking went on.7 In Holstein the lads on Stephen's Eve used
to visit their neighbours in a company, groom the horses, and ride
about in the farmyards, making a great noise until the people woke
up and treated them to beer and spirits.8 At the village of Walls-
büll near Flensburg the peasant youths in the early morning held
a race, and the winner was called Steffen and entertained at the
inn. At Viöl near Bredstadt the child who got up last on
December 26 received the name of Steffen and had to ride to a
neighbour's house on a hay-fork. In other German districts the
festival was called "the great horse-day," consecrated food was
given to the animals, they were driven round and round the fields
until they sweated violently, and at last were ridden to the blacksmith's and bled, to keep them healthy through the year. The
blood was preserved as a remedy for various illnesses.9

It is, however, in Sweden that the "horsy" aspect of the festival
is most obvious.10 Formerly there was a custom, at one o'clock
on St. Stephen's morning, for horses to be ridden to water that
flowed northward ; they would then drink "the cream of the
water" and flourish during the year. There was a violent race to
the water, and the servant who got there first was rewarded by
a drink of something stronger. Again, early that morning one

peasant would clean out another's stable, often at some distance from his home, feed, water, and rub down the horses, and then be entertained to breakfast. In olden times after service on St. Stephen's Day there was a race home on horseback, and it was supposed that he who arrived first would be the first to get his harvest in. But the most remarkable custom is the early morning jaunt of the so-called " Stephen's men," companies of peasant youths, who long before daybreak ride in a kind of race from village to village and awaken the inhabitants with a folk-song called *Staffansvisa*, expecting to be treated to ale or spirits in return.

The cavalcade is supposed to represent St. Stephen and his followers, yet the saint is not, as might be expected, the first martyr of the New Testament, but a dauntless missionary who, according to old legends, was one of the first preachers of the Gospel in Sweden, and was murdered by the heathen in a dark forest. A special trait, his love of horses, connects him with the customs just described. He had, the legends tell, five steeds : two red, two white, one dappled ; when one was weary he mounted another, making every week a great round to preach the Word. After his death his body was fastened to the back of an unbroken colt, which halted not till it came near Norrala, his home. There he was buried, and a church built over his grave became a place of pilgrimage to which sick animals, especially horses, were brought for healing.

Mannhardt and Feilberg hold that this Swedish St. Stephen is not a historical personage but a mythical figure, like many other saints, and that his legend, so bound up with horses, was an attempt to account for the folk-customs practised on the day dedicated to St. Stephen the first martyr. It is interesting to note that legendary tradition has played about a good deal with the New Testament Stephen ; for instance an old English carol makes him a servant in King Herod's hall at the time of Christ's birth :—

> " Stephen out of kitchen came,
>   With boarës head on hand,
> He saw a star was fair and bright
>   Over Bethlehem stand."

Thereupon he forsook King Herod for the Child Jesus, and was stoned to death.[11]

To return, however, to the horse customs of the day after Christmas, it is pretty plain that they are of non-Christian origin. Mannhardt has suggested that the race which is their most prominent feature once formed the prelude to a ceremony of lustration of houses and fields with a sacred tree. Somewhat similar "ridings" are found in various parts of Europe in spring, and are connected with a procession that appears to be an ecclesiastical adaptation of a pre-Christian lustration-rite.[12] The great name of Mannhardt lends weight to this theory, but it seems a somewhat roundabout way of accounting for the facts. Perhaps an explanation of the "horsiness" of the day might be sought in some pre-Christian sacrifice of steeds.

We have already noted that St. Stephen's Day is often the date for the "hunting of the wren" in the British Isles; it was also in England generally devoted to hunting and shooting, it being held that the game laws were not in force on that day.[13] This may be only an instance of Christmas licence, but it is just possible that there is here a survival of some tradition of sacrificial slaughter.

St. John's Day.

An ecclesiastical adaptation of a pagan practice may be seen in the *Johannissegen* customary on St. John's Day in many parts of Catholic Germany and Austria. A quantity of wine is brought to church to be blessed by the priest after Mass, and is taken away by the people to be drunk at home. There are many popular beliefs about the magical powers of this wine, beliefs which can be traced back through at least four centuries. In Tyrol and Bavaria it is supposed to protect its drinker from being struck by lightning, in the Rhenish Palatinate it is drunk in order that the other wine a man possesses may be kept from injury, or that next year's harvest may be good. In Nassau, Carinthia, and other regions some is poured into the wine-casks to preserve the precious drink from harm, while in Bavaria some is kept for use as medicine in sickness. In Styria St. John's wine is said to keep the body sound and healthy, and on his day even babes in the cradle are made to join in the family drinking.[14]

It appears that in the sixteenth and seventeenth centuries there was a great drinking on St. John's Day of ordinary, as well as consecrated, wine, often to excess, and scholars of that time seriously believed that *Weihnacht*, the German name for Christmas, should properly be spelt *Weinnacht*.[15] The *Johannissegen*, or *Johannisminne* as it was sometimes called, seems, all things considered, to be a survival of an old wine sacrifice like the *Martinsminne*. That it does not owe its origin to the legend about the cup of poison drunk by St. John is shown by the fact that a similar custom was in old times practised in Germany and Sweden on St. Stephen's Day.[16]

HOLY INNOCENTS' DAY.

Holy Innocents' Day or Childermas, whether or not because of Herod's massacre, was formerly peculiarly unlucky ; it was a day upon which no one, if he could possibly avoid it, should begin any piece of work. It is said of that superstitious monarch, Louis XI. of France, that he would never do any business on that day, and of our own Edward IV. that his coronation was postponed, because the date originally fixed was Childermas. In Cornwall no housewife would scour or scrub on Childermas, and in Northamptonshire it was considered very unlucky to begin any undertaking or even to do washing throughout the year on the day of the week on which the feast fell. Childermas was there called Dyzemas and a saying ran : " What is begun on Dyzemas Day will never be finished." In Ireland it was called " the cross day of the year," and it was said that anything then begun must have an unlucky ending.[17]

In folk-ritual the day is remarkable for its association with whipping customs. The seventeenth-century writer Gregorie mentions a custom of whipping up children on Innocents' Day in the morning, and explains its purpose as being that the memory of Herod's " murther might stick the closer ; and, in a moderate proportion, to act over the crueltie again in kind." [18]

This explanation will hardly hold water; the many and various examples of the practice of whipping at Christmas collected by Mannhardt [19] show that it is not confined either to Innocents' Day or to children. Moreover it is often regarded not as a cruel infliction, but as a service for which return must be made in good things to eat.

In central and southern Germany the custom is called " peppering " (*pfeffern*) and also by other names. In the Orlagau the girls on St. Stephen's, and the boys on St. John's Day beat their parents and godparents with green fir-branches, while the menservants beat their masters with rosemary sticks, saying :

> " Fresh green ! Long life !
> Give me a bright *thaler* [or nuts, &c.]."

They are entertained with plum-loaf or gingerbreads and brandy. In the Saxon Erzgebirge the young fellows whip the women and girls on St. Stephen's Day, if possible while they are still in bed, with birch-rods, singing the while :

> " Fresh green, fair and fine,
> Gingerbread and brandy-wine " ;

and on St. John's Day the women pay the men back. At several places in the Thuringian Forest children on Innocents' Day beat passers-by with birch-boughs, and get in return apples, nuts, and other dainties. Various other German examples of the same class of practice are given by Mannhardt. [20]

In France children who let themselves be caught in bed on the morning of Holy Innocents' came in for a whipping from their parents ; while in one province, Normandy, the early risers among the young people themselves gave the sluggards a beating. The practice even gave birth to a verb—*innocenter*. [21]

There can be little doubt that the Innocents' Day beating is a survival of a pre-Christian custom. Similar ritual scourging is found in many countries at various seasons of the year, and is by no means confined to Europe. [22] As now practised, it has often a harsh appearance, or has become a kind of teasing, as when in Bohemia at Easter young men whip girls until they give them something. Its original purpose, however, as we have seen in connection with St. Martin's rod, seems to have been altogether kindly. The whipping was not meant as a punishment or expiation or to harden people to pain, but either to expel harmful influences and drive out evil spirits or to convey by contact the virtues of some sacred tree.

CHAPTER XV

NEW YEAR'S DAY

CHAPTER XV

NEW YEAR'S DAY

Principle of New Year Customs—The New Year in France, Germany, the United States, and Eastern Europe—"First-footing" in Great Britain—Scottish New Year Practices—Highland Fumigation and "Breast-strip" Customs—Hogmanay and Aguillanneuf—New Year Processions in Macedonia, Roumania, Greece, and Rome—Methods of Augury—Sundry New Year Charms.

COMING to January 1, the modern and the Roman New Year's Day, we shall find that most of its customs have been anticipated at earlier festivals; the Roman Kalends practices have often been shifted to Christmas, while old Celtic and Teutonic New Year practices have frequently been transferred to the Roman date.*

The observances of New Year's Day mainly rest, as was said in Chapter VI., on the principle that "a good beginning makes a good ending," that as the first day is so will the rest be. If you would have plenty to eat during the year, dine lavishly on New Year's Day, if you would be rich see that your pockets are not empty at this critical season, if you would be lucky avoid like poison at this of all times everything of ill omen.

"On the Borders," says Mr. W. Henderson, "care is taken that no one enters a house empty-handed on New Year's Day. A visitor must bring in his hand some eatable; he will be doubly welcome if he carries in a hot stoup or 'plotie.' Everybody

---

* A remarkably clear instance of the transference of customs from Hollantide Eve (Hallowe'en) to the modern New Year is given by Sir John Rhys. Certain methods of prognostication described by him are practised by some people in the Isle of Man on the one day and by some on the other, and the Roman date is gaining ground.[1]

should wear a new dress on New Year's Day, and if its pockets contain money of every description they will be certain not to be empty throughout the year." [2]

The laying of stress on what happens on New Year's Day is by no means peculiarly European. Hindus, for instance, as Mr. Edgar Thurston tells us, " are very particular about catching sight of some auspicious object on the morning of New Year's Day, as the effects of omens seen on that occasion are believed to last throughout the year." It is thought that a man's whole prosperity depends upon the things that he then happens to fix his eyes upon.[3]

Charms, omens, and good wishes are naturally the most prominent customs of January 1 and its Eve. The New Year in England can hardly be called a popular festival ; there is no public holiday and the occasion is more associated with penitential Watch Night services and good resolutions than with rejoicing. But let the reader, if he be in London, pay a visit to Soho at this time, and he will get some idea of what the New Year means to the foreigner. The little restaurants are decorated with gay festoons of all colours and thronged with merrymakers, the shop-windows are crowded with all manner of *recherché* delicacies ; it is the gala season of the year.

In France January 1 is a far more festal day than Christmas ; it is then that presents are given, family gatherings held, and calls paid. In the morning children find their stockings filled with gifts, and then rush off to offer good wishes to their parents. In the afternoon the younger people call upon their older relations, and in the evening all meet for dinner at the home of the head of the family.[4]

In Germany the New Year is a time of great importance. Cards are far more numerous than at Christmas, and "New Year boxes " are given to the tradespeople, while on the Eve (*Sylvesterabend*) there are dances or parties, the custom of forecasting the future by lead-pouring is practised, and at the stroke of midnight there is a general cry of "Prosit Neu Jahr ! ", a drinking of healths, and a shaking of hands.[5]

New Year wishes and "compliments of the season " are

NEW YEAR'S DAY

familiar to us all, but in England we have not that custom of paying formal calls which in France is so characteristic of January 1, when not only relations and personal friends, but people whose connection is purely official are expected to visit one another. In devout Brittany the wish exchanged takes a beautiful religious form—"I wish you a good year and Paradise at the end of your days." [6]

New Year calling is by no means confined to France. In the United States it is one of the few traces left by the early Dutch settlers on American manners. The custom is now rapidly falling into disuse,[7] but in New York up to the middle of the nineteenth century "New Year's Day was devoted to the universal interchange of visits. Every door was thrown wide open. It was a breach of etiquette to omit any acquaintance in these annual calls, when old friendships were renewed and family differences amicably settled. A hearty welcome was extended even to strangers of presentable appearance." At that time the day was marked by tremendous eating and drinking, and its visiting customs sometimes developed into wild riot. Young men in barouches would rattle from one house to another all day long. "The ceremony of calling was a burlesque. There was a noisy and hilarious greeting, a glass of wine was swallowed hurriedly, everybody shook hands all round, and the callers dashed out and rushed into the carriage and were driven rapidly to the next house." [8]

The New Year calling to offer good wishes resembles in some respects the widespread custom of "first-footing," based on the belief that the character of the first visitor on New Year's Day affects the welfare of the household during the year. We have already met with a "first-foot" in the *polaznik* of the southern Slavs on Christmas Day. It is to be borne in mind that for them, or at all events for the Crivoscian highlanders whose customs are described by Sir Arthur Evans, Christmas is essentially the festival of the New Year : New Year's Day is not spoken of at all, its name and ceremonies being completely absorbed by the feasts of "Great" and "Little" Christmas.[9]

The "first-foot" superstition is found in countries as far apart as

Scotland and Macedonia. Let us begin with some English examples of it. In Shropshire the most important principle is that if luck is to rest on a house the " first-foot " must not be a woman. To provide against such an unlucky accident as that a woman should call first, people often engage a friendly man or boy to pay them an early visit. It is particularly interesting to find a Shropshire parallel to the *polaznik's* action in going straight to the hearth and striking sparks from the Christmas log,* when Miss Burne tells us that one old man who used to "let the New Year in " "always entered without knocking or speaking, and silently stirred the fire before he offered any greeting to the family." [10]

In the villages of the Teme valley, Worcestershire and Herefordshire, " in the old climbing-boy days, chimneys used to be swept on New Year's morning, that one of the right sex should be the first to enter; and the young urchins of the neighbourhood went the round of the houses before daylight singing songs, when one of their number would be admitted into the kitchen 'for good luck all the year.' " In 1875 this custom was still practised ; and at some of the farmhouses, if washing-day chanced to fall on the first day of the year, it was either put off, or to make sure, before the women could come, the waggoner's lad was called up early that he might be let out and let in again.[11]

The idea of the unluckiness of a woman's being the "first-foot" is extraordinarily widespread ; the present writer has met with it in an ordinary London restaurant, where great stress was laid upon a man's opening the place on New Year's morning before the waitresses arrived. A similar belief is found even in far-away China : it is there unlucky on New Year's Day to meet a woman on first going out.[12] Can the belief be connected with such ideas about dangerous influences proceeding from women as have been described by Dr. Frazer in Vol. III. of "The Golden Bough," [13] or does it rest merely on a view or woman as the inferior sex ? The unluckiness of first meeting a woman is, we may note, not confined to, but merely intensified on New Year's Day ; in Shropshire [14] and in Germany [15] it belongs to any ordinary day.

* See p. 252.

NEW YEAR'S DAY

As to the general attitude towards woman suggested by these superstitions I may quote a striking passage from Miss Jane Harrison's "Themis." "Woman to primitive man is a thing at once weak and magical, to be oppressed, yet feared. She is charged with powers of child-bearing denied to man, powers only half understood, forces of attraction, but also of danger and repulsion, forces that all over the world seem to fill him with dim terror. The attitude of man to woman, and, though perhaps in a less degree, of woman to man, is still to-day essentially magical."[16]

"First-foot" superstitions flourish in the north of England and in Scotland. In the northern counties a man is often specially retained as "first-foot" or "lucky bird"; in some parts he must be a bachelor, and he is often expected to bring a present with him—a shovelful of coals, or some eatable, or whisky.[17] In the East Riding of Yorkshire a boy called the "lucky bird" used to come at dawn on Christmas morning as well as on New Year's Day, and bring a sprig of evergreens[18]—an offering by now thoroughly familiar to us. In Scotland, especially in Edinburgh, it is customary for domestic servants to invite their sweethearts to be their "first-foots." The old Scotch families who preserve ancient customs encourage their servants to "first-foot" them, and grandparents like their grandchildren to perform for them the same service.[19] In Aberdeenshire it is considered most important that the "first-foot" should not come empty-handed. Formerly he carried spiced ale; now he brings a whisky-bottle. Shortbread, oat-cakes, "sweeties," or sowens, were also sometimes brought by the "first-foot," and occasionally the sowens were sprinkled on the doors and windows of the houses visited— a custom strongly suggesting a sacramental significance of some sort.[20]

Before we leave the subject of British "first-footing" we may notice one or two things that have possibly a racial significance. Not only must the "first-foot" be a man or boy, he is often required to be dark-haired; it is unlucky for a fair- or red-haired person to "let in" the New Year.[21] It has been suggested by Sir John Rhys that this idea rested in the first instance upon racial antipathy—the natural antagonism of an indigenous dark-haired people to a race of blonde invaders.[22]   Another curious requirement—in the Isle of Man and Northumberland—is that the "first-foot" shall not be flat-footed : he should be a person with a high-arched instep, a foot that "water runs under."   Sir John Rhys is inclined to connect this also with some racial contrast.   He remarks, by way of illustration, that English shoes do not as a rule fit Welsh feet, being made too low in the instep.[23]

Some reference has already been made to Scottish New Year customs.   In Scotland, the most Protestant region of Europe, the country in which Puritanism abolished altogether the celebration of Christmas, New Year's Day is a great occasion, and is marked by various interesting usages, its importance being no doubt largely due to the fact that it has not to compete with the Church feast of the Nativity.   Nowadays, indeed, the example of Anglicanism is affecting the country to a considerable extent, and Christmas Day is becoming observed in the churches.   The New Year, however, is still the national holiday, and January 1 a great day for visiting and feasting, the chief, in fact, of all festivals.[24]   New Year's Day and its Eve are often called the "Daft Days"; cakes and pastry of all kinds are eaten, healths are drunk, and calls are paid.[25]

In Edinburgh there are striking scenes on New Year's Eve. "Towards evening," writes an observer, "the thoroughfares become thronged with the youth of the city. . . . As the midnight hour approaches, drinking of healths becomes frequent, and some are already intoxicated. . . . The eyes of the immense crowd are ever being turned towards the lighted clock-face of 'Auld and Faithfu'' Tron [Church], the hour approaches, the hands seem to stand still, but in one second more the hurrahing, the cheering, the hand-shaking, the health-drinking, is all kept up as long as the clock continues to ring out the much-longed-for midnight hour. . . . The crowds slowly disperse, the much-intoxicated and helpless ones being hustled about a good deal, the police urging them on out of harm's way.   The first-footers are off and away, flying in every direction through the city, singing, cheering, and shaking hands with all and sundry."[26]

NEW YEAR'S DAY

One need hardly allude to the gathering of London Scots around St. Paul's to hear the midnight chime and welcome the New Year with the strains of "Auld Lang Syne," except to say that times have changed and Scotsmen are now lost in the swelling multitude of roysterers of all nationalities.

Drinking is and was a great feature of the Scottish New Year's Eve. " On the approach of twelve o'clock, a *hot pint* was prepared—that is, a kettle or flagon full of warm, spiced, and sweetened ale, with an infusion of spirits. When the clock had struck the knell of the departed year, each member of the family drank of this mixture ' A good health and a happy New Year and many of them ' to all the rest, with a general hand-shaking." The elders of the family would then sally out to visit their neighbours, and exchange greetings.[27]

At Biggar in Lanarkshire it was customary to "burn out the old year " with bonfires, while at Burghead in Morayshire a tar-barrel called the "Clavie " was set on fire and carried about the village and the fishing boats. Its embers were scrambled for by the people and carefully kept as charms against witchcraft.[28] These fire-customs may be compared with those on Hallowe'en, which, as we have seen, is probably an old New Year's Eve.

Stewart in his "Popular Superstitions of the Highlands of Scotland " tells how on the last night of the year the Strathdown Highlanders used to bring home great loads of juniper, which on New Year's Day was kindled in the different rooms, all apertures being closed so that the smoke might produce a thorough fumigation. Not only human beings had to stand this, but horses and other animals were treated in the same way to preserve them from harm throughout the year. Moreover, first thing on New Year's morning, everybody, while still in bed, was asperged with a large brush.[29] There is a great resemblance here to the Catholic use of incense and holy water in southern Germany and Austria on the *Rauchnächte* (see also Chapter VIII.). In Tyrol these nights are Christmas, New Year's, and Epiphany Eves. When night falls the Tyrolese peasant goes with all his household through each room and outhouse, his wife bearing the holy water vessel and the censer. Every corner of the buildings, every animal, every human being is purified with the sacred smoke and the holy sprinkling, and even the Christmas pie must be hallowed in this way. In Orthodox Greek countries something of the same kind takes place, as we shall see, at the Epiphany. To drive away evil spirits is no doubt the object of all these rites.[30]

The most interesting of Scottish New Year customs, considered as religious survivals, is a practice found in the Highlands on New Year's Eve, and evidently of sacrificial origin. It has been described by several writers, and has various forms. According to one account the hide of the mart or winter cow was wrapped round the head of one of a company of men, who all made off belabouring the hide with switches. The disorderly procession went three times *deiseal* (according to the course of the sun) round each house in the village, striking the walls and shouting on coming to a door a rhyme demanding admission. On entering, each member of the party was offered refreshments, and their leader gave to the goodman of the house the " breast-stripe " of a sheep, deer, or goat, wrapped round the point of a shinty stick.[31]

We have here another survival of that oft-noted custom of skin-wearing, which, as has been seen, originated apparently in a desire for contact with the sanctity of the sacrificed victim. Further, the " breast-stripe " given to the goodman of each house is evidently meant to convey the hallowed influences to each family. It is an oval strip, and no knife may be used in removing it from the flesh. The head of the house sets fire to it, and it is given to each person in turn to smell. The inhaling of its fumes is a talisman against fairies, witches, and demons. In the island of South Uist, according to a quite recent account, each person seizes hold of it as it burns, making the sign of the cross, if he be a Catholic, in the name of the Trinity, and it is put thrice sun-wise about the heads of those present. If it should be extinguished it is a bad omen for the New Year.[32]

The writer of the last account speaks of the " breast-strip " as the " Hogmanay," and it is just possible that the well-known Hogmanay processions of children on New Year's Eve (in Scotland and elsewhere) may have some connection with the ritual above described. It is customary for the poorer children to swaddle themselves in a great sheet, doubled up in front so as to form a vast pocket, and then go along the streets in little bands, calling out " Hogmanay " at the doors of the wealthier classes, and expecting a dole of oaten bread.   Each child gets a quadrant of oat-cake (sometimes with cheese), and this is called the " Hog-manay."   Here is one of the rhymes they sing :—

> "Get up, goodwife, and shake your feathers,
> And dinna think that we are beggars ;
> For we are bairns come out 'to play,
> Get up and gie's our hogmanay ! " [33]

The word *Hogmanay*—it is found in various forms in the northern English counties as well as in Scotland—has been a puzzle to etymologists.   It is used both for the last day of the year and for the gift of the oaten cake or the like ; and, as we have seen, it is shouted by the children in their quest. Exactly corresponding to it in sense and use is the French word *aguillanneuf*, from which it appears to be derived.   Although the phonetic difference between this and the Scottish word is great, the Norman form *hoguinané* is much closer.   There is, moreover, a Spanish word *aguinaldo* (formerly *aguilando*)=Christmas-box. The popular explanation of the French term as *au-guy-l'an-neuf* (to the mistletoe the New Year) is now rejected by scholars, and it seems likely that the word is a corruption of the Latin *Kalendae*.[34]

A few instances of *aguillanneuf* customs may be given.   Here are specimens of rhymes sung by the New Year *quêteurs* :—

> " Si vous veniez à la dépense,
> À la dépense de chez nous,
> Vous mangeriez de bons choux,
> On vous servirait du rost.
>   Hoguinano.
>
> Donnez-moi mes hoguignettes
> Dans un panier que voicy.
> Je l'achetai samedy
> D'un bon homme de dehors ;
> Mais il est encore à payer.
>   Hoguinano." [35]

PAGAN SURVIVALS

Formerly at Matignon and Ploubalay in Brittany on Christmas Eve the boys used to get together, carry big sticks and wallets, and knock at farmhouse doors. When the inmates called out, "Who's there?" they would answer, "The *hoguihanneu*," and after singing something they were given a piece of lard. This was put on a pointed stick carried by one of the boys, and was kept for a feast called the *bouriho*.[36] Elsewhere in Brittany poor children went round crying "*au guyané*," and were given pieces of lard or salt beef, which they stuck on a long spit.[37] In Guernsey the children's quest at the New Year was called *oguinane*. They chanted the following rhyme :—

> "Oguinâni ! Oguinâno !
> Ouvre ta pouque, et pis la recclios." * [38]

Similar processions are common in eastern Europe at the New Year. In some parts of Macedonia on New Year's Eve men or boys go about making a noise with bells. In other districts, early on New Year's morning, lads run about with sticks or clubs, knock people up, cry out good wishes, and expect to be rewarded with something to eat. Elsewhere again they carry green olive- or cornel-boughs, and touch with them everyone they meet.[39] We have already considered various similar customs, the noise and knocking being apparently intended to drive away evil spirits, and the green boughs to bring folks into contact with the spirit of growth therein immanent.

In Roumania on New Year's Eve there is a custom known as the "little plough." Boys and men go about after dark from house to house, with long greetings, ringing of bells, and cracking of whips. On New Year's morning Roumanians throw handfuls of corn at one another with some appropriate greeting, such as :—

> " May you live,
> May you flourish
> Like apple-trees,

---

* "Ope thy purse, and shut it then."

NEW YEAR'S DAY

> Like pear-trees
> In springtime,
> Like wealthy autumn,
> Of all things plentiful."

Generally this greeting is from the young to the old or from the poor to the rich, and a present in return is expected.[40]

In Athens models of war-ships are carried round by waits, who make a collection of money in them. "St. Basil's ships" they are called, and they are supposed to represent the vessel on which St. Basil, whose feast is kept on January 1, sailed from Caesarea.[41] It is probable that this is but a Christian gloss on a pagan custom. Possibly there may be here a survival of an old Greek practice of bearing a ship in procession in honour of Dionysus,[42] but it is to be noted that similar observances are found at various seasons in countries like Germany and Belgium where no Greek influence can be traced. The custom is widespread, and it has been suggested by Mannhardt that it was originally intended either to promote the success of navigation or to carry evil spirits out to sea.[43]

It is interesting, lastly, to read a mediaeval account of a New Year *quête* in Rome. "The following," says the writer, "are common Roman sports at the Kalends of January. On the Eve of the Kalends at a late hour boys arise and carry a shield. One of them wears a mask ; they whistle and beat a drum, they go round to the houses, they surround the shield, the drum sounds, and the masked figure whistles. This playing ended, they receive a present from the master of the house, whatever he thinks fit to give. So they do at every house. On that day they eat all kinds of vegetables. And in the morning two of the boys arise, take olive-branches and salt, enter into the houses, and salute the master with the words, 'Joy and gladness be in the house, so many sons, so many little pigs, so many lambs,' and they wish him all good things. And before the sun rises they eat either a piece of honeycomb or something sweet, that the whole year may pass sweetly, without strife and great trouble." [44]

Various methods of peering into the future, more or less like those described at earlier festivals, are practised at the New Year. Especially popular at German New Year's Eve parties is the custom of *bleigiessen*. "This ceremony consists of boiling specially prepared pieces of lead in a spoon over a candle ; each guest takes his spoonful and throws it quickly into the basin of water which is held ready. According to the form which the lead takes so will his future be in the coming year . . . ships (which indicate a journey), or hearts (which have, of course, only one meaning), or some other equally significant shape is usually discerned." 45

In Macedonia St. Basil's Eve (December 31) is a common time for divination : a favourite method is to lay on the hot cinders a pair of wild-olive-leaves to represent a youth and a maid. If the leaves crumple up and draw near each other, it is concluded that the young people love one another dearly, but if they recoil apart the opposite is the case. If they flare up and burn, it is a sign of excessive passion.46

In Lithuania on New Year's Eve nine sorts of things—money, cradle, bread, ring, death's head, old man, old woman, ladder, and key—are baked of dough, and laid under nine plates, and every one has three grabs at them. What he gets will fall to his lot during the year.47

Lastly, in Brittany it is supposed that the wind which prevails on the first twelve days of the year will blow during each of the twelve months, the first day corresponding to January, the second to February, and so on.48 Similar ideas of the prophetic character of Christmastide weather are common in our own and other countries.

Practically all the customs discussed in this chapter have been of the nature of charms ; one or two more, practised on New Year's Day or Eve, may be mentioned in conclusion.

There are curious superstitions about New Year water. At Bromyard in Herefordshire it was the custom, at midnight on New Year's Eve, to rush to the nearest spring to snatch the "cream of the well"—the first pitcherful of water—and with it the prospect of the best luck.49 A Highland practice was to send some one on the last night of the year to draw a pitcherful of water in silence, and without the vessel touching the ground. The water was drunk on New Year's morning as a charm against witchcraft and the evil eye.[50] A similar belief about the luckiness of "new water" exists at Canzano Peligno in the Abruzzi. "On New Year's Eve, the fountain is decked with leaves and bits of coloured stuff, and fires are kindled round it. As soon as it is light, the girls come as usual with their copper pots on their head ; but the youths are on this morning guardians of the well, and sell the 'new water' for nuts and fruits—and other sweet things." [51]

In some of the Aegean islands when the family return from church on New Year's Day, the father picks up a stone and leaves it in the yard, with the wish that the New Year may bring with it "as much gold as is the weight of the stone." [52] Finally, in Little Russia "corn sheaves are piled upon a table, and in the midst of them is set a large pie. The father of the family takes his seat behind them, and asks his children if they can see him. 'We cannot see you,' they reply. On which he proceeds to express what seems to be a hope that the corn will grow so high in his fields that he may be invisible to his children when he walks there at harvest-time." [53]

With a curious and beautiful old carol from South Wales I must bring this chapter to a close. It was formerly sung before dawn on New Year's Day by poor children who carried about a jug of water drawn that morning from the well. With a sprig of box or other evergreen they would sprinkle those they met, wishing them the compliments of the season. To pay their respects to those not abroad at so early an hour, they would serenade them with the following lines, which, while connected with the "new water" tradition, contain much that is of doubtful interpretation, and are a fascinating puzzle for folk-lorists :—

> "Here we bring new water
> From the well so clear,
> For to worship God with,
> This happy New Year.

PAGAN SURVIVALS

Sing levy-dew, sing levy-dew,
  The water and the wine ;
The seven bright gold wires
  And the bugles they do shine.

Sing reign of Fair Maid,
  With gold upon her toe,—
Open you the West Door,
  And turn the Old Year go :
Sing reign of Fair Maid,
  With gold upon her chin,—
Open you the East Door,
  And let the New Year in." [54]

CHAPTER XVI

EPIPHANY TO CANDLEMAS

CHAPTER XVI

EPIPHANY TO CANDLEMAS

The Twelfth Cake and the "King of the Bean "—French Twelfth Night Customs—
St. Basil's Cake in Macedonia—Epiphany and the Expulsion of Evils—The Befana
in Italy—The Magi as Present-bringers—Greek Epiphany Customs—Wassailing
Fruit-trees—Herefordshire and Irish Twelfth Night Practices—The "Haxey
Hood " and Christmas Football—St. Knut's Day in Sweden—Rock Day—Plough
Monday—Candlemas, its Ecclesiastical and Folk Ceremonies—Farewells to
Christmas.

THE EPIPHANY.

THOUGH the Epiphany has ceased to be a popular festival in England, it was once a very high day indeed, and in many parts of
Europe it is still attended by folk-customs of great interest.* For
the peasant of Tyrol, indeed, it is New Year's Day, the first of
January being kept only by the townsfolk and modernized
people.[1]

To Englishmen perhaps the best known feature of the secular
festival is the Twelfth Cake. Some words of Leigh Hunt's will
show what an important place this held in the mid-nineteenth
century :—

"Christmas goes out in fine style,—with Twelfth Night. It is a
finish worthy of the time. Christmas Day was the morning of the
season ; New Year's Day the middle of it, or noon ; Twelfth Night
is the night, brilliant with innumerable planets of Twelfth-cakes. The
whole island keeps court ; nay, all Christendom. All the world are

* It is probable that some customs practised at the Epiphany belong in reality to
Christmas Day, Old Style.

kings and queens. Everybody is somebody else, and learns at once to laugh at, and to tolerate, characters different from his own, by enacting them. Cakes, characters, forfeits, lights, theatres, merry rooms, little holiday-faces, and, last not least, the painted sugar on the cakes, so bad to eat but so fine to look at, useful because it is perfectly useless except for a sight and a moral—all conspire to throw a giddy splendour over the last night of the season, and to send it to bed in pomp and colours, like a Prince." [2]

For seventeenth-century banqueting customs and the connection of the cake with the " King of the Bean " Herrick may be quoted :—

> " Now, now the mirth comes
> With the cake full of plums,
> Where bean's the king of the sport here ;
> Besides we must know,
> The pea also
> Must revel as queen in the court here.
>
> Begin then to choose
> This night as ye use,
> Who shall for the present delight here
> Be a king by the lot,
> And who shall not
> Be Twelfth-day queen for the night here.
>
> Which known, let us make
> Joy-sops with the cake ;
> And let not a man then be seen here,
> Who unurg'd will not drink,
> To the base from the brink,
> A health to the king and the queen here." [3]

There are many English references to the custom of electing a Twelfth Day monarch by means of a bean or pea, and this "king" is mentioned in royal accounts as early as the reign of Edward II.[4] He appears, however, to have been even more popular in France than in England, and he probably still lingers in some of the remoter French provinces.

THE EPIPHANY

The method of choosing the Epiphany king is thus described by the sixteenth-century writer, Étienne Pasquier :—

"When the cake has been cut into as many portions as there are guests, a small child is put under the table, and is interrogated by the master under the name of Phebé [Phoebus], as if he were a child who in the innocence of his age represented a kind of Apollo's oracle. To this questioning the child answers with a Latin word : *Domine*. Thereupon the master calls on him to say to whom he shall give the piece of cake which he has in his hand : the child names whoever comes into his head, without respect of persons, until the portion where the bean is is given out. He who gets it is reckoned king of the company, although he may be a person of the least importance. This done, everyone eats, drinks, and dances heartily." [5]

In Berry at the end of the festive repast a cake is brought before the head of the household, and divided into as many portions as there are guests, plus one. The youngest member of the family distributes them. The portion remaining is called *la part du bon Dieu*, and is given to the first person who asks for it. A band of children generally come to claim it, with a leader who sings a little song.[6] There was formerly a custom of dressing up a king in full robes. He had a fool to amuse him during the feast, and shots were fired when he drank.[7]

Here is a nineteenth-century account from Lorraine :—

"On the Vigil of the Epiphany all the family and the guests assemble round the table, which is illuminated by a lamp hanging above its centre. Lots are cast for the king of the feast, and if the head of any-one present casts no shadow on the wall it is a sign that he will die during the year. Then the king chooses freely his queen : they have the place of honour, and each time they raise their glasses to their mouths cries of 'The king drinks, the queen drinks !' burst forth on all sides. . . . The next day an enormous cake, divided into equal portions, is distributed to the company by the youngest boy. The first portion is always for *le bon Dieu*, the second for the Blessed Virgin (these two portions are always given to the first poor person who presents him-self) ; then come those of relations, servants, and visitors. He who finds a bean in his portion is proclaimed king ; if it is a lady she chooses her

339

king, and he invites the company to a banquet on the Sunday following, at which black kings are made by rubbing the face with a
burnt cork." [8]

The use of the *gâteau des Rois* goes pretty far back.   At the
monastery of Mont-St.-Michel in the thirteenth century the
Epiphany king was chosen from among the monks by means of a
number of cakes in one of which a bean was placed.   At Matins,
High Mass, and Vespers he sat upon a special throne.[9]

It may be added that there is a quaint old story of a curate
" who having taken his preparations over evening, when all men
cry (as the manner is) *the king drinketh*, chanting his Masse the
next morning, fell asleep in his Memento : and, when he awoke,
added with a loud voice, *The king drinketh*." [10]

One more French " king " custom may be mentioned, though
it relates to Christmas Day, not Epiphany.   At Salers in the
centre of France there were formerly a king and queen whose
function was to preside over the festival, sit in a place of honour
in church, and go first in the procession.   The kingship was not
elective, but was sold by auction at the church door, and it is said
to have been so much coveted that worthy citizens would sell their
heritage in order to purchase it.[11]

It may be remarked that Epiphany kings and cakes similar to
the French can be traced in Holland and Germany,[12] and that the
" King of the Bean " is known in modern Italy, though there he
may be an importation from the north.[13]

How is this merry monarch to be accounted for ?   His resemblance to the king of the *Saturnalia*, who presided over the fun
of the feast in the days of imperial Rome, is certainly striking,
but it is impossible to say whether he derives directly from
that personage.   No doubt his association with the feast of the
Three Kings has helped to maintain his rule.   As for the bean, it
appears to have been a sacred vegetable in ancient times.   There
is a story about the philosopher Pythagoras, how, when flying
before a host of rebels, he came upon a field of beans and refused
to pass through it for fear of crushing the plants, thus enabling his
pursuers to overtake him.   Moreover, the *flamen dialis* in Rome
was forbidden to eat or even name the vegetable, and the

name of the Fabii, a Roman *gens*, suggests a totem tribe of the bean.14

In eastern Europe, though I know of no election of a king, there are New Year customs with cakes, closely resembling some of the French practices described a page or two back. "St. Basil's Cake" on New Year's Eve in Macedonia is a kind of shortbread with a silver coin and a cross of green twigs in it. When all are seated round the table the father and mother take the cake, " and break it into two pieces, which are again subdivided by the head of the family into shares. The first portion is destined for St. Basil, the Holy Virgin, or the patron saint whose icon is in the house. The second stands for the house itself. The third for the cattle and domestic animals belonging thereto. The fourth for the inanimate property, and the rest for each member of the household according to age. Each portion is successively dipped in a cup of wine." He who finds the cross or the coin in his share of the cake will prosper during the year. The money is considered sacred and is used to buy a votive taper.15

In Macedonia when the New Year's supper is over, the table, with the remnants of the feast upon it, is removed to a corner of the room in order that St. Basil may come and partake of the food.16 He appears to have been substituted by the Church for the spirits of the departed, for whom, as we have seen, food is left in the West on All Souls' and Christmas Eves. Probably the Macedonian practice of setting aside a portion of the cake for a saint, and the pieces cut in France for *le bon Dieu* and the Virgin or the three Magi, have a like origin. One may compare them with the Serbian breaking of the *kolatch* cake in honour of Christ " the Patron Namegiver." Is it irrelevant, also, to mention here the Greek Church custom, at the preparation of the elements for the Eucharist, of breaking portions of the bread in memory of the Virgin and other saints ?

In many countries the Epiphany is a special time for the expulsion of evils. At Brunnen in Switzerland boys go about in procession on Twelfth Night, with torches and lanterns, and make a great noise with horns, bells, whips, &c., in order to frighten away two wood-spirits. In Labruguière in southern France on the Eve of Twelfth Day the inhabitants rush through the streets, making discordant noises and a huge uproar, with the object of scaring away ghosts and devils.[17]

In parts of the eastern Alps there takes place what is called *Berchtenlaufen*. Lads, formerly to the number of two or three hundred, rush about in the strangest masks, with cowbells, whips, and all sorts of weapons, and shout wildly.[18] In Nuremberg up to the year 1616 on *Bergnacht* or Epiphany Eve boys and girls used to run about the streets and knock loudly at the doors.[19] Such knocking, as we have seen, may well have been intended to drive away spirits from the houses.

At Eschenloh near Partenkirchen in Upper Bavaria three women used to *berchten* on that evening. They all had linen bags over their heads, with holes for the mouth and eyes. One carried a chain, another a rake, and the third a broom. Going round to the houses, they knocked on the door with the chain, scraped the ground with the rake, and made a noise of sweeping with the broom.[20] The suggestion of a clearing away of evils is here very strong.

In connection with the *Kallikantzaroi* mention has already been made of the purification of houses with holy water, performed by Greek priests on the Epiphany. In Roumania, where a similar sprinkling is performed, a curious piece of imitative magic is added—the priest is invited to sit upon the bed, in order that the brooding hen may sit upon her eggs. Moreover there should be maize grains under the mattress ; then the hen will lay eggs in abundance.[21]

We noted in an earlier chapter the name *Berchtentag* applied in southern Germany and in Austria to the Epiphany, and we saw also how the mysterious Frau Berchta was specially connected with the day. On the Epiphany and its Eve in the Möllthal in Carinthia a female figure, " the Berchtel," goes the round of the houses. She is generally dressed in a hide, wears a hideous wooden mask, and hops wildly about, inquiring as to the behaviour of children, and demanding gifts.[22]

THE EPIPHANY IN FLORENCE.

To face p. 343.

THE EPIPHANY

Something of the terrible, as well as the beneficent, belongs to the " Befana," the Epiphany visitor who to Italian children is the great gift-bringer of the year, the Santa Klaus of the South. " Delightful," say Countess Martinengo, " as are the treasures she puts in their shoes when satisfied with their behaviour, she is credited with an unpleasantly sharp eye for youthful transgressions." 23 Mothers will sometimes warn their children that if they are naughty the Befana will fetch and eat them. To Italian youngsters she is a very real being, and her coming on Epiphany Eve is looked forward to with the greatest anxiety. Though she puts playthings and sweets in the stockings of good children, she has nothing but a birch and coal for those who misbehave themselves.24

Formerly at Florence images of the Befana were put up in the windows of houses, and there were processions through the streets, guys being borne about, with a great blowing of trumpets.25 Toy trumpets are still the delight of little boys at the Epiphany in Italy.

The Befana's name is obviously derived from *Epiphania*. In Naples the little old woman who fills children's stockings is called " Pasqua Epiphania,"* the northern contraction not having been acclimatized there.26

In Spain as well as Italy the Epiphany is associated with presents for children, but the gift-bringers for little Spaniards are the Three Holy Kings themselves. There is an old Spanish tradition that the Magi go every year to Bethlehem to adore the infant Jesus, and on their way visit children, leaving sweets and toys for them if they have behaved well. On Epiphany Eve the youngsters go early to bed, put out their shoes on the window-sill or balcony to be filled with presents by the Wise Men, and provide a little straw for their horses.27

It is, or was, a custom in Madrid to look out for the Kings on Epiphany Eve. Companies of men go out with bells and pots and pans, and make a great noise. There is loud shouting, and torches cast a fantastic light upon the scene. One of the men carries a large ladder, and mounts it to see if the Kings are

* *Pasqua* is there used for great festivals in general, not only for Easter.

coming. Here, perhaps, some devil-scaring rite, resembling those described above, has been half-Christianized.[28]

In Provence, too, there was a custom of going to meet the Magi. In a charming chapter of his Memoirs Mistral tells us how on Epiphany Eve all the children of his countryside used to go out to meet the Kings, bearing cakes for the Magi, dried figs for their pages, and handfuls of hay for their horses. In the glory and colour of the sunset young Mistral thought he saw the splendid train ; but soon the gorgeous vision died away, and the children stood gaping alone on the darkening highway—the Kings had passed behind the mountain. After supper the little ones hurried to church, and there in the Chapel of the Nativity beheld the Kings in adoration before the Crib.[29]

At Trest not only did the young people carry baskets ot dried fruit, but there were three men dressed as Magi to receive the offerings and accept compliments addressed to them by an orator. In return they presented him with a purse full of counters, upon which he rushed off with the treasure and was pursued by the others in a sort of dance.[30] Here again the Magi are evidently mixed up with something that has no relation to Christianity.

We noted in Chapter IV. the elaborate ceremonies connected in Greece with the Blessing of the Waters at the Epiphany, and the custom of diving for a cross. It would seem, as was pointed out, that the latter is an ecclesiastically sanctioned form of a folk-ceremony. This is found in a purer state in Macedonia, where, after Matins on the Epiphany, it is the custom to thrust some one into water, be it sea or river, pond or well. On emerging he has to sprinkle the bystanders.[31] The rite may be compared with the drenchings of human beings in order to produce rain described by Dr. Frazer in " The Magic Art." [32]

Another Greek custom combines the purifying powers ot Epiphany water with the fertilizing influences of the Christmas log—round Mount Olympos ashes are taken from the hearth where a cedar log has been burning since Christmas, and are baptized in the blessed water of the river. They are then borne to the vineyards, and thrown at their four corners, and also at the foot of apple- and fig-trees.33

This may remind us that in England fruit-trees used to come in for special treatment on the Vigil of the Epiphany. In Devonshire the farmer and his men would go to the orchard with a large jug of cider, and drink the following toast at the foot of one of the best-bearing apple-trees, firing guns in conclusion :—

"Here's to thee, old apple-tree,
Whence thou may'st bud, and whence thou may'st blow!
And whence thou may'st bear apples enow!
Hats full! caps full!
Bushel!—bushel—sacks full,
And my pockets full too! Huzza!"34

In seventeenth-century Somersetshire, according to Aubrey, a piece of toast was put upon the roots.35 According to another account each person in the company used to take a cupful of cider, with roasted apples pressed into it, drink part of the contents, and throw the rest at the tree.36 The custom is described by Herrick as a Christmas Eve ceremony :—

"Wassail the trees, that they may bear
You many a plum and many a pear;
For more or less fruits they will bring,
As you do give them wassailing."37

In Sussex the wassailing (or "worsling") of fruit-trees took place on Christmas Eve, and was accompanied by a trumpeter blowing on a cow's horn.38

The wassailing of the trees may be regarded as either originally an offering to their spirits or—and this seems more probable— as a sacramental act intended to bring fertilizing influences to bear upon them. Customs of a similar character are found in Continental countries during the Christmas season. In Tyrol, for instance, when the Christmas pies are a-making on St. Thomas's Eve, the maids are told to go out-of-doors and put their arms, sticky with paste, round the fruit-trees, in order that they may bear well next year.[39] The uses of the ashes of the Christmas log have already been noticed.

Sometimes, as in the Thurgau, Mecklenburg, Oldenburg, and Tyrol, the trees are beaten to make them bear. On New Year's Eve at Hildesheim people dance and sing around them,[40] while the Tyrolese peasant on Christmas Eve will go out to his trees, and, knocking with bent fingers upon them, will bid them wake up and bear.[41] There is a Slavonic custom, on the same night, of threatening apple-trees with a hatchet if they do not produce fruit during the year.[42]

Another remarkable agricultural rite was practised on Epiphany Eve in Herefordshire and Gloucestershire. The farmer and his servants would meet in a field sown with wheat, and there light thirteen fires, with one larger than the rest. Round this a circle was formed by the company, and all would drink a glass of cider to the success of the harvest.* This done, they returned to the farm, to feast—in Gloucestershire—on cakes made with caraways, and soaked in cider. The Herefordshire accounts give particulars of a further ceremony. A large cake was provided, with a hole in the middle, and after supper everyone went to the wain-house. The master filled a cup with strong ale, and standing opposite the finest ox, pledged him in a curious toast; the company followed his example with the other oxen, addressing each by name. Afterwards the large cake was put on the horn of the first ox.[43]

It is extremely remarkable, and can scarcely be a mere coincidence, that far away among the southern Slavs, as we saw in Chapter XII., a Christmas cake with a hole in its centre is likewise put upon the horn of the chief ox. The wassailing of the animals is found there also. On Christmas Day, Sir Arthur

---

* The custom of "burning the bush," still surviving here and there in Herefordshire, shows a certain resemblance to this. The "bush," a globe made of hawthorn, hangs throughout the year in the farmhouse kitchen, with the mistletoe. Early on New Year's Day it "is carried to the earliest sown wheat field, where a large fire is lighted, of straw and bushes, in which it is burnt. While it is burning, a new one is made ; in making it, the ends of the branches are scorched in the fire." Burning straw is carried over twelve ridges of the field, and then follow cider-drinking and cheering. (See Leather, " Folk-Lore of Herefordshire," 91 f.)

Evans relates, the house-mother " entered the stall set apart for the goats, and having first sprinkled them with corn, took the wine-cup in her hand and said, ' Good morning, little mother ! The Peace of God be on thee ! Christ is born ; of a truth He is born. May'st thou be healthy. I drink to thee in wine ; I give thee a pomegranate ; may'st thou meet with all good luck ! ' She then lifted the cup to her lips, took a sup, tossed the pomegranate among the herd, and throwing her arms round the she-goat, whose health she had already drunk, gave it the ' Peace of God '—kissed it, that is, over and over again." The same ceremony was then performed for the benefit of the sheep and cows, and all the animals were beaten with a leafy olive-branch.44

As for the fires, an Irish custom to some extent supplies a parallel. On Epiphany Eve a sieve of oats was set up, " and in it a dozen of candles set round, and in the centre one larger, all lighted." This was said to be in memory of the Saviour and His apostles, lights of the world.45 Here is an account of a similar custom practised in Co. Leitrim :—

" A piece of board is covered with cow-dung, and twelve rushlights are stuck therein. These are sprinkled with ash at the top, to make them light easily, and then set alight, each being named by some one present, and as each dies so will the life of its owner. A ball is then made of the dung, and it is placed over the door of the cow-house for an increase of cattle. Sometimes mud is used, and the ball placed over the door of the dwelling-house." 46

There remains to be considered under Epiphany usages an ancient and very remarkable game played annually on January 6 at Haxey in Lincolnshire. It is known traditionally as " Haxey Hood," and its centre is a struggle between the men of two villages for the possession of a roll of sacking or leather called the " hood." Over it preside the " boggans " or " bullocks " of Plough Monday (see p. 352), headed by a figure known as " My Lord," who is attended by a fool. The proceedings are opened on the village green by a mysterious speech from the fool :—

" Now, good folks, this is Haxa' Hood. We've killed two

bullocks and a half, but the other half we had to leave running about field : we can fetch it if it's wanted. Remember it's—

> 'Hoose agin hoose, toon agin toon,
> And if you meet a man knock him doon.'"

Then, in an open field, the hoods—there are six of them, one apparently for each of the chief hamlets round—are thrown up and struggled for. "The object is to carry them off the field away from the boggans. If any of these can get hold of them, or even touch them, they have to be given up, and carried back to My Lord. For every one carried off the field the boggans forfeit half-a-crown, which is spent in beer, doubtless by the men of the particular hamlet who have carried off the hood." The great event of the day is the struggle for the last hood—made of leather—between the men of Haxey and the men of Westwood-side—"that is to say really between the customers of the public-houses there—each party trying to get it to his favourite 'house.' The publican at the successful house stands beer." [47]

Mr. Chambers regards the fool's strange speech as preserving the tradition that the hood is the half of a bullock—the head of a sacrificial victim, and he explains both the Haxey game and also the familiar games of hockey and football as originating in a struggle between the people of two villages to get such a head, with all its fertilizing properties, over their own boundary.[48] At Hornchurch in Essex, if we may trust a note given by Hone, an actual boar's head was wrestled for on Christmas Day, and afterwards feasted upon at one of the public-houses by the victor and his friends.[49]

One more feature of the Haxey celebration must be mentioned (it points apparently to a human sacrifice) : the fool, the morning after the game, used to be "smoked" over a straw fire. "He was suspended above the fire and swung backwards and forwards over it until almost suffocated ; then allowed to drop into the smouldering straw, which was well wetted, and to scramble out as he could." [50]

Returning to the subject of football, I may here condense an account of a Welsh Christmas custom quoted by Sir Laurence Gomme, in his book " The Village Community," from the *Oswestry Observer* of March 2, 1887 :—" In South Cardiganshire it seems that about eighty years ago the population, rich and poor, male and female, of opposing parishes, turned out on Christmas Day and indulged in the game of football with such vigour that it became little short of a serious fight." Both in north and south Wales the custom was found. At one place, Llanwenog near Lampeter, there was a struggle between two parties with different traditions of race. The Bros, supposed to be descendants from Irish people, occupied the high ground of the parish ; the Blaenaus, presumably pure-bred Brythons, occupied the lowlands. After morning service on Christmas Day, " the whole of the Bros and Blaenaus, rich and poor, male and female, assembled on the turnpike road which divided the highlands from the lowlands." The ball was thrown high in the air, " and when it fell Bros and Blaenaus scrambled for its possession. . . . If the Bros, by hook or by crook, could succeed in taking the ball up the mountain to their hamlet of Rhyddlan they won the day, while the Blaenaus were successful if they got the ball to their end of the parish at New Court." Many severe kicks were given, and the whole thing was taken so keenly " that a Bro or a Blaenau would as soon lose a cow from his cowhouse as the football from his portion of the parish." There is plainly more than a mere pastime here ; the thing appears to have been originally a struggle between two clans.[51]

Anciently the Carnival, with its merrymaking before the austerities of Lent, was held to begin at the Epiphany. This was the case in Tyrol even in the nineteenth century.[52] As a rule, however, the Carnival in Roman Catholic countries is restricted to the last three days before Ash Wednesday. The pagan origin of its mummeries and licence is evident, but it is a spring rather than a winter festival, and hardly calls for treatment here.

The Epiphany is in many places the end of Christmas. In Calvados, Normandy, it is marked by bonfires ; red flames mount skywards, and the peasants join hands, dance, and leap through blinding smoke and cinders, shouting these rude lines :—

> " Àdieu les Rois
> Jusqu'à douze mois,
> Douze mois passés
> Les bougelées." [53]

Another French Epiphany *chanson*, translated by the Rev. R. L. Gales, is a charming farewell to Christmas :—

> "Noël is leaving us,
> Sad 'tis to tell,
> But he will come again,
> Adieu, Noël.
>
> His wife and his children
> Weep as they go :
> On a grey horse
> They ride thro' the snow.
>
> .   .   .   .
>
> The Kings ride away
> In the snow and the rain,
> After twelve months
> We shall see them again." [54]

Post-Epiphany Festivals.

Though with Twelfth Day the high festival of Christmas generally ends, later dates have sometimes been assigned as the close of the season. At the old English court, for instance, the merrymaking was sometimes carried on until Candlemas, while in some English country places it was customary, even in the late nineteenth century, to leave Christmas decorations up, in houses and churches, till that day.[55] The whole time between Christmas and the Presentation in the Temple was thus treated as sacred to the Babyhood of Christ ; the withered evergreens would keep alive memories of Christmas joys, even, sometimes, after Septuagesima had struck the note of penitence.

Before we pass on to a short notice of Candlemas, we may

glance at a few last sparks, so to speak, of the Christmas blaze, and then at the English festivals which marked the resumption of work after the holidays.

In Sweden Yule is considered to close with the Octave of the Epiphany, January 13, "St. Knut's Day," the twentieth after Christmas.

> "Twentieth day Knut
> Driveth Yule out"

sing the old folks as the young people dance in a ring round the festive Yule board, which is afterwards robbed of the viands that remain on it, including the Yule boar. On this day a sort of mimic fight used to take place, the master and servants of the house pretending to drive away the guests with axe, broom, knife, spoon, and other implements.[56] The name, "St. Knut's Day," is apparently due to the fact that in the laws of Canute the Great (1017–36) it is commanded that there is to be no fasting from Christmas to the Octave of the Epiphany.[57]

In England the day after the Epiphany was called St. Distaff's or Rock Day (the word Rock is evidently the same as the German *Rocken* = distaff). It was the day when the women resumed their spinning after the rest and gaiety of Christmas. From a poem of Herrick's it appears that the men in jest tried to burn the women's flax, and the women in return poured water on the men :—

> "Partly work, and partly play
> You must on St. Distaff's day :
> From the plough soon free your team,
> Then come home and fother them ;
> If the maids a-spinning go,
> Burn the flax and fire the tow.
>
> .   .   .   .   .
>
> Bring in pails of water then,
> Let the maids bewash the men ;
> Give St. Distaff all the right,
> Then bid Christmas sport good night ;
> And next morrow, every one
> To his own vocation." [58]

PAGAN SURVIVALS

A more notable occasion was Plough Monday, the first after Twelfth Day. Men's labour then began again after the holidays.59 We have already seen that it is sometimes associated with the mummers' plays. Often, however, its ritual is not developed into actual drama, and the following account from Derbyshire gives a fairly typical description of its customs :—

"On Plough Monday the ' Plough bullocks ' are occasionally seen ; they consist of a number of young men from various farmhouses, who are dressed up in ribbons. . . . These young men yoke themselves to a plough, which they draw about, preceded by a band of music, from house to house, collecting money. They are accompanied by the Fool and Bessy ; the fool being dressed in the skin of a calf, with the tail hanging down behind, and Bessy generally a young man in female attire. The fool carries an inflated bladder tied to the end of a long stick, by way of whip, which he does not fail to apply pretty soundly to the heads and shoulders of his team. When anything is given a cry of ' Largess ! ' is raised, and a dance performed round the plough. If a refusal to their application for money is made they not unfrequently plough up the pathway, door-stone, or any other portion of the premises they happen to be near." 60

By Plough Monday we have passed, it seems probable, from New Year festivals to one that originally celebrated the beginning of spring. Such a feast, apparently, was kept in mid-February when ploughing began at that season ; later the advance of agriculture made it possible to shift it forward to early January.61

CANDLEMAS.

Nearer to the original date of the spring feast is Candlemas, February 2 ; though connected with Christmas by its ecclesiastical meaning, it is something of a vernal festival.62

The feast of the Purification of the Virgin or Presentation of Christ in the Temple was probably instituted by Pope Liberius at Rome in the fourth century. The ceremonial to which it owes its popular name, Candlemas, is the blessing of candles in church and the procession of the faithful, carrying them lighted in their hands. During the blessing the " Nunc dimittis " is chanted, with the antiphon "Lumen ad revelationem gentium et gloriam plebis tuae Israel," the ceremony being thus brought into connection with the "light to lighten the Gentiles" hymned by Symeon. Usener has however shown reason for thinking that the Candlemas procession was not of spontaneous Christian growth, but was inspired by a desire to Christianize a Roman rite, the *Amburbale*, which took place at the same season and consisted of a procession round the city with lighted candles.[63]

The Candlemas customs of the sixteenth century are thus described by Naogeorgus :

" Then numbers great ot Tapers large, both men and women beare
　To Church, being halowed there with pomp, and dreadful words to heare.
　This done, eche man his Candell lightes, where chiefest seemeth hee,
　Whose taper greatest may be seene, and fortunate to bee,
　Whose Candell burneth cleare and brighte ; a wondrous force and might
　Doth in these Candells lie, which if at any time they light,
　They sure beleve that neyther storme or tempest dare abide,
　Nor thunder in the skies be heard, nor any devils spide,
　Nor fearefull sprites that walke by night, nor hurts of frost or haile." [64]

Still, in many Roman Catholic regions, the candles blessed in church at the Purification are believed to have marvellous powers. In Brittany, Franche-Comté, and elsewhere, they are preserved and lighted in time of storm or sickness.[65] In Tyrol they are lighted on important family occasions such as christenings and funerals, as well as on the approach of a storm [66] ; in Sicily in time of earthquake or when somebody is dying.[67]

In England some use of candles on this festival continued long after the Reformation. In 1628 the Bishop of Durham gave serious offence by sticking up wax candles in his cathedral at the Purification ; " the number of all the candles burnt that evening was two hundred and twenty, besides sixteen torches ; sixty of those burning tapers and torches standing upon and near the high Altar." [68]   Ripon Cathedral, as late as the eighteenth century, was brilliantly illuminated with candles on the Sunday before the festival.[69]   And, to come to domestic customs, at Lyme Regis in Dorsetshire the person who bought the wood-ashes of a family used to send a present of a large candle at Candlemas.   It was lighted at night, and round it there was festive drinking until its going out gave the signal for retirement to rest.[70]

There are other British Candlemas customs connected with fire.   In the western isles of Scotland, says an early eighteenth-century writer, " as Candlemas Day comes round, the mistress and servants of each family taking a sheaf of oats, dress it up in woman's apparel, and after putting it in a large basket, beside which a wooden club is placed, they cry three times, ' Briid is come ! Briid is welcome ! ' This they do just before going to bed, and as soon as they rise in the morning, they look among the ashes, expecting to see the impression of Briid's club there, which if they do, they reckon it a true presage of a good crop and prosperous year, and the contrary they take as an ill-omen." [71]   Sir Laurence Gomme regards this as an illustration of belief in a house-spirit whose residence is the hearth and whose element is the ever-burning sacred flame.   He also considers the Lyme Regis custom mentioned above to be a modernized relic of the sacred hearth-fire.[72]

Again, the feast of the Purification was the time to kindle a " brand " preserved from the Christmas log.   Herrick's Candlemas lines may be recalled :—

> "Kindle the Christmas brand, and then
>   Till sunne-set let it burne ;
> Which quencht, then lay it up agen,
>   Till Christmas next returne.
>
> Part must be kept wherewith to teend
>   The Christmas Log next yeare ;
> And where 'tis safely kept, the Fiend
>   Can do no mischiefe there." [73]

CANDLEMAS

Candlemas Eve was the moment for the last farewells to Christmas; Herrick sings :—

> " End now the White Loafe and the Pye,
> And let all sports with Christmas dye,"

and

> " Down with the Rosemary and Bayes,
> Down with the Misleto ;
> Instead of Holly, now up-raise
> The greener Box for show.
>
> The Holly hitherto did sway ;
> Let Box now domineere
> Until the dancing Easter Day,
> Or Easter's Eve appeare." [74]

An old Shropshire servant, Miss Burne tells us, was wont, when she took down the holly and ivy on Candlemas Eve, to put snowdrops in their place.[75]   We may see in this replacing of the winter evergreens by the delicate white flowers a hint that by Candlemas the worst of the winter is over and gone ; Earth has begun to deck herself with blossoms, and spring, however feebly, has begun. With Candlemas we, like the older English countryfolk, may take our leave of Christmas.

CONCLUSION

THE reader who has had patience to persevere will by now have gained some idea of the manner in which Christmas is, and has been, kept throughout Europe. We have traced the evolution of the festival, seen it take its rise soon after the victory of the Catholic doctrine of Christ's person at Nicea, and spread from Rome to every quarter of the Empire, not as a folk-festival but as an ecclesiastical holy-day. We have seen the Church condemn with horror the relics of pagan feasts which clung round the same season of the year ; then, as time went on, we have found the two elements, pagan and Christian, mingling in some degree, the pagan losing most of its serious meaning, and continuing mainly as ritual performed for the sake of use and wont or as a jovial tradition, the Christian becoming humanized, the skeleton of dogma clothed with warm flesh and blood.

We have considered, as represented in poetry and liturgy, the strictly ecclesiastical festival, the commemoration of the Nativity as the beginning of man's redemption. We have seen how in the carols, the cult of the *presepio*, and the religious drama, the Birth of the King of Glory in the stable at midwinter has presented itself in concrete form to the popular mind, calling up a host of human emotions, a crowd of quaint and beautiful fancies. Lastly we have noted the survival, in the most varied degrees of transformation, of things which are alien to Christianity and in some cases seem to go back to very primitive stages of thought and feeling. An antique reverence for the plant-world may lie, as we have seen, beneath the familiar institution of the Christmas-tree, some sort of animal-worship may be at the bottom of the

357

CONCLUSION

beast-masks common at winter festivals, survivals of sacrifice may
linger in Christmas feasting, and in the family gatherings round
the hearth may be preserved a dim memory of ancient domestic
rites.

Christmas, indeed, regarded in all its aspects, is a microcosm of
European religion. It reflects almost every phase of thought and
feeling from crude magic and superstition to the speculative
mysticism of Eckhart, from mere delight in physical indulgence
to the exquisite spirituality and tenderness of St. Francis.
Ascetic and *bon-vivant*, mystic and materialist, learned and
simple, noble and peasant, all have found something in it of
which to lay hold. It is a river into which have flowed tribu-
taries from every side, from Oriental religion, from Greek and
Roman civilization, from Celtic, Teutonic, Slav, and probably
pre-Aryan, society, mingling their waters so that it is often hard
to discover the far-away springs.

We have seen how the Reformation broke up the great
mediaeval synthesis of paganism and Christianity, how the
extremer forms of Protestantism aimed at completely destroying
Christmas, and how the general tendency of modern civilization,
with its scientific spirit, its popular education, its railways, its
concentration of the people in great cities, has been to root out
traditional beliefs and customs both Christian and pagan, so that
if we would seek for relics of the old things we must go to the
regions of Europe that are least industrially and intellectually
"advanced." Yet amongst the most sceptical and "enlightened"
of moderns there is generally a large residuum of tradition.
"Emotionally," it has been said, "we are hundreds of thousands
of years old ; rationally we are embryos" [1]; and many people who
deem themselves "emancipated" are willing for once in the year
to plunge into the stream of tradition, merge themselves in
inherited social custom, and give way to sentiments and im-
pressions which in their more reflective moments they spurn.
Most men are ready at Christmas to put themselves into an
instinctive rather than a rational attitude, to drink of the springs
of wonder, and return in some degree to earlier, less intellectual
stages of human development—to become in fact children again.

CONCLUSION

Many elements enter into the modern Christmas. There is the delight of its warmth and brightness and comfort against the bleak midwinter. A peculiar charm of the northern Christmas lies in the thought of the cold barred out, the home made a warm, gay place in contrast with the cheerless world outside. There is the physical pleasure of "good cheer," of plentiful eating and drinking, joined to, and partly resulting in, a sense of goodwill and expansive kindliness towards the world at large, a temporary feeling of the brotherhood of man, a desire that the poor may for once in the year "have a good time." Here perhaps we may trace the influence of the *Saturnalia*, with its dreams of the age of gold, its exaltation of them of low degree. Mixed with a little sentimental Christianity this is the Christmas of Dickens—the Christmas which he largely helped to perpetuate in England.

Each nation, naturally, has fashioned its own Christmas. The English have made it a season of solid material comfort, of good-fellowship and "charity," with a slight flavour of soothing religion. The modern French, sceptical and pagan, make little of Christmas, and concentrate upon the secular celebration of the *jour de l'an*. For the Scandinavians Christmas is above all a time of sport, recreation, good living, and social gaiety in the midst of a season when little outdoor work can be done and night almost swallows up day. The Germans, sentimental and childlike, have produced a Christmas that is a very Paradise for children and at which the old delight to play at being young again around the Tree. For the Italians Christmas is centred upon the cult of the *Bambino*, so fitted to their dramatic instincts, their love of display, their strong parental affection. (How much of the sentiment that surrounds the *presepio* is, though religiously heightened, akin to the delight of a child in its doll!) If the Germans may be called the good, industrious, sentimental children of Europe, making the most of simple things, the Italians are the lively, passionate, impulsive children, loving gay clothes and finery ; and the contrast shows in their keeping of Christmas.

The modern Christmas is above all things a children's feast, and the elders who join in it put themselves upon their children's

CONCLUSION

level. We have noted how ritual acts, once performed with serious purpose, tend to become games for youngsters, and have seen many an example of this process in the sports and mummeries kept up by the elder folk for the benefit of the children. We have seen too how the radiant figure of the Christ Child has become a gift-bringer for the little ones. At no time in the world's history has so much been made of children as to-day, and because Christmas is their feast its lustre continues unabated in an age upon which dogmatic Christianity has largely lost its hold, which laughs at the pagan superstitions of its forefathers. Christmas is the feast of beginnings, of instinctive, happy childhood; the Christian idea of the Immortal Babe renewing weary, stained humanity, blends with the thought of the New Year, with its hope and promise, laid in the cradle of Time.

NOTES AND
BIBLIOGRAPHY

NOTES AND BIBLIOGRAPHY

Bibliographical details are given with the first reference to each authority, and the titles and authors' names are there printed in heavy type. The particulars are repeated in the notes to Part II. when authorities are referred to again.

CHAPTER I.—INTRODUCTION

1. **G. K. Chesterton** in **"The Daily News,"** Dec. 26, 1903.

2. *Ibid.* Dec. 23, 1911.

3. Cf. **J. E. Harrison, "Themis : a Study of the Social Origins of Greek Religion"** (Cambridge, 1912), 139, 184.

4. Or plural *Weihnachten.* The name *Weihnachten* was applied in five different ways in mediaeval Germany : (1) to Dec. 25, (2) to Dec. 25–8, (3) to the whole Christmas week, (4) to Dec. 25 to Jan. 6, (5) to the whole time from Christmas to the Octave of the Epiphany. **G. Bilfinger, "Das germanische Julfest"** (Stuttgart, 1901), 39.

5. **A. Tille, "Die Geschichte der deutschen Weihnacht"** (Leipsic, 1893), 22. [Referred to as " D. W."]

6. **H. Usener, "Das Weihnachtsfest"** (Kap. i., bis. iii. 2nd Edition, Bonn, 1911), 273 f.

7. **L. Duchesne, "Christian Worship : its Origin and Evolution"** (Eng. Trans., Revised Edition, London, 1912), 257 f.

8. **J. Hastings, "Encyclopædia of Religion and Ethics"** (Edinburgh, 1910), iii. 601 f.

9. **E. K. Chambers, "The Mediaeval Stage"** (Oxford, 1903), i. 244. [Referred to as " M. S."]

10. **A. Tille, "Yule and Christmas : their Place in the Germanic Year"** (London, 1899), 122. [Referred to as " Y. & C."]

11. *Ibid.* 164.

12. Tille, " D. W.," 21.

13. Tille, " Y. & C.," 203.

14. **K. Lake** in Hastings's " Encyclopædia " and in **"The Guardian,"** Dec. 29, 1911 ; **F. C. Conybeare,** Preface to **"The Key of Truth, a Manual of the Paulician Church of Armenia "** (Oxford, 1898), clii. f. ; Usener, 18 f.

15. Usener, 27 f.

16. *Ibid.* 31 ; **J. E. Harrison, "Prolegomena to the Study of Greek Religion "** (Cambridge, 1903), 550.

17. Harrison, " Prolegomena," 402 f., 524 f., 550.

363

NOTES AND BIBLIOGRAPHY

18. Lake, and **G. Rietschel, "Weihnachten in Kirche, Kunst und Volksleben"** (Bielefeld and Leipsic, 1902), 10.

19. Conybeare, lxxviii.

20. **A. Lupi, "Dissertazioni, lettere ed altre operette"** (Faenza, 1785), i. 219 f., mentioned in article "Nativity" in **T. K. Cheyne's "Encyclopædia Biblica"** (London, 1902), iii. 3346.

21. Chambers, "M. S.," i. 234.

22. *Ibid.* i. 235 ; **F. Cumont, "The Monuments of Mithra"** (Eng. Trans., London, 1903), 190.

23. **G. Negri, "Julian the Apostate"** (Eng. Trans., London, 1905), i. 240 f.

24. Chambers, "M. S.," i. 235.

25. Duchesne, "Christian Worship," 265.

26. Tille, "Y. & C.," 146.

PART I

THE CHRISTIAN FEAST

CHAPTER II.—CHRISTMAS POETRY (I)

1. See especially for Latin, German, and English hymnody **J. Julian, "A Dictionary of Hymnology"** (New Edition, London, 1907), and the **Historical Edition of "Hymns Ancient and Modern"** (London, 1909).

2. **H. C. Beeching, "A Book of Christmas Verse"** (London, 1895), 3.

3. Beeching, 8.

4. **A. Gastoué, "Noël"** (Paris, 1907), 38.

5. **R. W. Church, "St. Anselm"** (London, 1870), 6.

6. *Ibid.* 3 f.

7. **W. R. W. Stephens, "The English Church from the Norman Conquest to the Accession of Edward I."** (London, 1901), 309.

8. **W. Sandys, "Christmastide: its History, Festivities, and Carols"** (London, n.d.), 216 ; **E. Rickert, "Ancient English Carols. MCCCC–MDCC"** (London, 1910), 133.

9. For the Franciscan influence on poetry and art see : **Vernon Lee, "Renaissance Fancies and Studies"** (London, 1895) ; **H. Thode, "Franz von Assisi und die Anfänge der Kunst der Renaissance in Italien"** (Berlin, 1885) ; **A. Macdonell, "Sons of Francis"** (London, 1902) ; **J. A. Symonds, "The Renaissance in Italy. Italian Literature,"** Part I. (New Edition, London, 1898).

10. **Thomas of Celano, "Lives of St. Francis"** (Eng. Trans. by A. G. Ferrers Howell, London, 1908), 84.

11. **P. Robinson, "Writings of St. Francis"** (London, 1906), 175.

12. **"Le poesie spirituali del B. Jacopone da Todi,"** con annotationi di Fra Francesco Tresatti (Venice, 1617), 266.

13. *Ibid.* 275.

14. *Ibid.* 867.

15. **"Stabat Mater speciosa,"** trans. and ed. by J. M. Neale (London, 1866).

NOTES AND BIBLIOGRAPHY

16. For German Christmas poetry see, besides Julian : **Hoffmann von Fallersleben, "Geschichte des deutschen Kirchenliedes bis auf Luthers Zeit"** (2nd Edition, Hanover, 1854) ; P. **Wackernagel, "Das deutsche Kirchenlied"** (Leipsic, 1867) ; and **C. Winkworth, "Christian Singers of Germany"** (London, n.d.).

17. R. M. Jones, **"Studies in Mystical Religion"** (London, 1909), 235, 237.

18. **"Meister Eckharts Schriften und Predigten,"** edited by H. Buttner (Leipsic, 1903), i. 44.

19. Translation by C. Winkworth, **"Christian Singers,"** 84. German text in Wackernagel, ii. 302 f.

20. **"Deutsches Weihnachtsbuch"** (Hamburg-Grossborstel, 1907), 125.

21. **"A Compendious Book of Godly and Spiritual Songs,"** reprinted from the Edition of 1567 by A. F. Mitchell (Edinburgh and London, 1897), 53. This translation is abridged and Protestantized. The mediaeval German text, which is partly addressed to the Virgin, is given in **Hoffmann von Fallersleben, "In Dulci Jubilo"** (Hanover, 1854), 46. For the music see **G. R. Woodward, "The Cowley Carol Book"** (New Edition, London, 1909), 20 f. [a work peculiarly rich in old German airs].

22. **K. Weinhold, "Weihnacht-Spiele und Lieder aus Süddeutschland und Schlesien"** (2nd Edition, Vienna, 1875), 385.

23. *Ibid.* 396. [For help in the translation of German dialect I am indebted to Dr. M. A. Mügge.]

24. *Ibid.* 400.

25. *Ibid.* 417.

26. E. K. Chambers, essay on "Some Aspects of Mediæval Lyric" in **"Early English Lyrics,"** chosen by **E. K. Chambers and F. Sidgwick** (London, 1907), 290. [Twenty-five of Awdlay's carols were printed by Messrs. **Chambers and Sidgwick** in **"The Modern Language Review"** (Cambridge), Oct., 1910, and Jan., 1911.]

27. *Ibid.* 293.

28. Quoted by **J. J. Jusserand, "A Literary History of the English People"** (2nd Edition, London, 1907), i. 218.

29. Rickert, 6 ; Beeching, 13.

30. No. lv. in Chambers and Sidgwick, "Early English Lyrics."

31. No. lix., *ibid.*

32. No. lxi., *ibid.*

33. No. lxx., *ibid.*

34. No. lxvii., *ibid.*

35. No. lxiii., *ibid.*

36. Rickert, 67.

CHAPTER III.—CHRISTMAS POETRY (II)

1. **Noël Hervé, "Les Noëls français"** (Niort, 1905), Gastoué, 57 f. ; **G. Gregory Smith, "The Transition Period"** (Edinburgh and London, 1900), 217.

2. Gregory Smith, 217.

3. **H. Lemeignen, "Vieux Noëls composés en l'honneur de la Naissance de Notre-Seigneur Jésus-Christ"** (Nantes, 1876), iii. 2 f.

4. *Ibid.* i. 10, 11.

5. *Ibid.* ii. 93, 95.

6. Hervé, 46.

7. Lemeignen, i. 55.

8. Lemeignen, i. 29.

9. "**Les Vieux Noëls**," in "**Nouvelle Bibliothèque Populaire**" (published by Henri Gautier, 55 Quai des Grands Augustins, Paris).

10. Lemeignen, i. 93.

11. **H. J. L. J. Massé, "A Book of Old Carols**" (London, 1910), i. 21.

12. Hervé, 86.

13. Lemeignen, i. 71.

14. "Hymns Ancient and Modern" (Historical Edition), 79. Translation is No. 58 in Ordinary Edition.

15. Hervé, 132.

16. A great number of these *villancicos* and *romances* may be found in **Justo de Sancha, "Romancero y Cancionero Sagrados**" (Madrid, 1855, vol. 35 of Rivadeneyra's Library of Spanish Authors), and there are some good examples in **J. N. Böhl de Faber, "Rimas Antiguas Castellanas** " (Hamburg, 1823).

17. Böhl de Faber, ii. 36.

18. **F. Caballero, "Elia y La Noche de Navidad** " (Leipsic, 1864), 210.

19. **A. de Gubernatis, "Storia Comparata degli Usi Natalizi** " (Milan, 1878), 90.

20. These three verses are taken from **Countess Martinengo-Cesaresco's** charming translation of the poem, in her "**Essays in the Study of Folk-Songs** " (London, 1886), 304 f.

21. Martinengo, "Folk-Songs," 302 f.

22. Latin text in Tille, "D. W.," 311 ; Italian game in De Gubernatis, 93.

23. Hervé, 115 f.

24. **W. Hone, "The Ancient Mysteries Described** " (London, 1823), 103.

25. *Ibid.* 103.

26. See Note 11.

27. **D. Hyde, "Religious Songs of Connacht**" (London, 1906), ii. 225 f.

28. "**The Vineyard**" (London), Dec., 1910, 144.

29. " Deutsches Weihnachtsbuch," 120 f.

30. "A Compendious Book of Godly and Spiritual Songs," 49 f. (spelling here modernized) ; Rickert, 82 f.

31. "Deutsches Weihnachtsbuch," 123, and most German Protestant hymnbooks.

32. Translation by Miles Coverdale, in Rickert, 192 f.

33. No. 5 in **Paulus Gerhardt, "Geistliche Lieder,**" ed. by P. Wackernagel and W. Tümpel (9th Edition, Gütersloh, 1907).

34. Translation by **C. Winkworth** in "**Lyra Germanica** " (New Edition, London, 1869), ii. 13 f.

35. " Deutsches Weihnachtsbuch," 128 f.

36. Translation (last verse altered) in "**The British Herald** " (London), Sept., 1866, 329.

37. "**Christmas Carols New and Old**," the words edited by **H. R. Bramley**, the music edited by **Sir John Stainer** (London, n.d.).

38. Beeching, 27 f.

39. *Ibid.* 67.

40. *Ibid.* 49.

41. *Ibid.* 76.

42. *Ibid.* 48.

43. *Ibid.* 45.

44. *Ibid.* 42 f.

366

NOTES AND BIBLIOGRAPHY

45. Beeching, 85 f.

46. **Selwyn Image, " Poems and Carols "** (London, 1894), 25.

47. **G. K. Chesterton** in **" The Commonwealth "** (London), Dec., 1902, 353.

CHAPTER IV.—CHRISTMAS IN LITURGY AND POPULAR
DEVOTION

1. Translation, " Creator of the starry height," in " Hymns A. and M." (Ordinary Edition), No. 45.

2. **J. Dowden, " The Church Year and Kalendar "** (Cambridge, 1910), 76 f.

3. **" Rational ou Manuel des divins Offices de Guillaume Durand, Évêque de Mende au treizième siècle,"** traduit par **M. C. Barthélemy** (Paris, 1854), iii. 155 f.

4. See translation of the Great O's in " The English Hymnal," No. 734.

5. Barthélemy, iii. 220 f.

6. **D. Rock, " The Church of Our Fathers "** (London, 1853), vol. iii. pt. ii. 214.

7. **J. K. Huysmans, " L'Oblat "** (Paris, 1903), 194.

8. Gastoué, 44 f.

9. **E. G. C. F. Atchley, " Ordo Romanus Primus "** (London, 1905), 71.

10. **" The Pilgrimage of S. Silvia of Aquitaine "** (Eng. Trans. by J. H. Bernard, London, 1891), 50 f.

11. **S. D. Ferriman** in **" The Daily News,"** Dec. 25, 1911.

12. **G. Bonaccorsi, " Il Natale : appunti d'esegesi e di storia "** (Rome, 1903), 73.

13. Gastoué, 41 f.

14. Bonaccorsi, 75.

15. **H. Malleson and M. A. R. Tuker, " Handbook to Christian and Ecclesiastical Rome "** (London, 1897), pt. ii. 211.

16. **Th. Bentzon, " Christmas in France "** in **" The Century Magazine "** (New York), Dec., 1901, 170 f.

17. **L. von Hörmann, " Tiroler Volksleben "** (Stuttgart, 1909), 232.

18. **M. J. Quin, " A Visit to Spain "** (2nd Edition, London, 1824), 126 f.

19. **" Madrid in 1835,"** by a **Resident Officer** (London, 1836), i. 395 f.

20. **W. S. Walsh, " Curiosities of Popular Customs "** (London, 1898), 237.

21. **G. Pitrè, " Spettacoli e feste popolari siciliane "** (Palermo, 1880), 444.

22. Tille, " D. W.," 70 f.

23. **F. H. Woods, " Sweden and Norway "** (London, 1882), 209 ; **L. Lloyd, " Peasant Life in Sweden "** (London, 1870), 201 f.

24. **J. E. Vaux, " Church Folklore "** (London, 1894), 222 f.

25. **M. Trevelyan, " Folk-Lore and Folk-Stories of Wales "** (London, 1909), 28.

26. Vaux, 262 f.

27. **R. F. Littledale, " Offices from the Service-Books of the Holy Eastern Church "** (London, 1863), 174 f.

28. **[Sir] A. J. Evans, " Christmas and Ancestor Worship in the Black Mountain,"** in **" Macmillan's Magazine "** (London), vol. xliii., 1881, 228.

29. Duchesne, 273.

30. Chambers, " M. S.," i. 245.

31. **" The Roman Breviary,"** translated by **John, Marquess of Bute** (New Edition, Edinburgh and London, 1908), 186.

32. See announcement in **" The Roman Mail "** in Jan., 1912.

33. Mary Hamilton, "Greek Saints and their Festivals" (London, 1910), 113 f.

34. H. Holloway, "An Eastern Epiphany Service" in "Pax" (the Magazine of the Caldey Island Benedictines), Dec., 1910.

35. Hamilton, 119 f.

36. Holloway, as above.

37. F. H. E. Palmer, "Russian Life in Town and Country" (London, 1901), 176 f.

38. Thomas of Celano, trans. by Howell, 82 f.

39. Countess Martinengo-Cesaresco, "Puer Parvulus" in "The Outdoor Life in the Greek and Roman Poets" (London, 1911), 248.

40. Chambers, "M. S.," ii. 41.

41. Bonaccorsi, 85 ; Usener, 298.

42. Usener, 290.

43. *Ibid.* 295, 299.

44. Rietschel, 55.

45. *Ibid.* 56 f.

46. *Ibid.* 60.

47. *Ibid.* 69 f. ; Tille, "D. W.," 59 f.

48. Music from **Trier** "**Gesangbuch**" (1911), No. 18, where a very much weakened text is given. Text from Weinhold, 114. Another form of the air is given in "The Cowley Carol Book," No. 36.

49. Text and music in Massé, i. 6.

50. Tille, "D. W.," 60.

51. *Ibid.* 61 f.

52. *Ibid.* 63.

53. Thomas Naogeorgus, "The Popish Kingdome," Englyshed by Barnabe Googe, 1570 (ed. by R. C. Hope, London, 1880), 45.

54. Tille, "D. W.," 68.

55. *Ibid.* 68.

56. Hörmann, "Tiroler Volksleben," 235.

57. *Ibid.* 235.

58. Tille, "D. W.," 64.

59. Rietschel, 75.

60. Martinengo, "Outdoor Life," 249.

61. Lady Morgan, "Italy" (New Edition, London, 1821), iii. 72.

62. Matilde Serao, "La Madonna e i Santi" (Naples, 1902), 223 f.

63. L. Caico, "Sicilian Ways and Days" (London, 1910), 192 f.

64. Information kindly given to the author by Mrs. C. G. Crump.

65. Information derived by the author from a resident in Messina.

66. Serao, *see* Note 62.

67. W. H. D. Rouse, "Religious Tableaux in Italian Churches," in "Folk-Lore" (London), vol. v., 1894, 6 f.

68. Morgan, iii. 76 f.

69. Bonaccorsi, 45 f.

70. A. J. C. Hare, "Walks in Rome" (11th Edition, London, 1883), 157.

71. Martinengo, "Outdoor Life," 253 ; Bonaccorsi, 110 f. ; R. Ellis Roberts, "A Roman Pilgrimage" (London, 1911), 185 f.

72. H. J. Rose, "Untrodden Spain" (London, 1875), 276.

73. See Note 18 to Chapter III.

NOTES AND BIBLIOGRAPHY

74. **T. F. Thiselton Dyer,** " **British Popular Customs** " (London, 1876), 464.

75. Vaux, 216.

76. Dyer, 464.

77. Cf. Chambers, " M. S.," i. 120.

CHAPTER V.—CHRISTMAS DRAMA

1. This account of the mediaeval Christmas drama owes much to Chambers, " The Mediaeval Stage," especially chaps. xviii. to xx., and to **W. Creizenach,** " **Geschichte des neueren Dramas** " (Halle a/S., 1893), vol. i., bks. ii.–iv. See also : **Karl Pearson,** essay on " **The German Passion Play** " in " **The Chances of Death, and other Studies in Evolution** " (London, 1897), ii. 246 f. ; **E. Du Méril,** " **Origines latines du théâtre moderne** " (Paris, 1849) ; **L. Petit de Julleville,** " **Histoire du théâtre en France au moyen âge. I. Les Mystères** " (Paris, 1880) ; and other works cited later.

2. Chambers, " M. S.," ii. 8 f.

3. *Ibid.* ii. 11.

4. Du Méril, 147.

5. Chambers, " M. S.," ii. 52.

6. Text in Du Méril, 153 f.

7. Chambers, " M. S.," ii. 44.

8. *Ibid.* ii. 52 f.

9. On the English plays see : Chambers, " M. S.," chaps. xx. and xxi. ; **A. W. Ward,** " **A History of English Dramatic Literature** " (London, 1875), vol. i. chap. i. ; Creizenach, vol. i. ; **K. L. Bates,** " **The English Religious Drama** " (London, 1893).

10. Chambers, " M. S.," ii. 129, 131, 139.

11. " **Ludus Coventriae,** " ed. by J. O. Halliwell (London, 1841), 146 f.

12. " **York Plays,** " ed. by L. Toulmin Smith (Oxford, 1885), 114 f.

13. " **The Chester Plays,** " ed. by T. Wright (London, 1843), 137.

14. *Ibid.* 138.

15. *Ibid.* 143.

16. " **The Towneley Plays,** " ed. by George England, with Introduction by A. W. Pollard (London, 1897). The first Shepherds' Play is on p. 100 f., the second on p. 116 f.

17. Text from Chambers and Sidgwick, " Early English Lyrics," 124 f.

18. Text in **T. Sharp,** " **A Dissertation on the Pageants or Dramatic Mysteries anciently performed at Coventry** " (Coventry, 1825).

19. Petit de Julleville, ii. 36 f and 431 f.

20. *Ibid.* ii. 620 f. ; " **Les marguerites de la Marguerite des princesses,** " ed. from the edition of 1547 by F. Frank (Paris, 1873), ii. 1 f.

21. Petit de Julleville, i. 441.

22. *Ibid.* i. 455. Text in Lemeignen, ii. 1 f.

23. Petit de Julleville, i. 79 f.

24. **P. Sébillot,** " **Coutumes populaires de la Haute-Bretagne** " (Paris, 1886), 177.

25. Martinengo, " Folk-Songs," xxxiii. f. In her essay, " Puer Parvulus," in " The Outdoor Life," 260 f., the Countess gives a charming description of a somewhat similar Piedmontese play.

26. Barthélemy, iii. 411 f.

27. Rietschel, 88 f. ; **O. von Reinsberg-Düringsfeld, "Das festliche Jahr"** (2nd Edition, Leipsic, 1898), 439 f.

28. Rietschel, 92 f.

29. An interesting book on popular Christmas plays is **F. Vogt, " Die schlesischen Weihnachtspiele "** (Leipsic, 1901).

30. Weinhold, 94.

31. *Ibid.* 95 f.

32. *Ibid.* 100 f.

33. *Ibid.* 96 f.

34. See Chambers, " M. S.," ii. 91 f. ; Symonds, " Renaissance," iv. 242, 272 f. ; A. d'Ancona, **"Origini del Teatro italiano "** (Florence, 1877), i. 87 f.

35. D'Ancona, " Origini," i. 126 f.

36. **A. d'Ancona, " Sacre Rappresentazioni dei secoli xiv, xv e xvi "** (Florence, 1872), i. 191 f.

37. *Ibid.* i. 192.

38. Latin original quoted by D'Ancona, " Origini," i. 91, and Chambers, " M. S.," ii. 93.

39. Creizenach, i. 347.

40. **J. Fitzmaurice-Kelly, "A History of Spanish Literature"** (London, 1898), 113.

41. **Juan del Encina, " Teatro Completo "** (Madrid, 1893), 3 f., 137 f.

42. See **G. Ticknor, "History of Spanish Literature "** (6th American Edition, Boston, 1888), ii. 283 f.

43. *Ibid.* ii. 208.

44. **"Archivio per lo studio delle tradizioni popolari "** (Palermo and Turin), vol. xxi., 1902, 381.

45. Pitrè, 448.

46. Fernan Caballero, " Elia y La Noche de Navidad," 222 f.

47. Lloyd, 213 f.

48. **H. F. Feilberg, " Jul "** (Copenhagen, 1904), ii. 242 f.

49. **E. Cortet, " Essai sur les fêtes religieuses"** (Paris, 1867), 38.

50. Sébillot, 215.

51. Feilberg, ii. 250 ; Reinsberg-Düringsfeld, 31 f. ; **T. Stratilesco, "From Carpathian to Pindus: Pictures of Roumanian Country Life"** (London, 1906), 195 f. ; **E. van Norman, " Poland : the Knight among Nations "** (London and New York, 3rd Edition, n.d.), 302 ; **S. Graham, " A Vagabond in the Caucasus. With some Notes of his Experiences among the Russians "** (London, 1910), 28.

52. Translation in **Karl Hase, " Miracle Plays and Sacred Dramas "** (Eng. Trans., London, 1880), 9 ; German text in Weinhold, 132.

53. Hörmann, " Tiroler Volksleben," 247 f.

54. Graham, 28.

55. Stratilesco, 195 f.

56. *Ibid.* 355 f.

57. Van Norman, 302.

58. Cortet, 42.

59. Barthélemy, iii. 411 f.

60. **Madame Calderon de la Barca, " Life in Mexico "** (London, 1843), 237 f.

POSTSCRIPT

1. **E. Underhill, " Mysticism : A Study in the Nature and Development of Man's Spiritual Consciousness "** (London, 1911), 305.

NOTES AND BIBLIOGRAPHY

PART II

PAGAN SURVIVALS

CHAPTER VI.—PRE-CHRISTIAN WINTER FESTIVALS

1. Karl Pearson, essay on "Woman as Witch" in "The Chances of Death and other Studies in Evolution" (London, 1897), ii. 16.

2. Cf. J. G. Frazer, "The Dying God" (London, 1911), 269.

3. J. A. MacCulloch, "The Religion of the Ancient Celts" (Edinburgh, 1911), 278.

4. Frazer, "Dying God," 266.

5. E. Anwyl, "Celtic Religion in Pre-Christian Times" (London, 1906), 1 f.

6. Ibid. 20 ; cf. E. K. Chambers, "The Mediaeval Stage" (Oxford, 1903), i. 100 f. [Referred to as "M. S."]

7. W. Robertson Smith, "Lectures on the Religion of the Semites" (New Edition, London, 1894), 16.

8. Chambers, "M. S.," i. 236 ; W. W. Fowler, "The Roman Festivals of the Period of the Republic" (London, 1899), 272.

9. "The Works of Lucian of Samosata" (Eng. Trans. by H. W. and F. G. Fowler, Oxford, 1905), iv. 108 f.

10. John Brand, "Observations on Popular Antiquities" (New Edition, with the Additions of Sir Henry Ellis, London, Chatto & Windus, 1900), 283.

11. "Works of Lucian," iv. 114 f.

12. Ibid. iv. 109.

13. J. G. Frazer, "The Golden Bough" (2nd Edition, London, 1900), iii. 138 f., and "The Magic Art and the Evolution of Kingship" (London, 1911), ii. 310 f.

14. W. W. Fowler, "The Religious Experience of the Roman People" (London, 1911), 107, 112.

15. Fowler, "Roman Festivals," 268, and "Religious Experience," 107 ; C. Bailey, "The Religion of Ancient Rome" (London, 1907), 70.

16. Chambers, "M. S.," i. 237 f. ; Fowler, "Roman Festivals," 278.

17. Quoted from "Libanii Opera," ed. by Reiske, i. 256 f., by G. Bilfinger, "Das germanische Julfest" (vol. ii. of "Untersuchungen über die Zeitrechnung der alten Germanen," Stuttgart, 1901), 41 f.

18. "Libanii Opera," iv. 1053 f., quoted by Bilfinger, 43 f.

19. Chambers, "M. S.," i. 237 f., 258.

20. A. Tille, "Yule and Christmas" (London, 1899), 96. [Referred to as "Y. & C."]

21. J. C. Lawson, "Modern Greek Folklore and Ancient Greek Religion" (Cambridge, 1910), 221 f. Cf. M. Hamilton, "Greek Saints and their Festivals" (London, 1910), 98.

22. Chambers, "M. S.," ii. 290 f.

23. Latin text in Chambers, "M. S.," ii. 297 f.

24. Ibid. i. 245.

25. Tille, "Y. & C.," 88 f. ; Chambers, "M. S.," ii. 303 f.

26. Tille, " Y. & C.," throughout ; Chambers, " M. S.," i. 288 f. ; **Chantepie de la Saussaye, "The Religion of the Ancient Teutons"** (Boston, 1902), 382. Cf. **O. Schrader,** in **Hastings's "Encyclopædia of Religion and Ethics"** (Edinburgh, 1909), ii. 47 f.

27. MacCulloch, " Religion of the Ancient Celts," 258 f. Cf. Chambers, " M. S.," i. 228, 234.

28. Tille, " Y. & C.," 203.

29. **[Sir] A. J. Evans, "Christmas and Ancestor Worship in the Black Mountain,"** in **"Macmillan's Magazine"** (London), vol. xliii., 1881, 363.

30. Chambers, " M. S.," i. 247.

31. Tille, " Y. & C.," 64.

32. Chambers, " M. S.," i. 232.

33. *Ibid.* i. 130 ; W. Robertson Smith, 213 f.

34. Frazer, " Dying God," 129 f.

35. See **N. W. Thomas** in **"Folk-Lore"** (London), vol. xi., 1900, 227 f.

36. Chambers, " M. S.," i. 132 f.

37. W. Robertson Smith, 437 f.

38. **J. E. Harrison, "Themis : A Study of the Social Origins of Greek Religion"** (Cambridge, 1912), 67. Cf. **E. F. Ames, "The Psychology of Religious Experience"** (London and Boston, 1910), 95 f.

39. Harrison, " Themis," 137.

40. *Ibid.* 110.

41. **S. Reinach, "Cultes, mythes, et religions"** (Paris, 1905), i. 93. For the theory that totems were originally food-objects, see Ames, 118 f.

42. Chambers, " M. S.," i. 133.

43. *Ibid.* i. 105 f., 144.

44. Harrison, " Themis," 507.

45. W. Robertson Smith, 255.

46. **Bede, "Historia Ecclesiastica,"** lib. i. cap. 30. Latin text in Bede's Works, edited by J. A. Giles (London, 1843), vol. ii. p. 142.

47. Frazer, " Golden Bough," iii. 143.

48. **Jerome, "Comm. in Isaiam,"** lxv. 11. Latin text in Chambers, " M. S.," ii. 294.

49. Chambers, " M. S.," i. 266.

50. Latin text in Chambers, " M. S.," ii. 306.

51. **Bede, "De Temporum Ratione,"** cap. 15, quoted by Chambers, i. 231. See also Tille, " Y. & C.," 152 f., and Bilfinger, 131, for other views.

52. Frazer, " Golden Bough," iii. 70 f.

53. See Frazer, " Magic Art," i. 52.

54. Cf. Frazer, " Golden Bough," iii. 300 f.

55. Latin text in **H. Usener, "Religionsgeschichtliche Untersuchungen,"** part ii. (Bonn, 1889), 43 f. See also A. Tille, **"Die Geschichte der deutschen Weihnacht"** (Leipsic, 1893), 44 f. [Referred to as " D. W."]

56. **Philip Stubbs, "Anatomie of Abuses"** (Reprint of 3rd Edition of 1585, edited by W. B. Turnbull, London, 1836), 205.

57. Quoted by **J. Ashton, "A righte Merrie Christmasse ! !"** (London, n.d.), 26 f.

58. *Ibid.* 27 f.

NOTES AND BIBLIOGRAPHY

CHAPTER VII.—ALL HALLOW TIDE TO MARTINMAS

1. **R. Chambers, "The Book of Days"** (London, n.d.), ii. 538 [referred to as "B. D."] ; **T. F. Thiselton Dyer, "British Popular Customs"** (London, 1876), 396 f.

2. **[Sir] J. Rhys, "Lectures on the Origin and Growth of Religion as illustrated by Celtic Heathendom"** (London, 1888), 514, **"Celtic Folklore : Welsh and Manx"** (Oxford, 1901), i. 321.

3. Tille, " Y. & C.," 57 f.

4. Rhys, " Celtic Folklore," i. 315 f.

5. **J. Dowden, "The Church Year and Kalendar"** (Cambridge, 1910), 23 f.

6. Cf. **J. G. Frazer, " Adonis, Attis, Osiris "** (2nd Edition, London, 1907), 315 f.

7. **E. B. Tylor, "Primitive Culture"** (3rd Edition, London, 1891), ii. 38.

8. Frazer, " Adonis," 310.

9. *Ibid.* 312 f.

10. **P. Sébillot, "Coutumes populaires de la Haute-Bretagne"** (Paris, 1886), 206.

11. **L. von Hörmann, "Tiroler Volksleben"** (Stuttgart, 1909), 193.

12. Frazer, " Adonis," 315.

13. **G. Pitrè, "Spettacoli e feste popolari siciliane "** (Palermo, 1880), 393 f. Cf. **H. F. Feilberg, "Jul"** (Copenhagen, 1904), i. 67.

14. **"Notes and Queries"** (London), 3rd Series, vol. i. 446 ; Dyer, 408.

15. Frazer, " Adonis," 250.

16. Dyer, 405 f.

17. *Notes and Queries*, 1st Series, vol. iv. 381 ; Dyer, 407.

18. **C. S. Burne and G. F. Jackson, "Shropshire Folk-Lore"** (London, 1883), 383.

19. *Ibid.* 381 f.

20. Quoted by Dyer, 410.

21. **O. von Reinsberg-Düringsfeld, "Das festliche Jahr der germanischen Völker"** (2nd Edition, Leipsic, 1898), 390.

22. **"Archivio per lo studio delle tradizioni popolari"** (Palermo), vol. viii. 574.

23. Hörmann, " Tiroler Volksleben," 189 f.

24. Frazer, " Adonis," 303 f.

25. *Ibid.* 306 f.

26. Evans, 363 f.

27. Dyer, 394.

28. *Ibid.* 398.

29. *Ibid.* 394. Cf. Chambers, " B. D.," ii. 519 f.

30. Dyer, 395.

31. *Ibid.* 399.

32. *Ibid.* 397 f.

33. **S. O. Addy, "Household Tales, with other Traditional Remains. Collected in the Counties of Lincoln, Derby, and Nottingham "** (London and Sheffield, 1895), 82.

34. *Ibid.* 85.

35. **W. Henderson, "Folk Lore of the Northern Counties of England and the Borders"** (2nd Edition, London, 1879), 101.

36. Dyer, 399.

37. *Ibid.* 403.

38. Rhys, " Celtic Folklore," i. 321, " Celtic Heathendom," 514.
39. Rhys, "Celtic Folklore," i. 328.
40. MacCulloch, " Religion of the Ancient Celts," 259, 261.
41. Rhys, "Celtic Heathendom," 515.
42. *Ibid.* 515.
43. *Ibid.* 515, "Celtic Folklore," i. 225.
44. MacCulloch, " Religion of the Ancient Celts," 262.
45. Brand, 211.
46. Dyer, 402.
47. *Ibid.* 394 f.
48. Frazer, " Golden Bough," iii. 299 f.
49. Burne and Jackson, 389.
50. Dyer, 409.
51. J. **Grimm**, **"Teutonic Mythology"** (Eng. Trans. by J. S. Stallybrass, London, 1880–8), i. 47.
52. **K. Weinhold, "Weihnacht-Spiele und Lieder aus Süddeutschland und Schlesien"** (Vienna, 1875), 6.
53. **U. Jahn, " Die deutschen Opfergebräuche bei Ackerbau und Viehzucht "** (Breslau, 1884), 262.
54. *Ibid.* 262.
55. Weinhold, 6.
56. Dyer, 472.
57. *Notes and Queries*, 1st Series, vol. i. 173 ; Dyer, 486.
58. Weinhold, 7.
59. *Ibid.* 10.
60. Reinsberg-Düringsfeld, 449.
61. Chambers, " M. S.," i. 166.
62. Dyer, 480.
63. Feilberg, ii. 228 f.
64. Reinsberg-Düringsfeld, 393.
65. **Tacitus, "Annales,"** lib. i. cap. 50, quoted by Tille, " Y. & C.," 25.
66. Tille, " Y. & C.," 26.
67. *Ibid.* 52.
68. *Ibid.* 27.
69. Brand, 216 f.
70. Reinsberg-Düringsfeld, 401 f.   For German Martinmas feasting, see also Jahn, 229 f.
71. Grimm, iv. 1838, for Danish custom ; Jahn, 235 f., for German.
72. **"The Folk-Lore Record"** (London), vol. iv., 1881, 107 ; Dyer, 420.
73. MacCulloch, " Religion of the Ancient Celts," 260.
74. Reinsberg-Düringsfeld, 403.
75. Jahn, 246 f.
76. *Ibid.* 246 ; Reinsberg-Düringsfeld, 403.
77. Tille, " Y. & C.," 34 f.
78. Reinsberg-Düringsfeld, 404 ; Jahn, 250.
79. Jahn, 247.
80. Angela Nardo-Cibele in *Archivio trad. pop.*, vol. v. 238 f., for Venetia ; Pitrè, 411 f., for Sicily.
81. Reinsberg-Düringsfeld, 405.

NOTES AND BIBLIOGRAPHY

82. Jahn, 240.
83. *Ibid.* 241 f.
84. *Ibid.* 241.
85. Reinsberg-Düringsfeld, 404.
86. Weinhold, 7.
87. Chambers, " M. S.," i. 268 ; Weinhold, 7 ; Tille, " D. W.," 25.
88. Reinsberg-Düringsfeld, illustration facing p. 406.
89. *Ibid.* 405.
90. *Ibid.* 404.
91. *Ibid.* 410 ; Tille, " D. W.," 26 f. ; **W. Mannhardt, " Der Baumkultus der Germanen und ihrer Nachbarstämme "** (Berlin, 1875. Vol. i. of " Wald- und Feldkulte "), 273.
92. Cf. Mannhardt, " Baumkultus," 303, and Reinach, i. 180.
93. *Archivio trad. pop.*, vol. v. 238 f., 358 f.
94. Mannhardt, " Baumkultus," 274.

CHAPTER VIII.—ST. CLEMENT TO ST. THOMAS

1. Dyer, 423.
2. *Notes and Queries*, 1st Series, vol. viii. 618 ; Dyer, 425.
3. Brand, 222 f.
4. Henderson, " Folk Lore of the Northern Counties," 97.
5. *Notes and Queries*, 3rd Series, vol. iv. 492 ; Dyer, 423.
6. Dyer, 425.
7. Brand, 222.
8. *Ibid.* 223.
9. *Notes and Queries*, 2nd Series, vol. v. 47 ; Dyer, 427.
10. Dyer, 426 f.
11. Reinsberg-Düringsfeld, 415.
12. **J. N. Raphael** in **" The Daily Express,"** Nov. 28, 1911.
13. Dyer, 430.
14. *Ibid.* 429.
15. Tille, " D. W.," 148.
16. **B. Thorpe, " Northern Mythology "** (London, 1852), iii. 143.
17. *Ibid.* iii. 144.
18. Reinsberg-Düringsfeld, 416 f. Cf. Grimm, iv. 1800.
19. Reinsberg-Düringsfeld, 417. Cf. Thorpe, iii. 145.
20. Reinsberg-Düringsfeld, 418.
21. Thorpe, iii. 145.
22. **F. S. Krauss, " Sitte und Brauch der Südslaven "** (Vienna, 1885), 179.
23. **T. Stratilesco, " From Carpathian to Pindus : Pictures of Roumanian Country Life "** (London, 1906), 189.
24. *Ibid.* 188 f.
25. Reinsberg-Düringsfeld, 416.
26. *Ibid.* 420 f.
27. *Ibid.* 425.

NOTES AND BIBLIOGRAPHY

28. **Thomas Naogeorgus, "The Popish Kingdome,"** Englyshed by Barnabe Googe, 1570 (ed. by R. C. Hope, London, 1880), 44.

29. **G. F. Abbott, "Macedonian Folklore"** (Cambridge, 1903), 76.

30. **P. M. Hough, "Dutch Life in Town and Country"** (London, 1901), 96.

31. Cf. Frazer, "Golden Bough," iii. 90, and also the Epiphany noise-makings described in the present volume.

32. Reinsberg-Düringsfeld, 426.

33. Hörmann, "Tiroler Volksleben," 218 f.

34. Tille, "D. W.," 30.

35. Chambers, "M. S.," i. 370.

36. Hamilton, 30. Cf. article on St. Nicholas by Professor Anichkof in *Folk-Lore*, vol. v., 1894, 108 f.

37. Reinsberg-Düringsfeld, 428 f.

38. Tille, "D. W.," 35 f. ; Reinsberg-Düringsfeld, 430.

39. Hörmann, "Tiroler Volksleben," 209 f.

40. Reinsberg-Düringsfeld, 430.

41. Weinhold, 9.

42. Mannhardt, "Baumkultus," 326.

43. Weinhold, 9.

44. Reinsberg-Düringsfeld, 431 f.

45. Hörmann, "Tiroler Volksleben," 212 f.

46. Reinsberg-Düringsfeld, 433.

47. *Ibid.* 433.

48. Chambers, "M. S.," i. 369.

49. **W. S. Walsh, "Curiosities of Popular Customs"** (London, 1898), 753 f. Cf. Chambers, "B. D.," ii. 664.

50. Feilberg, i. 165, 170.

51. *Ibid.* i. 169 f.

52. *Ibid.* i. 171.

53. **L. Caico, "Sicilian Ways and Days"** (London, 1910), 188 f.

54. Feilberg, i. 168.

55. Reinsberg-Düringsfeld, 434.

56. *Ibid.* 434 f.

57. Grimm, iv. 1867.

58. Feilberg, i. 108 f.

59. *Ibid.* i. 111.

60. N. W. Thomas in *Folk-Lore*, vol. xi., 1900, 252.

61. Ashton, 52.

62. Dyer, 72 f.

63. Reinsberg-Düringsfeld, 436 f.

64. *Ibid.* 437.

65. *Ibid.* 438.

66. *Ibid.* 439.

67. Dyer, 439.

68. *Ibid.* 438 f. ; Chambers, "B. D.," ii. 724.

69. Abbott, 81.

70. *Notes and Queries*, 2nd Series, vol. v. 35 ; Dyer, 439.

NOTES AND BIBLIOGRAPHY

CHAPTER IX.—CHRISTMAS EVE AND THE TWELVE DAYS

1. Tille, "D. W.," 32 f.
2. Reinsberg-Düringsfeld, 446.
3. *Ibid.* 448.
4. *Ibid.* 449.
5. *Ibid.* 448 ; Weinhold, 8 f.
6. Evans, 229.
7. Weinhold, 8.
8. Tille, "Y. & C.," 116.
9. Reinsberg-Düringsfeld, 444 f.
10. *Ibid.* 442 f.
11. *Ibid.* 444.
12. **W. R. S. Ralston, "Songs of the Russian People"** (1st Edition, London, 1872), 186 f.
13. Sébillot, 216.
14. Walsh, 232.
15. Burne and Jackson, 406 ; Henderson, "Folk Lore of the Northern Counties," 311 ; **Sir Edgar MacCulloch, "Guernsey Folk Lore"** (London, 1903), 34 ; Thorpe, ii. 272.
16. Walsh, 232.
17. Henderson, "Folk Lore of the Northern Counties," 311.
18. MacCulloch, "Guernsey Folk Lore," 34 f. Cf. for Germany, Grimm, iv. 1779, 1809.
19. Grimm, iv. 1840.
20. Ralston, 201.
21. **A. Le Braz, "La Légende de la Mort chez les Bretons armoricains"** (Paris, 1902), i. 114 f.
22. Thorpe, ii. 89.
23. Lloyd, 171.
24. Feilberg, ii. 7 f.
25. *Ibid.* ii. 14.
26. Bilfinger, 52.
27. Feilberg, ii. 3 f.
28. *Ibid.* ii. 20 f.
29. **A. F. M. Ferryman, "In the Northman's Land"** (London, 1896), 112.
30. Feilberg, ii. 64.
31. Grimm, iv. 1781, 1783, 1793, 1818.
32. Krauss, 181.
33. Accounts of the carols used in Little Russia are given by Mr. Ralston, 186 f., while those sung by the Roumanians are described by Mlle. Stratilesco, 192 f., and those customary in Dalmatia by Sir A. J. Evans, 224 f.
34. Ralston, 193.
35. Stratilesco, 192.
36. Ralston, 197.
37. Chambers, "M.S." i. 244.
38. **Shakespeare, "Hamlet," Act I. Sc. I.**
39. Bilfinger, 37 f.
40. Henderson, "Folk Lore of the Northern Counties," 132.

NOTES AND BIBLIOGRAPHY

41. Tylor, i. 362.

42. **W. Golther, "Handbuch der germanischen Mythologie"** (Leipsic, 1895), 283 f.

43. Tille, "D. W.," 173.

44. Henderson, "Folk Lore of the Northern Counties," 132.

45. MacCulloch, "Guernsey Folk Lore," 33 f.

46. Burne and Jackson, 396 f., 403.

47. **R. T. Hampson, "Medii Aevi Kalendarium"** (London, 1841), i. 90.

48. Grimm, iv. 1836; Thorpe, ii. 272.

49. Burne and Jackson, 405.

50. *Ibid.* 405; MacCulloch, "Religion of the Ancient Celts," 166.

51. **E. H. Meyer, "Mythologie der Germanen"** (Strassburg, 1903), 424; Golther, 491; Reinsberg-Düringsfeld, 22 f.

52. Golther, 493.

53. Meyer, 425 f.

54. *Ibid.* 425 f.

55. Grimm, iii. 925 f.

56. *Ibid.* i. 268, 275 f.

57. Reinsberg-Düringsfeld, 22.

58. Grimm, i. 275; Reinsberg-Düringsfeld, 23.

59. *Ibid.* 23.

60. Meyer, 425; Grimm, i. 281.

61. Reinsberg-Düringsfeld, 21.

62. Golther, 493.

63. Reinsberg-Düringsfeld, 24.

64. Grimm, i. 274.

65. Meyer, 428.

66. **R. H. Busk, "The Valleys of Tirol"** (London, 1874), 116.

67. *Ibid.* 118.

68. *Ibid.* 417.

69. The details given about the *Kallikantzaroi* are taken, unless otherwise stated, from Lawson, 190 f.

70. Abbott, 74.

71. Hamilton, 108 f.

72. *Ibid.* 109.

73. Abbott, 218.

74. *Ibid.* 73 f.

75. Meyer, 85 f.

76. **G. Henderson, "Survivals of Belief among the Celts"** (Glasgow, 1911), 178.

77. *Ibid.* 177.

78. **F. H. E. Palmer, "Russian Life in Town and Country"** (London, 1901), 178.

CHAPTER X.—THE YULE LOG

1. Evans, 221 f.; Mannhardt, "Baumkultus," 224 f. Cf. the account of the Servian Christmas in **Chedo Mijatovitch, "Servia and the Servians"** (London, 1908), 98 f.

2. Same sources.

NOTES AND BIBLIOGRAPHY

3. Mannhardt, " Baumkultus," 236.
4. Frazer, " Magic Art," ii. 208.
5. *Ibid.* ii. 232.
6. Evans, 219, 295, and 357.
7. *Ibid.* 222.
8. Mannhardt, " Baumkultus," 237.
9. Cf. Frazer, " Magic Art," ii. 233.
10. *Ibid.* ii. 365 f.
11. Mannhardt, " Baumkultus," 226 f.
12. **" Memoirs of Mistral "** (Eng. Trans. by C. E. Maud, London, 1907), 29 f.
13. Mannhardt, " Baumkultus," 226 f.
14. Sébillot, 218.
15. **A. de Gubernatis, " Storia Comparata degli Usi Natalizi "** (Milan, 1878), 112.
16. C. Casati in *Archivio trad. pop.*, vol. vi. 168 f.
17. Jahn, 253.
18. *Ibid.* 254.
19. *Ibid.* 257.
20. Brand, 245 ; Dyer, 466.
21. **[Sir] G. L. Gomme, " Folk Lore Relics of Early Village Life "** (London, 1883), 99.
22. Ashton, 111.
23. Burne and Jackson, 402.
24. *Ibid.* 398 f.
25. *Notes and Queries*, 1st Series, vol. iv. 309 ; Dyer, 446 f.
26. **" The Gentleman's Magazine,"** 1790, 719.
27. Hampson, i. 109.
28. Feilberg, i. 118 f.
29. *Ibid.* i. 146.
30. *Ibid.* ii. 66 f.

CHAPTER XI.—THE CHRISTMAS-TREE, DECORATIONS, AND GIFTS

1. **I. A. R. Wylie, " My German Year "** (London, 1910), 68.
2. **Mrs. A. Sidgwick, " Home Life in Germany "** (London, 1908), 176.
3. Tille, " D. W.," 258. For the history and associations of the Christmas-tree see also **E. M. Kronfeld, " Der Weihnachtsbaum "** (Oldenburg, 1906).
4. Tille, " D. W.," 259.
5. *Ibid.* 261.
6. *Ibid.* 261 f.
7. **G. Rietschel, " Weihnachten in Kirche, Kunst und Volksleben "** (Bielefeld and Leipsic, 1902), 153.
8. *Ibid.*, 153.
9. Tille, " D. W.," 270.
10. Rietschel, 151.
11. *Ibid.* 151.
12. Tille, " D. W.," 267.

13. Dyer, 442 ; **E. M. Leather, "The Folk-Lore of Herefordshire"** (London, 1912), 90.

14. Rietschel, 154.

15. Ashton, 189.

16. *Ibid.* 190.

17. Tille, "D. W.," 271.

18. *Ibid.* 272.

19. *Ibid.* 277 ; Rietschel, 254.

20. Information supplied by the Rev. E. W. Lummis, who a few years ago was a pastor in the Münsterthal.

21. **L. Macdonald** in **"The Pall Mall Gazette"** (London), Dec. 28, 1911.

22. Tille, "Y. & C.," 174.

23. *Ibid.* 175 f.

24. Rietschel, 141.

25. Tille, "Y. & C.," 175.

26. *Ibid.* 172 f. ; Chambers, "B. D.," ii. 759.

27. Latin text in Chambers, "M. S.," ii. 290.

28. Mannhardt, "Baumkultus," 244.

29. Frazer, "Magic Art," ii. 65.

30. Mannhardt, "Baumkultus," 244.

31. *Ibid.* 241 ; Reinsberg-Düringsfeld, 18.

32. Lloyd, 168.

33. Dyer, 35.

34. **W. F. Dawson, "Christmas : its Origin and Associations "** (London, 1902), 325.

35. Harrison, "Themis," 321.

36. Frazer, "Magic Art," ii. 55 f.

37. Frazer, "Magic Art," ii. 48.

38. Mannhardt, "Baumkultus," 242 f.

39. Chambers, "M. S.," i. 251.

40. Latin text, *ibid.* ii. 300.

41. **J. Stow, "A Survay of London,"** edited by Henry Morley (London, 1893), 123.

42. Chambers, "M. S.," i. 251.

43. Grimm, iii. 1206 ; Frazer, "Golden Bough," iii. 327 ; MacCulloch, "Religion of the Ancient Celts," 162, 205.

44. MacCulloch, "Religion of the Ancient Celts," 162 f.

45. Grimm, iii. 1206.

46. Burne and Jackson, 246 ; **Laisnel de la Salle, "Croyances et légendes du centre de la France"** (Paris, 1875), i. 58.

47. Frazer, "Golden Bough," iii. 451 f.

48. **Washington Irving, "The Sketch-Book "** (Revised Edition, New York, 1860), 245.

49. *Notes and Queries,* 5th Series, vol. viii. 481.

50. Reinsberg-Düringsfeld, 472.

51. Henderson, "Folk Lore of the Northern Counties," 100.

52. Burne and Jackson, 245.

53. Henderson, "Folk Lore of the Northern Counties," 226.

54. **E. K. Chambers and F. Sidgwick, "Early English Lyrics"** (London, 1907), 293 ; **E. Rickert, "Ancient English Carols "** (London, 1910), 262.

55. Rickert, 262.
56. Burne and Jackson, 245 f., 397, 411.
57. Lloyd, 169.
58. Van Norman, 300.
59. Evans, 222.
60. Van Norman, 300 f.
61. Frazer, "Golden Bough," ii. 286 f.
62. Grimm, iv. 1831.
63. Chambers, "M. S.," i. 238. Cf. Tille, "Y. & C.," 104.
64. Reinsberg-Düringsfeld, 420.
65. Tille, "D. W.," 195.
66. *Ibid.* 197.
67. Bilfinger, 48.
68. **Th. Bentzon, "Christmas in France"** in **"The Century Magazine"** (New York), Dec., 1901, 173.
69. Feilberg, ii. 179 f.
70. Pitrè, 167, 404.
71. Feilberg, i. 196 ; Reinsberg-Düringsfeld, 453 f. ; Wylie, 77 f.
72. Lloyd, 172.
73. **W. Sandys, "Christmas Carols, Ancient and Modern"** (London, 1833), xcv.
74. Walsh, 240 f. ; Ashton, 194 f.

CHAPTER XII.—CHRISTMAS FEASTING AND SACRIFICIAL SURVIVALS

1. Chambers, "M. S.," i. 257.
2. Rickert, 259.
3. **W. Sandys, "Christmastide : its History, Festivities, and Carols"** (London, n.d.), 112.
4. Chambers, "M. S," i. 133.
5. **J. A. H. Murray, "A New English Dictionary"** (Oxford, 1888, &c.) iv. (1) 577.
6. Addy, 103.
7. Dawson, 254.
8. Addy, 104.
9. Burne and Jackson, 407.
10. Brand, 283.
11. Cf. *Folk-Lore*, vol. xi., 1900, 260.
12. Addy, 103.
13. Cf. carols in Brand, 3, and Rickert, 243 f.
14. Brand, 3.
15. Dyer, 464.
16. Feilberg, i. 119, 184 ; Lloyd, 173.
17. Jahn, 265.
18. Stratilesco, 190.
19. Ralston, 193, 203.
20. Mijatovich, 98.
21. Jahn, 261.
22. Rietschel, 106. Cf. Weinhold, 25, and Reinsberg-Düringsfeld, 463.
23. Sébillot, 217.

24. Laisnel, i. 7 f.

25. *Ibid.* i. 12 f.

26. *Ibid.* i. 11.

27. **E. Cortet, "Essai sur les Fêtes religieuses"** (Paris, 1867), 265.

28. Frazer, " Golden Bough," ii. 286 f.

29. **M. Höfler, "Weihnachtsgebäcke. Eine vergleichende Studie der germanischen Gebildbrote zur Weihnachtszeit " in " Zeitschrift für österreichische Volkskunde,"** Jahrg. 11, Supplement-Heft 3 (Vienna, 1905).

30. Jahn, 280 f.

31. Burne and Jackson, 406 f.

32. **" The Mirror of Perfection,"** trans. by Sebastian Evans (London, 1898), 206.

33. Mannhardt, " Baumkultus," 233 f.

34. Lloyd, 170 f.

35. Jahn, 276.

36. *Ibid.* 276.

37. Lloyd, 168.

38. Evans, 231 f. ; for the ox-custom, see Evans, 233.

39. Abbott, 76.

40. Hörmann, " Tiroler Volksleben," 244 f., 238, 245.

41. Dawson, 339.

42. **S. Graham, "A Vagabond in the Caucasus. With some Notes of his Experiences among the Russians "** (London, 1910), 25 f.

43. Stratilesco, 190.

44. Van Norman, 299 f.

45. Jahn, 267.

46. Frazer, " Golden Bough," ii. 442 f., where other examples, British and Continental, of the wren-hunt are given. Cf. Dyer, 494 f.

47. *Folk-Lore,* vol. xviii., 1907, 439 f.

48. MacCulloch, " Religion of the Ancient Celts," 221.

49. See Frazer, " Golden Bough," ii. 380, 441, for examples of similar practices with sacred animals.

50. *Folk-Lore,* vol. xi., 1900, 259.

51. Brand, 272.

52. *Folk-Lore,* vol. xi., 1900, 262.

53. Lloyd, 181 f.

54. *Ibid.* 181.

55. Thorpe, ii. 49 f.

56. Ralston, 200.

CHAPTER XIII.—MASKING, THE MUMMERS' PLAY, THE FEAST OF FOOLS, AND THE BOY BISHOP

1. Chambers, " M. S.," i. 390 f.

2. **The Works of Ben Jonson,** ed. by Barry Cornwall (London, 1838), 600.

3. **Shakespeare, " Henry VIII.,"** Act I. Sc. IV.

4. Chambers, " M. S.," i. 403 f.

5. *Ibid.* i. 227, 402.

6. *Ibid.* i. 402. Cf. Burne and Jackson, 410.

7. For a bibliography of texts of the mummers' plays see Chambers, " M. S.," i. 205 f.

NOTES AND BIBLIOGRAPHY

8. This account of the plays and dances is based upon Chambers, " M. S.," i. 182 f. (chapters ix. and x.).

9. **Tacitus, "Germania,"** cap. xxiv. (Eng. Trans. by W. Hamilton Fyfe, Oxford, 1908).

10. Cf. Harrison, " Themis," 43 f.

11. Professor Gilbert Murray in " Themis," 341 f.

12. Harrison, " Themis," 232.

13. Chambers, " M. S.," i. 226.

14. Chambers, " M. S.," i. 192, 213 f.

15. *Ibid.* i. 220 f.

16. Lawson, 223 f.

17. *Notes and Queries*, 5th Series, vol. x. 482.

18. This account of the Feast of Fools and the Boy Bishop is mainly derived from Chambers, "M. S.," i. 274–371, and from **Mr. A. F. Leach's** article, **"The Schoolboys' Feast,"** in **"The Fortnightly Review"** (London), vol. lix., 1896, 128 f.

19. Chambers, " M. S.," i. 294.

20. Full text in Chambers, " M. S.," ii. 280 f.

21. Chambers, " M. S.," i. 372 f.

22. **"Two Sermons preached by the Boy Bishop at St. Paul's,"** ed. by J. G. Nichols, with an Introduction by E. F. Rimbault (London, printed for the Camden Society, 1875).

23. *Ibid.* 3.

24. Quoted by **F. J. Snell, "The Customs of Old England "** (London, 1911), 44.

25. Chambers, " M. S.," i. 366.

26. **J. Aubrey, "Remaines of Gentilisme and Judaisme"** (1686–7), ed. by J. Britten (London, 1881), 40 f.

27. Chambers, " M. S.," i. 350.

28. Feilberg, ii. 254.

CHAPTER XIV.—ST. STEPHEN'S, ST. JOHN'S, AND HOLY INNOCENTS' DAYS

1. Hörmann, " Tiroler Volksleben," 237 f.

2. Dyer, 492.

3. **L. von Hörmann, " Das Tiroler Bauernjahr "** (Innsbruck, 1899), 204.

4. *Ibid.* 204.

5. *Ibid.* 204 f.

6. Feilberg, i. 212.

7. Mannhardt, " Baumkultus," 402.

8. Feilberg, i. 211.

9. Mannhardt, " Baumkultus," 402 f.

10. *Ibid.* 402 f. ; Feilberg, i. 204 f. ; Lloyd, 203 f.

11. **H. C. Beeching, " A Book of Christmas Verse "** (London, 1895), 21 f.

12. Mannhardt, " Baumkultus," 406.

13. Henderson, " Folk Lore of the Northern Counties," 67.

14. Jahn, 269 f.

15. *Ibid.* 270 f.

16. *Ibid.* 273.

NOTES AND BIBLIOGRAPHY

17. Dyer, 497 f.
18. *Ibid.* 498 ; Brand, 290.
19. Mannhardt, "Baumkultus," 264 f.
20. *Ibid.* 265 f.
21. *Ibid.* 268.
22. Frazer, "Golden Bough," iii. 129 f.

CHAPTER XV.—NEW YEAR'S DAY

1. Rhys, "Celtic Folklore," i. 320 f.
2. Henderson, "Folk Lore of the Northern Counties," 72.
3. E. Thurston, "Omens and Superstitions of Southern India " (London, 1912), 17 f.
4. Walsh, 742.
5. Wylie, 81.
6. Sébillot, 176.
7. A. Maurice Low, "The American People " (London, 1911), ii. 6.
8. Walsh, 739 f.
9. Evans, 229.
10. Burne and Jackson, 315 f.
11. *Notes and Queries*, 5th Series, vol. iii. 6.
12. Information given by the Rev. E. J. Hardy, formerly Chaplain to the Forces at Hongkong.
13. Frazer, "Golden Bough," iii. 204 f.
14. Burne and Jackson, 265.
15. Grimm, iv. 1784.
16. Harrison, "Themis," 36.
17. Henderson, "Folk Lore of the Northern Counties," 72 f.
18. Addy, 205.
19. G. Hastie in *Folk-Lore*, vol. iv., 1893, 309 f.
20. J. E. Crombie in same volume, 316 f.
21. Addy, 106 ; Burne and Jackson, 314 ; Rhys, "Celtic Folklore," i. 337.
22. Rhys, "Celtic Folklore," i. 339.
23. *Ibid.* 339 f. ; W. Henderson, 74. Cf. *Folk-Lore*, vol. iii., 1892, 253 f. ; vol. iv., 1893, 309 f.
24. Hastie (see Note 19), 311.
25. Walsh, 738.
26. Hastie, 312.
27. Chambers, " B. D.," i. 28.
28. *Ibid.* ii. 789 f. ; *Notes and Queries*, 2nd Series, vol. ix., 322 ; Dyer, 506.
29. Ashton, 228.
30. Hörmann, "Tiroler Volksleben," 230 f.
31. J. G. Campbell, "Witchcraft and Second Sight in the Highlands and Islands of Scotland " (Glasgow, 1902), 232. Cf. the account given by Dr. Johnson, in Brand, 278.
32. Henderson, "Survivals of Belief among the Celts," 263 f.
33. R. Chambers, "Popular Rhymes of Scotland " (Edinburgh, 1847), 296, and " B. D.," ii. 788.

NOTES AND BIBLIOGRAPHY

34. "New English Dictionary," v. (1) 327.
35. Cortet, 18.
36. Sébillot, 213.
37. *Ibid.* 213.
38. MacCulloch, "Guernsey Folk Lore," 37.
39. Abbott, 80 f.
40. Stratilesco, 197 f.
41. Hamilton, 103.
42. *Ibid.* 104.
43. Mannhardt, "Baumkultus," 593 f.
44. Latin text from Ducange in Chambers, "M. S.," i. 254.
45. Wylie, 81.
46. Abbott, 78.
47. Grimm, iv. 1847.
48. Sébillot, 171.
49. Dyer, 7.
50. Ashton, 228.
51. A. Macdonell, "In the Abruzzi" (London, 1908), 102.
52. Abbott, 77.
53. Ralston, 205.
54. "The Athenæum" (London), Feb. 5, 1848 ; *Notes and Queries*, 1st Series, vol. v., 5.

CHAPTER XVI.—EPIPHANY TO CANDLEMAS

1. Hörmann, "Tiroler Volksleben," 240 f.
2. Leigh Hunt, "The Seer; or, Common-Places Refreshed" (London, 1850), part ii. 31.
3. Beeching, 148 f.
4. Chambers, "M. S.," i. 261.
5. E. Pasquier, "Les Recherches de la France" (Paris, 1621), livre iv., chap. ix. p. 375.
6. Cortet, 33.
7. *Ibid.* 34.
8. *Ibid.* 43.
9. E. Du Méril, "Origines latines du théâtre moderne" (Paris, 1849), 26 f.
10. Brand, 13.
11. A. de Nore, "Coutumes, mythes et traditions des provinces de France" (Paris, 1846), 173.
12. Reinsberg-Düringsfeld, 29 f. ; Brand, 13.
13. Matilde Serao, "La Madonna e i Santi" (Naples, 1902), 128.
14. Reinach, i. 45 f.
15. Abbott, 77.
16. *Ibid.* 78.
17. Frazer, "Golden Bough," iii. 93.
18. Hörmann, "Tiroler Volksleben," 246 ; Reinsberg-Düringsfeld, 21.
19. Reinsberg-Düringsfeld, 21.
20. *Ibid.* 21 f.

NOTES AND BIBLIOGRAPHY

21. Stratilesco, 198.

22. Reinsberg-Düringsfeld, 21.

23. **Countess Martinengo-Cesaresco, "Essays in the Study of Folk-Songs"** (London, 1886), 334.

24. **D. N. Lees, "Tuscan Feasts and Tuscan Friends"** (London, 1907), 87.

25. *Ibid.* 83.

26. Serao, 127 f.

27. **E. de Olavarría y Huarte, "El Folk-Lore de Madrid,"** 90. [Vol. ii. of "Biblioteca de las Tradiciones Populares Españolas" (Seville, 1884).]

28. *Ibid.* 92.

29. "Memoirs of Mistral," 32 f.

30. Nore, 17.

31. Abbott, 87.

32. Frazer, "Magic Art," i. 275 f.

33. Hamilton, 118.

34. Brand, 16 ; Chambers, "B. D.," i. 56 ; Dyer, 21.

35. Aubrey, 40.

36. Brand, 16.

37. Beeching, 147.

38. Ashton, 87 f.

39. Hörmann, "Tiroler Volksleben," 225.

40. Tille, "D. W.," 254.

41. Hörmann, "Tiroler Volksleben," 230.

42. **W. S. Lach-Szyrma in "The Folk-Lore Record"** (London), vol. iv., 1881, 53.

43. Brand, 17 ; Chambers, "B. D.," i. 55 f. ; Dyer, 22 f. Several accounts have been collected by Mrs. Leather, "Folk-Lore of Herefordshire," 93 f.

44. Evans, 228.

45. Dyer, 24.

46. *Folk-Lore*, vol. v., 1894, 192.

47. *Ibid.* vol. vii., 1896, 340 f.

48. Chambers, "M. S.," i. 149 f.

49. W. Hone, "Every Day Book" (London, 1838), ii. 1649.

50. *Folk-Lore*, vol. vii., 1896, 342.

51. **[Sir] G. L. Gomme, "The Village Community"** (London, 1890), 242 f.

52. Busk, 99.

53. Dawson, 320.

54. **"The Nation"** (London), Dec. 10, 1910.

55. Burne and Jackson, 411.

56. Lloyd, 217.

57. Bilfinger, 24.

58. Brand, 18 f.

59. Dyer, 37.

60. Quoted from **"Journal of the Archæological Association,"** vol. vii., 1852, 202, by Dyer, 39.

61. Chambers, "M. S.," i. 113.

62. *Ibid.* i. 114.

63. Usener, 310 f.

64. Naogeorgus, 48.

65. Sébillot, 179 f.

NOTES AND BIBLIOGRAPHY

66. Hörmann, "Tiroler Volksleben," 7.

67. Usener, 321.

68. Brand, 25. Cf. **G. W. Kitchin, "Seven Sages of Durham"** (London, 1911),. 113.

69. *The Gentleman's Magazine*, 1790, 719.

70. Dyer, 55 f.

71. Quoted by Dyer, 57, from **Martin's "Description of the Western Isles of Scotland"** (1703), 119.

72. Gomme, "Folk-Lore Relics," 95.

73. Brand, 26.

74. *Ibid.* 26.

75. Burne and Jackson, 411.

CONCLUSION

1. E. Clodd in Presidential Address to the Folk-Lore Society, 1894. See *Folk-Lore*,. vol. vi., 1895, 77.

INDEX

INDEX

391

INDEX

INDEX

INDEX

INDEX

395

INDEX

Howison, 234
Hubert, St., his Day, 202
Hunt, Leigh, 337–8
Huysmans, J. K., 93
Hymns, Latin, 31–4, 42

ICELAND, "Yule host" in, 240
Image, Prof. Selwyn, 85
"In dulci jubilo," 44–5
Incense used for purification, 183, 225, 244–5, 327–8
Ireland, Christmas carols in, 69–70; All Souls' Eve in, 192; Hallowe'en customs in, 197–8; Martinmas slaughter in, 203–4; "hunting of the wren" in, 292; Holy Innocents' Day in, 315; Epiphany in, 350
Italy, Christmas poetry in, 36–42, 67; presepio in, 105–7, 112–6, 359; Christmas drama in, 146–8, 152; All Souls' in, 192, 194; Martinmas in, 204; Christmas log in, 256; Santa Lucia in, 278; Christmas fare in, 287, 289–91; Epiphany in, 343
Ivy, 272, 275–6

JACOPONE DA TODI, 36, 39–42, 146
James, St., Gospel of, 124
Jerome, St., 181
Jerusalem, Christmas at, 22, 94–5
John, St., Evangelist, his Day, 302, 314–5
Johnson, Lionel, 85
Johnson, Richard, 301
Jonson, Ben, 298
Julebuk, 202
Julian the Apostate, 23
Julklapp, 278–9

KALENDS of January, the Roman festival, 24, 165, 167–71, 200, 269; made a fast, 101, 170–1. *See also* New Year's Day
Kallikantzaroi, 244–7
Kindelwiegen, 108–11
King of the Bean, 180, 338–41
"Kissing-bunch," 274
Kissling, K. G., 266
Klapperbock, 201
Klaubauf, 219

Klöpfelnächte, 216–7
Knecht Ruprecht, 220, 231–2
Kore, 21
Krampus, 219

LABRUGUIÈRE, Epiphany in, 342
Lake, Prof. K., 20, 24
La Monnoye, 62–3
Lancashire, Hallowe'en in, 198
Latin Christmas poetry, 31–4, 42, 63–4, 68–9
Lawson, Mr. J. C., 247, 301
Lead-pouring, 215, 237, 332
Leather, Mrs., 269, 346
Le Moigne, Lucas, 56–8
Libanius, 168–9, 269
Liberius, Pope, 107, 352–3
Lima, Christmas Eve at, 98
Lithuania, feast of the dead in, 195; New Year's Eve in, 332
Log customs. *See* Yule log
Lombardy, Christmas log in, 256
London, Greek Epiphany ceremonies in, 103; Italian Christmas in, 116–7, 291; Christmas in, under Puritans, 185; German Christmas in, 265; Boy Bishop in, 306–7; New Year in, 322, 327
Lord Mayor's day, 202
Lord of Misrule, 298
Lorraine, cake customs in, 287, 339–40
Lucia, St., her festival, 221–3, 268
Lucian, 166–7
Ludlow, Guy Fawkes Day at, 199
Lullabies, 51, 67–9, 83–4, 109–10
Luther, Martin, 70–3, 265
Lyme Regis, Candlemas at, 354

MACEDONIA, Christmas Eve in, 217; New Year's Eve in, 226, 330, 332; *Kallikantzaroi* in, 245; folk-play in, 300; Epiphany in, 344
Macée, Claude, 141
Madrid, 97–8, 153, 343
Magi in drama, 125–6, 128–9, 151–3; as present-bringers, 343
Magic, 163
Man, Isle of, carol-singing in, 99; *Hollantide* in, 189, 198, 321;

INDEX

INDEX

Otfrid of Weissenburg, 42
Oxford, boars head at, 284

PALMER, Mr. F. H. E., 104
Parcae, 181
Paris, Christmas in, 98 ; All Souls' Eve
   in, 191 ; St. Catherine's Day in, 213 ;
   Christmas-tree in, 267 ; New Year in,
   277 ; Feast of Fools in, 302–3
Paschal, Françoise, 61–2
Pasquier, Étienne, 339
Pearson, Dr. Karl, 161–2
Pellegrin, Abbé, 63
Pelzmärte, 206–8, 217
Perchta, 181, 241–4, 342
Perun, 254
Peterborough, St. Catherine's Day at, 213
Philocalian Calendar, 20
Pifferari, 112
Pillersee, Advent mummeries at, 218
Pliny, 273
Plough Monday, 300
Plum-pudding, 284–5
Plygain, 99
Poland, the " star " in, 152 ; puppet-shows
   in, 153 ; werewolves in, 246 ; Christ-
   mas straw in, 276 ; Christmas wafers
   in, 291
Polaznik, 231, 252, 323–4
Presents, at the Roman Kalends, 168–71,
   276–7 ; on All Souls' Eve, 192 ; at
   Martinmas, 205–8 ; on St. Nicholas's
   Day, 218–20 ; at Christmas, 183, 230,
   277–9 ; at New Year and other seasons,
   277–8 ; at Epiphany, 343
Presepio. See Crib
" Prophetae," 127
Protestantism, effects of, on Christmas, 27,
   70–8, 111, 138, 141, 185–6, 229–30
Provence, remains of Christmas drama in,
   141, 154 ; Christmas log in, 255 ; Magi
   in, 344
Prudentius, 32
Puppet-plays, 153 f.
Purification, feast of the. *See* Candlemas
Puritans, their attitude towards Christmas,
   77, 180, 184–5, 298
Pyramids, 266

QUAINTON, blossoming thorn at, 268

" RAGING host," 240, 242
Ragusa, Christmas log customs at, 252
Ramsgate, hodening at, 200–1
Rauchnächte, 225, 327–8
Rhys, Sir John, 189, 321, 325–6
Ripon, St. Clement's Day at, 212 ; Yule
   candles at, 259 ; Candlemas at, 354
Risano, Christmas log customs at, 252
Rolle, Richard, 48
Rome, Christmas established in, 20–1 ;
   pagan winter festivals in, 23–4, 165–71 ;
   Christmas services and customs in, 95–6,
   112–6, 289–90 ; mediaeval New Year
   quête in, 331
Rossetti, Christina, 85
Rouen, religious plays at, 124–5, 138–40
Roumania, the " star " in, 152 ; Christmas
   drama in, 153 ; St. Andrew's Eve in,
   215–6 ; Christmas songs in, 238 ; Christmas fare in, 287, 291 ; New Year in,
   330–1 ; Epiphany in, 342
Russia, Epiphany ceremonies in, 104, 246 ;
   the " star " in, 152 ; Christmas Eve in,
   232–3, 237 ; fire superstitions in, 253 ;
   Christmas fare in, 287, 291 ; Christmas
   games in, 294 ; mummers in, 302 ; New
   Year in, 333

SABOLY, 62
Sacrifice, theories of, 174–8 ; connected
   with festivals, 178–9 ; survivals of, 199,
   283–7, 292–4, 328, 347–9
Salers, Christmas king at, 340
Samhain, 172, 204
Sant' Andrea della Valle, Rome, 102
Santa Klaus, 220
Santa Maria Maggiore, Rome, 95–6, 107,
   114–5
Saturnalia, 24, 113, 165–7, 180, 359
Schiller, 266
Schimmel and *Schimmelreiter*, 199–200, 206,
   231
Schoolboys' festival, 223–4. *See also* Boy
   Bishop
Scotland, Christmas carols in, 70 ; Hal-
   lowe'en customs in, 197–8 ; sowens
   eaten in, 285 ; " firstfoot " in, 325–6 ;
   other New Year customs in, 326–9,
   332–3 ; Candlemas in, 354

398

INDEX

INDEX